NO-BODY HOMICIDES

No-Body Homicides: The Evolution of Investigation and Prosecution examines how police and prosecutors have become more successful in obtaining convictions for homicide when the remains of the victim are unavailable as evidence. Based on an examination of over 600 cases in the United States and Canada, this book shows the length some killers will go to avoid punishment and the determination of police and prosecutors to bring them to justice.

For over 300 years, murderers in the United States and Canada could avoid prosecution by successfully disposing of the body of their victim. *No-Body Homicides* provides the reader with a historical overview of prosecutions in which a killer destroyed or hid the body of the victim. It explains why prosecutions were once extremely rare, and how legal, attitudinal, and technical changes have made them more common. The book also explores how the logic of no-body homicide prosecutions differs from body-present homicides. It allows police and prosecutors to draw on the accumulated experience of hundreds of prosecutions. For criminology students, it provides fascinating insights into the process of investigating and prosecuting homicides – as well as a glimpse into the motivations and practices of killers who are so determined to avoid punishment that they remove the bodies of their victims.

No-Body Homicides will be of practical interest to police or prosecutors confronted with a missing person's case that could be sinister. It is also written to be appropriate as a supplementary text in an undergraduate criminology class or for an aficionado of "True Crime."

Mark Stobbe teaches Sociology at Lakeland College in Lloydminster, Canada. He is the author of *The "Mr. Big" Sting: The Cases, The Killers, The Controversial Confessions* and *Lessons from Remand.*

NO-BODY HOMICIDES

The Evolution of Investigation and Prosecution

Mark Stobbe

Routledge
Taylor & Francis Group
NEW YORK AND LONDON

Designed cover image: Manuel Velasco

First published 2023
by Routledge
605 Third Avenue, New York, NY 10158

and by Routledge
4 Park Square, Milton Park, Abingdon, Oxon, OX14 4RN

Routledge is an imprint of the Taylor & Francis Group, an informa business

Library of Congress Cataloging-in-Publication Data
Names: Stobbe, Mark, author.
Title: No-body homicides : the evolution of investigation and prosecution / Mark Stobbe.
Description: New York, NY : Routledge, 2023. | Includes bibliographical references and index.
Identifiers: LCCN 2022055398 (print) | LCCN 2022055399 (ebook) | ISBN 9781032444260 (hardback) | ISBN 9781032440705 (paperback) | ISBN 9781003372134 (ebook)
Subjects: LCSH: Homicide--Case studies. | Homicide investigation--Case studies. | Trials (Murder)--Case studies. | Dead--Identification. | Dead bodies (Law)
Classification: LCC HV8079.H6 S76 2023 (print) | LCC HV8079.H6 (ebook) | DDC 363.25/9523--dc23/eng/20221117
LC record available at https://lccn.loc.gov/2022055398
LC ebook record available at https://lccn.loc.gov/2022055399

ISBN: 978-1-032-44426-0 (hbk)
ISBN: 978-1-032-44070-5 (pbk)
ISBN: 978-1-003-37213-4 (ebk)

DOI: 10.4324/9781003372134

Typeset in Bembo
by Deanta Global Publishing Services, Chennai, India

"A very strong addition to a rapidly growing and evolving field of criminology: no-body murder investigations and prosecutions."

Thomas A. (Tad) DiBiase, author of No-Body Homicide Cases: A Practical Guide to Investigating, Prosecuting, and Winning Cases When the Victim Is Missing

CONTENTS

FIGURES

ACKNOWLEDGMENTS

The research for this book was conducted by examining court documents, news articles, and "true crime" accounts of homicide prosecutions in which the killer hid or destroyed the body of their victim. This task was intrinsically solitary and somewhat bleak. The task could not have been completed without the support and good humor of my wife, Marilyn Totten, my two sons, Nicholas and Jacob Stobbe, and my mother, Margaret Munro.

Isaac Newton once said that his work was made possible by standing on the shoulders of giants. In writing this book, I stood on the shoulders of Thomas (Tad) DiBiase and Meaghan Good.

The compilation of no-body cases for this book was anchored in the list compiled by Thomas A. (Tad) DiBiase (2015) in *No Body Homicide Cases: A Practical Guide to Investigating, Prosecuting and Winning Cases When the Victim is Missing* (Boca Raton, FL: CRC Press) and updated on his website www.nobodycases.com. I expanded on his list, primarily with the addition of Canadian cases, but without the work of Mr. DiBiase as a foundation, this book would not have been possible in its present form.

Another invaluable source has been the compilation of "cold" missing persons cases compiled and maintained by Meaghan Good and found at www.charleyproject.org. Ms. Good's site contains information on over 15,000 missing persons' cases. In researching this book, I used her work to cross-check the accuracy of my own research. Her industry, accuracy, and commitment to justice for the missing are remarkable.

1

INTRODUCTION

Homicides and Missing Bodies

Homicide is as old as humanity. So are homicide cases in which the body of the victim has disappeared. These can be called "no-body" homicide cases.

In the Bible, homicide reared its ugly head in the fourth book of Genesis. According to this narrative, the second generation of people on earth started killing each other when Cain dispatched his brother Abel. God served as the detective, asking Cain, "Where is Abel thy brother?" When Cain denied knowledge, God replied, "the voice of thy brother's blood crieth unto me from the ground."[1] This early homicide was a no-body case, with God relying on circumstantial (Abel was gone) and forensics (blood in the soil) to determine that Cain was a victim of fratricide.

No-body cases appeared early in other early societal origins stories. According to legend, Rome was founded by the twins Remus and Romulus. The two quarreled over the location of their new city. Romulus bumped off Remus. If the murder of Remus was Rome's first murder, it did not take long before the city had its first no-body case. According to Livy, Romulus was reviewing the Roman army when a storm blew up a cloud of dust. When the weather settled, Romulus was gone. One theory was that the founder and first king of Rome had been raised to the heavens by Mars, God of War. The other was that Romulus was murdered and dismembered by the senators who carried away in pieces of the body under their clothing. Livy presents both theories for the disappearance of Romulus, but argues that accession to the heavens was more likely than homicide because of post-disappearance events (Rome continued to conquer and grow) and the lack of forensic evidence (killing and dismemberment should have left blood).[2]

We have no way of knowing how many no-body homicides have been committed since the murder of Abel and the possible killing of Romulus, but there have probably been many. Despite this, successful prosecutions of no-body cases were extremely rare for centuries. Destroying or hiding the body of a victim was an almost infallible way of getting away with murder. This has changed over the past five decades. More people are now successfully prosecuted for homicide even when the victim's body is unavailable to police. This book explores the history of no-body prosecutions (with a focus on the United States and Canada), analyzes the type of homicides most likely to become no-body cases, and examines why successful no-body prosecutions have become more common.

DOI: 10.4324/9781003372134-1

Homicide Investigations and Bodies

Most homicide investigations begin with the discovery of a body which is examined to determine the medical cause of death. Let us take the hypothetical (but common) case of a corpse found with extensive head injuries. A pathologist conducting an autopsy determines that death was caused by a blow to the head which fractured the skull and sent bone fragments into the brain. The pathologist typically provides an assessment of the physical dimensions of the object that struck the head, how many blows were struck, and the direction of the blow. But this is just the beginning of the process. The medical determination of the cause of death does not provide a legal one. The pathologist does not determine whether the fatal blow was the result of an accident or an intentional killing. The task of determining whether the death was a culpable homicide is a task for detectives rather than doctors. If the fatal blow to the head was from an object being wielded by a human being – that is, a homicide – the circumstances and motivations must also be assessed. There are many potential scenarios:

- Was it an accident? Did the victim walk into the path of a sledgehammer wielded by someone driving in a spike?
- Was it self-defense? Was the person wielding the object fighting off an aggressive attacker?
- Was it manslaughter? Did an attacker mean to injure, but not to kill?
- Was it murder? Did an attacker swing the object with the conscious intention of caving in the skull and killing the person?
- Was it premeditated murder? Did the attack come in a spontaneous quarrel or a fit passion, or was it planned?

In answering these questions, the investigating detectives start by discovering the "who" – which person, out of the billions inhabiting the earth, wielded the object that struck the head, caved in the skull, and caused death? From there, motive and circumstances are examined to assess the degree of criminal culpability, if any.

Police often answer this "who" question with relative ease.[3] There might be witnesses. The killer might still be on the scene. There could be compelling forensic evidence – the blood of the victim on someone's clothes, fingerprints on the murder weapon, or DNA on the victim in places where it had no innocent reason to be. Sometimes there is incriminating circumstantial evidence. Possession of the victim's wallet and using the victim's credit cards makes a person a suspect. Sometimes a killer will immediately and spontaneously confess, often with a plea for mitigation and understanding. British criminologist Martin Innes calls homicide investigations in which the who is readily apparent "self-solvers."[4]

Self-solvers are, by definition, "easy" to solve, but police must still assemble evidence sufficient for a prosecutor to extract a guilty plea or convince a jury to convict.[5] Some self-solvers are difficult or impossible to prove in a court of law. What is more, sometimes the obvious solution is wrong. Things are not always as they seem. The innocent as well as the guilty flees a crime scene. The innocent sometimes confesses to acts they did not commit. An apparent self-solver can be transformed into the second kind of homicide identified by Innes – the "whodunnit." These cases do not solve themselves. The investigators must identify a suspect before proceeding to the step of gathering evidence to build a provable case.[6] On other occasions, the problem can be too many suspects. In the Agatha Christie novel *Murder on the Orient Express*, the homicide victim had been stabbed 12 times. The detective, Hercule Poirot, identified 12 passengers with both motive and opportunity. He concluded that all were guilty; all had taken a turn at stabbing the very objectional victim.[7] Real homicides are not like those in Agatha Christie novels. It is not common for all the suspects to be guilty. Finding out which one is guilty can be a challenging task.

Determining the medical cause of death, converting it to the legal categories of manslaughter or murder, identifying the guilty person, and generating sufficient evidence to allow a prosecutor to prove a case can be challenging for investigators. No-body cases present investigators with one more tough challenge. The investigators must start by proving that death has occurred.

In "no-body" homicide cases, police do not begin the investigation with the discovery of a body.[8] They begin with an absence. Someone is gone. In these cases, police must find evidence showing that absence was the result of death. They must then establish that death was the result of homicide; that a specific person was the killer; and the killing was a "culpable" homicide. Four cases show the possible problems for investigators.

On April 26, 2005 Jennifer Wilbanks went jogging. The woman from Duluth, Georgia was to be married in four days. When Jennifer did not return home, her fiancé called police. The police initially downplayed the disappearance, suggesting that the bride-to-be might have a case of "cold feet" over her wedding. The police chief told reporters that "there is no indication that a crime has been committed."[9] Jennifer's family and friends were indignant. They said this was impossible. Citing Jennifer's character and the fact that she had not taken her engagement ring, cell phone, or keys, family members suspected foul play. They posted a $100,000 reward for information about her disappearance. The police responded by turning the missing person's case into a criminal investigation. Searchers found a clump of hair and some jogging clothes. The media concluded that Jennifer's fiancé had murdered her and hidden her body.[10] Four days after Jennifer disappeared – on the day her wedding was scheduled – she phoned her fiancé from Albuquerque, New Mexico. Jennifer claimed she had been kidnapped, sexually assaulted, and finally released after a 1,400-mile journey.[11] During questioning by the FBI, Jennifer changed her story, confirming the preliminary assessment of the police. Jennifer said she had been stressed by her impending wedding. She disguised herself by cutting her hair, changed her clothes, got on a Greyhound bus, and left town.[12]

At about 3:00 am on October 12, 2002, Eduardo Sanchez disappeared in Winnipeg, Manitoba. The 21-year-old disc jockey had finished his night's work at a popular nightclub. Everyone else went home. Eduardo just disappeared. It looked like murder, but the police were frustrated. Many people had been at the nightclub, but nobody was identified as the last person seen with Eduardo. There was no forensic evidence. There was no identified motive. Eduardo had no enemies, no angry lovers, and no debts to drug dealers. The investigation went nowhere until, 11 months later, the City of Winnipeg banned smoking in restaurants and nightclubs. People living near the nightclub started complaining about an unpleasant smell. When this was investigated, Eduardo's body was found. He was wedged in a narrow space between the nightclub's stone foundation and a newer wall. Until the new tobacco ban was passed, cigarette smoke masked the odor produced by Eduardo's body. Police could not explain why Eduardo had squeezed himself into the crawlspace, but an autopsy showed his death was not a homicide. Eduardo had died of positional asphyxiation.[13] He had crawled into a tight space, gotten stuck, and suffocated. But for the change in legal and social attitudes towards smoking, Eduardo's fate might never have been known.

August 16, 2005, was a Sunday. Alicia Ross spent the afternoon and evening with her boyfriend in Markham, Ontario. At about midnight, Alicia walked her boyfriend to his car and kissed him goodnight. When the boyfriend got home, he called Alicia to say good night again but got no answer. The next morning, he tried telephoning again. There was still no answer. The boyfriend drove to Alicia's house. Everything was as it had been the night before – except Alicia was gone. The boyfriend phoned 911 to report Alicia's disappearance. The police quickly concluded that Alicia had been "abducted by someone she knew – and not by a stranger." Hundreds of volunteers mobilized to help in a search.[14]

The police were careful not to publicly identify a suspect. Alicia's parents were not as reticent. They accused the boyfriend. The media joined in. Headlines proclaimed the police were canvassing the boyfriend's neighbors and announcing the police viewed him as a "person of interest." The boyfriend confirmed he was being treated as the "prime suspect."[15] This was interpreted as a sign of guilt. The boyfriend stopped speaking to the media. This was treated as confirming his guilt. Alicia's mother told the media she telephoned the boyfriend "begging him to go to the police, to help our family." She told the media that he hung up on her. The boyfriend was convicted in the court of public opinion.[16]

About the only ones without tunnel vision were the police. A month after Alicia's disappearance, they asked Alicia's neighbors to take polygraph tests. This caused Alicia's next-door neighbor to confess. Daniel Sylvester had the habit of peeping into the windows of his female neighbors and fantasizing about raping them. He told police Alicia spotted him hiding in the shrubbery. Sylvester said Alicia called him a "loser." He responded by beating her to death.[17] After killing Alicia, Sylvester cleaned up the crime scene, put her in the trunk of his car, and dumped her body in a field. Three weeks later, he moved her remains to the forest near his family's cottage. Police believe Sylvester sexually assaulted Alicia both pre- and post-mortem. Sylvester denied this, but confessed to visiting her corpse at least ten times and masturbating. Sylvester gave the police detailed confessions and reenacted the killing. He took police to the two locations where he had stored Alicia's body. Sylvester's wallet and clothing – stained with Alicia's blood and his semen – were at one location. Alicia's body was at the second. Medical examiners found 33 fractured bones, including several ribs, her nose, a cheekbone, her breastbone, and three neck vertebrae.[18] Sylvester was charged with second-degree murder. He attempted to plead guilty to manslaughter, but the prosecutor refused to accept this plea. Sylvester was convicted on the murder charge.[19]

On February 24, 2008, Dennis Cornish abruptly disappeared. The 37-year-old from 100 Mile House, British Columbia, was a drug dealer. Along with his partner, Dennis operated marijuana grow-ops and sold cocaine. The partner told friends that Dennis had decided to go away "for awhile," hinting that debt avoidance was the reason for the disappearance. Dennis's parents were not convinced. They began putting up posters asking for information and filed a missing person report with the police. The police noted Dennis and his partner telephoned or texted each other several times a day. The partner stopped texting or phoning Dennis the day of the disappearance. Police became even more suspicious when they found the partner had appropriated Dennis's property. The police suspected the partner murdered Dennis and disposed of the body, but nothing could be proven until the police launched a "Mr. Big" operation (discussed in detail in Chapter 14). The partner was tricked into believing he is being recruited into an imaginary criminal gang. He told the boss of the gang – "Mr. Big" – that Dennis died after being shot and that he (the partner) burned the body and dumped the ashes into a garbage dumpster. However, the partner said the death was an accident – that Dennis had been fronted "a bunch of fucking cocaine from this guy, and fucken, and lost it." This created cash flow problems for the two drug-dealing partners. As the pair argued about the situation, Dennis pulled a gun. The two wrestled for control of it. The gun went off. Dennis died. At least that is the story the partner told Mr. Big. The prosecutor decided it was impossible to proceed with a murder or manslaughter charge. The incident, as described, was self-defense. The partner was charged and convicted of committing an indignity to Dennis's body. Ironically, Dennis's partner benefited from the undercover Mr. Big operation. If he told this story to police during an interrogation, it probably would have been dismissed as a self-serving lie. Because he told it Mr. Big – the leader of a powerful (if imaginary) criminal gang – the partner's story was deemed credible.[20]

The disappearances of Jennifer Wilbanks, Eduardo Sanchez, Alicia Ross, and Dennis Cornish looked a lot like murders. In all these cases, someone inexplicably disappeared. There appeared to be no plausible explanation other than foul play. In three cases, there was a primary suspect. It seemed obvious that Jennifer and Alicia were killed by their boyfriends. It seemed even more obvious that Dennis's drug-dealing business partner had dissolved the partnership. Eduardo's case was a genuine "whodunnit." Foul play was the obvious explanation for his disappearance, but there were no clues and nobody seemed to have a motive. The police were stymied.

None of these cases were what they seemed. Jennifer was still alive. Eduardo was dead, but was the victim of a weird accident. Alicia had been cruelly murdered, but not by the "obvious" suspect. Dennis was killed by the person suspected by the police, but the homicide was ruled self-defense rather than murder.

No-body homicides present investigators with special challenges. The first is proving that the victim is dead without a body to be identified and examined. Chapter 2 will look at one aspect of the history of this challenge. People who disappeared and were presumed dead had the awkward habit of reappearing in an untimely manner. It is embarrassing to the authorities when a murder trial is visited by the victim. It is worse when the reappearance occurs after conviction and execution. This has happened; not often, but the memory of these legal fiascos remains. More common are reports of sightings of the missing person during an investigation. During the evening of April 21, 2002, a young woman in Brandon, Manitoba, named Erin Chorney was murdered by her boyfriend, Mike Bridges. He buried Erin in another woman's freshly dug grave.[21] Two years later, police tricked Bridges into telling them where Erin's body was located.[22] There is absolutely no question that Erin was murdered on April 21, 2002, and buried the following night.[23] Despite this, in the two years following her disappearance, over 160 people called police to report seeing her alive. If her body had not been found, these "witnesses" could have been used to convince a jury that Erin was still alive – and hence that Bridges was innocent.

A missing body destroys a lot of evidence. In his book *No-Body Homicide Cases: A Practical Guide to Investigating, Prosecuting and Winning Cases When the Victim Is Missing*, Thomas A [Tad] DiBiase points out that normally "the victim's body remains the single most important piece of evidence in any murder case."[24] It can tell investigators the manner of death. Wounds can be matched with weapons. The body of the victim will often hold forensic evidence from the killer. The lack of a body can prevent investigators from locating the crime scene with all of the resulting evidentiary loss. A missing body can make it impossible to determine the time of death, leading to complications in finding potential witnesses or confirming alibis. Temporal problems can be even more basic. Investigation will not begin until the victim is reported missing. The killer often influences or controls this process. In 1970, Wayne Roberts killed his four-year-old stepdaughter and buried her in a shallow grave. Surrette Clarke was not reported missing until 1994. Roberts was convicted of manslaughter in 1996, but he had a 24-year head start on homicide investigators.[25]

There is another, more intangible, factor that makes it difficult for police to investigate cases where the body of the victim has been successfully hidden or destroyed. It lies in the attitude of the killer. These guys (and almost all of them are guys) do not want to get caught. The effort a killer puts into avoiding detection matters.[26] No-body killers put a lot of effort into concealment.[27]

After Glenn Franz strangled his ex-wife, he carried her body to the manure treatment lagoon of a dairy farmer. Franz cut off his victim's head and dismembered her body. He threw the head off a bridge into a river and the body parts into the manure lagoon. The aeration activity dissolved them completely.[28]

Adam Strong lured a young prostitute to his basement suite. After killing her, he dismembered the young woman and took the organs such as lungs, stomach, and intestines out of the body cavity before dumping her torso into Lake Ontario. This was designed to prevent the bloating that causes bodies to rise to the surface. Strong cut up his victim's organs and flushed them down his toilet. He also flushed his victim's flesh down the toilet. It is not known what he did with her bones, but whatever Strong did was permanent. He got away with murder – until he killed a second time. On this occasion, the sewer line plugged up. The people living in another apartment complained when their sewer backed up. The landlord called a plumber who used a "snake" to clear the line. The plumber was shocked at what he began to pull up. The police were called. Strong ruefully complained to police that he was "foiled by inadequate plumbing."[29] Killers like Glenn Franz and Adam Strong put a lot of effort into avoiding detection. This determination makes them hard to catch and prosecute.

Most homicide investigations begin with someone calling police to report the discovery of a corpse[30], but DiBiase reports that 1 in 34 begin as a missing person report. The police begin by looking for, and find, a live person. If the missing person is a homicide victim, a different kind of investigation is needed. DeBiase argues, "one of the biggest mistakes made in a no-body investigation is to treat the case like a missing persons case for too long."[31] This statement is true, but it obscures a problem. Police get a lot of missing persons reports. In the five-year period from 2015 to 2019, the FBI's National Crime Information Centre[32] (NCIC) reports that 631,142 people were reported missing (in the United States – every year [annual average for the period]). In Canada, the National Centre for Missing Persons and Unidentified Remains (NCMPUR) reports that police received an annual average of 73,874 missing persons reports annually during this same five-year period.[33] During this same five-year time period, there were an annual average of 16,146 homicides in the United States[34] and 646 in Canada[35] – that is, 39 missing persons reports for every homicide in the United States and 114 in Canada. There is a danger in waiting too long to convert a missing person case into a homicide investigation, but overly hasty conversion would overwhelm the capacity of police forces. We do not have enough police officers – and as a society, we probably do not want to have that many – to treat all missing persons reports as homicide investigations.

But there is more to the matter than the issue of resources. Missing persons investigations are different than homicide investigations. A missing person's investigation is not a criminal inquiry; in most cases, no crime has been committed. The objective is finding a person to ensure their safety. In a homicide investigation, the objective is finding, arresting, and convicting a killer.[36] In missing persons cases, the person making the report – usually family members or friends of the missing person – are treated as partners in the investigation. In homicide investigations, these people are treated as suspects. Information is shared when looking for a missing person. When investigating a homicide, information is jealously guarded by police to avoid compromising a prosecution. When looking for a missing person, privacy is honored as much as possible. When investigating a homicide, police put the person's life under a microscope.[37] Homicide investigations are extremely destructive to almost everyone touched by one. The combination of police secrecy and intrusiveness is a necessary evil when attempting to catch killers, but it would produce pathological results if these techniques were applied to every missing person's report. If people knew that reporting someone missing would mean being subjected to a harsh interrogation, having your home ripped apart by a forensics team, having your car seized for examination, and all your friends and relatives questioned as to whether you were having affairs, financial problems, or substance abuse issues, very few people would report a missing person to police.

All of this means that police must make choices.[38]

"Triage" is the sorting of cases into the categories of immediate, urgent, and non-urgent according to pre-established criteria. The practice was developed in France by Baron Dominique Jean Larrey, Surgeon in Chief to Napoleon's Imperial Guard. Napoleon's battles generated so many wounded men that they overwhelmed the medical treatment capacity of the army. Larrey created assessment criteria to quickly sort the incoming wounded to determine who would first receive treatment.[39] Police use a variant of the triage system for missing persons reports. They are assessed against established criteria to determine how quickly and vigorously a response will be organized. The three basic categories for police are missing persons cases that are benign and innocuous, those that are urgent but non-criminal, and those in which foul play is a real possibility.

Let us begin with the benign and innocuous. A child goes to a friend's house after school without telling a parent. Someone takes an unplanned trip. A car breaks down. In many cases, the problem is a simple failure of communications. The number of missing persons reports has dropped during the past two decades because of the widespread adoption of the cell phone. In the United States, missing persons reports peaked in 1998 with 980,712 missing persons reports. As 2G digital cell phones became common, missing persons reports dropped to 836,131 in 2006. Apple released the iPhone on June 29, 2007. Within five years, the number of missing persons reports to police had dropped to 661,593.[40] As more people carried cell phones, fewer people went missing. Even with the connectedness provided by mobile telephones, benign and innocuous explanations are common.

In other cases, the missing person does not want to be "found." A woman might be fleeing an abusive relationship. A teenager might be running away from parents deemed too strict. A person might just leave. I had a friend whose brother disappeared. His mother sent him to the store to buy a loaf of bread. He disappeared. Twenty-three years later, he suddenly reappeared at his parent's home. He had been living and working a few hundred miles away. The long-lost person decided to leave on a whim. As time passed, coming home to explain his absence got progressively more embarrassing; so, he procrastinated.

Sometimes the missing person does not realize they are missing. In 1868, the Scottish missionary and explorer Dr. David Livingstone set off from Zanzibar to find and map the source of the Nile River. Nobody in Europe or America heard from him for six years. The *New York Herald* dispatched a reporter, Henry Stanley, to find the "lost" explorer. Livingstone was "found" on the shores of Lake Tanganyika. He denied being lost or missing.[41]

In most missing persons cases, the best investigative tool is patience.

Other missing persons reports are treated as urgent, but non-criminal. Police gear up for immediate and urgent action. If a small child or someone suffering from dementia disappears, a search is immediately launched. The discovery of an empty boat or overturned canoe will have the same effect. The police treat the missing person as being at risk and often mount an immediate, intense search utilizing police officers, volunteers, tracking dogs, and, often, technical assists such as helicopters. If the person is not found within normal survival-time parameters, the search will continue, but it becomes a search for a body. Cadaver dogs replace tracking dogs. Lakes and rivers are dragged and divers are sent underwater.

Occasionally, the circumstances of a disappearance are intrinsically suspicious. These cases are immediately treated as probable homicide cases. Irene Silverman was an 82-year-old woman with a close network of friends, employees, and acquaintances when she suddenly disappeared. It was inconceivable that she had voluntarily gone away without telling anyone. What is more, Irene had been telling her friends and employees that a new tenant in the building she owned was behaving in a weird and suspicious manner. There was a trail of blood drops from her front door to a parking spot down the block. When Irene disappeared, it was treated as the equivalent of a homicide investigation from the beginning; complete with a primary suspect.[42]

Some disappearances are self-solving homicide cases. Doug Snider was a physician in Fairview, Alberta. He and the other doctors in the town were having acrimonious disputes with a colleague, Abraham Cooper. On the evening of May 5, 1999, Doug kissed his wife goodbye and set off for a meeting with Cooper to resolve their differences. He never returned. Police found blood on Cooper's shoes and clothing – and in the trunk of Cooper's car. DNA testing showed the blood was Doug's. Cooper was convicted of manslaughter after a trial in which he claimed Doug had staged his own disappearance in order to frame him (Cooper) of murder.[43]

For the police, the triage process for missing persons reports sometimes is simple. It did not take Sherlock Holmes to deduce that the disappearances of Irene Silverman or Doug Snider were intrinsically suspicious. In each of these cases there was also an obvious (and guilty) suspect at hand. On other occasions, the triage process is more difficult. Hard judgment calls are made on incomplete information. It is these cases that DiBiase is referring to when he suggests that waiting too long to convert from missing persons to homicide investigation protocols makes solving a crime and getting a conviction more difficult. Let us briefly look at a few of the complexities of this triage.

In the 1990s and early 2000s, serial killer Robert Pickton preyed on prostitutes and street people from skid-row in Vancouver. Numerous missing persons reports were filed – and treated as missing persons cases. It took years before the sheer volume of the missing persons reports forced police to treat the disappearances as linked homicides.[44] A comparison of the disappearances of Pickton's victims and Irene Silverman reveals a conundrum faced by the police in their triage process. The people who are least likely to go missing for benign and innocuous reasons are the most likely to have their disappearances immediately treated as possible homicides. All of Irene's many friends were adamant that she would not have gone away on her own volition without telling anyone. As a result, foul play was the natural inference of her absence. It was very different with Pickton's victims. Many worked as street prostitutes. To make their living, they got into vehicles with strangers and temporarily disappeared. Some lived a transient lifestyle. Temporary, unexplained absences were common. The idea that the disappearances were the result of foul play – and the possibility that a serial killer was at work – was resisted by police because there were plausible and benign explanations for many individual disappearances. It took the accumulated weight of many long absences for a serious homicide investigation to be launched. The cruel reality is that those most likely to be murdered are often the very ones whose disappearance will ring the fewest alarm bells.

There is even more complexity. Police do not take missing persons reports from everyone. On November 17, 1980, a 13-year-old girl named Christine Weller disappeared while riding a bicycle borrowed from a friend. Christine's father reported her to police as a "runaway." She had left before; often to go stay with friends or relatives. Neither the police nor Christine's father took her disappearance seriously. One person became concerned – the father of the friend from whom the bicycle was borrowed. At first, the man just wanted the bicycle back. As he searched for Christine to recover the bicycle, he became disturbed by her disappearance. He attempted to file a missing person report with the police, but was ignored. The young girl had been drugged, raped, strangled, and stabbed by serial killer Clifford Olson.[45] In retrospect, the fact that police ignored the complaint from the friend's father seems incompetent and shocking. In reality, it was understandable, if not inevitable. The man had never even met the missing girl. He had no legal standing to report her missing.

In cases of intimate partner homicides and the killing of children, the person with the legal standing to file a missing person report is often the killer. They have no interest in haste or in providing accurate information. We have already seen how Wayne Roberts delayed the start of any investigation into his killing of his stepdaughter for 24 years. In Chapter 4, we will examine in detail how wife-killers John Bayerl, Michael Clark, and Paul Calnen delayed the launch of an investigation by delaying the filing of a missing person report. In Chapter 9, we will see how Perry March used the same tactic, and in Chapter 11 we will look at the strategy of Robert Bierenbaum. Not only did these wife-killers delay the start of an investigation, they fabricated a reason for the absence. In these cases (and many others), the homicidal husband told police that they had quarreled with their spouse, who then left. The "disappearance" was portrayed as a voluntary "leaving." Unless forensic evidence is found, only the passage of time creates certainty the missing person is dead; that is, to transform an innocent and benign missing persons case into a homicide investigation.

Cases initially triaged as urgent but non-criminal can also become murky with the passage of time.

On June 7, 1967, James Brady and Absolum Halkett were dropped off on the shore of a lake in northern Saskatchewan to do some prospecting. Nine days later, their boss flew out to check on their progress. He found a deserted camp. The two men were gone. A massive search effort eventually found their canoe, but there was no sign of James and Absolum. The police theory that the two got lost attempting to walk out of the bush was dismissed by the locals since the two were experienced in the wilderness. Rumors began to circulate that the pair had been murdered. Theories proliferated. Some cited political motives, others centered on mining company greed, and still others pointed to sexual jealousies and personal paybacks. Those dismissing the murder theories pointed out that James had both diabetes and heart trouble. A fatal medical crisis was not impossible. More than half a century later, it is still a mystery as to whether the disappearances were the result of a tragic accident or a cunning murder.[46]

The triage of missing persons cases can move between categories. In August of 1989, a professional hockey player from Saskatoon, Saskatchewan named Duncan MacPherson was on his way to a coaching job in Scotland. He stopped in Germany to visit a friend, rented a car to do some sightseeing, and disappeared. At first, benign and innocuous explanations seemed most likely. Then Duncan's rented car was found in the parking lot of a ski resort near Innsbruck, Austria. The last sightings of Duncan had him snowboarding on a glacier. The police moved from a benign explanation to theorizing that Duncan had accidently died either hiking in the mountains or falling into a glacial crevice. When Duncan's body was not located, various foul play scenarios were developed. Almost 24 years after Duncan disappeared, his body was found. It had been in a glacial crevice all along. Because it was in ice, Duncan's body was well preserved. It was badly mangled. The police again attributed Duncan's death and disappearance to an accident, with the condition of the body caused by the movement of the glacier. However, others argued that the body's condition was inconsistent with glacier movement. John Leake theorizes that Duncan's death was due to a combination of events. He speculates that Duncan broke his leg in a snowboarding accident and then was accidentally run over by a snow grooming machine. Leake suggests that the snow-grooming machine operator then pushed Duncan's body into a crevice and covered it up with snow, either inadvertently or to cover up his carelessness.[47] We will never actually know what happened. Disappearance and the passage of time can create unsolvable mysteries, even when the body is eventually found.

No-Body Homicide Cases in North America

This book is about the investigation and prosecution of no-body homicides in the United States and Canada. Building on work of DiBiase,[48] no-body cases were identified using a snowball technique building references to other no-body cases in news articles and court rulings. Keyword searches were also conducted in media and court databases. A total of 487 successful prosecutions of no-body cases in the United States and 32 in Canada were identified. In addition, another 14 Canadian cases in which the killer was tricked into showing an undercover police officer the location of a hidden body are included in the study. These cases represent the best available tabulation of no-body cases, but are incomplete. Some cases involve multiple victims or killers, but the killer might be convicted only for some of their murders. As we will see in Chapter 7 with sexually motivated serial killers and Chapter 8 dealing with criminal gang killings, police and prosecutors are often forced to choose the best cases – that is, the most provable cases – to prosecute. Sometimes nobody except the killer knows how many people they have killed. Sometimes even the killer cannot remember. Memory is not infallible when someone kills in volume. We can also learn from failure, so in Chapter 15 we will examine "misfire" prosecutions; that is, no-body prosecutions in which charges were laid but which resulted in an acquittal either at trial or overturned on appeal. In researching this book, 70 misfires have been identified in the United States and 4 in Canada. In some misfires, the accused was clearly innocent. In others, the result was ultimate acquittal despite significant evidence of guilt.

The successful prosecution of no-body homicide cases remained very rare in the United States and Canada until late in the 20th century. Chart 1.1 shows the number of these successful prosecutions in the United States and misfires by decade. The number of prosecutions started to climb in the 1960s and accelerated in the 1970s and afterward (the final numbers for the 2010 to 2019 period will be higher than shown as investigations are completed and cases work their way through the legal system). In addition to an increase in the number of no-body prosecutions, the success rate also increased. In the 19th century, only 64 percent of no-body prosecutions resulted in an ultimate conviction. As police and prosecutors began to launch more of these prosecutions in the 1970s, they had a success rate of 75 percent. By the decade beginning in 2010, no-body prosecutions had a success rate of 95 percent.

The history of Canadian no-body cases follows a similar pattern. There appear to have been only two successful no-body prosecutions in the 1800s. A fur trader was convicted of killing and burning the body of his partner in 1904.[49] The next no-body prosecution was launched in 1947, with one case in the 1960s and one in the 1970s. There were two successful Canadian prosecutions in the 1980s; 10 in the 1990s, 3 in the 2000s, and 11 in the 2010s. Four Canadian no-body prosecutions have misfired. The earliest of these was launched in 1989.

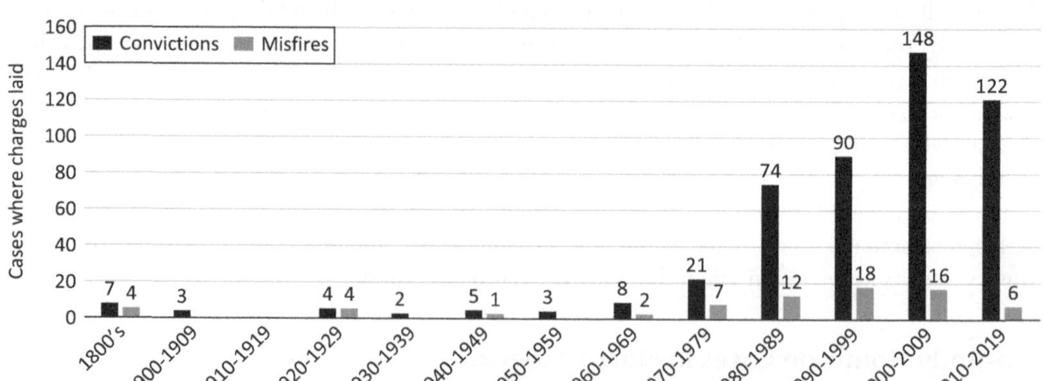

FIGURE 1.1 "No-Body" Homicide Cases by Decade Charges Laid: United States of America

We have no way of knowing how many people have "gotten away with murder" by successfully disposing of the body, but the extreme rarity of prosecutions prior to the 1970s means that tactics such as burying or burning a body was a virtual guarantee against prosecution. For reasons discussed in Chapter 12, this began to change. We do not know how many killers still adopt the strategy of body disposal, but the increasing number of successful prosecutions means that successful body disposal is no longer a "stay out jail free" card for killers. The increase in successful no-body prosecutions occurred in an era when clearance rates for homicide, in general, dropped. In the 1960s, police in Canada and the United States "cleared" (usually with an arrest) over 90 percent of reported homicides. Clearance rates then began to drop. By the mid-1990s, about a quarter of all reported homicides in Canada remained unsolved and unpunished.[50] It was (and is) worse in the United States where about one in three reported homicides is not cleared.[51] Since the mid-1990s, clearance rates for reported homicides have remained stable despite advances in police technology such as DNA identification and much more sophisticated forensics.[52] As police and prosecutors have become more successful at solving no-body homicides, they have remained frustrated in a lot of traditional homicide investigations.

The pattern of homicides in successful no-body prosecutions is different than that of homicides in general.

The first difference is gendered. Compared with homicides in general, there are more female victims and more male killers in no-body cases.

Every year, 20 to 25 percent of homicide victims in the United States are female.[53] In the 487 successful no-body prosecutions identified, 61 percent involved female victims and another 4 percent were cases of multiple killing with both female and male victims. It is similar in Canada. Every year, between 20 and 25 percent of homicide victims are female,[54] but 50 percent of the no-body cases had female victims exclusively and another 11 percent had both female and male victims.

While the victims in no-body cases are disproportionately female, the killers are disproportionately male. In the United States, 88 percent of killers in cleared homicide cases are male.[55] In no-body cases, 93 percent of the cases featured a male killer and other 2 percent involved a male/female killing tandem. In Canada, tendency of no-body cases to feature a male killer is even more pronounced. About 80 percent of killers in cleared homicide cases are male,[56] while those convicted in no-body cases have been 98 percent male. The exception to the overwhelming masculinity of killers in no-body cases is when the victim is a child. In these cases, females account for almost half of the convictions.

Assessing the statistical distribution of the nature of relationship between killer and victim in homicide cases is intrinsically difficult because of the number of cases that remain unsolved. If the police are unable to identify the killer, the nature of their relationship with the victim also remains unknown. This likely results in an overstating of the proportion of intimate partner homicides or acquaintance homicides along with a corresponding understating of "stranger" killings since police use identified motives as a starting point for investigation. With this cautionary caveat in mind, the relationship profile in no-body cases appears different than that for homicides in general. The most important difference is that no-body cases are twice as likely to be intimate partner homicides. In both the United States and Canada, about one in five solved homicide cases features an intimate partner as the killer.[57] Intimate partners account for about two in five no-body cases. Killing of other family members and criminal associates are also more common in no-body cases than for homicides in general.

Killers in no-body cases also tend to kill people differently than in ordinary homicide cases. Chart 1.2 presents the comparative data for means of killing in the United States, and Chart

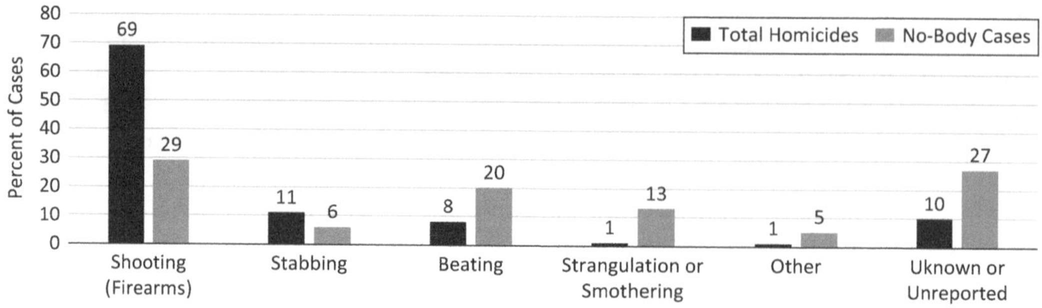

FIGURE 1.2 Means of Killing Comparison: U.S. Homicides (2014–2018) vs. U.S. No-Body Cases

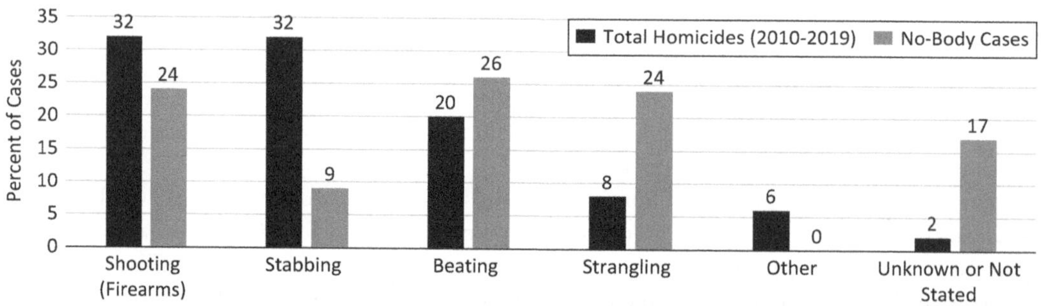

FIGURE 1.3 Means of Killing Comparison: Canadian Homicides (2010–2019) Vs. Canadian No-Body Cases

1.3 presents this data for Canada. In both countries, killers who dispose of their victim's bodies are more likely to kill via beating and strangulation rather than the generally more popular methods of shooting or stabbing.[58] In about one in five no-body cases, the method of killing remains unknown. In the absence of eyewitnesses, a confession, or a body on which to conduct an autopsy, prosecutors are forced to convince a jury that the suspect is guilty of killing without being able to describe how the deed was done. This hurdle is difficult, but not impossible, for prosecutors to clear.

These differences between no-body homicides and "normal" homicides derive from the difficulties inherent in disposing of a body. To hide or destroy the body of their victim, the killer must either bring their victim, while still alive, to the ultimate disposal site or transport a corpse. The first option usually means having some sort of relationship with the victim. The transport of victims while still living is more possible for intimate partner homicides and the killing of family members. Moving the body after the killing requires physical strength to move a "dead weight." Differentials in the size and strength between males and females make it easier for a man to move the corpse of a woman. Women can handle the smaller corpses of children. To make body disposal a viable strategy, privacy for the act of killing is required. It makes no sense to attempt to remove the body if there are non-culpable witnesses to the killing. The prevalence of strangulation in no-body cases speaks to the difference in both size and strength between killer and victim in no-body cases. Strangulation is neater than shooting or stabbing. People who are strangled do not bleed. This makes crime scene clean-up easier.

The Reason for This Book and Notes on Approach

In 2000, my wife was the victim of a homicide. Eight years later, I was charged with murder for her death. In 2012, a jury reached the correct decision and rendered a verdict of "not-guilty." The identity of my wife's killer remains unknown and he (it's almost certainly a he) remains at large. This set of experiences left me with two deep and personal convictions. I believe murderers should be caught and punished. Seeing people "get away with murder" is offensive. I also believe that it is very important that the right person be convicted. Conviction of the wrong person is an offense to both the person unjustly convicted and to the memory of the victim. As a result, I want both vigorous investigation and prosecution in homicide cases AND due regard for the rights of the accused. In homicide cases, the criminal justice system should be stern and unforgiving, but it must also be careful to get things right. The goal of this book is to help advance both these causes. Killers should not be able to get away with murder simply because they have successfully done away with the body, along with the life, of their victims. Police and prosecutors have become more aggressive in pursuing no-body cases. I hope this book helps encourage this trend. At the same time, the possibility of misfires in no-body cases is real. The cases of Jennifer Wilbanks, Eduardo Sanchez, Alicia Ross, and Dennis Cornish reveal some of the hazards of a rush to judgment in no-body cases. As we will see in the next chapter, people have been convicted (and even executed) for killing people who were not dead. It has not happened often, but it has happened. It should make us cautious about our certainty in an ambiguous situation.

This book is based primarily on court documents and media coverage of no-body cases. In addition, a lot of "true crime" books have been written about no-body cases. The appendix lists these book-length true-crime accounts that contributed to the facts and analysis presented in this book.

This book discusses many cases. This means there are a lot of names involved in these stories. To name everyone involved in every case would make the book incomprehensible. As a result, except for killers and victims, I have largely dispensed with naming names. Most people are identified only by their role in the case. Accomplices are described as accomplices. Family members are brothers, sisters, husbands, wives, and children. Police officers are police officers. Defense lawyers and prosecutors are lawyers. Judges are judges. The exceptions to this anonymity are killers, victims and, sometimes, those formally charged but acquitted. The first time these individuals are named, the full name will be used. In the ongoing narratives, subsequent references to these individuals will use the first names of the victims and the last names of the killers. This is intended to reflect a more personal and sympathetic portrayal of victims while being less respectful of killers. For those who were charged, but never convicted, anonymity will be provided or first names will be used throughout. These people are innocent in the eyes of the law and often in fact. They deserve a different treatment than those convicted of evil deeds.

This brings us to a final important point. In this book, I do not relitigate cases. I was on the jury of none of these cases. I have no privileged knowledge of the facts. There would be no grounds but arrogance to presume that I have a better understanding of the truth in these cases than those entrusted with making the momentous decision of adjudicating guilt or innocence. As a result, the final decision of the legal process will be treated as established fact. Sometimes this is difficult. Chapter 15 deals with misfires in no-body prosecutions. One reality is that some of these accused in these cases were guilty but were acquitted or had charges dropped. The other reality is that I do not *know* which of these individuals were factually guilty and which ones were innocent. Humility and honesty require that I respect the outcomes of the justice system.

Structure of the Book

We begin the book with a look at some cases that demonstrated a primary reason for a reluctance to prosecute for homicide in cases where the body of the victim was gone. Chapter 2 outlines some cases, both famous and obscure, in which the person allegedly murdered was found still alive. The embarrassment arising from these cases helped create a reluctance to prosecute no-body cases. In Chapter 3, we look at the key cases in the United States and Canada that began to change the legal framework governing no-body prosecutions. These cases received a lot of publicity. This began to create an inspirational effect for police and prosecutors by showing conviction was possible without a body in the coffin.

As we noted earlier, the profile of no-body homicides is different than for homicides in general. The next seven chapters discuss major categories of no-body homicide. We begin the relationship between killer and victim. Chapter 4 examines no-body homicides where killer and victim are intimate partners, and Chapter 5 looks at the killing and disposal of children by those entrusted with their care. Chapter 6 examines no-body homicides in which the commercial buying and selling of sexual services created a deadly relationship. In all these categories of no-body homicide, the killing usually occurs in a private location controlled by the killer and there is a size difference between killer and victim. These two factors make body disposal viable as a detection avoidance strategy. In cases involving intimate partners and children, the killer can hinder police investigation by delaying or eliminating the filing of a missing person report. In most cases involving those involved in the commercial sex trades, a lack of an established, ongoing relationship between killer and victim creates obstacles for police. These three categories of killer–victim relationship account for most no-body homicide cases.

In Chapters 7 and 8, we move from victim relationship to motive by looking at two types of killers producing disproportionate numbers of unsolved no-body cases. Serial killers and contract killers employed by criminal organizations are rare, but they kill a lot of people. In these chapters, we will examine how body disposal is one detection avoidance strategy utilized. When these killers are caught, they are often prosecuted for body-present cases, even though authorities suspect them of being guilty in no-body cases as well.

We then turn to the characteristics of the killers in some high-profile no-body cases. Chapter 9 looks at people who respond to a mid-life crisis with homicide. Chapter 10 looks at cases where the impulse to kill was created by the combination of different personality types; a group of people (usually two) become lethal only in a synergistic combination. Mid-life crisis and synergistic no-body cases are relatively rare, but generate a disproportionate number of books, made-for-television movies, and true-crime podcasts. As a result, these atypical cases unduly influence how we view no-body homicides and their prosecution.

We then switch gears to examine the issues associated with no-body investigations and prosecutions.

In Chapter 11, we deal with how police, prosecutors, judges, and juries arrive at a legal determination of guilt in the absence of a body. No-body cases have a different epistemological foundation than do traditional homicide cases. In Chapter 12, we will examine the reasons for the increase in the number of no-body homicide prosecutions – they've gone from being almost nonexistent to something that, if not yet common, is no longer rare. This transition was caused by a combination of legal changes, inspirational examples, and technological changes. In Chapter 13, we'll examine how hiding or destroying the body of their victim gives the killer a powerful secret that sometimes gives them advantages in dealing with the legal system – and sometimes creates a Kafkaesque trap for the innocent. In Chapter 14, we'll look at "Mr. Big," a made-in-Canada approach to investigating no-body homicides. In Chapter 15 we'll look at the prosecutions that did not result in convictions. In some cases, a prosecutorial misfire results in justice being partially served; an innocent person was not convicted. However, these misfired prosecutions usually mean the actual killer avoided punishment. Other misfires are disconcerting because a person was ultimately acquitted, even though factual guilt was probable. In Chapter 16 we will wrap it all up by reviewing the special challenges and opportunities in punishing killers who hide or destroy the body of their victim.

Notes

1 Gn 4:10 AV.
2 Livy, Titus Livius, *The Rise of Rome: Books One to Five* trans. by Torrey James Luce (Oxford, UK: Oxford University Press, 1998.
3 Addington, Lynn A., "Using National Incident-Based Reporting System Murder Data to Evaluate Clearance Predictors" *Homicide Studies* 10, No. 2 (2006): 140–152; Brookman, Fiona & Martin Innes, "The Problem of Success: What Is a 'good' Homicide Investigation?" *Policing and Society* 23, No. 2 (2013): 292–310; Brookman, Fiona, Edward R. Maguire and Mike Maguire, "What Factors Influence Whether Homicide Cases Are Solved? Insights From Qualitative Research With Detectives in Great Britain and the United States" *Homicide Studies* 23, No. 2 (2019): 145–174; Hawk, Shila René, Dean A. Dabney and Brent Teasdale, "Reconsidering Homicide Clearance Research: The Utility of Multifaceted Data Collection Approaches" *Homicide Studies* 25, No. 3 (2020): 195–219; Keel, Timothy G., John P. Jarvis and Yvonne E. Muirhead, "An Exploratory Analysis of Factors Affecting Homicide Investigations: Examining the Dynamics of Murder Clearance Rates" *Homicide Studies* 13, No 1 (2009): 50–68; Pastia, Christina, Garth Davies and Edith Wu, "Factors Influencing the Probability of Clearance and Time to Clearance of Canadian Homicide Cases, 1991-2011" *Homicide Studies* 21, No. 3 (2017): 199–218.
4 Innes, Martin, *Investigating Murder: Detective Work and the Police Response to Criminal Homicide* (Oxford, UK: Oxford University Press, 2003): 197.
5 Innes, *Investigating Murder*, 197–220.
6 Innes, *Investigating Murder*, 221–240.
7 Christie, Agatha, *Murder on the Orient Express* (London, UK: Collins, 1934).
8 Beauregard, Eric and Melissa Martineau, "No Body, No Crime? The Role of Forensic Awareness in Avoiding Police Detection in Cases of Sexual Homicide," *Journal of Criminal Justice* 42, No. 2 (2014): 213–220.
9 Hart, Ariel, "Bride-to-be Goes for a Jog and Disappears," *New York Times*, April 29, 2005.
10 "Foul Play Suspected in Case of Missing Bride-to-be in Georgia," *AccessWDUN*, April 28, 2005.
11 Kaye, Randi, "Missing Bride to be Found in Albuquerque, New Mexico," *CNN*, April 30, 2005.
12 Hart, Ariel, "Runaway Bride Is Indicted," *New York Times*, May 26, 2005.
13 Wattie, Chris, "DJ's Mummified Body Found in Wall Behind Club; Winnipeg Mystery," *National Post*, December 6, 2004.
14 Diebel, Linda and Morgan Campbell, "'Abducted by someone she knew'; Tips Lead to Search: Police Speculate Alicia Ross Was not Taken by Strangers: Residents Asked to Check Property Lines, Bush Lots, Fencelines," *Toronto Star*, August 6, 2005.
15 Campbell, Morgan and Alejando Bustos, "Police Expand Search for Woman; Boyfriend Says He's 'prime suspect'; 25-Year-Old Last Seen on Tuesday; Helicopters Scan Area in Markham," *Toronto Star*, August 19,2005.
16 Bustos, Alejandro, "Put an End to This for the Family," *Toronto Star*, August 28, 2005.
17 Kohler, Nicholas, "'Feeling Remorse' in Toronto Death," *National Post*, September 22, 2005.
18 Mitchell, Bob, "'It's not a whodunnit' Crown Says; Argument Led to Alicia Ross's Death Says Prosecutor Describing Spat with Neighbour," *Toronto Star*, May 8, 2007.
19 Shannon, Kari, "NO PAROLE FOR AT LEAST 16 YEARS; Ross killer; Judge Concludes Attack Was Sexually Motivated," *National Post*, July 7, 2007.
20 R v. Randle, 2014 BCSC 1990.
21 McIntyre, Mike, *To the Grave: Inside a Spectacular RCMP Sting* (Winnipeg, MB: Great Plains, 2006).
22 Q v. Bridges (No.2), 2005 MBQB 142.
23 Pritchard, Dean, "Killer Who Hid Ex-girlfriend's Body in Grave Applies for Early Release," *Winnipeg Free Press* (Winnipeg, MB), October 21, 2019.
24 DiBiase, Thomas A (Tad), *No-body Homicide Cases: A Practical Guide to Investigating, Prosecuting, and Winning Cases When the Victim Is Missing* (Boca Raton, FL: CRC Press, 2015), xii.

25 Sakal, Mike, "Police ID Remains of 4-year-Old Girl Buried Under Tempe Bridge," *East Valley Tribune* (East Valley, AZ), August 5, 2010.
26 Brookman, Fiona, "Killer Decisions: The Role of Cognition, Affect and 'expertise' in Homicide," *Aggression and Violent Behavior* 20 (2015): 42–52.
27 Beauregard, Eric and M. Bouchard, "Cleaning Up Your Act: Forensic Awareness as a Detection Avoidance Strategy," *Journal of Police and Criminal Psychology* 28 (2010): 1160–1166.
28 R v. Franz, 2000 BCSC 802.
29 R v. Strong, 2021 ONSC 1906.
30 Greenwood, P., J. Chaiken, and J. Petersilia, *The Criminal Investigation Process* (Lexington, MA: Lexington Books, 1977.
31 DeBiase, *No-Body Homicide Cases*, xvii.
32 Compiled from National Crime Information Centre, *NCIC Missing Person and Unidentified Person Statistics* (annual), https://www.fbi.gov/file-repository.
33 Compiled from National Centre for Missing Persons and Unidentified Remains, Fast Fact Sheets (annual) https://www.canadasmissing.ca/pubs.
34 Compiled from Federal Bureau of Investigation, *Crime in the United States, Table 12*, (Annual), https://ucr.fbi.gov/crime-in-the-u.s.
35 Compiled from Statistics Canada, *Number of homicide victims and persons accused of homicide, by Indigenous Identity, age and gender,* (Annual) Table 35-10-0060-01. https://www150.statcan.gc.ca/.
36 Foy, Shaunagh, "A Profile of Missing Persons: Some Key Findings for Police Officers," in *Handbook of Missing Persons,* ed. Stephen J. Morewitz and Caroline Sturdy Colls (Gewerbestrasse, CH: Springer, 2016): 8.
37 Kim, Joyce, Jackie Leach Scully, and Sara Huston Katsanis, "Ethical Challenges in Missing Persons Investigations," in Morewitz and Colls, *Missing Persons*, 163–176; Taylor, Rae, "Slayed and Slandered: A Content Analysis of Femicide in Crime News," *Homicide Studies* 13, No. 1 (2009): 21–49.
38 Newiss, Geoff, "Estimating the Risk Faced by Missing Persons: A Study of Homicide Victims as an Example of an Outcome-based Approach," *International Journal of Police Science and Management* 6, No. 1 (2004): 27–36.
39 Skandalakis, Panagiotis N., Pianagiotis Lainas, Odyseas Zoras, John E. Skandalakis, and George L. Sternback, "'To afford the wounded speedy assistance': Dominique Jean Larray and Napoleon," *World Journal of Surgery,* 30, No. 8 (August 2006): 1392–1399.
40 National Crime Information Centre, *NCIC Missing Person and Unidentified Person Statistics* (annual), https://www.fbi.gov/file-repository.
41 Gallop, Alan, *Mr. Stanley, I Presume?: The Life and Explorations of Henry Morton Stanley* (Cheltenham, UK: The History Press, 2004).
42 Havill, Adrian, *The Mother, The Son, and the Socialite: A True Story of a Mother-Son Crime Spree* (New York, NY: St. Martins, 1999); McQuillan, Alice, *They Call Them Grifters: The True Story of Sante and Kenneth Kimes* (New York, NY: Onyx, 2000).
43 R v. Cooper, 2000 ABQB 656; R v. Cooper 2002 ABCA 236.
44 Cameron, Stevie, *The Pickton File* (Toronto, ON: Knopf Canada, 2007); Cameron, Stevie, *On the Farm: Robert William Pickton and the Tragic Story of Vancouver's Missing Women* (Toronto, ON: Knopf Canada, 2011); Shenher, Lori, *That Lonely Section of Hell: The Botched Investigation of a Serial Killer Who Almost Got Away* (Vancouver, BC: Greystone, 2015).
45 Worthington, Peter, *Predator: The Life and Crimes of Serial Killer Clifford Olson* (E-Book, 2012); Mulgrew, Ian *Final Payoff: The True Price of Convicting Clifford Robert Olson* (New York, NY: Seal, 1991); Broderick, Elizabeth, *Clifford Olson: The Beast of British Columbia* (Toronto: RJ Parker Publishing, 2016); Holmes, William Leslie, *Where Shadows Linger: The Untold Story of the RCMP's Olson Murder Investigation* (Victoria, BC: Heritage House, 2010).
46 Nest, Michael, Deanna Reder and Eric Bell, *Cold Case North: The Search for Jim Brady and Absolom Halkett* (Regina, SK: University of Regina Press, 2020).
47 Leake, John, *Cold a Long Time: An Alpine Mystery* (Self-published, 2012).
48 DiBiase, Thomas A. (Tad), n.d. "No-body Murder Trials," accessed August 29, 2022. https://www.nobodycases.com/wp-content/uploads/2020/11/Nobodytablelatest-Nov-2020.pdf.
49 The King v. Charles King, Supreme Court of the North-West Territories, *Canadian Criminal Cases* Vol. IX (1905): 426–447.
50 Pastia, Christina, Garth Davies and Edith Wu, "Factors Influencing the Probability of Clearance and Time to Clearance of Canadian Homicide Cases, 1991–2011," *Homicide Studies* 21, No. 3 (2017): 199–218; Trussler, Tanya, "Explaining the Changing Nature of Homicide Clearance in Canada," *International Criminal Justice Review* 20, No. 4 (2010): 336–383.

51 Ousey, Graham C. and Mathew R. Lee, "To Know the Unknown: The Decline in Homicide Clearance Rates, 1980–2000," *Criminal Justice Review* 35, No. 2 (2010): 141–158. Riedel, Mark "Homicide Arrest Clearances: A Review of the Literature," *Sociology Compass* 2, No. 4 (2008): 1145–1164; Riedel, Marc and John Jarvis, "The Decline of Arrest Clearances For Criminal Homicide: Causes, Correlates, and Third Parties," *Criminal Justice Policy Review* 9, No. 3&4 (1999):279–306.

52 Keel, Timothy G., John P. Jarvis and Yvonne E. Muirhead, "An Exploratory Analysis of Factors Affecting Homicide Investigations: Examining the Dynamics of Murder Clearance Rates," *Homicide Studies* 13, No. 1 (2009): 50–68; Litwin, Kenneth J., "A Multilevel Multivariate Analysis Of Factors Affecting Homicide Clearances," *Journal of Research in Crime and Delinquency* 41, No. 4 (2004): 327–351; Pizzaro, Jesenia M., William Terrill and Charles A. LoFaso, "The Impact of Investigation Strategies and Tactics on Homicide Clearance," *Homicide Studies* 24, No. 1 (2020): 3–24; Puckett, Janice L. and Richard J. Lundman, "Factors Affecting Homicide Clearances: Multivariate Analysis of a More Complete Conceptual Framework," *Journal of Research in Crime and Delinquency* 40, No. 2 (2003): 171–193; Roberts, Aki, "Predictors of Homicide Clearance by Arrest: An Event History Analysis of NIBRS Incidents," *Homicide Studies* 11, No. 2 (2007): 82–93; Rydberg, Jason and Jesenia M. Pizarro (2014) "Victim Lifestyle as a Correlate of Homicide Clearance," *Homicide Studies* 18, No. 4 (2014): 342–362; Schroeder, David A. and Michael D. White (2009) "Exploring the Use of DNA Evidence in Homicide Investigations Implications for Detective Work and Case Clearance," *Police Quarterly* 12, No. 3(2009): 319–342; Braga, Anthony A. and Desiree Dusseault (2018) "Can Homicide Detectives Improve Homicide Clearance Rates?," *Crime & Delinquency* 64, No. 3 (2009): 283–315.

53 U.S. Department of Justice, annual, Crime in the United States: Expanded Homicide Data Table 1: Murder Victims by Race, Ethnicity and Sex.

54 Statistics Canada, Table 35-10-0060-10. Number of homicide victims and persons accused of homicide by indigenous identity, age group and gender.

55 U.S. Department of Justice, annual, Crime in the United States: Expanded Homicide Data Table 3: Murder Offenders by Age, Sex, Race, and Ethnicity.

56 Statistics Canada, Table 35-10-0060-10. Number of homicide victims and persons accused of homicide by indigenous identity, age group and gender.

57 U.S. Department of Justice, annual, Crime in the United States: Expanded Homicide Data Table 10: Murder, Circumstances by Relationship; Statistics Canada, Table 35-10-0073-01: Number of victims of solved homicides, by type of accused-victim relationship.

58 U.S. Department of Justice, annual, Crime in the United States: Expanded Homicide Data Table 7: Murder, Types of Weapons Used; Statistics Canada, Table 35-10-0069-01. Number of homicide victims, by method used to commit the homicide.

2

GONE BUT NOT DEAD

Mark Twain provided a fictional account of disappearance and return. Tom Sawyer convinced his friends, Joe Harper and Huckleberry Finn, that their future lay in piracy. The boys "borrowed" a raft and made their way to an island in the Mississippi River. They spent almost a week fishing, swimming, and planning a piratical career. The raft drifted away and was found downstream. When a search was unsuccessful, people assumed the boys had drowned. That Sunday, the church service became a funeral during which "the minister related many a touching incident in the lives of the departed, too, which illustrated their sweet, generous natures." It was an emotional affair. "The whole company broke down and joined the weeping mourners in a chorus of anguished sobs." At this point, the three pirates (who had been hiding in the gallery listening to their own funeral service) marched up the aisle. Twain reported that "Tom got more cuffs and kisses that day – according to Aunt Polly's varying moods – than he earned before in a year." [1]

Mark Twain's story of disappearance, presumed death, and return is entertaining. For the criminal justice system, the story reveals a real problem. A century ago, it was easy to disappear. If disappearance was believed to be caused by death, action would be taken. In this case, the action was a funeral and an outpouring of emotion. But suppose the community and the legal system attributed the boys' disappearance to a more sinister cause. Tom was always in trouble with his guardian, Aunt Polly. Joe's mother had recently whipped him over a false accusation of cream drinking. Someone could have seen these incidents and assigned sinister interpretations. Aunt Polly and Joe's mother could have faced an accusation that the boys had been murdered rather than drowned. Some disreputable character in the village could have been accused. The boys' dramatic reappearance could have prevented a hanging rather than a funeral. Indeed, if the boys mistimed their arrival, someone falsely accused would have paid a high price for the pirate adventure.

This scenario was not always fictional. A case with long-lasting legal implications occurred in the English village of Campden.[2] On August 6, 1660, William Harrison set off to collect rents on behalf of the local lord and landowner. When Harrison failed to return, his servant – John Perry – was dispatched to look for him. The next day, Harrison's son joined the search. He encountered Perry, who said he had gotten lost and slept in a hedge. The two found Harrison's hat and comb. They were cut and bloody. Foul play was suspected. Perry immediately became the primary suspect. After a vigorous interrogation, he gave a detailed confession. Perry claimed

DOI: 10.4324/9781003372134-2

his brother and mother had instigated a plot to rob and kill Harrison. Perry said that they threw Harrison's body into a bog or "sink."

The sink and nearby ponds were searched, but nothing was found. When Perry's brother was arrested, he attempted to discard some string with a slipknot at the end. The brother said it was his wife's hair lace, but Perry claimed it was used to strangle Harrison. At trial, Perry recanted his confession. With this, the authorities stopped the prosecution of the murder charge. All three members of the Perry family then admitted to burgling Harrison's house a year earlier. The timing of this admission and guilty plea was strategic. Oliver Cromwell had died and the Stuart monarchy was being restored. As part of the general tidying up of turmoil arising from the English Civil War, *An Act of Free and Generall Pardon Indempnity and Oblivion* (archaic spelling) pardoned those convicted of crimes except murder, piracy, rape, "the detestable and abominable Vice of Buggery committed with Mankind or Beast," and "the wilfull taking away or marrying any Maid Widow or Damzel against her will, or without the assent or agreement of her Parents."[3] With their strategically timed guilty plea, the Perry family got a "get out of jail free" card for the burglary and theft. It also undermined their credibility in the village and with the authorities.

A year passed. There was no sign of Harrison. The Perry family was again arrested and charged with murder. Despite their protestations of innocence, they were all convicted, primarily based on Perry's original confession and accusation. They were sentenced to hang. It was believed that the mother was a witch and had cast a spell on her sons to keep them from confessing. To save the souls of her two sons, she was hanged to remove her spell and allow her sons to confess. They continued to maintain their innocence. The trap door on the gallows opened beneath them as well. A contemporary report stated, "Mother and sons passed to their account amid the execrations of a rude assembly and the pen of public feeling seemed to record that they well deserved their fate."[4]

Another year passed. Suddenly William Harrison disembarked in England off a ship from Lisbon. Accompanied by great excitement and tumult, he returned to Campden. Harrison said he had been kidnapped by a press gang and sold into slavery in Turkey. After two years, his master died, allowing Harrison to escape to Lisbon and make his way back to England. Harrison's employer returned him to his former position. Others doubted the story. There were whispers that Harrison absconded to London with the rent money and returned after it was spent.

Despite doubts about Harrison's story, one core fact was inescapable. The Perry family had not murdered him. Three people had been hanged for a crime they did not commit. It was embarrassing for the criminal justice system of the day.

In an unrelated case about the same time, an uncle/guardian was seen punishing his niece so severely that she begged for her life. The niece then disappeared. The uncle was ordered to produce his niece to the authorities. He presented an imposter. It was assumed he had murdered his niece. He was promptly hanged. His niece then emerged from hiding to claim her inheritance.[5]

These cases were cited by the jurist Lord Mathew Hale to justify his much-quoted observation that "I would never convict any person of murder or manslaughter, unless the fact were proved to be done, or at least the body found dead."[6] Hale also argued that attempts to conceal a crime should be interpreted as an indication of guilt, but this qualification has generally been ignored. Nonetheless, Hale's dictum had so much impact because the putative victims of homicides had the embarrassing habit of returning to life on a reasonably regular basis.

One example was described by Abraham Lincoln. In 1841, Lincoln was a young lawyer in Springfield, Illinois. A somewhat simple-minded man named Fisher boarded with three brothers (who were unrelated to Fisher). The brothers were relatively prosperous; Fisher was not. Since Fisher never spent any money, people believed he was wealthy. Fisher disappeared. A few weeks later, one of Fisher's landlords was rumored to have spent gold coins. He was arrested, vigorously interrogated, and eventually gave a statement blaming his brothers for the disappearance. He claimed they took Fisher into a wood and emerged without him. The other two brothers were arrested. An intense search was conducted, complete with the draining of a mill pond. There was no sign of Fisher or his body. Nonetheless, all three brothers faced a trial for murder. One hired Lincoln as his lawyer. The brothers' future looked grim until Lincoln located the missing Fisher in the next county, disorientated and feeble, but alive. Fisher was delivered to the court in Springfield. The murder charges were dropped.[7] Lincoln ended up being a little bitter about the affair. His biographer, Carl Sandberg, reports his client "couldn't or wouldn't pay the fee of his lawyer and best friend in the hours a noose was knotted for his neck."[8] When his former client died of natural causes four years later, Lincoln successfully sued the estate to collect his fee of $100.

In other cases, the reappearance of the murder victim came after conviction.

In 1928 in Alabama, Louise Butler was a poor, black single parent with two children of her own and guardianship of two nieces. She had a violent quarrel with her 14-year-old niece, Topsy Warren. After the quarrel, Topsy abruptly disappeared. Rumors spread that she had been murdered. When the sheriff investigated, Louise said she had given the girl a "good whipping." The other niece and Louise's daughter told a more sinister story. They claimed Louise killed Topsy while administering the whipping. The two girls went on to say that Louise enlisted the aid of a friend, George Yelder. According to the girls, Louise and George cut Topsy's arms off with an ax, put her in a bag, and disappeared in the direction of a river half a mile distant. Upon return, George washed the ax while Louise Butler made supper.

Louise confessed. She showed the sheriff where Topsy's body had been thrown into the river. Louise described how George became tangled in vines while carrying out the gruesome disposal. The two were arrested and charged with murder. At her trial, Louise recanted her confession, but her daughter and niece repeated their story. After short trials, Louise and George were convicted and sentenced to life imprisonment. A week later, the sheriff was told that Topsy was living with other relatives only 20 miles away. He investigated and found Topsy alive and well. She had run away following her "good whipping" and did not know she had been murdered. Further investigation revealed that an enemy of George had taken advantage of Topsy's disappearance to convince the two young girls to lie. The girls did not understand the implications of the prank until their mother and guardian did not come home after the trial. Louis's temporary confession was attributed to a desire to do what the "white folk" were demanding. Alabama's governor granted pardons.[9]

On occasion, locating the person believed to have been murdered came too late for the accused.

In 1886, George Watkins disappeared from Arkansas. Andrew Hudspeth was having an affair with Watkins's wife. Mrs. Watkins was interrogated about her husband's disappearance. She eventually blamed her lover, saying that the killing was designed to clear the way for their marriage. Hudspeth was arrested and convicted of murder. The conviction was overturned on appeal,[10] but Hudspeth was convicted in a second trial and was hanged. Mrs. Watkins was charged with being an accessory but died in jail while awaiting trial.

Six months after Hudspeth was hanged, his lawyer reported finding George Watkins alive in Kansas. Given that both his putative murderers were dead, the authorities did not have much enthusiasm for confirming or disproving George's continued existence. There was no follow-up. The case remains murky.[11]

Sometimes a person reappeared even after "their" body was found and their murderer convicted. There was a mistaken identification of the body. We can call these "wrong-body" homicide cases rather than "no-body" ones.

In 1872, William Marion and John Cameron traveled and worked together in railroad construction. While in Nebraska, William appeared wearing John's boots and driving his wagon. There was no sign of John. William was suspected of murdering his friend, so he prudently left the state. A few months later, a skeleton was found. The skull had been shattered by three bullets. Everyone agreed that the skeleton was wearing John Cameron's clothing. It was assumed William killed and robbed his friend, but it took the law a decade to catch up to him. In 1883, William was found in a Kansas jail waiting for trial on a theft charge. He was brought back to Nebraska, tried for murder, convicted, and sentenced to death. This was overturned on appeal on the grounds that the death sentence should have been imposed by the jury rather than the judge. On the do-over trial, a jury showed itself to be just as harsh. William Marion was hanged on March 25, 1887. The *Omaha Daily Bee*, in a story titled "Death on the Scaffold: John Marion Hustled Hence with Hemp at Beatrice," proclaimed, "there seems to be no doubt but that he is guilty." For good measure, William was accused of having committed other unidentified murders in Oklahoma.[12]

Four years later, the headline in the same paper proclaimed, "HANGED AN INNOCENT MAN: Sensational Developments in an Old Murder Case at Beatrice – THE SUPPOSED VICTIM IS FOUND ALIVE."[13] John Cameron had surfaced. He explained his absence by saying he had been worried about a paternity allegation. Rather than marry the pregnant woman, John sold his belongings to his friend and fled – first to Mexico and then to Alaska. John was unaware of his putative death until 1890 – three years after William's hanging. John further delayed coming forward because of fear he would be blamed for the entire mess. William Marion was finally pardoned by Nebraska's governor on the 100th anniversary of his hanging.[14]

In 1908, Jenny Wilson left her husband, Bill Wilson. She took their 19-month-old child with her, leaving Bill with two older children. Jenny moved back to her parents' home. A few months later, she disappeared. Four years later, the skeletons of an adult and a child were discovered. It was assumed this was an indigenous burial site until a former employee of Bill's father got involved. He spread the rumor that the skeletons belonged to the missing Jenny and her child. He also claimed he saw Jenny on her way to visit her husband the night she disappeared. The disgruntled ex-employee also claimed to have discovered bloody children's clothing after the disappearances. Bill was charged with murdering his wife and child. Experts testified that the skeletons had been buried longer than four years, and that the child's jaw contained a mixture of children and adult teeth. This, the experts said, made it exceptionally unlikely the skeleton came from a child under the age of two. Despite this, Bill was convicted by a jury and sentenced to life imprisonment.

The case against Bill was so weak that the presiding judge wrote to Alabama's governor asking that the sentence be commuted. Bill's lawyer eventually found Jenny Wilson alive, well and remarried in Indiana. Upon learning of her first husband's incarceration for her murder, she returned to Alabama to verify her identity and account for her movements. After three and a half years in prison, Bill received a pardon. The Alabama State Legislature awarded him $3,500 compensation. Bill's luck remained bad. The trustee administering this money stole most of it and left the state.[15]

In 1908, Rev. James Smith and Rev. Ernest Lyons were engaged in a bitter dispute as to who would provide spiritual leadership to the primarily black congregation of a church in Reid's Ferry, Virginia. The two traveled to a regional church conference. James was carrying $45 in church funds. Ernest returned from the trip; James did not. As a result, Ernest assumed the sole pastorship of the church – until the decomposed body of a black man the size of James was discovered in a river. The body was identified as James Smith because of a distinctive ring. Ernest was charged with murder. At his three-day trial, members of the congregation testified about the un-Christian hostility between the two men of God. Ernest was convicted of second-degree murder. His lawyer wanted to appeal. The judge proposed an unorthodox procedure. An appeal hearing would be granted if the lawyer told his client that the appeal had been denied. The convicted pastor was then asked if he wanted to confess for the good of his soul. If he refused to confess, an appeal hearing would be granted. To the lawyer's surprise, Ernest confessed to the murder – and implicated several members of the congregation. All had testified against him at the trial. They were dismayed when arrested. The authorities were skeptical about the veracity of the confession/accusation. The pastor was asked to swear an oath, saying, "If I have told a lie, may God strike me dead."[16] He refused. The congregants were told to go home, and their pastor was returned to prison.

The matter appeared to be finished until a court clerk located Rev. James Smith, alive, well, and living in North Carolina. James said he had absconded with the church funds. He was aware of his colleague's arrest, trial, and conviction but had not come forward because he feared prosecution for the theft. Ernest Lyons was pardoned by the governor after serving three years of an 18-year sentence.[17]

In 1925, Mary Vickery disappeared from the small mining town of Coxton, Kentucky. A taxi driver, Condy Daubey, was questioned about whether he had given her a ride. He convinced the police he had nothing to do with the disappearance. Nine months later, a United States Marshall investigated a rumor that a still was producing moonshine in an abandoned mine. He discovered some clothing and a badly decomposed body. Mary's father tentatively identified the body as his daughter, but was so uncertain of his identification that he did not attend her funeral. At this point, a woman came forward to claim that the taxi driver had given Mary a ride and murdered her. Another witness testified that Condy once made a cryptic comment suggestive of guilt. Despite the weakness of the case against him, Condy Daubey was convicted of murder and sentenced to life imprisonment.

A year later, a police officer in Williamsburg, Kentucky (some 75 miles from Coxton), noticed that a Mary Vickery was registered in a hotel. The name sounded familiar, so he sought her out and recognized Mary from newspaper photographs. Mary immediately confirmed her identity. Mary explained that she left home because of disputes with her stepmother. She was working in a woolen mill in Cincinnati when she heard someone had been convicted for her murder. Mary said she procrastinated before deciding to return home to establish that she had not been murdered. Her trip was interrupted by the alert police officer. Condy was pardoned and the woman who accused him was charged with perjury. Two explanations were presented for the accusation. The first was a desire for the $500 in reward money. The second was bitterness toward Condy because he had refused to leave his wife to take up with her. These explanations are not mutually exclusive.[18]

These cases of "wrong-body" homicide cases have been discussed because they point to two problems for investigators. It was easy for someone to disappear, and identification of the dead was difficult and imprecise. With the exception of the Watkins/Hudspeth case in which Andrew Hudspeth's hanging removed any incentive for follow-up, in one respect these cases were relatively simple. When the person presumed to be dead reappeared, there was no controversy about their identity. In the cases of Russell Colvin and Connie Franklin, the identity of the living/murdered person was controversial.

The "Dead Alive" and "The Ghost of the Ozarks"

On May 10, 1812, Russell Colvin was observed having an argument with his brothers-in-law, Stephen and Jesse Boorn, in a field near Manchester, Vermont. Everyone in the community agreed that Russell was a couple of furrows short of a fully plowed field. The Boorn brothers were of the opinion – not unfounded – that their parents' support for Colvin, his wife (their sister), and their offspring was a drain on the family's wealth and a threat to their eventual inheritance. The argument turned violent. Russell's son reported that his father hit one of the brothers with a stick. Russell's brother-in-law used a bigger stick. Russell was knocked to the ground motionless and lay still. Russell's son ran away. His father disappeared.

At the time, not much attention was paid to Russell's disappearance. He had a history of aimless wandering and lengthy disappearances. Further, the War of 1812 with England had begun. Rumors had Russell joining the army. Years passed. By 1816, rumors began to circulate that Russell had come to a bad end. In 1919, these rumors intensified when Stephen and Jesse's uncle reported a dream in which Russell claimed he had been murdered. In this dream appearance, Russell reported being buried in an old cellar.[19] Word spread. Mass hysteria set in as others reported seeing Russell's ghost. Jesse Boorn was arrested while community leaders attempted to discover whether a crime had taken place. The cellar was searched, revealing a coat button and two knives. Russell's wife identified one of the knives as belonging to her missing husband. The coat button matched her description of those on his coat. Jesse responded by confirming Russell's murder but blaming his brother. A posse was dispatched to arrest Stephen. When he was brought back to Manchester and thrown into the primitive jail along with his brother, another prisoner claimed that Stephen confessed. Villagers conducted an intensive search for Russell's body, during which a dog located some burned bones in a hollow tree stump.

Public feeling ran high. Dozens of people reported seeing Russell Colvin's ghost wandering forlornly over the hills and fields. Those seeing the apparition said that Russell's spirit could not rest until his murderers were convicted and executed. The trial was quick and emphatic. Even though Jesse recanted his confession and Stephen denied having made one, the brothers were convicted and sentenced to death. Appeals to the state legislature resulted in Jesse's sentence being commuted to life imprisonment with hard labor. No mercy was shown toward Stephen. He was scheduled to be hanged at the end of January 1820.

The strange case got even stranger. Stephen Boorn's lawyer took out an advertisement in a small newspaper, the *Rutland Herald*. Under the headline "MURDER," the ad read:

> Printers of newspapers thro' out the United States are desired to publish, that Stephen Boorn, of Manchester, in Vermont, is sentenced to be executed for the murder of Russel Colvin, who has been absent about seven years. Any person who can give information of said Colvin may save the life of the innocent by making immediate communication. Colvin is about five feet high, light complexion, light coloured hair, blue eyes, about forty years of age. Manchester, Vt. Nov. 25, 1819.[20]

The advertisement went viral. It was published by one newspaper after another and eventually ended up in the *New York Evening Post*. A New Jersey reader wrote the paper to report that a farm laborer matching the description had appeared in his area "in a state of mental derangement" some seven years earlier. A New York pub owner originally from Vermont (and was a friend of the Boorn family) traveled to New Jersey to fetch the putative Russell Colvin. The two made a slow triumphal trip to Manchester, Vermont. The publicity and excitement built as Russell's identity was confirmed in community after community – by people who had never met him. The two arrived in Manchester. The farm laborer submitted to an examination and responded to questions in order to confirm his identity. Community leaders in Manchester declared him to be the missing Russell Colvin, previous ghostly appearances notwithstanding. Public opinion shifted abruptly. The Boorn brothers were declared innocent and released. Russell Colvin returned to New Jersey to resume his work as a farm laborer. On his way home, he profited by charging admission for the people to look at him.[21]

The affair received extensive publicity as an exemplar of the dangers of convicting without a body. It was cited as a case of justice ultimately being served. But perhaps justice was avoided. A hundred and seventy years after the "dead alive" Russell Boorn appeared, University of Massachusetts (Amherst) historian Gerald McFarland took a close look at the affair. He discovered some problems with the generally accepted narrative.[22]

McFarland's first discovery was that the timing did not line up. The original newspaper advertisement first appeared in Vermont on November 25, 1819. The *New York Evening Post* "reprinted" it the next day. In 1819, it was impossible to get from Vermont to New York that quickly. The first telegraph was not invented for another quarter century. The pub owner who produced the missing Russell Colvin was a family friend of the Boorns and had the local knowledge to provide a good briefing to an imposter. By making a slow, well-publicized trip to Manchester, the certification of the man's authenticity was established prior to his arrival. Preconceptions matter. The structure of the Manchester community also played a role in the acceptance of a possible imposter. Russell Colvin and his in-laws lived at the fringes of the community. The town leaders had the task of deciding whether the man was genuinely Russell Colvin – but they had not really known him. Those who did were members of the Boorn family and their neighbors. They, of course, had a strong incentive to declare him genuine. The most compelling identification came from Russell's wife. However, if she said the man before her was a stranger, she would be condemning one brother to the gallows and one to life in prison.

McFarland makes a strong circumstantial case that the man who presented himself as Russell Colvin was an imposter. But there is more.

After being released from jail, Jesse Boorn made his way to Ohio. He became a counterfeiter. In 1860, a deputy U.S. Marshall went undercover to infiltrate the counterfeiting gang. Jesse bragged to the undercover police officer that he and his brother murdered Russell Colvin but avoided punishment by producing an imposter. Jesse's trial for producing counterfeit coinage included testimony that he had once successfully produced a counterfeit brother-in-law.

Jesse Boorn's claim that he had successfully duped people in Vermont was dismissed back home as a fabrication. The good folk of Manchester had been mocked for their earlier belief that the ghost of Russell Colvin had appeared to seek justice. Forty years later, they were unwilling to admit they had been duped a second time – and it is possible that a living Russell had reappeared. McFarland makes a strong case that the "dead alive" murder victim was an imposter, but there can be no definitive answer after two centuries.

A hundred and ten years after Russell Colvin may or may not have been alive after people were convicted of killing him, another controversy about the identity of a possible murder victim bubbled up in the Arkansas Ozarks. A man known as Connie Franklin became famous as the "Ghost of the Ozarks."[23]

Late in January of 1929, a drifter calling himself Connie Franklin appeared in Stone County, Arkansas. Connie was a good-time boy soon known for his singing and harmonica playing more than his reliability as an employee. He worked for a few local farmers and entertained the locals. Six weeks after his appearance in the area, a poverty-stricken 16-year-old girl agreed to marry him. The couple walked to the home of the nearest justice of the peace. He was elsewhere. The disappointed lovebirds started walking back to the girl's home. Connie Franklin disappeared. At first, nobody noticed or cared that he was gone. By mid-summer, rumors began to spread that Connie had come to a bad end. A neighbor of Connie's fiancé reported having heard screams. Another directed the sheriff to a site where the brush had been burned. A search revealed no clues until the first neighbor produced a box with some small pieces of charred bones. She claimed these came from the ashes. Most of the fragments were too small to identify, but a doctor said one piece came from a human skull. The neighbor also produced a bloody hat allegedly belonging to Connie.

About eight months after the disappearance, Connie's bride-to-be told authorities an extraordinary story. While the two were walking back to her family's cabin, five of her neighbors appeared. The bride-to-be said they attacked Connie, beating him with a rock, a stick, and brass knuckles. The young woman said she was forced into the woods, raped, and forced to watch as her finance was burned in a roaring fire, dismembered, and burned again. The smoldering remains were then put in a sack and tossed into a nearby creek. The young woman said she was held prisoner for two weeks in a cabin and repeatedly raped. Connie's fiancé said she was warned she would be killed if she ever revealed what happened.

Five men were arrested and charged with Connie's murder. Two were also charged with rape. The lurid story went viral. Within a few days, the *New York Times* ran a story under the headline of "Murder by Torture Laid to Arkansans."[24] Media outlets closer to home were not as restrained. The *St. Louis Journal-Post* ran headlines such as "BURNING ALIVE CLIMAXES EVIL."[25] There was little regard for the presumption of innocence. An editorial in the *Arkansas Democrat* asked, "Could the depths of human depravity, the bestiality of mankind be plumbed deeper than by this act of barbarism?" Additional "eyewitnesses" to the crime came forward. As reporters gathered in Stone County, a class element was added to the coverage. Connie, his fiancé, and the key witnesses were poor and marginalized by any standard. The five accused of killing Connie were far from wealthy, but affluent by the standards of the Arkansas Ozarks at the beginning of the Depression. They owned more than one mule. This was transformed into sensationalistic depictions of class division and oppression. The *St. Louis Journal-Post* led the way with a story titled "OZARK MURDER REVEALS SYSTEM OF PEIONAGE: "BARONS' SAID TO BACK OF BRUTAL CRIME."[26] *Time* magazine said Stone County was dominated by an "Ozark Oligarchy" in which "two intermarrying, farm-owning clans on Dry and Cajun Creeks hold baronial sway over the hilly domain. With hickory whips and squirrel rifles they drive indigent, illiterate citizens to farm work as serf's wages."[27] *Time*'s theory of the crime was that Connie objected to the claim of "seigniorial 'first right'" to his bride-to-be. These portrayals were highly exaggerated, if not fantastical, but were based on a kernel of fact.[28] Missouri State University historian Brooks Blevins argues that the accused were part of a system of a vigilante enforcement of social norms.[29] As such, while the actual economic divisions were much more modest than portrayed (everyone was poor), the accused and accusers were on different ends of the stick used to enforce "appropriate" behavior.

By the time the trial began in December 1929 (the wheels of justice turned quickly back then), the town of Mountain View contained more reporters than whiskey stills. All were trying to outdo their colleagues in producing the most sensational description of the vile crime. Suddenly the story changed. Connie Franklin reappeared. The father of one of the accused posted a thousand-dollar reward for anyone producing a live Connie. A traveling cotton buyer and seller of crank-powered radios located Connie working on a farm in about a hundred and fifty miles away. The salesman took Connie back to Stone County. The farmer and his sons were in hot pursuit, outraged at being cheated out of the reward money.

Connie's sensational reappearance caused considerable controversy. The accused immediately recognized him as the missing man. Their accusers did not. Community and media opinion was divided. Connie gave three explanations for his sudden departure from Stone County. The first was that he had been beaten and encouraged to leave by rival bootleggers. The second was that he had fallen, hit his head on a rock, drank heavily, and left for no reason. The third was that he had a dispute with his fiancé. According to this version, the absence of the justice of the peace generated a quarrel. Connie wanted to get married the next day, while his bride-to-be decided she wanted to wait till spring. When she refused to share his sense of urgency, Connie left.

Since he had only been in the county for six weeks before disappearing and eight months had passed, it was difficult for people to say with certainty whether the current claimant to Connie Franklin's name was the same person as the old one. It was decided that his former fiancé was the best person to judge. A line-up was arranged, with the fiancé in a group with other young women. Connie promptly identified her, but the fiancé said she was uncertain, declaring, "If it's Connie, he's changed some since I saw him." Connie shared details of their time together and sang for her. She still refused to confirm he was her former suitor. The fiancé's father was also skeptical even after the ghost played the harmonica for him. Uncertainty soon hardened into a hard and active denunciation that the man was an imposter.

The man claiming to be Connie Franklin presented a detailed and reasonably coherent description of his travels after disappearing. His "front-story" or explanation of what he had done prior to his six-week stay in Stone County was murkier. Investigations eventually revealed that he was a man named Frank Rogers and was married with two children.[30] He'd abandoned his family several years earlier and drifted until being incarcerated in Arkansas's State Mental Hospital. After escaping from this institution, he arrived in Stone County to find true, if short-lived, love. The question of who Connie Franklin was before his disappearance was controversial but legally irrelevant. The essential question was whether he was the man attempting to get married before disappearing. Had that person been murdered, dismembered, and burned? Or had he just wandered off, regardless of motivation? The question was left to a jury to decide.

The trial began a week after Connie Franklin's reappearance. It was the biggest event in Mountain View's history. A dozen reporters and hundreds of curious hillbillies converged on the courthouse. The Associated Press strung a telegraph line into town to ensure prompt dissemination of the news. At the time of the trial, the town was a construction site. A new state highway was being built so the buildings on one side of main street had been jacked up so they could be moved to widen the road allowance. The Ozark Café was on a rolling pallet. The owners hooked the restaurant up to a mule team so it could move up and down the street selling meals to those in town for the trial.

The trial focused on the question of whether Franklin/Rogers was the same person who had been singing and harmonica playing nine months earlier or whether he was an imposter. The issue of identification became even more important when the only piece of forensic evidence – the small, charred piece of someone's skull – disappeared. The box of bones had been accessible to media inspection. The sheriff suggested someone had taken it as a souvenir.

The key prosecution witness was Connie's teenage former fiancé. She repeated her lurid story of love, assault, rape, and murder. Pointing at Frank Rogers, she proclaimed "he claims he's Connie, but he hain't my Connie." Upon cross-examination, she could not swear her that Connie was dead the last time she saw him. She said his last words were "they have killed me." Such a proclamation would be at best premature. The account of dismemberment and body burning disappeared from her account. A parade of witnesses pointed to discrepancies between their recollection of Connie Franklin and the current reality of the man now identified as Frank Rogers. The defense countered with a similar parade of witnesses to testify to the contrary. Frank Rogers took the stand and provided colorful, often contradictory, testimony that left observers understanding why he had been incarcerated in the State Mental Hospital. However, he was firm on the essential point. Earlier in the year, he had been the person known locally as Connie Franklin – and that he had not been murdered.

After several hours of deliberation, the jury emerged to tell the judge they were deadlocked, with six in favor of conviction and six for acquittal. The judge told them to try harder to reach a consensus decision. Several hours later they reemerged to report that they were deadlocked over the rape charges. The judge reminded them that the rape charges were not at issue in this trial – they would be dealt with at a future trial. A short time later, the jury emerged to announce acquittals on the murder charges.[31]

Frank Rogers proclaimed the verdict was vindication of his claim to be Connie Franklin. He bought a new harmonica with his witness fee and attempted to monetize his notoriety with a vaudeville act in which he played the harmonica while a narrator told the story of the Ghost of the Ozarks. In those days, people were desperate for entertainment, but not that desperate. The show failed. A proposed movie was never made. Connie Franklin resumed his wandering ways. He died just over three years after coming back from the dead. Back in Stone County, opinion remained divided as to whether he had been an imposter.

No-Body Murders and Resurrection

The cases discussed in this chapter show problems for homicide investigators in no-body and wrong-body cases. William Harrison, Fisher, and Topsy Warren went missing and were believed murdered until they showed up alive. George Watkins may or may not have reemerged after his disappearance. John Cameron, Jenny Wilson and her child, Mary Vickery, and James Smith disappeared with foul play suspected. When a body – the wrong body – was discovered, suspects were charged, convicted, and, in one case, hanged. Russell Colvin and Connie Franklin reappeared – or maybe they did not.

In today's world, it is easy to forget about the difficulty of identification. Our existence is caught in a tight web of financial transactions, government regulations, cell phone tracking, and social media posting. A hundred years ago, none of this existed. Most people did not have a bank account – let alone a social insurance number. When a person arrived in a town, their name was what they said it was. Nobody could prove otherwise. The isolating effects of distance were much greater. Fisher was living only 15 miles from where he was believed to have been murdered. Topsy Warren was in the next county. It took weeks for news of their putative murder to travel this distance. There were no fingerprint records or dental records until early in the 20th century – and DNA matching did not come until the end. Even memory of physical appearance was imprecise until Kodak's box camera became ubiquitous following its introduction in 1888.[32] Until then, people had to rely on personal memory and physical descriptions. It is hard to give precise and distinctive descriptions. This was the reason tattoos first became popular with sailors. During the Napoleonic wars, the British navy would stop American ships and press into service any sailor believed to be a British subject. American sailors carried letters from officials and community leaders describing them and attesting to their American citizenship. Since the British naval officer's acceptance of these descriptions was directly proportional to their manpower needs, sailors began to get distinctive tattoos in order to provide a unique description of themselves.[33]

People disappeared and reappeared quite regularly. The reasons were usually simple and benign. On occasion, suspicious circumstances would create the suspicion that murder had occurred. This could be buttressed by eyewitness testimony or a confession. Even with this, prosecution was risky. The putative murder victim could return at the most awkward and embarrassing moments. Because the prosecution of no-body homicide cases was very rare, these embarrassments were also rare, but when they occurred, publicity was extensive.

Today, it is much harder for a person to disappear without a trace. As a result, police and prosecutors are less likely to be embarrassed by the dead returning to life during a trial or after a conviction.

But there is still a risk; prosecutors in Australia learned this in 2003 in the case of Leonard Fraser.[34]

In 1999, Fraser was released from prison. He had spent 20 of the previous 22 years in prison after being convicted of four vicious rapes. Fraser celebrated his freedom by going on a killing spree. He was caught and convicted for the rape and murder of nine-year-old Keyra Steinhardt. This put him behind bars. However, police in Queensland were left with unsolved cases. Three other women had been found raped and murdered in the area. A 14-year-old girl, Natasha Ryan, was missing and presumed dead. Until he was in prison for Keyra's death, Fraser refused to admit any involvement in the other four cases. After he was locked up, this changed. Fraser confessed to four more murders – including Natasha – in exchange for being placed in protective custody. Fraser was charged in these deaths. Just as the trial was about to begin, police received a tip that Natasha was still alive. They raided a house and discovered Natasha hiding in a closet. She had run away from home five years earlier to live with her boyfriend.[35] Natasha said that when the search for her began, she was too embarrassed to reveal herself. As a result, she had spent five years living indoors. When company came over, she hid in a closet. Natasha reported that she used cutup towels for sanitary products so that her boyfriend would not be seen purchasing these feminine products.

The prosecutor dropped the charge of murdering Natasha. Fraser was convicted of the three murders. He died in prison of natural causes. Reaction toward Natasha was mixed. Police were unhappy. They had spent five years and $400,000 investigating her case. The prosecutor was unhappy. The reemergence of Natasha cast doubt on Fraser's confessions and threatened to derail the prosecution for the other three murders. Because he had told police that he did not know where Natasha was, her boyfriend was convicted of perjury and sentenced to three years in prison. Natasha was found guilty of causing a false investigation and fined $1,000. Amid all this unhappiness, the press was delighted. They made sure that crime paid for the two lovers. Two magazines and a television show paid a reported $250,000 for the rights to their story. After the boyfriend got out of jail, the two got married. Media outlets reportedly paid another $200,000 for their wedding pictures.[36]

The possibility of the dead returning to life is always present in a no-body prosecution. It led to the apocryphal story of the defense lawyer who, when giving his closing argument, suddenly turned to the door and exclaimed the name of the person believed to have been murdered. When everyone looks, the lawyer proclaims to the jury, "You looked. That means you thought the person might have entered – you must acquit because you demonstrated a reasonable doubt the person is dead." In the story, the prosecutor always responds by saying, "everyone looked but the accused. There is one person that knew absolutely the person would not be entering the room, and that is the accused." The highly publicized stories of purported murder victims reappearing contributed to an extreme reluctance by prosecutors to proceed to trial in the absence of the victim's body. This did not begin to change until the last half of the 20th century.

Notes

1 Twain, Mark, *The Adventures of Tom Sawyer* (Oxford, UK: Oxford University Press, 2007).
2 Clark, George (ed.), *The Campden Wonder* (London, UK: Oxford University Press, 1959).
3 "Charles II, 1660: An Act of Free and Generall Pardon Indempnity and Oblivion," in *Statutes of the Realm: Volume 5, 1628-80*, ed. John Raithby (s.l: Great Britain Record Commission, 1819), 226–234. *British History Online*, accessed February 20, 2021, http://www.british-history.ac.uk/statutes-realm/vol5/pp226-234.
4 Clark, *Campden Wonder*, 107.

5 Greene, Francis Paul, "I Ain't Got No Body: The Moral Uncertainty of Bodiless Murder Jurisprudence in New York After People v. Birenbaum," *Fordham Law Review* 71, no. 6 (2003): 2868.
6 Cited in Greene, "I Ain't Got No Body", 2868.
7 Helmuth, Laura, "Abraham Lincoln, True Crime Writer," *Smithsonian Magazine*, February 10, 2010.
8 Sandberg, Carl, *Abraham Lincoln: The Prairie Years (vol. 1)* (Norwalk, CT: Easton Press, 1995): 293.
9 Borchard, Ewin M., *Convicting the Innocent: Sixty-five actual errors of criminal justice* (Garden City, NY: Garden City Publishing Company, 1932): 39–44.
10 Hudspeth vs State, 50 Ark 534, 9 S.W. 1 (1888).
11 Wrongfully Convicted Database Record, n.d. "Andrew J. Hudspeth," Accessed June 18, 2022. Andrew J. Hudspeth - Innocents Database of Exonerations.
12 "Death on the Scaffold," *The Omaha Daily Bee*, March 26, 1887.
13 "Hanged an Innocent Man," *The Omaha Daily Bee*, August 4, 1891.
14 ExecutedToday.com, n.d. "In the Matter of a Posthumous Pardon to William Jackson Marion," accessed July 14, 2022. http://www.executedtoday.com/images/William_Jackson_Marion_pardon.jpg.
15 Borchard, *Convicting the Innocent*, 303–310.
16 Borchard, *Convicting the Innocent*, 146.
17 Borchard, *Convicting the Innocent*, 144–148.
18 Borchard, *Convicting the Innocent*, 50–57.
19 Pearson, Edmund Lester, *Studies in Murder* (Garden City, NY: MacMillan, 1924): 265–285.
20 Reproduced in McFarland, Gerald, *The Counterfeit Man: The True Story of the Boorn-Colvin Murder Case* (New York, NY: Pantheon Books, 1990): 117.
21 McFarland, *Counterfeit Man*, 119–143.
22 McFarland, *Counterfeit Man*, 178–208.
23 Blevins, Brooks, *Ghost of the Ozarks: Murder and Memory in the Upland South* (Champaign, IL: University of Illinois Press, 2017).
24 "Murder by Torture Laid to Arkansans," *New York Times*, November 25, 1929.
25 Secrist, William G., "Burning Alive of Farm Hand Climaxes Evils," *Kansas City Journal-Post*, December 1, 1929.
26 Secrist, William G. "OZARK MURDER REVEALS SYSTEM OF PEIONAGE: "BARONS' SAID TO BACK OF BRUTAL CRIME," *Kansas City Journal-Post*, November 28, 1929.
27 "Ozark Oligarchy," *Time*, December 9, 1929.
28 Blevins, Brooks, "The Arkansas Ghost Trial: The Connie Franklin Case and the Ozarks in the National Media," *The Arkansas Historical Quarterly* 68, No. 3 (Autumn, 2009): 245–271.
29 Blevins, *Ghost of the Ozarks*.
30 Allen, Dean, "Man at Batesville Identified as Franklin," *Arkansas Democrat*, December 8, 1929.
31 Chenout, Fletcher, "Four Cleared of Slaying Franklin," *Arkansas Democrat*, December 20, 1929.
32 Fineman, Mia, "Kodak and the Rise of Amateur Photography" Metmuseum.org. (October 2004). https://www.metmuseum.org/toah/hd/kodk/hd_kodk.htm#:~:text=By%20far%20the%20most%20significant,100%2Dexposure%20roll%20of%20film.
33 Dye, Ira, "The Tattoos of Early American Seafarers, 1796 – 1818," *Proceedings of the American Philosophical Society* 133, No. 4 (December 1989): 520–554.
34 Doneman, Paula, *Things a Killer Would Know: The True Story of Leonard Fraser* (Crows Nest, NSW, AU: Allen & Unwin, 2006).
35 Molloy, Shannon, "The 'dead' Girl Who Fooled a Nation," *Fraser Coast Chronicle*, December 23, 2018.
36 Davies, Hannah, "'Girl in Cupboard' Marries Crime Partner," *news.com.au*. October 23, 2009.

3

OPENING THE DOOR TO PROSECUTING NO-BODY HOMICIDES

Fears about the reappearance of the dead contributed to a reluctance to pursue murder charges when someone disappeared, no matter how suspicious the circumstances. As we saw in Chapter 1, in the 19th century, there appear to have been only seven no-body homicides successfully prosecuted in the United States. Canada witnessed only two no-body prosecutions during that century. During the first half of the 20th century, no-body prosecutions remained extremely rare. We will look at two cases from the 19th century to illustrate why prosecutors were reluctant to prosecute these cases. We will then in turn examine three cases from the mid-20th century that were pivotal in making prosecutions more common.

In 1844, Edward Rulloff worked as a naturopathic doctor and teacher in upstate New York. His career and residence choices had been made under duress. Rulloff started as a lawyer in the British colony of New Brunswick, but embezzlement charges caused a change in his country of residence and career. This had unfortunate consequences. Rulloff was not a great doctor. His sister-in-law and his niece died while under his care.

Rulloff married a woman named Harriet and had a young daughter named Priscilla. It was not a happy marriage. Rulloff was insanely jealous. He threatened to poison his wife after he saw her kiss a cousin goodbye. Shortly after this incident, neighbors noted that the shutters on the Rulloffs' house remained closed all day. The next day, Rulloff borrowed a horse and wagon. He got help loading a heavy trunk into the wagon and was seen putting a sack beside it. He disappeared for a day. When Rulloff returned, he was observed carrying the trunk into his house. It looked much lighter. Visitors observed the house was disordered. Harriet's clothing and Priscilla's toys remained in the house, but there was no sign of Rulloff's wife or daughter. Rulloff gave contradictory explanations for their absence. When rumors spread that he had murdered Harriet and Priscilla, Rulloff fled.

In 1844, criminal justice retained a significant element of self-help. Harriet's brother pursued Rulloff to Ohio, arrested him, and brought him back to New York for prosecution. The prosecutor believed it would be impossible to obtain a conviction for murder without a body, so Rulloff was tried and convicted for kidnapping his wife. He got ten years in prison. When his term expired, Rulloff was re-arrested and charged with murdering his wife but successfully argued this constituted double jeopardy. The prosecutor then charged Rulloff for the murder of his daughter. Rulloff was convicted. While waiting for his appeal, Rulloff taught school to local children inside the jail. He cultivated a relationship with the jailer's teenage son; he then

DOI: 10.4324/9781003372134-3

convinced the jailer's wife to help him escape. Rulloff fled with the jailer's wife and son but was caught and returned to jail. The escape had been unnecessary. The appeal court ruled either a body or an eyewitness was needed to convict.[1] When Rulloff was released from jail, he partnered with the jailer's son in a career of burglary. This resulted in sporadic jail terms. In 1870, Rulloff, the jailer's son and third person attempted to burgle a dry-goods store in Binghamton, New York. Two clerks were sleeping on the premises. A struggle ensued. Rulloff shot and killed one of the clerks. The robbers fled and attempted to escape by swimming across a river. Rulloff's partners drowned, but Rulloff was caught. He was tried for murder, convicted, and hanged on May 18, 1871.

Rulloff's trial for killing the clerk would normally have received only local interest. It was, after all, just a shooting arising from an incompetent burglary. Such events were common and attracted little notice. It was different for Rulloff. His trial attracted crowds of 2,000 people per day and generated saturation coverage in New York's newspapers. One reason was Rulloff's earlier trials for the kidnapping and murder of his wife and child. The second was that the media declared Rulloff a genius. While serving his ten-year sentence for kidnapping his wife, Rulloff spent his time studying languages, primarily Greek and Latin. He theorized that before people developed language, they invented universal linguistic rules. Understanding these rules would allow anyone to learn a new language in a few days. In 1869, Rulloff presented a book manuscript to the American Philological Society and offered to sell it for $500,000. The Society dismissed his ideas as the work of a crank. A year later, after Rulloff was again charged with murder, newspapers published excerpts of his manuscript. Nobody could understand what he was saying, so Rulloff was proclaimed a genius. In his description of the case, Edmund Pearson said "Rulloff was described as 'a great philologist,' which means, probably, a great philologist, – for a murderer... [he was] not far removed from the man who seeks to find perpetual motion, or to square the circle."[2] Nonetheless, the media certified Rulloff as a genius. Horace Greeley, publisher of the *New York Tribune* and soon-to-be presidential candidate, declared that someone with Rulloff's intellect was too valuable to execute regardless of guilt. When this argument failed to impress the hangman, Rulloff's brain was put on display at Cornell University. It was the largest brain ever measured.[3]

Before his execution, Rulloff gave a detailed confession to the editor of the *Binghamton Leader*, R.H. Freeman, admitting to murdering his wife and daughter. Rulloff's account confirmed the essential features of the prosecutor's theory. Rulloff beat his wife to death, put her in a trunk, and used the borrowed wagon to transport her to a lake. He then surreptitiously borrowed a rowboat, and sent her to the bottom. Rulloff told Freeman he gave his daughter morphine to "stop her from crying" but denied killing the girl. Another reporter claimed Rulloff confessed strangling the girl, but Rulloff denied making this confession. This denial generated rumors that Rulloff placed his daughter with relatives. A woman named Pricilla Rulofson was identified by some newspapers as being Rulloff's daughter. The woman and her family "utterly denied" any connection to Rulloff. There was no evidence to support the alleged relationship except a general similarity in the name. The unfortunate little girl probably joined her mother in a watery grave.

Rulloff was mentally unstable and regularly committed criminal acts, both violent and non-violent. There was a strong circumstantial case that he murdered his wife and daughter. Despite this, he was initially charged with kidnapping his wife rather than murdering her. A later jury was quite willing to convict for murdering his daughter, but the conviction was overturned on appeal. Unlike the jury, the appeal court judges required a body (or a witness) to establish murder. Circumstantial evidence, no matter how powerful, was not enough. In 1871, as he approached his date with the hangman for a different murder, Rulloff confirmed that he should have been hanged a quarter century earlier. He did not completely "get away" with these crimes; he served ten years in prison for kidnapping his wife and a couple of years in jail for murdering his daughter, but he did not face the penalty prescribed by law for the two murders.[4]

Half a century after Rulloff murdered his wife and daughter, another high-profile no-body murder case resulted in a failure of the criminal justice system. In New Mexico, the killers of a father and his son avoided punishment.[5]

On February 1, 1896, Albert Jennings Fountain and his youngest son, eight-year-old Henry, were traveling in a buckboard wagon from Lincoln, New Mexico, to their home in Las Cruces. Today the trip takes less than two and a half hours. In 1896, it was a three-day journey. The pair were almost home when they met a mail carrier traveling the other direction. Albert reported that three mysterious riders had been following him. The mail carrier urged Fountain to return to a nearby stage-coach station to ensure their safety. Albert refused, saying his son had a cold and needed his mother's care. Albert and Henry were never seen again. When they did not arrive home, a posse was hastily organized. It found a spot where tracks and empty cartridge cases marked an ambush. The buckboard was found abandoned. It contained two pools of blood, several empty cartridge cases, and Henry's blood-soaked handkerchief knotted around two coins. Tracks from three men led away from the wagon. When the men camped, they left an indentation made by a heavy object wrapped in a blanket – something about as heavy as a body. The tracks eventually petered out, and the posse abandoned pursuit.

It was clear that Albert and Henry were murdered. Albert's slaying came as no surprise. He had enemies. Henry's murder was more unexpected. Nobody expected that Albert's enemies would be "low enough" to murder a child. Indeed, Henry's mother sent the boy to Lincoln with his father on the expectation the child's presence would offer protection to the father. It was a tragic miscalculation.

Albert Jennings Fountain arrived in New Mexico during the Civil War as part of the 1st California Infantry Regiment of the Union Army. After the war, he settled in El Paso, Texas, and was active in the state's reconstruction government; serving as a tax collector, election judge, administrator of confiscated Confederate property, and member of the Texas legislature. By 1873, the Reconstruction Republicans lost power in Texas. Albert decided it was safer to move his growing family into the New Mexico Territory. They settled in his wife's hometown of Mesilla, New Mexico, 45 miles from El Paso. The new location was safer and politically more congenial. Albert became the leading citizen in Southern New Mexico. He led campaigns against the Apaches, served in the territorial legislature, and served as assistant district attorney. In his spare time, he founded a newspaper, a dramatic society, and an opera house. Albert's day job was a successful legal practice which included defending Billy the Kid on a murder charge.

The issue that got Albert and Henry murdered was cattle rustling. New Mexico was home to open range ranching; ranchers could graze their cattle anywhere. Wealth came from ownership of the cattle and the control of water supplies. The large ranchers and corporate cattle companies weaponized their herds. Large herds could eat out the range used by smaller ranchers. On the other hand, the smaller ranchers viewed the cattle belonging to the large cattle companies as an excellent opportunity for enrichment. The result was a bubbling cauldron of violence that approached the intensity of a war.

In 1894, the large cattle companies formed the Southeastern New Mexico Stock Growers' Association to fight the smaller ranchers/rustlers. Some called it a land grab by the big, rich companies. Others called it a fight against rustling. The Association hired Albert Fountain as a special investigator and prosecutor. University of Oklahoma historian Arrell Gibson says that when Albert took this job, "he in effect signed his death warrant."[6] Within a year, Albert and the Stock Growers' Association sent 15 people to jail for rustling. The trip to Lincoln was to obtain more indictments. Albert was explicitly warned against proceeding when a messenger arrived in court delivering an anonymous note reading, "If you drop this we will be your friends. If you go on with it you will never reach home alive."[7] Albert ignored the note and obtained 32 criminal indictments. He never reached home – dead or alive.

In the circumstances, it did not take Sherlock Holmes to deduce who, generally, was responsible for the bloody disappearance of Albert Fountain and his son. Reports soon emerged of earlier, unsuccessful, conspiracies to ambush and kill Albert. But which individuals were directly responsible? Had the small ranchers/rustlers hired contract killers or had they done the foul deed themselves? The primary suspects claimed to have been at home at the time of the attack, but a witness reported that the three leading suspects did not arrive at their ranch until late that night – on tired horses. This testimony was undermined when the witness admitted he was promised a share of a $10,000 reward for his testimony.

The Stock Growers' Association engineered the hiring of Pat Garrett, the killer of Billy the Kid, as sheriff. The suspects went into hiding. Given Garrett's reputation for six-shooter trials, this was deemed prudent. In July of 1898 – almost two and a half years after Albert and Henry's disappearance – Garrett and his deputies caught up with the suspects. In the ensuing gunfight, Garrett withdrew after one of his deputies was mortally wounded. The suspects were finally arrested eight months later. After much legal maneuvering about jurisdiction, the location of the trial, and the basket of charges, Oliver Lee and Jim Gililland were charged with murdering eight-year-old Henry Fountain. No charges were laid for the murder of Albert Fountain.

The trial took place in the small and isolated mining town of Hillsboro, population around 200. It was the biggest event in the history of the town. The Territorial government constructed a tent city to house court officials and witnesses. The defense team constructed another temporary city on the other side of town to house friends and well-wishers of the accused. The Western Union Telegraph Company installed a telegraph line to let reporters send out their stories. Newspapers from El Paso, the Hearst syndicate, and the Associated Press reporters covered the trial.

The prosecution case introduced the history of threats against Albert Fountain from the small ranchers/rustlers and the witness claiming the accused had not been home at the time of the ambush. The core of the case, however, was testimony from posse members about their observations of tracks, blood, and spent cartridges. The defense argued that the accused were victims of a long-stand conspiracy by the corporate cattle companies against small, honest ranchers. The credibility of the anti-alibi witness was attacked with the suggestion his recollection was affected by greed for the reward money. These arguments were sideshows. The defense attacked the forensic evidence presented by the posse members. Could they distinguish human blood from animal blood? Could they determine whose feet created tracks in the sandy soil? How many guns in the Territory used the same type of cartridges as were found? Most importantly, where was Henry's body? Rumors that Albert Fountain had been seen in distant cities swirled around the trial.

The jury deliberated for eight minutes before reaching a verdict to acquit. With that, the authorities abandoned their efforts. Nobody was ever charged for the disappearance and presumed murder of Henry's father.

Professor Charles Sonnichsen of the University of Texas at El Paso argues that the acquittal was partly due to the hostility of small ranchers toward the large corporate cattle companies.[8] Further, the small ranchers did not talk to outsiders. As a result, while it was generally assumed the small ranchers were behind the disappearance, individual attribution of guilt was difficult. These factors likely contributed to the acquittals, but the absence of Henry's body contributed to the acquittal. The jury was not sequestered during the trial, and there were constant rumors that Albert and Henry had been sighted in cities such as St. Louis and New Orleans. The absence of a body created doubt. In the absence of either an eyewitness or a confession, a conviction was unlikely even if the circumstantial case had been stronger.

In 1844, Harriet and Pricilla were undoubtably murdered by Edward Rulloff. In 1896, Albert and Henry were undoubtably murdered, although the identity of the killers remains uncertain. Both cases were extremely high profile. The disappearance of the Fountains generated publicity equivalent to the disappearance of Jimmy Hoffa almost seven decades later. The subsequent failure to convict anyone for the crime even contributed to a delay in New Mexico being granted statehood as the case was cited as an indication that the Territory was too lawless to become a full member of the Union.[9] These cases seemed to confirm the accuracy of the proposition that anyone could remain unpunished for murder if they successfully disposed of the body.

Opening the Door to No-Body Prosecutions

The number of prosecutions and convictions for no-body homicides began to increase in the last half of the 20th century. In Chapter 12, we will explore some technological and investigative reasons for the change, but three cases were crucial in changing the social and legal approach to no-body prosecutions. These cases changed perceptions about the possibilities of obtaining convictions without a corpse. The technological improvements in investigations came after the change in attitude and precedent created by these cases.

In Georgia, the prosecution of John Wallace for the 1948 murder of Wilson Turner changed the perception of *how much* of a body was necessary to successfully prosecute. Wallace was sent to the electric chair, even though he burned Wilson's body and dumped the ashes in a stream.[10]

In California, police and prosecutors sent L. Ewing Scott to prison for the murder of his wife, Evelyn Scott, without forensic evidence, witnesses, or a confession. Scott was convicted and sentenced to life based on his behavior and actions following his wife's disappearance. It was described as the first no-body conviction obtained purely based on circumstantial evidence.[11]

In the late 1940s, John Wallace was a wealthy landowner in rural Georgia. The family wealth came from distilling illegal whiskey and bootlegging. After serving prison time for bootlegging, Wallace downsized the illegal operation to concentrate on his dairy herd and supervising sharecroppers growing cotton and corn. Some people who are successful in other endeavors become "hobby farmers." By the end of the 1940s, Wallace was a successful farmer who was a hobby bootlegger.

Wallace received a tip from the county's sheriff that federal revenue agents were planning a raid. He ordered his associates to dismantle the still and dump the whiskey. For Wallace, risk aversion was more important than income maximization. He had been to prison, and he had enough money. Wilson Turner's math was different. Wilson was a white sharecropper and junior partner in Wallace's bootlegging operation. He was poor, ambitious, and had a young family. Rather than dumping the whiskey, Wilson took it to town to sell. Wallace was outraged. Georgia journalist Margaret Anne Barnes reports that Wallace was generous, but insisted on receiving absolute obedience. Wallace seized the money Wilson received from the sale of the whiskey and evicted him just before Wilson's crop could be harvested. Wilson responded by stealing two of Wallace's dairy cows and hiding them in a different county until they could be sold.

Wilson was caught with one of the cows and arrested. Wallace arranged for him to be transferred to his home county to face the theft charges. Wilson was terrified by the move. He believed Wallace was bringing him home in order to kill him. As they say, just because you are paranoid does not mean they are not out to get you. Wallace arranged for Wilson's truck to be parked outside the jail with the gas tank drained. The sheriff agreed to release Wilson from jail. Wallace and three friends were waiting on the street. They planned to "capture" Wilson as he was "escaping" from jail. It is unclear whether Wallace intended to kill Wilson or merely administer a severe beating. His friends later claimed that homicide was not the intent, but there was a high-voltage reason for them to deny premeditation.

Regardless of intent, the plan was incompetently implemented. Wilson was released a few minutes too soon. He got to his truck before Wallace and his helpers were in position. A chase ensued. Wilson made it past the county line before running out of gas. He abandoned his truck in the parking lot of a restaurant and sought shelter inside. The pursuit was too close. As Wilson screamed for help, Wallace and his associate grabbed him. They dragged a struggling Wilson to their car. Wallace hit Wilson over the head with a shotgun. With this, Wilson stopped moving. He was stuffed into the car. As the car drove away, Wallace was seen continuing to beat Wilson with the shotgun. Wallace later threw Wilson's body down an abandoned well.

Quite naturally, the incident perturbed the restaurant owner and his seven patrons. They summoned their sheriff, who started a homicide investigation. It was not much of a "whodunnit." Eight witnesses identified Wallace. The sheriff launched a search for both the body and the culprits.

Wallace's lawyer proposed an audacious strategy based on jurisdiction. The lawyer proposed that Wallace admit to killing Wilson but claim the death happened later, in his home county. The cooperative sheriff would arrest Wallace and the legal process would be in a jurisdiction where the legal authorities were friendly. Wallace rejected this advice. After being told that nobody in Georgia had been convicted for murder without a body being found, Wallace recruited two black sharecroppers to pull Wilson's body from the well, transport it to a large hole that once contained a still, burn the body, and throw the ashes into a nearby stream. Wallace and his lawyer then traveled to meet the sheriff of the county from which Wilson had been kidnapped. He arrived in the car used in the chase and kidnapping. It had been imperfectly cleaned.

The sheriff promptly arrested Wallace, who proclaimed that conviction was impossible without a body. The sheriff launched a massive search. Nothing was found. The sheriff arrested two of Wallace's associates. One panicked and confessed. Finally, the sheriff located the two sharecroppers who helped burn the body. They showed the sheriff the well that had been Wilson's temporary grave and the cremation site. A human brain was found in the bottom of the well. At the cremation site, ashes were found between the firepit and the stream. A small piece of charred bone was in the stream. In a movie made about the case in 1983, Johnny Cash played the sheriff. In the movie the sheriff was asked what he had found. "The body of Wilson Turner" was the reverent reply.[12]

And so, it was, legally speaking.

The trial attracted dozens of journalists and hundreds of spectators. Objectively, the evidence against Wallace was overwhelming. Eight witnesses had seen him kidnap and assault Wilson. Two other witnesses described how they had been forced to help burn the body. There was blood in the car and at the top of the well. The clothes Wallace was wearing were found in his closet – covered in bloodstains. A parade of witnesses testified about the motive and the scheme to create a faked jailbreak and capture. There was even a fortune teller who Wallace consulted to help relocate the well into which Wilson had been dumped in and to ask if he would get caught. But there was almost nothing of Wilson Turner; just his brain and a small piece of charred bone. It was enough. Wallace was convicted and sentenced to death. After a few years of appeals,[13] he sat in a hot and uncomfortable chair for the last time.

Despite the evidence, there was doubt that Wallace would be convicted or executed. He was the richest man, up to that point, ever to be executed in Georgia. Many expected that his wealth and power would protect him. The two sharecroppers who testified how they helped burn the body were black. Never had a white person in Georgia been convicted of murder based on the testimony of a black witness. There was also the question of jurisdiction. Wallace took the stand to claim that Nelson was alive and (relatively) well after being hit over the head with the shotgun. He made the bizarre claim that Wilson asked to be thrown down the well as punishment, but was killed when the shotgun accidentally went off. The defense argued that this meant Wallace had been charged in the wrong offence in the wrong jurisdiction. This defense was undermined by the refusal of Wallace's accomplices to support of this version of events and by the fact that the body was no longer available to ascertain whether Wilson had been killed by a blow to the head or by a shotgun blast.

The issues of wealth, race, and jurisdiction all established important precedents for justice in Georgia. However, for no-body prosecutions in general, the issue of "how much body is needed?" had the most long-term impact. Wallace was convicted, even though there was very little of Wilson Turner left. An autopsy to establish the cause of death was impossible. The ability to gain a conviction with a small piece of a body would become more important as forensic techniques improved. By the 1990s, improved forensics and DNA techniques meant that a single cell from a victim's body could be enough to help convict a murderer.

But there is even more. Dot Moore argues that it was the destruction of the body that caused Wallace to be executed.[14] She argues that the killing of a poor cow thief by a wealthy and powerful man would, by itself, not have been dealt with particularly harshly. If Wallace had followed his lawyer's initial advice, he would likely have been acquitted by a friendly jury or, at worst, served a few years in prison for manslaughter. There is evidence supporting this contention. Wallace's colleagues were convicted of murder, sentenced to life, and then paroled a few years later. The desecration of Wilson's body through incineration may have been more responsible for Wallace's execution than the actual act of murder.

John Wallace committed murder in front of eight eyewitnesses. An accomplice confessed. Two people he forced to help him destroy the body testified at his trial. There was a wealth of forensic evidence, including Wilson's brain at the bottom of the well and the charred bone in the stream. There was a trail of blood – in the car used to transport the body, on Wallace's clothing and at the top of the well. This cornucopia of direct evidence was absent when L. Ewing Scott was prosecuted in California a decade later for the murder of his wife, Evelyn Throsby Scott.[15]

Evelyn was a wealthy widow living in the Los Angeles suburb of Bel Air. She had a net worth of about a million dollars; roughly the equivalent of ten million today. In 1950, at the age of 58, she married Leonard Ewing Scott. On May 16, 1955, Evelyn disappeared.

Scott was a few years younger than his wife. He dressed well, was a good dancer, and could be an attentive companion. These qualifications enabled him to marry frequently. Scott carried business cards describing himself as an "investment broker" but had no training, experience, or clients. His documented work experience included clerking in a paint store and self-publishing a self-help book for women, titled *How to Fascinate Men*. The printer was never paid. Despite this spotty record in the business world, after marrying Evelyn, Scott began to take control of her finances. He argued that cash would be key to survival in the event of nuclear war to convince his wife to sell $223,000 worth of stocks and bonds. The cash was stored in safety deposit boxes. From a previous husband, Evelyn had inherited an apartment building in Milwaukee. Scott convinced her to change the property management company. The new firm took direction from Scott.

On May 15, 1955, the Scotts took a new Cadillac for a test drive. The car salesman was, other than Scott, the last person known to see Evelyn alive. The next day, Scott canceled his wife's regular appointment at a beauty salon. Two days later, he forged his wife's signature to get access to her safety deposit boxes. He began to open accounts at different banks and deposit large amounts of cash. Scott instructed the Milwaukee property management company to deposit the rental income to one of these new accounts. Scott began to sell his wife's clothing and fired her housekeeper and handyman. He told them Evelyn had "gone east" and no longer needed their services.

Scott told Evelyn's friends, her lawyer, and her relatives' contradictory stories to explain her absence. The most common explanation was that his wife was a mentally unstable alcoholic and was getting treatment in an eastern sanatorium; sometimes he said Baltimore, other times New York. Evelyn's friends and family were skeptical. They had never seen any sign of mental instability or alcoholism. Sometimes Scott claimed he did not know the exact location of the sanatorium. On other occasions, he cited a need to protect Evelyn's privacy to keep the location a secret. Scott gave a completely different story to another widow he began courting; she was told that his wife had simply disappeared. When the woman asked why he did not get a divorce, Scott replied that he was waiting seven years to have Evelyn legally declared dead. Scott also took up with a younger, poorer, prettier woman. She became a frequent overnight guest and traveled with him to Las Vegas using the name Mrs. Scott. She received Evelyn's jewelry, luggage, and furniture as gifts.

Evelyn's friends were suspicious of Scott, but her disappearance was not reported to the police until her brother returned from the South Pacific. The brother accused Scott of killing his sister. Scott denied that Evelyn was dead. He claimed she had disappeared, but communication was ongoing. According to Scott, he and his wife left notes for each other under a vase outside the house. Evelyn's brother was skeptical. He went to the police in March 1956 to report his sister's disappearance and his suspicions about her husband.

When interviewed by the police, Scott told another story. He now claimed that Evelyn had sent him to the store to purchase tooth powder eight months earlier. When he returned home, she was gone. The police searched the Scotts' home. They could find no forensic evidence within the house. There was a firepit in the backyard. Sifting through the ashes, they found some fabric, belt buckles, and snaps for hosiery fasteners. Against the fence in the neighbor's yard, the police found Evelyn's dentures and eyeglasses hidden by branches and leaves. A search of bank records was more productive. Scott had clearly been forging Evelyn's signature and draining her assets. He was indicted on 13 counts of forgery and theft. While waiting trial, Scott was released on a $25,000 bail. He promptly disappeared, but was arrested a year later at the Canadian border crossing between Detroit and Windsor, Ontario. Scott had been hiding in Canada but went to Detroit to buy a new car. He was extradited to California to face trial on a charge of murdering Evelyn.

The prosecution presented circumstantial evidence to make two arguments.

The first argument was that Evelyn was dead. There was no body – not even a charred fragment of bone. There was no autopsy report identifying a cause of death. Instead of this kind of direct physical evidence, Evelyn's absence was used to convince the jury she was dead. She had been a woman of regular habits, with scheduled appointments at hair dressers, dentists, and doctors. Evelyn had a lot of friends who she phoned and visited regularly. She kept close track of her wealth and consulted frequently with her lawyer and accountant. All this suddenly ended. The prosecutor argued that in an orderly life, there was only one explanation for her absence. She was dead.

The second strand of the prosecution's case was to argue that if Evelyn was dead, there was no rational explanation but that Scott had murdered her. He had given many implausible and contradictory stories about her disappearance. He had embezzled her money. He had given away her belongings. He took a mistress into her home and started courting a replacement wealthy widow. These actions suggested that Scott knew Evelyn was dead. If she was dead, he must have killed her. With this, the prosecutor walked past traditional elements of proving a murder such as showing the jury the murder weapon and autopsy reports. He argued that it was not necessary to prove *how* he had killed her, but just that he had. Perhaps the best summation of the prosecution's case came later from the Appeal Court:

> The theory of the People can be stated as follows: It would be utterly unreasonable to believe that Mrs. Scott would have run away from her home, her husband and her friends; it would have been an irrational thing for her to do. If it was unreasonable to believe that she would have left home voluntarily that would have been a circumstance tending logically to prove that she did not leave of her own accord. The People's theory then proceeds to the activities of appellant both before and after his wife's disappearance. It is contended that the evidence proved that he had a motive for doing away with his wife, he coveted her large estate, attempted to prepare her friends for an explanation of her disappearance at some future time, was pleased and satisfied when she disappeared, did everything in his power to deceive her friends and the authorities in order to prevent an investigation, promptly set about through forgeries and thefts to steal her property, and fled the country when he feared that he would be charged with her murder.[16]

The defense claimed Evelyn was still alive. To support this contention, they produced several witnesses offering dubious accounts of seeing her. For example, a railroad ticket seller testified that he sold Evelyn a ticket to New York City on July 20, 1955 – over a month after her disappearance. The ticket seller said that he read media reports of Evelyn's disappearance about nine months later and recalled selling her the ticket. Aside from the implausibility of this level of recollection, this testimony was contradicted by the railroad's records. The Court of Appeal later dismissed the "But Mrs. Scott may still be alive" defense as "some mythical or miraculous hypothesis" and noted that "the law is reason; it does not proceed upon fantasy or remote and unrealistic possibilities."[17]

Scott was sentenced to life imprisonment in 1957. He spent the next few decades protesting his innocence and mounting appeals. Scott accumulated over 500 pounds of legal papers and files in his cell. The California prison system attempted to parole him in 1974, but Scott refused to accept release on the grounds that it might be construed as an admission of guilt. In 1978, the California prison system had enough of Scott and kicked him out of prison against his will. His determined denial of guilt abruptly ended in 1984. Journalist Diane Wagner had completed research for a book on the case. She interviewed Scott several times. After she informed Scott that she would not be visiting again, he asked for one more visit. Scott then gave a detailed, tape-recorded confession. Scott said that Evelyn had been lying in bed when he hit her on the head with a hard rubber mallet. He then wrapped her body in a tarpaulin, put her in the trunk of his car, drove into the desert near Las Vegas, and buried her in an unmarked grave.[18]

The successful prosecution of Scott received a lot of media attention. Perhaps more importantly, the legal community took notice of a precedent that convictions for homicide could be obtained and upheld solely based on circumstantial evidence.

Opening the Door to No-Body Prosecutions in Canada

A few days before Christmas in 1946, nine-year-old Marion Rusnak was sent to the store to buy milk. The shopkeeper gave the girl a gift along with one for her brother. Marion set off for home. A short time later, a neighbor saw her talking to a man. That was the last time the

St. Catherine's, Ontario, girl was ever seen. After Marion did not return home, a huge search was organized. The searchers found no sign of her, dead or alive.

A week after Marion disappeared, the superintendent of a nearby factory found Sydney Chambers bloody and unconscious. Chambers, the watchman and stationary engineer for the factory, had slit his wrists. Chambers lived in a suite in the factory. The police found a jug of milk and the wrapping paper for two gifts in his residence. The shopkeeper said the milk and paper was identical to what she had given Marion. After his wounds were treated, Chambers was charged with the criminal offence of attempting suicide and questioned about Marion's disappearance. He promptly confessed to killing her. Chambers said he kidnapped the girl and was holding his hand over her mouth to prevent a scream when she died. Chambers said he burned Marion's body in the factory's furnace.[19]

Chambers was charged with murder and quickly brought to trial. He recanted his confession, claiming he confessed to complete his suicide attempt. "Suicide by policeman" is a well-documented phenomenon. Chambers claimed he had attempted suicide by hangman, but was now of sound mind and wished to live. The jury did not buy Chambers's new story. He was convicted of murder and sentenced to hang.

Chambers appealed. He argued that his suicide attempt should not have been treated as evidence of his guilt, and that his confession should not have been admitted because it was not supported by a corpus delicti – evidence that the crime had occurred. The Ontario Court of Appeal ruled in his favor on the first argument but not on the second.[20] The result was a new trial. Chambers was once again convicted. He was hanged on December 16, 1947 – only 51 weeks after Marion disappeared. With this case, Hale's dictum against convicting for murder without a body was rejected. Like the Scott case in California, the Chambers conviction established the corpus delicti could be established by circumstantial evidence rather than by a corpse or eyewitness.

Cracking Open the Door on No-Body Homicide Prosecutions

The unsuccessful prosecutions for murder of the Rulloffs and the Fountains demonstrated how difficult it was to obtain a homicide conviction without a body. Making things even worse, the dead (or their proxies) had an occasional, but embarrassing habit of turning up alive when the legal system did prosecute. For both these reasons, prosecutions in no-body homicides were rare. A murderer was almost certain to avoid punishment by successfully disposing of the body.

In Canada, the successful prosecution of Chambers created a precedent that the body of evidence demonstrating a crime occurred did not mean the body of the deceased was required.

The successful prosecution of Wallace created the potential of establishing death with a small piece of the body. It was no longer necessary to have a corpse with a gunshot or knife wound or a bashed-in skull to show the victim had been murdered. All that was necessary was a small fragment of the person along with other evidence pointing to guilt. It was impossible to determine whether Wilson Turner had been killed with an intentional blow to the head or shot with a shotgun. The jury decided this question did not matter. The appeal courts agreed. With this, evidence such as a bloodstain in the trunk of a car could, in the right circumstances, become strong presumptive evidence in a homicide case. The technical capacity to identify the remains of people from fragments emerged in the 1990s with DNA technology, but the legal capacity to use this evidence dates to Wallace's conviction in 1948.

The conviction of Scott took things one step further. As an article about the case in the *California Law Review* stated, "since circumstantial evidence alone may adequate proof of the identity of the criminal, it is submitted that it would illogical to hold that the corpus delecti could not be proven with circumstantial evidence."[21] In the right circumstances, the fact of disappearance could be deemed proof of homicide. In times past, this would have been a very dangerous assumption but by the 1950s, someone like Evelyn Scott lived a well-documented life. Strong inferences could be made from her absence. At the time, Evelyn's life was still unusual in the extent to which her existence – and therefore the implications of her absence – could be documented. However, the case occurred on the cusp of a massive expansion in the bureaucratic surveillance of individuals. Within a few decades, it was easier to document an individual's habitual existence and therefore make inferences from their disappearance. As in the case of Wallace, the change in the legal interpretation foreshadowed a change in the technical capacity of law enforcement agencies.

The ground was laid for more prosecutions in no-body cases.

Notes

1 Ruloff v. The People, 18 N.Y. 179 (N.Y. 1858).
2 Pearson, Edmund, *Instigation to the Devil* (New York, NY: Charles Scribner's Sons, 1930), 46.
3 Godwin, Dwayne, "Big Head, Dark Heart: The Notorious Head of Edward H. Rulloff," *BrainFacts.Org,* December 2, 2012.
4 Pearson, *Instigation to the Devil*; Freeman, *E.H., Edward H. Rulloff: The Veil of Secrecy Removed* (Binghamton, NY: Carl and Freeman, 1871.); Wisely, Jr., Herbert A., "The Life and Death of Edward H. Rulloff," *The Crooked Lake Review*, May, 1993; Bailey, Richard W., *Rogue Scholar: The Sinister Life and Celebrated Death of Edward H. Rulloff* (Ann Arbor: MI, 2003).
5 Gibson, A.M., *The life and death of Colonel Albert Jennings Fountain* (Norman, OK: University of Oklahoma Press, 1965); Sonnichsen, C.L., *Tularosa: Last of the Frontier West* (Albuquerque, NM: University of New Mexico Press, 1960); Recko, Corey, *Murder on the White Sands: The Disappearance of Albert and Henry Fountain* (Denton, TK: University of North Texas Press, 2008).
6 Gibson, *Life and Death*, 220.
7 Gibson, *Life and Death*, 229.
8 Sonnichsen, *Tularosa*, 173–191.
9 Recko, *Murder on the Whitesands*, 197–199.
10 Barnes, Margaret Anne, *Murder in Coweta County* (New York, NY: Pelican, 1983); Moore, Dot, *No Remorse: The Rise and Fall of John Wallace* (Montgomery, AB: NewSouth Books. 2011).
11 Poland, W. Charles, "Criminal Procedure - Proof of Corpus Delicti by Circumstantial Evidence" *William and Mary Review of Virginia Law* 2, No. 2 (1955): 170–173.
12 Nelson, Gary, dir. *Murder in Coweta County* (New York, NY: CBS).
13 Wallace vs. State, 204 GA 679 (GA 1949).
14 Moore, *No Remorse*, 62–69.
15 Wagner, Dianne, *Corpus Delicti* (New York, NY: St. Martin's Press, 1986); "In the Teeth of the Evidence," *The Daily Mirror*, October 18, 1957; Hill, Gladwin, "Coast 'Murder' Lacks Only Body" *New York Times*, April 28, 1957.
16 The People vs. Leonard Ewing Scott, 176 Cal.App.2d 458, 1 Cal.Rptr. 600.
17 The People vs. Leonard Ewing Scott, 176 Cal.App.2d 458, 1 Cal.Rptr. 600.
18 Wagner, *Corpus Delecti*, 284–290.
19 Maksymchuk, Andrew F., *Champions of the Dead: OPP Crime-Fighters Seeking Proof of the Truth* (Victoria, BC: Friesen, 2014), 71–83.
20 Rex v. Chambers, [1947] O.R. 443–454.
21 Willmarth, Francis, "Criminal Law: Murder: Proof of Corpus Delicti by Circumstantial Evidence," *California Law Review* 48, No. 5 (1960): 852.

4

"TILL DEATH DO US PART"

Intimate Partner Homicides and Body Disposal

On the evening of Friday, November 11, 2011, Dorothy "Dot" Woods spent a few hours in a lounge with a friend. She returned home and kept her children company while they finished watching a movie. Just before midnight, her children went to bed. Nobody has admitted to ever seeing Dorothy alive again.[1]

When with her friend, the Saskatoon, Saskatchewan woman talked about her marriage. It was not good. In the spring, Dorothy and her husband, David Woods, agreed to an "open marriage." Each would be free to have other sexual partners as long as discretion was practiced. Dorothy used internet dating sites to find a few lovers while her husband relied on prostitutes. The arrangement was not working. Woods believed that "openness" should be one-sided and harassed Dorothy's lovers. Woods was also a racist. Dorothy said her husband warned he would kill her if she ever had sex with a black man. Despite the warning, Dorothy spent the night of November 10 with a black lover. Her husband had "caught" her. Dorothy told her friend that she wanted out of the marriage, but did not have enough money to leave.

When Dorothy's children woke up on Saturday morning, their mother was gone. By Sunday, others noticed her absence. Woods told Dorothy's brother that Dorothy had left, adding there was no need to file a missing person's report. By Monday, more people became concerned. Dorothy operated a home-based day care (The Artsey Fartsey Day Care). When parents arrived to drop off their children, the door was locked. Dorothy had a lot of friends. They were phoning each other to exchange information and rumors. On Tuesday, November 15, Woods finally phoned the police to report Dorothy missing. The police also received a report from one of Dorothy's lovers who had received racist, threatening, and abusive texts from Dorothy's phone. The sender identified himself as "Dot's husband."

Woods told police Dorothy had left – likely with a lover – taking with her a makeup bag, purse, identification, and credit cards. He said Dorothy was wearing a black star-fish-shaped ring when she left. After the interview, the police arrested Woods for sending the threatening text messages and obtained a search warrant for the Woods' home. Hidden in the garage was Dorothy's purse, identification, and credit cards. Her ring was in a hidden safe. The clothes Dorothy had been wearing the previous Saturday were in a garbage can in the garage. On top of them was a partial roll of polyethylene, a bag that had once contained rope, and a receipt from a hardware store. Woods had purchased the polyethylene and 50 feet of rope the day Dorothy disappeared. The police also found Woods had 11 firearms and a set of brass knuckles. Five guns

DOI: 10.4324/9781003372134-4

were illegally stored. One was an illegal sawed-off shotgun. More charges were laid against Woods.

As police glowered suspiciously at Woods, Dorothy's friends organized a massive search. Hundreds of volunteers combed fields and the riverbank. No sign of Dorothy was found. Woods, facing charges for the threats and firearms, was released on bail. The case quickly reached an impasse. Dorothy was gone. Every passing day increased the probability she was dead. There was circumstantial evidence against Woods, but prosecutors said it was not enough to support a murder charge. The police watched Woods, placing a GPS tracking device in his truck.

Early in January, the case broke. An unidentified dead woman was found south of Saskatoon. The discovery was reported on radio newscasts. The police officer monitoring the GPS tracker on Woods's truck saw it took a strange trip into an isolated rural area immediately after the newscast. The police retraced the route. At the endpoint of the trip, the police found Dorothy's body. She was in a culvert filled with ice. Dorothy was naked. Her hands were tied, and there was rope tightly knotted around her neck. She had been wrapped in polyethylene; it was secured with green tape. The end of the tape matched perfectly with a partial roll of green tape found in Woods's garage.

In 1991, the 5,300-year-old body of a man known as Ökzi the Iceman was found so well preserved in ice in the Italian Alps that coroners could conduct an autopsy.[2] Dorothy had only been frozen for six weeks. For the coroner, it was as if she died the day before. He reported that Dorothy had been knocked unconscious with a blow to the head. Her hands had been tied. Then she had been strangled with the rope.

Woods was arrested and charged with murder. At his trial, Woods claimed the police planted Dorothy's wallet and ring in his house. Woods admitted to taking the suspicious truck trip, but said he discovered a hand-drawn map under his windshield wiper. Believing it an attempt by the police to set him up, he drove the route outlined on the map. Woods could not explain why, if he believed the map was a police setup, he obligingly followed its instructions. When asked to produce the map, Woods said he had lost it. One news report described the prosecutor's cross-examination as a "barbeque." The jury reached a guilty verdict before stopping for a coffee break. Woods appealed, claiming his defense lawyer had been incompetent. For example, he said the lawyer had not forced the police officer monitoring the GPS tracking device to admit that there was no way of determining who was driving the truck. In an affidavit responding to the allegations of incompetence, the lawyer pointed out that Woods admitted to being the driver. The defense lawyer also said that Woods admitted guilt after the trial.[3] The Saskatchewan Court of Appeal upheld Woods's conviction.[4]

Woods's lawyer was not incompetent. The trial was the legal equivalent of a basketball game between the Harlem Globetrotters and the Washington Generals. The two teams played about 17,000 times. Washington won once. By one point.[5] Given the evidence in the Woods case, the match between prosecutor and defense lawyers was as competitive as a Globetrotters/Generals game. Woods was convicted because he was guilty and because he was an incompetent murderer. He created a mountain of circumstantial evidence. He demonstrated both a guilty knowledge and a guilty conscience by leading the police to Dorothy's body. Woods carefully wrapped up Dorothy's body to protect it from the elements and preserved her in ice. He left forensic evidence that linked her body with his garage. Woods created a flashing neon "convict me" sign over his head.

But let us construct a contra-factual scenario. Let us imagine that Woods did everything exactly the same except for body disposal. There were some limitations on successfully disposing of Dorothy's body. It was November in Saskatchewan. Digging a grave or throwing her in a body of water was out. The ground was frozen and the lakes covered with ice. Effective options remained. If Woods dumped her in some isolated stand of trees, Dorothy's body would have been pulled apart by coyotes and other animals. If Woods threw Dorothy's body in a garbage dumpster, she would have been buried in Saskatoon's landfill. What would have happened if Woods had opted for one of these two simple body disposal methods?

Woods would not have been charged when he was. Despite the circumstantial case, Woods was not charged for murder until Dorothy's body was found. Police were convinced Dorothy was dead, but wanted to remove any possible doubt. The longer Dorothy was missing, doubt diminished. At some point, the prosecutor may have authorized charges but caution might prevail. Without Dorothy's body, it is possible Woods would never have been charged.

The police would have continued to monitor Woods. Since this crime occurred in Canada, Woods could have become the target of a "Mr. Big" operation; almost exactly four years after Dorothy was murdered, another Saskatchewan woman named Sheree Fertuck disappeared in suspicious circumstances.[6] Undercover police officers convinced Greg Fertuck that he was being recruited into a powerful criminal gang. He gave a detailed disclosure to the boss of the gang – "Mr. Big" – and took undercover officers on a two-day search looking for Sheree's body.[7] The search was unsuccessful, but Fertuck was charged because of his disclosures to Mr. Big.[8] Without Dorothy's body, the Woods case was tailor-made for Mr. Big. Woods would probably have fallen for it, but he might have been a little smarter and more cautious than Fertuck.

If Mr. Big was unsuccessful, the prosecutor might have eventually proceeded with the circumstantial case. Dorothy disappeared from the Woods home. The marriage was on the rocks. Woods had threatened to kill Dorothy and threatened her lover – after her disappearance and using her phone. He lied to police about her purse, identification, credit cards, and ring being gone. The clothes she was last wearing were in the garbage can in the garage. It probably would have convinced a jury, but would not have been the slam-dunk that the case became after Woods led police to Dorothy's body. The bottom line: Woods might have been convicted, but there was also a chance he would have avoided conviction.

Intimate Partner Homicides and No-Body Cases

In both the United States and Canada, the official homicide statistics suggest that about one in five homicides involves intimate partnership as the relationship between killer and victim. This ratio changes in no-body cases. In the United States, intimate partner homicides account for two in five of the successful prosecutions. In Canada, if we include the Mr. Big cases in which the killer led police to the body, one in three successfully prosecuted no-body cases involved an intimate partner relationship between killer and victim.[9]

There are many reasons body disposal is an attractive strategy for killers of their intimate partner. These killings usually occur in a residence. The killer controls the crime scene after the killing. This creates time for cleanup and disposal strategies. Blankets, tarpaulins, large suitcases, duffel bags, picnic coolers, and garbage bags are generally readily at hand. Fleeing the scene does not separate the killer from his crime. To avoid arrest, the killer must choose between staging the scene to point suspicion in other directions and moving his victim's body.

The means of killing affects the ability of the killer to use body disposal as a strategy to avoid arrest. In the United States, less than 1 percent of all homicide victims are strangled.[10] Among successful no-body prosecutions of intimate partners, at least 15 percent of the victims were strangled. In Canada, just under 8 percent of all homicides are strangulations[11] compared to half the prosecutions for no-body intimate partner homicides. Strangulation sets the stage for body disposal because it is relatively neat. Blood is not shed so it becomes easier to avoid creating forensic evidence as the body is removed and the crime scene cleaned up.

Probably the biggest incentive for murderous husbands or boyfriends to get rid of the body is that it allows them to delay the launch of a police investigation. In some cases, the killer can even prevent a homicide investigation from beginning. The disappearance might not ever be reported to police, or it might remain defined as a missing person's case.

Most intimate partner homicides are quickly cleared. The police start the investigation with an identified suspect. Many are "self-solvers" as defined by Innes. The gathering of evidence is focused on establishing guilt. It is different with no-body cases. Prolonged absence is needed to establish the fact of death. When Dorothy Woods disappeared, police quickly concluded she was dead and her husband was the killer, but doubt remained. It was conceivable Dorothy had gone off with a lover as Woods claimed. Without the recovery of her body, doubt would only be dissipated with the passage of time.

A measure of the effectiveness of body disposal as an arrest-avoidance strategy is the length of many intimate partner no-body cases. Even when police and prosecutors ultimately obtain a conviction, it often takes a long time. Of the 195 successful prosecutions of intimate partner no-body homicides in the United States identified in this study, charging occurred more than three years after the killing in 91 of the cases. In 33 cases, the delay between killing and charging was longer than a decade. The delay was longer than two decades in 11 cases. Five of these took three decades or longer before charges were laid. In Canada, in the six cases examined for this book there was a gap of more than three years between murder and arrest in five. In two cases, the gap was over a decade.

We will explore the challenges of investigating no-body intimate partner homicides by looking at the five cases that took at least three decades to solve. John Bayerl, Johnny Wright, Jose Rodriquez-Cruz, Michael Clark, and Eugene Zapata avoided arrest for over 10,000 days. That is a long time. The first American serviceman killed in Vietnam was Lt. Col. Peter Dewey in 1945. The last fatal casualties from U.S. military involvement in Vietnam came when two Marines – Corporal Charles McMahon and Lance-Corporal Darwin Judge – were killed on April 29, 1975. The "endless war" lasted 10,807 days – less time it took to charge these killers for their murders. Despite the delay, juries convicted three of these killers while two pleaded guilty. Why did these cases take so long? Why were charges eventually filed? What changed to trigger charges? Could prosecution have happened earlier? What do these cases tell us about the investigation and prosecution of no-body intimate partner body cases?

The Coldest of Cold Cases: Justice Delayed for Decades

The last time anyone saw DonaMae Bayerl was on May 6, 1979. Her husband, John Bayerl, was arrested 14,530 days later on February 15, 2019.[12]

After the Wisconsin woman disappeared, Bayerl waited three days before reporting her missing. Bayerl told police the two had argued about an unfixed television set and DonaMae drove away to "cool off." Bayerl said he went to bed and heard the car return about an hour later. In the morning, the car was in the garage but his wife was gone. Her clothes and personal belongings were not missing. Relatives and friends reported that DonaMae was a doting mother to her two daughters. One had chicken pox, making it even more unlikely her mother's departure was voluntary.

After DonaMae was reported missing, an extensive search found no sign of her. Police did find incriminating evidence inside the home. There was blood in the garage, the car, and on a rug inside the house. Circumstantial evidence pointed at Bayerl. Relatives reported he suddenly showed an unprecedented interest in doing laundry and housecleaning between DonaMae's disappearance and the filing of the missing person's report. DonaMae had complained of being physically abused and Bayerl's first wife had obtained a divorce by citing cruelty and abuse. Bayerl admitted he hit his wife and that he was having an affair. Despite the suspicious forensic and circumstantial evidence, Bayerl was not charged.

Three months after DonaMae disappeared, Bayerl filed for divorce. In DonaMae's absence, it was uncontested. Bayerl promptly remarried. No trace of DonaMae, either dead or alive, was ever discovered.

In 2009, Bayerl told one of his daughters that he was sure DonaMae was dead. Nine years later, he spoke to cold case investigators and said he had been a "bad husband" but had not killed his wife. In 2019, as part of a periodic review, the blood on the rug was tested for DNA. In 1979 Bayerl claimed he had been the one to bleed on the rug. The technology did not exist to test the veracity of this claim. Four decades later, it did. The DNA was DonaMae's. With this Bayerl was arrested.[13]

At trial, the prosecutor presented evidence of DonaMae's attachment to her daughters, Bayerl's 2009 statement she was dead, and the DNA evidence. Friends and relatives testified about DonaMae's complaints of abuse. Bayerl's first and third wives testified he had abused them. Bayerl did not testify. His lawyer did not call any witnesses. Instead, he argued the prosecutor had not proven Bayerl killed DonaMae. The jury disagreed. Bayerl was sentenced to life in prison; since he was then 79, his life sentence will be a short one.[14]

In the summer of 1976 Rebecca Doisy worked as a server in a Missouri steakhouse. A regular customer, Johnny Wright, kept asking her for a date. He seemed charming; Rebecca had no way of knowing he had an arrest record for rape, burglary, assault, and drug possession. On August 5, Rebecca agreed to go out with him. She was never seen alive again. On September 23, 2009 – 12,102 days later – Wright was arrested in Georgia and charged with Rebecca's murder.[15]

This was not really an intimate partner homicide; it was more of an aspirational intimate partner homicide. Further, it did not take three decades for the police to build a case. More than two thirds of the gap between Rebecca's murder and her killer's arrest occurred because Wright also disappeared.

Immediately after Rebecca's disappearance, police were stymied but in the early 1980s, they began hearing reports that Wright was bragging about killing Rebecca. In 1985, police located Wright's former roommate, who said Wright showed him Rebecca's body stuffed in the trunk of a car. Wright bragged that he "offed" the young woman. With this testimony, police obtained a warrant to arrest Wright for second-degree murder. Unfortunately, Wright heard the pitter-patter of police footsteps behind him. He fled Missouri for Washington State, then Texas, and, ultimately, Georgia. Wright settled down under the name of Errol Rodney Edwards. In 2007, computers at Georgia's Department of Driver's Services noticed that Wright's Social Security number did not match with the Edwards name. His driver's license was canceled. Wright used his own name to get a driver's license. Two years' later, Wright applied for a job requiring a background check. Wright went to a police station and paid $15 to get a letter for his prospective employer. Instead, he got arrested when the background check turned up the outstanding warrant dating back to 1985. One police officer told the media that "he basically paid $15 to get extradited to Missouri."[16]

At trial, the primary evidence against Wright was the absence of any sign of Rebecca's existence since August 5, 1979; testimony from two witnesses reporting his disclosures of guilt; and Wright's hiding from the law for 24 years.[17] Flight can be considered evidence of guilt. Wright was convicted and sentenced to 30 years in prison but died of natural causes after serving four years.[18]

The last reported sighting of Marta Rodriquez was on May 25, 1989. On October 18, 2019 –11,103 days later – Jose Rodriquez-Cruz was charged with her murder.[19]

Two months before Marta disappeared, a police officer saw Rodriquez-Cruz dragging his estranged wife down the street. The young Virginia woman was bound and gagged. Rodriquez-Cruz told the police officer that "if I can't have her, no one else will. She's mine." Rodriquez-Cruz was charged with kidnapping and assault, but the charges were dropped when Marta did not appear to testify. The police conducted a missing person investigation but closed the file after Florida authorities reported Marta was living there. In fact, it was not Marta. Rodriquez-Cruz had given Marta's identification to an illegal immigrant looking for an American identity. Authorities in Florida were fooled.

Marta's skeleton was discovered in 1991, but since she was no longer on the missing persons list, it was not identified.[20]

The fact of Marta's murder was discovered because Rodriquez-Cruz killed again. In 2009, he dated a woman named Pamela Butler in Washington D.C. She disappeared on Valentine's Day. Butler was a security fanatic. Her house had burglar alarms, exterior motion-activated lights, and video surveillance cameras covering the doors. The security video showed that Rodriquez-Cruz and Pamela entered the house together, but only Rodriquez-Cruz left. He returned a few times, but always left by himself. Pamela's disappearance resulted in an intense police investigation and extensive media coverage. Rodriquez-Cruz was the primary suspect, but police were stymied. Pamela had gone into her own home and vanished; there was no forensic evidence or sign of violence. The case went cold. Pamela was legally declared dead in 2016.[21]

In 2017, eight years after Butler disappeared, a cold case investigator took another run at the case. He found an acquaintance of Rodriquez-Cruz willing to testify about a guilty disclosure. The investigator also found other women willing to testify that Rodriquez-Cruz had been violent with them. With this, Rodriquez-Cruz was charged with murdering Pamela.

The prosecutor did not have the strongest case in the world, so when Rodriquez-Cruz offered to plead guilty to second-degree murder with a recommendation for a 12-year sentence, the proposal was accepted on the condition he tell police where Pamela's body was hidden. Rodriquez-Cruz told police that Pamela broke off the relationship so he strangled her. He turned off the motion-activated exterior lights and dropped Pamela's body out of a window. This enabled him to move the body without being caught on the video camera. After putting the corpse in his car, Rodriquez-Cruz returned to the house to turn the motion-detectors back on. Rodriquez-Cruz told the police he dumped Pamela's body near the Interstate I-95 in Virginia.[22]

There had been a lot of road construction along this interstate highway, and Pamela's remains were never found. However, one of the Virginia police officers remembered that the skeleton of an unidentified woman was found in the same location in 1991. It obviously could not be Pamela, but police wondered if Rodriquez-Cruz had returned to a familiar location for a second body disposal. They looked more closely at Marta's case and discovered the woman in Florida using Marta's identity was not Marta. DNA tests showed the skeleton was. Rodriquez-Cruz was charged with Marta's murder. He pleaded guilty.[23]

On March 30, 1981, Carol Lubahn had an argument with her husband, Michael Clark, about whether to sell their home. Carol wanted a bigger house. Clark did not. The California woman was never seen again. On April 12, 2011 – 10,970 days later – Clark was arrested and charged with Carol's murder.[24]

Prior to Carol's disappearance, there was tension in the marriage. In addition to an ongoing argument about the house, both husband and wife had a few affairs. Despite this, the marriage appeared stable and reasonably happy. There was no sign of abuse.

The morning after Carol's disappearance, Clark enlisted her parents to help care for the couple's two children. He waited a week before reporting her absence to the police. Clark claimed they had quarreled but he expected her back. Clark claimed that some of Carol's clothing and money had been removed from the home while he was at work. The investigation was superficial. A detective interviewed Clark twice before placing the case in the inactive file; he noted there was no sign of foul play and highlighted "divorce problems." Carol's car was found parked outside a restaurant a few miles away. Eight months later, Clark filed for divorce. It was granted in Carol's absence.

The case was reactivated in 1987. Police received a request for Carol's dental records after an unidentified skeleton was discovered in another state. The detective handling the request discovered that Carol had never reappeared. A search of government and financial records revealed "no indication of existence." Clark was interviewed again, and the backyard of the former family home was searched. Nothing came of this. In 2003, a review of cold case files resulted in another interview of Clark, again with no result. In 2011, the case came up again for review by the cold case squad. Clark was interviewed again. This time, the interview resulted in Clark's arrest and a murder charge.

At trial, the case against Clark was entirely circumstantial. Carol was gone. There had been no sign of her existence. Her children, relatives, and friends testified she would not have voluntarily abandoned her children. There were inconsistencies in the various versions of the story Clark had given to the police and media over the years. Clark took the stand to describe the night of March 30, 1981, and denied he had killed Carol.[25] The jury convicted him of second-degree murder.[26]

Prior to sentencing, Clark admitted to killing Carol, but claimed it was an accident. Clark said he and Carol argued about her affair as well as about selling the house. Clark said he pushed his wife. She fell, hit her head on the coffee table, and died.[27] Clark said he hid her body in the garage while he drove her car to the restaurant parking lot. After walking home, he tied a concrete block to her body, put her in the trunk of his car, drove to the ocean, used a raft to take her several hundred feet offshore, and sent her to Davy Jones's locker. Clark was given a polygraph test. It indicated that he was being partially deceitful. Clark then admitted to punching his wife instead of just pushing her.

Clark was sentenced to 15 years. He appealed his conviction, but was unsuccessful.

On October 11, 1976, Eugene Zapata murdered his wife Jeanette. He was not arrested and charged for 10,914 days.[28]

In the spring of 1976, Jeanette Zapata discovered her husband published semi-nude photos of her in a "swingers" magazine. She was displeased and filed for divorce.[29] Zapata moved out of the family home, but did not deal well with the situation. In September, Jeanette obtained a restraining order to keep him away from her and her home.

On the morning of October 11, 1976, Jeanette attempted to call her divorce lawyer from her home. The lawyer returned the call an hour later. Zapata answered. By being in the house, he was in violation of the restraining order. Zapata told the lawyer that Jeanette was not home but that her car was there and that her purse was on the table. He promised to let his wife know the lawyer had called. When the couple's three children returned home from school, Zapata told them their mother had gone away for a few weeks. Over time, this was transformed into a claim that Jeanette had abandoned the children. Three days after Jeanette's disappearance, her co-worker reported her missing to police. A few days later, a police officer visited the house. He saw no sign of violence or disturbance, but was suspicious of Zapata's demeanor. Zapata agreed to take a polygraph test. He denied knowing where his wife was or having anything to do with her disappearance. Zapata passed the test. With that, the investigation ended. Zapata moved back into the family home. The children were discouraged from mentioning their mother. On February 27, 1977 – just 139 days after Jeanette disappeared – the couple's divorce was finalized. Zapata promptly remarried. The children grew up. In 2001 Zapata and his second wife moved to Nevada. Jeanette never reappeared.

In 2004, more than a quarter century after Jeanette disappeared, a friend wrote to the police inquiring about the status of the investigation. A cold squad officer pulled the file and was dissatisfied with what she saw, or more accurately, by what she did not see. It had not been a case in which no stone had been left unturned. The officer checked official government databases. Jeanette's social security number had not been used since 1976. She had not used a credit card, done any banking, or renewed her pilot's license. The cold squad officer concluded Jeanette was dead. With the permission of the current owners, the police used a cadaver dog to search a crawlspace under Zapata's old house. The dog indicated it found the scent of a cadaver.

Zapata heard about the stirring of interest in the case. He made an unannounced trip back to Wisconsin. Using cell phone and financial records, the police determined he bought cleaning supplies, cleaned out a storage locker, and dumped something at a landfill 80 miles away.[30] A cadaver dog indicated the scent of a corpse in the storage locker. The police enlisted the assistance of Zapata's daughter. In a taped telephone call, she asked her father about Jeanette's death.[31] Zapata said Jeanette was dead but said he had nothing to do with it. The police discovered Zapata was renting a safety deposit box. They got a warrant to search it. Inside were four thick envelopes marked "Destroy. Do Not Read." The police disobeyed these instructions. Inside were detailed notes from the spring and summer of 1976. After Jeanette had filed for divorce, Zapata had stalked her. He had searched through her garbage and hired a private investigator to track her movements. He broke into Jeanette's house to sniff the crotch of her pants to see if he could smell spermicidal jelly. Zapata kept meticulous notes.[32]

After the discovery of his notes, Zapata was charged with murder.[33] The judge refused to admit the cadaver dog evidence.[34] The prosecutor's case was built on the long-term absence of Jeanette, the lawyer's call putting Zapata in the house the day of the disappearance, his record of stalking behavior, and the suspicious trip to the storage locker and landfill. It was not enough. A mistrial was declared after the jury deliberated four days without reaching a decision.

The prosecutor geared up for a second trial.[35] Just before it started, Zapata offered to confess and plead guilty to reckless homicide.[36] The proposal was accepted. Zapata said he was at the family home arguing with Jeanette when he "lost it." He hit her over the head with a paperweight and then strangled her. Zapata stored Jeanette's body in the crawlspace for a few days before burying her on land he owned. When he and his second wife moved to Nevada, the land was sold. To prevent discovery, Zapata dug up Jeanette's body and stored her in the storage locker. Permanent disposal was made after the police investigation was reactivated. Zapata had been like Coleridge's ancient mariner; instead of being bound to a murdered albatross he had been carrying around his murdered wife.

Zapata was sentenced to five years in prison following his plea bargain.[37] If he had left Jeanette's body lying where it fell, he would likely have received a life sentence. Because Zapata hid his wife's body, justice was delayed for three decades and was incomplete when delivered.

Turning Cold Cases into Hot Ones

Of these five cases, the only one with a "breakthrough" of completely new and unavailable evidence was that of Jose Rodriquez-Cruz for the murder of his wife, Marta. By giving her identification for another person to use, Rodriquez-Cruz successfully caused the original missing person's investigation to be closed. For almost three decades, police did not look for Marta because they did not know she was gone. This caused police to miss the connection when her skeleton was discovered in 1991. The breakthrough came when Rodriquez-Cruz killed again – and dumped Pamela's body in the same place as he had dumped Marta's. When he confessed to his second murder, Rodriquez-Cruz activated the investigation into his first. If a Virginia police officer did not remember that an unidentified skeleton had been discovered in the same area over two decades earlier, the police would not have discovered the person living under Marta's name was someone else.

There were no dramatic breakthroughs leading to arrests in the cases of John Bayerl, Michael Clark, and Eugene Zapata. In these cases, the passage of time and the long memories of cold squad investigators (or friends of the victim) resulted in charges eventually being laid. In all three cases, the length of the victim's disappearances transformed an initial categorization from "missing person" to "homicide." People often go missing for a day. Absences of a week are less common. The passage of months, years, and decades creates a kind of certainty that the person is no longer living.

In Bayerl's case, the passage of time was added to similar fact evidence of violence in other relationships. Regular periodic review by the cold case squad eventually resulted in the "new" evidence that sparked charges; the DNA that demonstrated it was DonaMae's blood on the rug. This kind of test was not available in 1979 when she was murdered. However, DNA testing was available for a quarter century before the test was performed. The case did not rest on the DNA test, but conducting it was the trigger for charges.

In Clark's case, the passage of time and periodic review created evidence in the form of contradictory statements. Clark told slightly different stories over the decades. Eventually a prosecutor decided these contradictions constituted evidence. The jury agreed. Clark was convicted on a weak case, but his pre-sentence confession removed any concerns about a false conviction.

Zapata would likely have gotten away with murder had it not been for a friend of Jeanette possessing a long memory. Jeanette's disappearance was initially investigated in a superficial fashion. Unlike the cases of Bayerl and Clark, it did not receive regular review by cold case investigators. The real investigation into Jeanette's disappearance did not start for over a quarter century. The activation of an investigation provoked Zapata into post-offence behavior that ultimately caused him to be arrested and charged.

In these four cases, the three most important factors preventing timely arrest and charging were the ability to kill without leaving easily visible forensic evidence, the ability to delay the filing of a missing person's report, and the difficulty police had in moving from a missing person's investigation to a homicide investigation. In the end it was the prolonged and otherwise inexplicable absence of the victim that made a conviction possible.

Wright's case was different. Within a decade of Rebecca's disappearance, police determined who was responsible. Then Wright disappeared. Not every disappearance is caused by homicide or even by death. Wright disappeared by choice. Over two decades later, he was caught. His arrest came because of the increasing computerization and linkage of data sets. It is harder for a motivated living person to stay hidden in the twenty-first century than it was in the past. In addition to catching Wright, this development makes it much easier to move forward with no-body homicide cases. If it is harder to hide, it is easier to develop a convincing case that a long-term absence means the person is dead. When a woman abruptly disappears, particularly in circumstances that are suggestive of a domestic homicide, the inability to hide makes it easier to infer foul play.

The five cases discussed here took longer for police to solve than it took for the United States to lose the Vietnam War. The causes of this delay point to some challenges police face in clearing no-body domestic homicides. However, we can also learn by looking at cases that were quick to solve.

Solving No-Body Domestic Homicides Quickly

On March 18, 2013, Reita Jordan packed her belongings while preparing to leave her common-law husband, Paul Calnen. She sent her texts to her mother and sister to tell them about her plans. With that, the Nova Scotia woman disappeared. Ten days later, her mother reported her disappearance to police. On June 17, just 92 days after Reita disappeared, Calnen was arrested and charged with second-degree murder.[38]

The police began their investigation by questioning Calnen. He claimed to know nothing; Reita had been home when he left for work in the morning but was not there when he returned home. The police did not buy this story. On April 11 – 25 days after Reita disappeared – police told Calnen the case was being treated as a homicide investigation. Two days later, police searched Calnen's house. Nothing of forensic value was discovered. Nonetheless, by mid-June police and prosecutors believed the circumstances were sufficient for an arrest.

After his arrest, Calnen was subjected to a lengthy and vigorous interrogation. Calnen stuck to his story. The police brought Reita's mother into the interrogation. She pleaded with Calnen to tell where her daughter's body was located. Calnen changed his story. He said he returned home on March 18 to discover Reita packed and ready to leave. Calnen said he became upset – not at her leaving, but because she was taking a laptop and a ring belonging to him. The two quarreled. Calnen said Reita demanded money and became physically aggressive. Calnen claimed death occurred because Reita threw a punch, missed, fell down the stairs, and hit her head. Calnen said he panicked. Instead of calling an ambulance, he wrapped her in a rug. He dumped Reita's body and her belongings off a logging road. The next day, he returned to burn her belongings and dragged her body further into the woods.

In Chapter 3, we saw how John Wallace responded to police pressure by burning his victim's body. Calnen did the same. After the police told him Reita's disappearance was being treated as a homicide, he picked up her body, took it to a more isolated location, built a big fire, and threw her in. While transporting her body, he got stuck and phoned a tow truck. While he was burning Reita, the police phoned to ask for a meeting. Calnen says he doused the fire, put Reita's charred remains in a canvas bag, put her in the back of his truck, and went off to meet the police. He reports that she was in the back of his truck – parked in his driveway – while the search of his home was conducted. Calnen said that after he was questioned by police, he finished burning Reita's body in a firepit in his yard. He dumped the ashes and other remains into a nearby lake.

If events had unfolded as Calnen described, he would be guilty of committing an indignity to a dead body. This would have carried a sentence of up to five years, but the death itself would have been an accident rather than homicide. Calnen was unsuccessful in convincing the police and prosecutor – and ultimately a jury – that this part of his story was true. Calnen was convicted of second-degree murder. He appealed. In a split decision, the Nova Scotia Court of Appeal overturned the conviction. The Appeal Court judges said the trial judge had failed to properly instruct the jury about how to evaluate post-offence behavior. They also said no evidence had been presented about Calnen's intent to kill. The appeal court said Calnen should face a new trial for manslaughter rather than for murder.[39] The prosecutor appealed this decision. The Supreme Court of Canada overturned the appeal court's decision and reinstated Calnen's murder conviction. The Supreme Court pointed out that Calnen "made a calculated decision to burn Ms. Jordan's body, thereby destroying the only evidence capable of establishing the cause of her death."[40] It was not unreasonable for a jury to conclude that he was attempting to cover up his guilt. It is worth noting that the only evidence of the multiple burnings of Reita's body comes from Calnen himself. It is possible that Reita's remains still lay undiscovered in the forest. The story of incineration could have been designed to prevent a coroner from establishing a cause of death consistent with homicide rather than falling down stairs. The absence of forensic evidence was significant. It is unlikely that hitting one's head on a stair hard enough to kill would not result in any bleeding or hair loss. The absence of this evidence is more consistent with strangulation.

Only 92 days passed between Reita's disappearance and Calnen's arrest. Because 10 days passed between her disappearance and the first report to police, the reality is that the case was "cleared" in 82 days. It then took 2,067 days for the case to be definitively resolved by Canada's judicial system.

When compared with the five cases discussed earlier, the quickness with which Calnen was charged shows delay is not always because of the evidence. Objectively, Calnen did a good clean job of murder. There were no witnesses. Unlike Jose Rodriquez-Cruz and Eugene Zapata, he did not have a documented history of violence against his partner. Unlike John Bayerl, he left no forensic evidence. Unlike Michael Clark, he presented a plausible story that was easy to keep consistent. It could neither be proven nor be disproven. Unlike Eugene Zapata he quickly and permanently disposed of the body. Calnen was better at murder than the others, but he was charged within weeks. The key difference was in the orientation of police. When Reita disappeared, the police did not accept the claim she had gone off on her own. They quickly treated the case as a homicide investigation. This placed pressure on Calnen. Ultimately it was the shock of his arrest and the pressure of his interrogation (with a big assist from Reita's mother) that caused him to change his story and admit to disposing of Reita's body. Once that admission was made, conviction was almost inevitable. Bayerl, Zapata, Rodriquez-Cruz, Clark, and Wright were all able to grow old while remaining free. Justice delayed is justice partially denied. Calnen will move from middle-age to old-age while in prison.

Gender and No-Body Intimate Partner Homicides

One final observation on no-body intimate partner homicides.

Attempting to avoid detection by disposing of the body of a murdered intimate partner is highly gendered. In intimate partner homicides involving opposite-sex couples, about three in four cases involve a male killing a female.[41] This ratio holds true in both Canada and the United States. It is different in no-body cases. In the United States, 95 percent of no-body intimate partner homicides have a male killer and a female victim. In Canada, there appears to be only one intimate partner no-body case in which the female was the killer and the male the victim.

There may be gendered differences in the psychological makeup of men and women that helps account for the male propensity to hide or destroy the body, but there are two more plausible explanations.

The first is the physical disparity between men and women. Men tend to be bigger and stronger than women. Just as this difference makes it easier for a man to strangle a woman, it is easier for a male killer to move a female body. In half of the American cases in which the female partner was the killer, male assistance was obtained for the killing itself, for the disposal of the body, or for both. In the only Canadian case in which a woman disposed of her husband's body after killing him, she obtained the assistance of a male friend to do the heavy lifting.[42] Intimate partner homicides usually occur in a home. To become a no-body case, the body of the victim must be removed. In most relationships, the man is more capable of this task than the woman.

Another possible explanation for the gender gap could be a stereotyped perception of gender relations on the part of police and prosecutors. Patricia Pearson argues that women in violent relationships are seen as the victims rather than potential perpetrators. Pearson documents how this stereotyped perception affects charging, conviction, and sentencing decisions in cases where the woman was the aggressor and instigator of violence.[43] It is possible this results in an undercounting of cases in which a woman killed an intimate partner and disposed of the body. When a woman in a troubled relationship goes missing without explanation, police are usually quick to consider the possibility of foul play and body disposal by a male partner. The disappearance of a male from a troubled relationship is more likely to be interpreted as "abandonment." People are more likely to condemn a man for abandoning his familial obligations than they are to wonder if he was murdered and thrown into a garbage dumpster or buried in a hidden grave. To the extent this explanation is true, the gender gap in intimate-partner no-body cases may be a misleading statistical artifact created by our biases and preconceptions.

These two explanations for the overwhelming male predominance as killers in no-body prosecutions are not mutually exclusive. Both can be true, but not exclusively true. The differences in size and strength between male and female make it more likely that men will use body disposal as a detection-avoidance strategy – and some women may use gender stereotypes to prevent a homicide investigation into their partner's disappearance. Given the intrinsic unknowns, empirical resolution is impossible.

Notes

1 R v. Woods 2019 SKCA 84.
2 Fowler, Brenda, "For 5,300-Year-Old Iceman, Extra Autopsy Tells the Tale," *New York Times*, August 17, 2001.
3 Polischuk, Heather, "David Woods's Former Lawyer Says the Man Admitted to Killing Wife," *Regina Leader-Post*, August 31, 2018.
4 R v. Woods 2019 SKCA 84.
5 Posnanski, Joe, "Losers Lament," *NBC Sports*, Aug 12, 2015. https://sportsworld.nbcsports.com/washington-generals-folding-harlem-globetrotters/.
6 De Ryk, Tara, "Former Keneston Woman Reported Missing," *The Davidson Leader*, December 9, 2016.
7 McAdam, Bre, "Crown Says Fertuck Confessed," *Toronto Sun*, September 8, 2021.
8 McAdam, Bre, "Greg Fertuck Murder Trial: A Timeline," *Saskatoon Star-Phoenix*, December 24, 2021.
9 We need to treat statistics on the relationship between killers and their victims cautiously since about one third of homicides in the United States and one quarter in Canada remain "uncleared" by police. In these cases, the relationship is, by definition, unknown. The official statistics likely (but not certainly) overstate the proportion of homicides committed by an intimate partner since this type of homicide is more likely to be cleared than those committed by a stranger or criminal associate.
10 U.S. Department of Justice, annual, Crime in the United States: Expanded Homicide Data Table 7: Murder, Types of Weapons Used.
11 Statistics Canada, Table 35-10-0069-01. Number of homicide victims, by method used to commit the homicide.
12 Henson, Stacey, Bruce Vielmetti and Gina Barton, "Man Arrested in Fort Myers in Connection with Wife's Death in Wisconsin in 1979," *USA Today*, February 21, 2019.
13 "Husband Who Claimed Wife Ran Away in Night Caught by DNA Test on Rug 40 Years on," *Daily Mirror*, May 24, 2020.
14 Staudinger, Stephanie, "John Bayerl Sentenced to Life in Prison for 1979 Murder of Wife," *WDJT-TV*, August 30, 2019.
15 Stevens, Alexis, "Missouri Murder Suspect Nabbed 33 Years Later in Lawrenceville," *The Atlanta Journal-Constitution*, August 10, 2012.
16 Stevens, "Missouri Murder Suspect Nabbed."
17 Slavit, Mark, "Update: Jury Finds Wright Guilty of Murder," *KRGC-TV*, January 24, 2011.
18 Deutsch, Jill, "Johnny Wright Dies Four Years into Sentence for Becky Doisy's Murder," *The Missourian*, January 23, 2015.
19 Duggan, Paul, "Three Decades after His Wife Disappeared, a Virginia Man Admits He Killed Her," *The Washington Post*, November 16, 2020.
20 Alexander, Keith, L and Dana Hedgpeth, "Remains Found in 1991 Identified as Those of Missing Arlington Woman," *The Washington Post*, June 13, 2018.
21 Duggan, Paul, "DC Woman's Disappearance Leaves a Trail with No End," *The Washington Post*, November 24, 2009.
22 Alexander, Keith L., "Suspect in Death of Pamela Butler Told Witness It Was 'easy' to Get Rid of Body," *The Washington Post*, April 25, 2017.

23 Epp, Keith, "Man Pleads Guilty to Killing Wife, Dumping Body in Stafford 30 Years Ago," *The Free Lance Star* November 16, 2020.
24 Emery, Sean, "Huntington Beach Man Arrested in 30-Year-Old Killing of His Wife," *Orange County Registrar,* April 14, 2011.
25 Morino, Douglas, "Accused Husband Takes the Stand in Carol Lubahn Murder Trial in Torrance," *Daily Breeze,* October 16, 2012.
26 People vs. Clark, No. B246263, Court of Appeals of California, Second District, Division Eight (September 13, 2014).
27 Shyong, Frank, "A Murderer's Latest Account of What Happened Three Decades Ago," *Los Angeles Times,* January 8, 2013.
28 Leonard, Brian, Daria Hirsch, and Sara Ely Hulse, "Into Thin Air: A Mother Disappears Leaving Behind a Mystery That Would Take Her Daughter 30 Years to Solve," *CBS News: 48 Hours,* October 18, 2008.
29 Cullen, Sandy, "Ex-cop Says Zapata Told of Fight with Ex-wife," *Madison State Journal,* September 9, 2007.
30 Treleven, Ed, "Zapata Murder Case Drawing to a Close: Detective Testifies about all the Efforts Made to Find Human Remains, None of Which Were Successful," *Madison State Journal,* September 13, 2007.
31 Trelven, Ed, "Zapata Jury to Hear Phone Conversations: Police Had Recorded Two Phone Conversations between Zapata and His Daughter," *Madison State Journal,* May 5, 2007.
32 Treleven, Ed, "Jury Hears Portions of Zapata's 'stalking diary': The Diary Has Details of Jeanette Zapata's Movements in 1976 as Gathered by Her Husband," *Madison State Journal,* September 12, 2007.
33 Longobardy, Joshua, "Why Do Criminals Flock Here? Zapata Is Arrested and Charged with Out-of-State Crimes," *Las Vegas Weekly,* September 7, 2006.
34 Treleven, Ed, "Zapata Jury Won't Hear of Dog's Search for Remains," *Madison State Journal,* September 1, 2007.
35 Treleven, Ed, "Another Trial for Zapata; His Son Disappointed, Saying the Stress Is Taking a Toll on the 69-Year-Old," *Madison State Journal,* October 3, 2007.
36 "Former Wisconsin Man Admits Killing His Wife in 1976," *ABC 11 Eyewitness News,* February 19, 2008.
37 "Man Says He Would Have Admitted Killing Wife – After His Death," *Twin Cities Pioneer Press,* March 11, 2008; Treleven, ed., "Zapata Admits to Killing Wife, Gets 5 Years: The Former Madison Man Pleads Guilty to 1976 Murder," *Madison State Journal,* February 19, 2008.
38 R. v. Calnen, 2019 SCC 6.
39 R. v. Calnen, 2017 NSCA 49.
40 R. v. Calnen, 2019 SCC 6.
41 U.S. Department of Justice, annual, Crime in the United States: Expanded Homicide Data Table 10: Murder, Circumstances by Relationship; Statistics Canada, Table 35-10-0073-01: Number of victims of solved homicides, by type of accused-victim relationship.
42 R. v. Black, 2007 BCSC 1105.
43 Pearson, Patricia, *When She Was Bad: How and Why Women Get Away with Murder* (Toronto, ON: Vintage, 2021).

5

MISSING ARE THE CHILDREN

Disposing the Most Vulnerable

Women in abusive violent relationships are common victims in no-body homicide cases. So too are children. In the United States, about 8 percent of all homicide victims are children. In no-body cases resulting in a successful prosecution, children account for 12 percent of victims – that is, 50 percent more than for homicides in general. In Canada, just over 9 percent of all homicide victims are children, compared with almost 18 percent in no-body cases. Children are disproportionately more likely to have their bodies hidden or destroyed after they are murdered.

Let us begin by looking at one case.

On May 25, 1979, six-year-old Etan Patz set off for school in New York City. For the first time in his life, Etan was permitted the "big boy" activity of walking to the bus stop by himself. He was never seen again.

Etan's disappearance was noticed when he did not return home from school. His parents, police, friends, and volunteers launched a massive search.[1] Nothing was found. It was as if Etan had been abducted by aliens flying an invisible spaceship. Over the days, weeks, months, years, and decades to come, Etan's disappearance generated extraordinary amounts of publicity. Etan was from a white, middle-class home in a part of New York normally deemed safe. As importantly, his father was a professional photographer. As in the case of Jon Benet Ramsey, there was an inexhaustible supply of good pictures for newspapers and television. This helped keep Etan on the front pages.

Etan's parents were determined to find their son and to focus awareness on the issue of child abduction. Their efforts helped establish the National Centre for Missing and Exploited Children. Etan was the first missing child to have his picture on a milk carton. President Ronald Reagan declared May 25, the anniversary of Etan's disappearance, National Missing Children's Day.[2] Academics say Etan's disappearance is a major reason six-year-old children are no longer allowed to walk by themselves on city streets.[3]

Police and prosecutors worked on Etan's case with remarkable persistence, determination, and imagination. Publicity generated thousands of false sightings of the child. Over 300 psychics claimed to know where Etan's body was. None of these sightings or visions were useful.[4]

The first suspect was Etan's father, largely because family members are always suspects. The number of photos of Etan was deemed suspicious; perhaps it suggested an unhealthy fixation on his son. The reality was more mundane. The father was a professional photographer. Etan liked having his picture taken. This combination made the boy useful for such tasks as adjusting lighting in the studio.[5]

DOI: 10.4324/9781003372134-5

The second primary suspect was a local handyman. Etan hung around to watch him work and was occasionally rewarded with a dollar for "helping." No good deed goes unpunished. The handyman's reward for being friendly to a young boy was the unpleasantness of being a suspect in a high-profile homicide investigation.[6]

Three years after Etan's disappearance, suspicion focused on a homeless pedophile living in a drainage culvert.[7] When arrested after trying to lure two boys into the culvert, pictures of Etan were discovered in his possession. Further investigation revealed that when Etan disappeared, the man was dating a woman hired to walk neighborhood children to school. Over the next several years, the man was arrested several times for child molestation offenses. He eventually told investigators that on the day Etan disappeared he had sex with a young boy – but took the child to a subway station afterward. The self-confessed child abuser said he was "90 percent" certain this child was Etan – but also gave a different name for him. This suspect was convicted of molesting a young boy in Pennsylvania[8] and given a ten- to twenty-year sentence. While he was in prison, investigators placed two informants in the man's cell. They reported the suspect confessed to molesting Etan but not to murdering him. One informant reported that the suspect said, "Etan is dead, there is no body, and there never will be a body."[9] When the District Attorney in Manhattan refused to prosecute, Etan's father launched a civil action against the suspect. In 2004, a judge ruled the pedophile was responsible for Etan's death.[10]

Despite believing the pedophile was guilty, New York's police continued to follow up on other leads. In 2012, they learned the handyman – the second suspect – may have lied about his alibi. Police dug up a basement in a nearby building.[11] They found nothing, but this search serendipitously solved the case. The media coverage about the excavation prompted a New Jersey man to tell police his brother-in-law, Pedro Hernandez, had repeatedly claimed to have killed a child in New York. Police questioned Hernandez. To their amazement, Hernandez gave a detailed confession. He was arrested and charged. Follow-up investigation revealed that Hernandez had told many people he killed a child, but these vague disclosures were ignored. A few disclosures had been reported to police, but because of a lack of detail, no follow-up investigation occurred.

Hernandez said he was working in a bodega or convenience store. Etan came into the store to buy a soda. For no apparent reason, Hernandez strangled the boy. He put Etan in a garbage bag. The bag went in a box. The box went into a garbage dumpster. With that, Etan disappeared forever.

Once he got a lawyer, Hernandez recanted his confession. His lawyer argued the confession was generated by a combination of police interrogation techniques, low intelligence, and mental illnesses. The defense lawyer also pointed to the pedophile as the more likely killer. The prosecution countered with the video-taped confession and a parade of witnesses testifying about Hernandez's past disclosures. A first trial resulted in a hung jury.[12] The second resulted in a conviction. Hernandez appealed. On March 26, 2020, the Appellate Court rejected the appeal.[13] It was 14,917 days after Etan Patz disappeared.

Etan Patz's murder received more media coverage than any other child victim in a no-body homicide case in North America. People think of him when they hear a child has disappeared and is believed murdered.[14] But Etan's case is atypical. When the police suspected Etan's father, they were playing the statistical odds.

In the United States, there have been 56 successful no-body prosecutions for the murder of children. Thirty-nine featured a family member (usually a parent) as the killer; 11 of the killers were an acquaintance of the family. The killer was a stranger in only 6 of these cases.

The pattern is different in Canada. Six successful prosecutions had a child as at least one of the victims. In three of these cases, the killer was a stranger to the victim. In one case, the killer was an acquaintance of the victim. In the fifth case, the killer had a grudge against the child's grandfather. When the killer carried out his murderous revenge plan, a five-year-old child was having a sleepover at his grandparents. He became a victim.[15] The only successful no-body prosecution of a family member for the murder of a child in Canada came after James Warner hit his teenage stepdaughter over the head with a hammer and dumped her body in the local landfill. At trial, the prosecution presented evidence showing she planned to report him for sexual molestation. The prosecution argued that Warner killed his stepdaughter to conceal his behavior. Warner was convicted, but his appeal was successful.[16] Before his second trial began, Warner pleaded guilty to manslaughter. He denied sexual improprieties and claimed the killing occurred in a quarrel over the girl's telephone usage.[17]

Invisible Children: The Unknown Unknown's

We will look at the dynamics of investigating and prosecuting stranger child-victim no-body cases in Chapter 7 when we examine sexually motivated serial killers. In the rest of this chapter, we will focus on cases where a child was the victim of a parent, guardian, or other family member. The chilling conclusion is that these cases may be more common than we know. The cases successfully prosecuted serve as a warning about the vulnerability of children to those responsible for their well-being.

In 2010, Lauryn Dickens's grandmother grew concerned. She had not seen the nine-month-old girl for a week. Lauryn's mother, Shakara Dickens, appeared unconcerned. Dickens said she gave the child to a strange woman who appeared with an offer to look after the child. Dickens said the woman was sent by Lauryn's incarcerated father, but that she did not know the woman's name, address, or phone number. Lauryn's grandmother insisted her daughter file a missing person's report. The police questioned Lauryn's father. He had not sent the woman, and had no idea who she might be. Lauryn's father reported being unable to contact his daughter – Dickens was blocking his calls. The police searched the Dickens's apartment. Cadaver dogs identified the scent of human remains in the apartment and in Dickens's car.[18] With this, Dickens was arrested and charged with child neglect and endangerment. The charges were upgraded to murder after Dickens's cellmate reported hearing a confession.[19]

Dickens pled not guilty. The evidence against her were inconsistent stories, the cadaver dog's behavior, and the testimony of the cellmate. The defense lawyer pointed to the lack of a body or forensic evidence. Dickens was convicted.[20] She then confessed, saying that she smothered Lauryn because the baby was crying.[21] Dickens disposed of Lauryn's body by putting it in the garbage.

Lauryn's murder resulted in a prompt investigation, charge, and conviction because someone noticed the baby was gone and acted. If Lauryn's grandmother had not forced Dickens to file a missing person's report, the police might never have heard about the baby's disappearance. Lauryn's father was trying to monitor his daughter's well-being, but was in jail. He did not know his daughter was gone.

This case reveals a chilling reality about no-body homicides when children are killed by a parent or guardian. Most no-body homicide investigations begin as a missing person investigation. To use the terminology of former U.S. defense secretary Donald Rumsfeld, these cases present police with a known unknown.[22] It is different if the child is not reported missing. The murderer will not be punished because the murder remains invisible to authorities. The disappearance is an unknown unknown. As Rumsfeld observed, "it is the latter category that tends to be the difficult ones."

Lauryn was reported missing a week after she was murdered. In other cases, the investigation did not occur for years or decades.

In 1970, four-year-old Surrette Clark got out of the family car when she was not supposed to. Her stepfather, Wayne Clifford Roberts, shook Surrette so hard she died. Roberts buried Surrette in a shallow grave under a bridge in Arizona. He forced Surrette's mother (who was pregnant) to move to Canada with him. Roberts threatened to kill Surrette's mother if she went to police. Surrette's death and disappearance remained invisible.[23] In 1979, her body was found. She was renamed as "Little Jane Doe." Neither her identity nor the cause of death could be determined. The child's neck was broken, but that could have been as a result of post-mortem trauma.

Over the years, Roberts told several family members he killed his stepdaughter. In 1994, his sister went to the police. This was the first indication they had that Surrette was missing. Roberts was charged with murder and convicted in 1996. The primary evidence against him was testimony from family members combined with the absence of the girl.[24] Another decade and a half passed before cold case investigators looking at the "Little Jane Doe" case realized she could be Surrette Clark. DNA testing provided confirmation. Forty years after Surrette was murdered and fourteen years after her killer was convicted, Surrette was buried under her own name.[25]

Roberts was convicted because he told people about his crime. Police could not act until this was reported to them. A missing person's report is a precondition of an investigation. This essential report can be both helped and hindered by custody disputes between parents.

In the mid-1990s, Karen Huster and her husband were in a tumultuous marriage marked by several separations and reconciliations. In 1995, the Oregon couple separated for the last time. Divorce proceedings were launched the next year. The couple's son went with his father while Huster retained custody of nine-year-old Elisabeth. During the marital disputes, Huster accused her husband of assaulting her. He admitted guilt and was sentenced to two years' probation. More importantly, a restraining order preventing contact with his wife was issued.

Elisabeth Huster was last seen on August 31, 1996. Four months later, her father reported the girl missing. He had been unable to contact his daughter and discovered she was not enrolled in school. The police investigated. Huster told them her daughter was living with relatives but refused to divulge who they were and where they lived. Eventually, Huster was charged with custodial interference for denying Elisabeth's father court-ordered visitation rights. Huster claimed she was protecting her daughter from possible abuse. She served two years in jail rather than tell where her daughter was. This made police suspicious. These suspicions hardened when several inmates reported Karen disclosed she killed her daughter and bragged the body would never be found.[26] Fourteen months after release from jail, Huster was indicted for murder. She responded by disappearing. She fled to California and hid by posing as the wife of a 73-year-old man. The relationship proved to be too much for him. After six months living with Huster, the old man died of a heart attack. Huster dismembered him and stored his body in the deep freezer. Police received a tip, searched the apartment, and discovered both the body and Huster's fugitive status.[27]

At her murder trial, Huster testified that she shot her daughter, dismembered her, and threw the body parts in the ocean. Huster said she disposed of the body in this unorthodox manner because she lacked money for a funeral. Her lawyer argued Huster was temporarily insane when she killed her daughter – that Huster was psychotic as a result of the stress of divorce and financial problems. Huster told the judge she was concerned her daughter had inherited a propensity for mental illness and killed her as a form of therapy.[28] The prosecution argued Huster killed Elisabeth to punish her husband. Whatever the motive, the judge ruled that Huster was sane at the time of the killing and sentenced her to 25 years to life.[29]

Elisabeth's disappearance was noticed by a concerned non-custodial parent. Huster's inability to comply with an access order after she shot, dismembered, and dumped her daughter in the ocean created circumstantial evidence that she killed her daughter. The police reasoned that if Huster was willing to go to jail for two years to keep Elisabeth's location secret, there must be a compelling and sinister reason to do so. Once Huster was in jail, other inmates came forward with real or imagined disclosures of guilt.

When the death of a child goes unnoticed, their very existence can be contested by the person accused of killing them.

In 1931, Eleanor Roosevelt founded the Gold Rule Foundation to honor mothers.[30] Anita Vega would never be a candidate for this award. In 1970, her three-year-old daughter, Anna Marie, wet her bed. Vega beat her, refused to provide breakfast, and locked her naked in a cold room. A nine-year-old sister was ordered to stay home from school to help impose discipline. When Anna Marie put on some shorts, Vegas ordered the older sister to fill the bathtub with cold water. Vegas beat and kicked the younger child. The nine-year-old filled the tub with warm water, but was ordered to refill it with cold. Anna Marie was ordered into the tub. She stood there shivering, refusing to sit. Her mother knocked her down and held her head under the water. The nine-year-old informed her mother that Anna Marie appeared dead. Vegas disagreed with this diagnosis and left the three-year old on an unheated porch. Whether death occurred in the bathtub or the porch, Anna Marie was dead by the time the other children returned home from school. They were told their sister had died and a funeral had already been held. When Vegas's husband returned home from work, he was ordered to dispose of his daughter's remains. He complied, but complained it was hard to dig in frozen ground.

More than two decades passed. The nine-year-old daughter remained, quite naturally, troubled by her memory of the affair. In 1992, she went to the police and told the story. The police could find no documentary evidence of Anna Marie's existence except for a birth certificate issued in 1967. Vegas was questioned. She denied that the girl ever existed. After being confronted with the birth certificate, Vegas acknowledged the girl's existence, death, and surreptitious burial but claimed the girl died from unidentified natural causes. She was charged with involuntary manslaughter. The jury believed the daughter's story rather than the mother's. The Court of Appeals in Indiana upheld this decision.[31]

If the Vegas case showed a child can be killed without anyone noticing, a Florida case showed a child can be killed and disposed of under the eye of child protection authorities.

In 2000, Florida's Department of Children and Families placed four-year-old Rilya Wilson and her baby sister into the care of Geralyn Graham. Their mother had substance abuse issues; she was unable to provide care for the two girls. Workers at the child protection agency believed Graham was the girl's grandmother. In fact, according to Rilya's mother, Graham was the mother of a friend she met through Narcotics Anonymous. Screening was minimal. Social workers did not notice Graham had an extensive criminal record for various fraud offenses. Court records from earlier lawsuits showed she had been diagnosed with dementia and suffered from hallucinations.[32]

Rilya disappeared in January 2001. Her absence went undetected for fifteen months.[33] The social worker responsible for her monitoring was working another job. Rather than visiting Graham's home, the social worker fabricated reports indicating the girl was "thriving." In April 2002, a different social worker was assigned to Rilya's file. When she conducted a home visit, there was no Rilya.[34] Graham claimed a worker from the Department of Children and Families had taken the child for an evaluation and never returned her. There was no record this occurred and Graham could not provide the name of the worker. Fingers were pointed in many directions. Rilya's sister was removed from the home. The moonlighting and report-fabricating social worker resigned; she was charged with official misbehavior and theft. The case of the "missing baby" became an election issue in Florida's gubernatorial election. While seeking reelection, Governor Jeb Bush signed a law to make falsifying child custody records a felony.[35]

The controversy left the question of Rilya's fate unanswered. Her case was featured on the television show *America's Most Wanted*.[36] A $100,000 reward for information about her whereabouts was posted.[37] No verifiable leads resulted. The body of a decapitated girl about the same age and size as Rilya was found in Kansas City, but DNA testing showed that this was not Rilya.

In 2004, Graham, her partner, and two others were charged with fraud. They collected money for Rilya's care for 15 months before her disappearance was discovered. Graham claimed she repeatedly called the funding agencies to tell them she no longer had Rilya, but no record of these calls existed. The fraud charges loosened the tongue of Graham's partner. She told police a story of abuse and mistreatment, belatedly reporting Graham kept Rilya locked in a dog cage and often tied the child to her bed with plastic flex cuffs. Graham's partner told police she came home from work to find Rilya missing. When she picked up the phone to file a missing person's report, Graham threatened her with a hammer. When Rilya's absence was noticed by the authorities, Graham ordered her partner to confirm the story of a social worker picking up the child.

Graham was charged with kidnapping and child abuse. While being held in jail prior to trial, her cellmate claimed Graham confessed to killing Rilya. According to the cellmate's version, Graham described the child as a "demon" and said she smothered Rilya with a pillow. The cellmate said Graham claimed she threw Rilya's body in a canal near her home, but would not disclose the exact location because "no body no murder." Graham's cellmate was not particularly credible, and she wanted a lot for her testimony. Facing a life sentence for armed robbery, the cellmate demanded a sentence recommendation of three years; the prosecutor offered twenty. No deal was struck, and the cellmate was sentenced to life.[38] Graham was charged with murder. A deal reduced the cellmate's sentence to ten years in exchange for her testimony at Graham's trial. Two other inmates also reported Graham had confessed. One was an inmate who described herself as a law clerk. She said Graham asked about the concept of corpus delicti and whether she could be indicted for murder without a body being found.[39]

The wheels of justice turned slowly. Graham was indicted on a murder charge in 2005. Her trial did not begin until 2012 – over a decade after Rilya's disappearance was discovered. The primary evidence against her was testimony from her partner and the jailhouse informants. Graham was convicted on the kidnapping and child abuse charges, but the jury deadlocked on the murder charge. One juror held out for acquittal after Graham's lawyer argued that Rilya may have been sold rather than murdered. At the age of 67, Graham was sentenced to 55 years in prison. While not convicted of murder, the sentence had the same practical effect.[40]

There are two disturbing postscripts to the tragic story of Rilya Wilson.

The fact that Rilya, a ward of the State of Florida, was dead for 15 months before anyone noticed she was missing created a political controversy. The governor ordered an audit of children in the care of the Department of Children and Families. Over 400 could not be found. The authorities asserted most were runaways who were, likely, still alive. This was probably true, but some may have been murdered without official notice or investigation.[41]

The discovery that Rilya was missing in Florida generated interest in Missouri. In April 2001 the naked, headless corpse of a small girl was found in a wood in Kansas City. A few days later, the girl's head was found in a garbage bag. A year later, when it was discovered that Rilya was missing, it was believed that she may have been killed and decapitated in Kansas City. DNA testing showed this child, called "Precious Doe" by police and the media, was not Rilya.[42] This meant there was another murdered child whose disappearance had not been reported to police.

In 2005, "Precious Doe" was finally identified when the girl's grandfather told police that Erica Green had been killed by her stepfather, Harrell Johnson. When the police followed up, both Johnson and his wife quickly confessed. They said Erica stood up when she was supposed to be in bed. Johnson kicked her in the head. Erica was knocked unconscious. Neither Johnson nor his wife called an ambulance because both had outstanding arrest warrants. About ten hours later, Erica died. Johnson cut off her head with hedge clippers. Erica's body was thrown into the woods. Her head, in a garbage bag, was initially tossed in a dumpster at a nearby church. Erica's mother worried that parishioners might smell Erica's head before the dumpster was emptied, so the stepfather moved it to the woods. Relatives were told that Erica had gone to live with an acquaintance in Oklahoma. This explanation satisfied everyone except Erica's grandfather, who eventually accused Johnson of murder. Johnson admitted he had killed the girl, but claimed it was an accident. Erica's grandfather called the police.

Erica's mother was convicted of second-degree murder, and Johnson was convicted of first-degree. He appealed, arguing his kick was caused by a mixture of PCP and alcohol rather than premeditation. The Missouri Court of Appeals denied this appeal, pointing to testimony that prompt medical attention would have saved Erica's life. The cause of death was not the kick but the intentional refusal to call an ambulance or take Erica to a hospital.[43] The prosecution of Erica's mother and stepfather was not a no-body case, but the case is another graphic indicator of how easy it is for a guardian to kill a child without triggering an investigation. All it takes is the disposal of a small body and a refusal to acknowledge the child is dead.

Newborn infants present special challenges for authorities. Existence must be established before homicide can be proven. This can be difficult.

On July 18, 1943, a young woman named Jesse Warmke got off the bus in a small town in Kentucky carrying a small baby and a suitcase. It was raining. Warmke took shelter in the town's drugstore. The pharmacist lent her a coat to wrap the baby in. Warmke departed, leaving her suitcase. That evening, she returned the coat and picked up the suitcase. The next morning, she arrived at a relative's house. The small-town gossip-mill established that Warmke arrived in town with a baby, but did not have it when arriving at her relatives. The town marshal was notified. Warmke first denied the existence of the baby. Then she said she was crossing a railroad bridge over the river when she accidentally dropped it. Warmke's third version was that she left home to hide her pregnancy. After giving birth, she was on her way home but threw the baby in the river to prevent her family from learning she had been pregnant. Warmke was charged with manslaughter. She recanted her confession and went back to denying the existence of the baby.

By the time Warmke went to trial, authorities had documented the baby's existence. Warmke went back to her second version of events; the baby had been dropped into the river by accident. The prosecution centered on her behavior, both before the baby died and afterward. It was the post-disappearance behavior that was most damning. In upholding her conviction, the Court of Appeals of Kentucky said that of all this behavior, "most illuminating of all is her failure to notify any one that she had dropped the baby from the trestle, if it was dropped accidentally." Warmke's lawyer argued that because the baby's body was never found, there was no proof it had drowned. Perhaps someone had found it and imitated Queen Bithia in secretly raising the baby Moses. The appeal court judges dismissed this suggestion as "beyond the bounds of possibility that that the baby survived this ordeal and was never thereafter heard of."[44] Warmke was sentence to nine years in prison. But consider this. If the sun had been shining when she got off the bus, Warmke would never have been prosecuted for her infanticide. Because it was raining, she took shelter in the drugstore. The pharmacist became the link in establishing the transition from "with baby" to "without baby." Without this, the child would not have been reported missing.

The potential for the undocumented life and death of a baby has not gone away. Samantha Heiges became pregnant about July of 2004. This was not welcomed by the young Minnesota woman and her boyfriend. During the pregnancy, the couple attempted to induce a miscarriage. Samantha's method was to consume large amounts of drugs and alcohol. Her boyfriend's contribution was attempts to kill the unborn child by punching Heiges in the abdomen. The couple told few people Samantha was pregnant. Neighbors and Samantha's co-workers just noticed a temporary transition to baggy clothing. Heiges delivered the baby in her apartment bathroom in May of 2005. The newborn girl was drowned in the bathtub and put in a shoebox. Heiges's boyfriend put the shoebox in a garbage bag and tossed the child down the garbage disposal chute of the apartment building. From there, the newborn child was compacted and dumped in a landfill.

The short life of Heiges's baby would have gone unnoticed but for a combination of a new boyfriend, remorse, and alcohol. After the birth and killing of her baby, Heiges broke up with her boyfriend and started dating someone else. On New Year's Day, 2006 this boyfriend found Heiges drunk and tearful. She said she had a baby but did not any longer. The boyfriend assumed the child had been put up for adoption. He attempted to console Heiges by saying that she could visit the child in the future. With this, Heiges became hysterical and told the story of the bathroom birth, drowning, and disposal down the garbage chute. The new boyfriend was horrified. The next day, he confirmed the story when Heiges was sober; then he went to the police. When interviewed, Heiges repeated the story in detail. She told the same story in three subsequent interviews. The ex-boyfriend and father of the child confirmed the birth, death, and disposal of the child. The two differed on culpability. Heiges said she helped kill the baby because she feared her boyfriend. The boyfriend's version was that he had not threatened Heiges or helped drown the baby. He claimed his participation was limited to disposal.

Heiges's trial came first. The evidence was her confessions to police. Both Heiges and her boyfriend testified. As with their confessions to police, they agreed on how the baby was disposed of, but differed on culpability for the death. Heiges was convicted of second-degree murder.[45] Then came the trial of the boyfriend. Heiges refused to testify.[46] The prosecutor was forced to withdraw the murder charge. Without Heiges's testimony, there was no evidence the baby existed or was killed.

Heiges appealed. Her lawyers argued that while Heiges had voluntarily confessed to police, these confessions were not sufficiently corroborated to be admissible as evidence. In short, her lawyers denied the existence of the baby. The Supreme Court of Minnesota ruled Heiges's were sufficiently corroborated and upheld her conviction. With this, Heiges was sent to prison for 299 months.[47] Because Heiges refused to testify at his trial, the boyfriend escaped a similar fate.

Proving the existence of a newborn child can be complicated. On one occasion, a young woman came close to getting convicted for the murder of an imaginary baby.

In 2010, A.S.[48] got herself into a predicament. The young woman was charged with murdering a child who never existed. A.S. came from a large family that combined birth children, adoptive children, and foster children. She never got a lot of attention. This changed when A.S. missed a period. A home pregnancy test showed positive. When A.S. broke the news to her family, everyone was excited and happy. For the first time in her life, A.S. was the center of attention. Then A.S. had a second test at a clinic and learned she was not pregnant. To maintain her new status in the family, she kept quiet about the second test and faked a growing abdomen. This plan was intrinsically flawed since pregnancies are time-limited affairs. Eventually, A.S. would need an exit strategy. One day, she told her family the baby had been stillborn at the local hospital. Her sisters attempted to claim the body so it could be given a proper funeral. Staff at the hospital denied any knowledge of the birth. A.S. changed her story. She worked at a motel. A.S. claimed she delivered a stillborn baby in a motel room and put it in a garbage dumpster.

With this, her predicament worsened. Family members notified the authorities.[49] A.S. was interrogated by police. Still unwilling to confess her pregnancy was faked, A.S. eventually said the baby was born alive; she had smothered it before throwing it in the dumpster. A.S. was charged with murder. When facing a life sentence, A.S. changed her story again. She confessed to faking the pregnancy. Nobody believed her. She had been too successful in fooling her family members. The police conducted a massive search of the local garbage dump. They dug up two acres of garbage between ten and fifteen feet deep.[50] No dead baby was discovered. No blood was found in a motel room. Despite these evidence problems, the prosecutor proceeded with the case. After all, A.S.'s own family insisted she had been pregnant. Now she was not, but there was no baby in sight.

A.S. came close to being convicted. At her first trial, 11 jurors voted to convict. Only one held out for acquittal. After four days, the judge declared a mistrial.[51] At her second trial, A.S's defense lawyers appear to have taken the case more seriously. They pointed to the second, negative, pregnancy test. A physician testified that A.S. did not have the normal physical signs associated with delivering a baby. A.S. took the stand and showed how she had created the appearance of a swollen belly.[52] Combined with the lack of forensic evidence, all this convinced the jury. After a short deliberation, A.S. was acquitted.[53] Her relationship with her duped family remained strained.

Known Unknowns: Blaming Others to Explain Disappearances

We have seen that one strategy for parents who kill a child is to hide the disappearance (or even the existence) of the child. This delays an investigation, and sometimes prevents it from occurring. When homicidal parents use this strategy, it simplifies the identification of a suspect. After all, few people have an innocent reason for not reporting that their child is missing. The lies and evasions necessary to hide the disappearance become compelling evidence of guilt of causing the death. When a parent or guardian kills a child, an alternative strategy for evading detection is to promptly report the child missing and visibly participate in the efforts to find them. The more concern a homicidal parent shows, the better their chance of directing suspicion elsewhere.

It is not surprising that police view grieving parents with suspicion. A child is much more likely to be killed by a parent than a stranger. When Etan Patz did not return home from school, his parents immediately reported his disappearance and helped launch a search. When it became clear something was seriously wrong, his parents became suspects in a homicide investigation. They were given polygraph tests and subjected to intense interrogations. Every aspect of their lives was scrutinized through the bleak suspicious eyes of big city homicide detectives. The police were not acting irrationally, even though Etan's parents had not, objectively, acted in a suspicious way. The police were playing the odds. The problem for both parents and police is that it can be difficult to prove a negative proposition.

The reality is that some parents or guardians who kill their children go to great lengths to stage a disappearance. We will look at a few of these cases.

In 1991, four-year-old James Johnson lived with his mother and his baby sister. Unfortunately, James's mother had a boyfriend, Maurice Martin, living with the family. Martin had a documented record of physically abusing both James and his mother.[54]

One Friday evening, James urinated on the curb outside their home. Martin "disciplined" the child by making him stand on a crate for at least four hours. The next morning, James's mother checked on her son before going to work. James was sleeping but snoring unusually loudly. Over the next day and a half, several people saw James. He was always lying still; people assumed he was sleeping. On Sunday morning while James's mother was at work, Martin telephoned to ask if he should go grocery shopping. She told him not to. Despite this, Martin arrived at the grocery store carrying James's baby sister. He bought a few groceries and left the store. Martin returned a minute later to announce James had gone missing from the car. The police were summoned. A massive search involving both police and hundreds of volunteers was organized. No sign of James was ever found.

Martin said James must have either wandered off or been kidnapped. The police were skeptical. Several people said they saw the car, but no boy. Martin gave contradictory explanations for leaving James in the car. A re-creation demonstrated that Martin could not have seen the car from the vantage point from which he first announced James was missing. Several people saw James between the discipline exercise and the disappearance, but none saw the child standing, sitting, walking, or talking. A neurosurgeon said loud snoring and long periods of sleep were consistent with a subdural hematoma caused by a blow to the head. This internal bleeding in the brain could be fatal if untreated. Police noted Martin's history of physically abusing James. Blood spots were found on the ceiling of the apartment. With that, Martin was charged with murder. While Martin was in jail awaiting trial, another inmate claimed he had heard Martin telling someone over the phone that James was in the city garbage dump. Police recalled that some volunteer searchers proposed searching the dump, but Martin told them the dump operator denied permission. The manager of the dump denied receiving any request from Martin.

At trial, Martin presented contradictory arguments. He argued that James had been alive and well until he went missing from the car. Despite this, Martin's lawyer argued that if James had been killed at home, the fatal blow could have been struck by his mother. The jury convicted Martin of murder. The verdict was upheld by the Superior Court of Pennsylvania.[55]

A parent can claim a child has wandered off or been kidnapped even if their death was likely the result of an accident.

On March 18, 1991, two-year-old Thomas Gibson was playing in his family's yard. His father, Larry Gibson, went for a jog. After returning from his run, Gibson reported Thomas had gone missing. Gibson worked as a deputy sheriff. The sheriff ordered him to stay off duty while the search was organized – Gibson was told to function as a parent rather than as a police officer. Despite these instructions, Gibson left his home driving his police car for seven miles that remained unaccounted for in the vehicle log. Gibson said he traveled to a highway rest area to look for his son. Other actions appeared odd. The strangest was a suggestion the search be suspended because it began to snow. Gibson's actions made him the primary suspect in his son's disappearance. Gibson resigned from the sheriff's department. He and his family moved to Montana.[56]

The impasse in the investigation was broken by divorce. In 1994, Gibson's oldest daughter, who was four at the time of her brother's disappearance, said she saw Gibson hit Thomas and put him in the trunk of the police car. This story was supported by Gibson's ex-wife. Gibson was charged with second-degree murder. Before the trial began, Gibson's half-sister disclosed that Gibson called on the day of the disappearance to confess killing his son and asking for a loan to post bail if he was arrested.[57]

The prosecution theorized that Gibson killed his son accidentally. The neighborhood was infested with stray cats. Gibson had the habit of shooting them. A shot was heard about the time Thomas disappeared, and a dead cat with a bullet wound was found nearby. The prosecutor suggested Thomas was hit after the bullet passed through the cat. A more sinister alternative theory was also proposed. In this second scenario, Gibson shot the cat, causing Thomas to investigate. Gibson lost his temper and fatally hit his son. Both theories had Gibson putting Thomas in the trunk of his police car, calling the sheriff's office to activate a search, and disposing of the body under the guise of searching the rest area.[58] Gibson denied all culpability. According to him, his ex-wife, half-sister, and daughter were all lying, with his daughter being coached by his vindictive ex. The jury convicted Gibson of manslaughter, suggesting they accepted the accidental shooting scenario.[59] Police believe Thomas was thrown into a body of water known as Swamp Creek, but his body was never found.

Sometimes a combination strategy of both denying and reporting a disappearance is followed. In 2006, nine-year-old Colton Clark and his twelve-year-old brother received foster care from their uncle and aunt, Rex and Rebecca Clark. Their parents had addictions problems. The Clarks lived on a farm and were homeschooling the two boys, whose contact with the community was limited. Social workers attempted to see the boys for a regular wellness check visit, but the Clarks stalled for six weeks. An appointment was finally scheduled. That morning the visit was to occur, the foster parents reported Colton was missing. They claimed the boy feared the social worker's visit and ran away. Colton's backpack and favorite shoes disappeared when he did. The disappearance was treated as a missing person's case, generating a massive search using police officers, professional searchers, and dogs. Colton was not found. Colton's brother was moved to a different foster home.[60] The case went cold.

In 2015, the police officer who originally took the missing person's complaint reopened the case. His efforts to find out what happened to Colton were reported by an online news agency called the *Red Dirt Report*.[61] Colton's brother, now in his early 20s, saw the article and called police. He reported that he and Colton had been regularly beaten and "disciplined" with cattle prods by the Clarks. Colton was accused of stealing a ring and was beaten to death. Colton's brother reported he had remained silent because of fear of the Clarks.[62] Subsequent searches of the Clark's farm revealed no sign of the boy's remains or any other forensic evidence.

The Clarks were charged with murdering Colton. The primary direct evidence against them was the testimony of Colton's brother. The defense lawyers introduced witnesses claiming they saw Colton alive in the days before his disappearance was reported. The trial became a test of credibility. The jury convicted the Clarks of first-degree murder, influenced by a witness who had no direct knowledge about the case. In 2013, a contractor installed a storm shelter on the farm. Before the contractor began the job, Rex Clark described his service in Vietnam and said he would shoot anyone coming on his property. The contractor warned Clark not to shoot his employee. He meant it as a semi-serious joke, but was taken aback by Clark's response.

> Well, if I do, I'll know what to do with the body. I'll cut it up, put in a barrel, cook it up, kick it over, feed it to my five dogs and gather up the bones and the rest of it and throw it in the river.[63]

In a trial wherein credibility was crucial, this story probably did not help Clark's cause. Both Rex and Rebecca Clark were convicted of murder.

Children and No-Body Homicides

As we saw at the beginning of the chapter, children constitute a disproportionate number of victims in no-body homicide cases. The cases discussed reveal some reasons for this. One is logistical. They are small. They can be easily carried and disposed of. The ease of body disposal ensures some killers will use this to attempt to avoid detection. Lauryn Dickens, James Johnson, and Samantha Heiges's unnamed baby were just tossed in the garbage. Rilya Wilson, Surrette Clark, Elisabeth Huster, Anna Marie Vega, and Thomas Gibson were easy to transport to some hidden or watery grave. The ease of disposal is likely a major reason a woman is far more likely to be the killer in no-body cases in which the victim is a small child.

But there is more. Children are more disposable socially as well as physically. Their existence is not yet embedded in many bureaucratic record systems. They pay no income tax and have no bank accounts. If they are too young to be in school, there are no teachers to notice they are gone. If they are homeschooled, this educational invisibility can continue for years. Even if the child is in school, a note to the principal saying the family has moved is enough to prevent inquiry. Many children who become victims of homicides have been previously abused and are, at least in theory, being monitored by child protection agencies. As we have seen, this can be a weak rope on which to cling. In most cases, a child is visible only to a relatively small and insular group of family and friends. The children most at risk of being killed are usually from the most socially isolated, transient, and dysfunctional families. When killed, they can disappear without any outside adult noticing or caring. The person legally entrusted with the power to report the child missing is often the person who killed them. When a child is murdered, their fate can remain an unknown unknown with chilling ease.

The border between Canada and the United States is a line that marks a significant difference in no-body homicide prosecutions in cases involving children. South of this border, most of these cases feature a parent, guardian, or other care-giver as the killer. North of the line, this kind of prosecution is essentially nonexistent. One possible explanation could be that Canada has a superior child-protection system such that a murdered child is less likely to be disposed of like a piece of garbage. Another is that the Canadian child protection system is worse – that the killing and disposing of children escapes official notice. I do not know which explanation is more correct, but the fact it is a question without an answer highlights the special vulnerability of children.

Notes

1 Rule, Sheila, "300 Police Search for Missing Boy as "No. 1" Task," *New York Times*, May 31, 1979; Goodman, George, "Volunteers Take Major Role in Search for Missing 6-Year Old SoHo Boy," New York Times, May 28, 1979.
2 Gross, Jane, "As Missing-Children Campaign Grows, Sorrow the Patz Family Lingers," *New York Times*, May 20, 1985.
3 Renfrew, Paul M., *Stranger Danger: Family Values, Childhood and the American Carceral State* (New York, NY: Oxford University Press, 2020); Wilson, Michael, "The Legacy of Etan Patz: Wary Children Who Became Watchful Parents," *New York Times*, May 8, 2015.
4 Cohen, Lisa R., *After Etan: The Missing Child Case That Held America Captive* (New York, NY: Grand Central, 2014).
5 Cohen, *After Etan*.
6 Barron, James and William K. Rashbaum, "In Basement, Hopes to Solve '78 Case of Missing Boy," *New York Times*, April 19, 2012.
7 Wolff, Craig, "Police Say 'Unstable' Drifter is Chief Suspect in Patz Case," *New York Times*, August 18, 1990.
8 "Patz Suspect Arraigned in Pennsylvania Case," *New York Times*, August 31, 1990.
9 Vega, Tanzina, "Jailhouse Informant Points to Alternate Suspect at Patz Trial," *New York Times*, March 27, 2015; Varga, Tanzina, "Defense at Patz Trial Presents Jury with Alternate Suspect, via an Old Video," *New York Times,* March 23, 2015.
10 Saulny, Susan, "Judge Rules that a Convicted Molester, Now in Prison, Is Responsible for Etan Patz's Death," *New York Times*, May 5, 2004.
11 Goldstein, Joseph, "Missing Child Case in SoHo, All but Closed, Was Revived by a New Agent," *New York Times*, April 23, 2012.
12 Sirois, Adam, "Why I Said Not Guilty: Etan Patz Jury's Lone Holdout Speaks," *New York Post*, May 10, 2015.
13 People v Hernandez 2020 NY Slip Op 02100 Decided on March 26, 2020 Appellate Division, First Department.
14 Cohen, *After Etan*; Renfrew, *Stranger Danger.*
15 R. v. Garland, 2019 ABCA 479.

16 R. v. Warner, 21 O.R. (3d) 136 (1994).
17 "Step-Father Admits to Murder," *Kingston Whig-Standard*, November 30, 1995.
18 The Charley Project, "Lauryn Dickens," https://charleyproject.org/case/lauryn-dickens, June 27, 2012.
19 Buser, Lawrence, "Fellow Prisoner Testifies in Trial," *The Commercial Appeal*, March 23, 2012.
20 Brown, George, "Guilty Verdict in Shakera Dickens Murder Trial," *WREG-TV Memphis*, March 23, 2012.
21 Jacobson, Kelsey, "Mother Who Killed Her Baby: 'I put my hand over her nose and mouth,'" *WCM-TV News*, June 22, 2012.
22 Rumsfeld, Donald, *Known and Unknown: A Memoir* (New York, NY: Sentinel, 2011).
23 Holland, Katherine, "Police Identify Remains of Child Murdered Almost 40 Years Ago," *United Press International*, August 5, 2010.
24 DiBiase, *No-Body Homicide Cases*, 240.
25 After 40 years, Tempe Police Identify Girl's Body," *Boston Herald*, August 9, 2010.
26 The Charley Project, "Elisabeth Ann Huster," https://charleyproject.org/case/elisabeth-ann-huster. January 21, 2010.
27 Fausset, Richard, "Woman Held in Body-Parts Case is Wanted in Oregon," *Los Angeles Times*, November 12, 2000.
28 "Woman Admits Shooting and Cutting Up Daughter," *Seattle Post-Intelligencer*, January 8, 2002.
29 "Woman Is Found Guilty of Killing Her Daughter," *Deseret News*, February 9, 2002.
30 "1935 Mother of the Year," *American Mothers*, accessed September 21, 2022, https://www.americanmothers.org/1935-national-mother-of-the-year/.
31 Vega v. State, 656 N.E.2d 497 (1995).
32 Canedy, Dana, "2 Charged With Fraud in Missing Girl Case," *New York Times*, October 3, 2002.
33 Canedy, Dana, "Miami 5-Year-Old Missing For Year Before Fact Noted," *New York Times*, May 1, 2002.
34 Canedy, Dana, "Florida Judge Says State Worker Lied in Court About 5-Year-Old Girl Who Vanished," *New York Times*, May 7, 2002.
35 Canedy, Dana, "National Briefing/South: Florida: Law Bans Fake Child-Custody Papers," *New York Times*, May 16, 2002.
36 America's Most Wanted, "Rilya Shanese Wilson," https://web.archive.org/web/20060128204142/http://www.amw.com/missing_children/brief.cfm?id=25448. Accessed September 21, 2022.
37 Reward Upped for Missing Girl," *Orlando Sentinel*, July 31, 2002.
38 "Bombshell in Defense of Child Murder Suspect Geralyn Graham," *Channel 5 CBS Miami*, January 10, 2013.
39 Graham v. State, No 3D13-561 (March 11, 2015).
40 Graham v. State, No 3D13-561 (March 11, 2015).
41 Canedy, Dana, "Children Suffer as Florida Agency Struggles," *New York Times*, July 1, 2002.
42 Canedy, Dana, "DNA Tests Show Girl's Body Is Not That of Miami Child," *New York Times*, May 11, 2002.
43 State v. Johnson, Missouri Court of Appeals, Western District, No. WD 70392 (May 25, 2010).
44 Warmke v. Commonwealth, 297 KY 694 (Ky. Ct. App. 1944).
45 State v. Heiges, 806 N.W.2d 1 (Minn. 2011).
46 Melo, Frederick, "Coons Rapids Woman Convicted of Killing Baby Won't Testify Against Baby's Dad," *Twin Cities Pioneer Press*, August 2, 2009.
47 State v. Heiges, 806 N.W.2d 1 (Minn. 2011).
48 Because A.S. was not convicted, her name is not being used in this book, even though it is a matter of public record.
49 Boer, Katie, "I'm Really Mad at Aunt Angie, But Is It Okay If I Still Love Her?" *KVAL News*, December 10, 2010.
50 "Springfield Police Search Landfill for Murdered Baby's Body," *KGW8*, December 10, 2010.
51 "Mistrial Declared for Woman Accused in Newborn's Death," *Albany Democrat-Herald*, February 9, 2012.
52 "Oregon Woman Accused of Killing Baby Says She Lied," *Salon.com*, February 2, 2012.
53 "Oregon Woman Acquitted in Baby-Death Retrial," *The Spokesman Review*, June 1, 2012.
54 Com. v. Martin, 433 Pa. Superior Ct. 280 (1994).
55 Com. v. Martin, 433 Pa. Superior Ct. 280 (1994).
56 Andrews, Mea, "Tommy's Missing: Mystery Surrounds the Disappearance of a Little Boy Whose Parents Still Search for Him," *The Missoulian*, August 9, 1992.
57 "Doubts Raised About 'confession'," *Albany (OR) Democrat-Herald*, February 25, 1995.

58 Bernard, Jeff, "Deliberations Start in Rosenberg Toddler's Death," *The World*, March 15, 1995.
59 The Charley Project, "Thomas Dean Gibson," https://charleyproject.org/case/thomas-dean-gibson, June 30, 2017.
60 The Charley Project, "Colton Levi Clark," https://charleyproject.org/case/colton-levi-clark, November 15, 2019.
61 Wood, Mindy Ragan, "Missing Boy Not Forgotten: Colt Clark," *Red Dirt Report*, September 15, 2015.
62 Wood, Mindy Ragan, "Disturbing Abuse Allegations in Colt Clark Case," *Red Dirt Report*, April 13, 2016.
63 Clay, Nolan, "Seminole Couple Convicted in Gruesome 'no-body' Case," *The Oklahoman*, October 11, 2017.

6

SOCIETY'S EXPENDABLES

Sex Trade Workers and No-Body Homicides

Catherine Todd was a successful musician until she developed an addiction to drugs. The Ontario woman turned to part-time prostitution, advertising her availability online. In March of 2013, she agreed to meet James Parise in her apartment; presumably she did not know Parise had a history of violence, including beating a man with a baseball bat. A fee of $210 was agreed upon. Catherine arranged to have cocaine delivered to her apartment for her customer. Parise arrived. Catherine was never seen again.[1]

A week after Catherine's assignation with Parise, her boyfriend filed a missing persons report. Police found her dog hungry and frantic in her apartment. There were bloodstains and the strong smell of bleach. Catherine's love seat was gone. So was Catherine. Her disappearance was immediately treated as a homicide investigation. It was a self-solver. Catherine's cell phone records led directly to Parise as her last scheduled visitor. Security camera video showed Parise and a friend carrying the love seat out of the apartment. There was a bundle under the cushions.

When questioned by police, the friend was horrified to learn that he may have helped dispose of Catherine's body. He told police that Parise recruited him to help throw the love seat into a garbage dumpster. Parise's girlfriend was a more reluctant witness, but said Parise recruited her to purchase cleaning supplies. The girlfriend drove Parise (he had no driver's license because of impaired driving convictions) to Catherine's apartment building and watched while Parise used a ladder to enter through the balcony door. She told police Parise took five garbage bags and a wooden table out of the apartment. They took this material to a remote location, doused it with gasoline, and burned it. The girlfriend said Parise told her he had killed a prostitute. Police conducted a six-week search of the local landfill, but were unable to find Catherine's body.[2]

Parise was charged with murder. He initially denied all involvement, but the evidence was so overwhelming that he gave up denial a few days into his preliminary hearing. Parise pleaded guilty to manslaughter.[3] He claimed that the cocaine dealer delivering his drugs robbed him; in frustration and rage, he beat Catherine to death. Parise also blamed steroid and cocaine use for his homicidal rage. In the statement of facts accompanying his guilty plea, the prosecutor noted that the only evidence the robbery occurred was Parise's statement and that, if it occurred, there was no evidence that Catherine had been in any way complicit.[4] Even if Parise's self-serving version was true, she was just a handy outlet for his temper.

DOI: 10.4324/9781003372134-6

Sex Trade Workers and No-Body Homicide Prosecutions

We left Chapter 5 with a queasy feeling. There are a lot of children among the victims in successful prosecutions of no-body homicides. Some of these cases demonstrate how vulnerable children are. The ease with which some killers of children delayed any substantive investigation makes us view these cases akin to a ship's captain coming near an iceberg. Something is seen, but there is more that is invisible; we do not know how much. This queasy feeling continues when we look at the no-body homicides of sex trade workers. There is a scattering of cases in the list of successful prosecutions. These cases suggest there are more, but we do not know how many.

Working in the sex trades is one of the most hazardous occupations in North America. Different studies have produced different estimates of the risk of homicide, but there is consensus, however, that people working in the sex trades are much more likely to be murdered than any other occupational group.[5]

The quick arrest of James Parise is an anomaly among no-body homicides of sex trade workers. Text messages on Catherine Todd's cell phone established that Parise was her last client. The homicide took place in an easily identified location. Some of Parise's post-offence behavior was captured on security camera video. The two people he recruited for body disposal and crime scene cleanup were willing to talk to police. Parise made guilty disclosures which were reported to police. Catherine's homicide was a self-solver. Most such cases are not. Criminologists Eric Beauregard and Melissa Martineau point out that sex trade workers are among the few people who regularly get into cars with strangers or meet them alone behind closed doors. Sex trade workers are often mobile, live transitory lifestyles, and less likely to inform friends or family when they move.[6] Their disappearances are often slow to be reported to police – if they are reported missing at all. Because prostitution is tangled in a web of criminal laws, sex trade workers and their clients are often very reluctant to talk to police. Abduction, killing, and body disposal for sex trade workers often occurs in different policing jurisdictions. This hinders investigations even more. As will be discussed in Chapter 7 when we look at the case of Robert Pickton, serial killers who prey on sex trade workers can create extraordinary numbers of victims before being caught.

As a society, we do not care that much about what happens to sex trade workers.[7] There is not a lot of public pressure to investigate their disappearances. When their killers use body disposal as a detection avoidance strategy, sex trade workers often become the "missing missing"[8] – missed by nobody except for a few friends and family members, uncounted in the official homicide (and often in the missing persons) statistics. Gary Ridgeway, "The Green River Killer" preyed on sex trade workers in the Washington state and dumped the bodies of his victims in selected, isolated locations.[9] This resulted in the discovery of clusters of bodies; effectively small, personalized, unmarked cemeteries. From the clusters of bodies discovered, we know Ridgeway had at least 48 victims; there could be more if other disposal sites remained undiscovered. Of these 48 known victims:

- Four had been reported missing, but the investigation was closed after police received false reports that they were sighted alive;
- Four were reported missing but their cases were accidentally deleted from the state's missing persons database;
- Two were never reported missing;
- One was only reported missing five years after disappearing.

Eleven of Ridgeway's known victims had no ongoing missing persons investigation into their disappearance. But there is more. Another five victims remain unidentified.[10] We do not know whether any of these women were reported missing in another state or country. As with children, the successful prosecutions of no-body homicides of sex trade workers present a flashing warning sign that there are more which remain uncounted and unsolved.

Sex trade workers are uniquely vulnerable to serial killers. In Chapter 7, we'll look at how Robert Pickton was only caught after a friend turned police informer because he needed rent money. Cory Legebokoff was caught because he had the bad luck to encounter a police officer on a lonely highway while leaving the site of a murder and body dump.[11] Serial killers preying on sex trade workers can use body disposal to avoid detection long enough to kill many before being caught. We will never know the exact number killed by Gary Ridgeway or Robert Pickton, but both probably killed about 50. Perhaps there were many more.

Kenneth McDuff was a prolific serial killer. In 1966, he kidnapped three teenagers. After taking them to an isolated location, he killed the two boys before raping and killing the girl. McDuff was sentenced to death, but got a reprieve when the U.S. Supreme Court ruled that existing capital punishment laws were unconstitutional. McDuff was paroled in 1989 and promptly went on a killing spree. He kidnapped, raped, and murdered women before dumping their bodies in isolated locations. The bodies of some victims were found; others were not. McDuff was convicted for two of these murders. One was clerking at a convenience store and one working at a car wash when kidnapped by McDuff. One body was found; one was prosecuted successfully as a no-body case. McDuff also murdered several sex trade workers. He was never prosecuted for these killings and we do not know how many there were, but prior to his execution McDuff told police where the bodies of two of these victims were hidden.[12]

While deadly and depraved, Garry Ridgeway, Robert Pickton, Cody Legebokoff, and Kenneth McDuff were not cunning and clever in the mold of the fictional Hannibal Lector. They did not have to be. Their choice of victim and body disposal methods was enough to allow a long run of homicidal success.

Serial killers present a special danger to sex trade workers. As James Parise demonstrated, so do "ordinary" customers. It's unlikely that Parise planned to kill Catherine Todd when he went to her apartment. The killing was spontaneous. The decision to avoid detection by throwing her body in a garbage dumpster came after the crime had been committed. Parise was exceptionally incompetent at avoiding detection. In other cases, the combination of a sex trade worker as victim and body disposal can make it almost impossible for a case to be solved by police or successfully prosecuted.

To highlight these problems, let us look at the prosecution of Leonard Lipsky after the 1976 disappearance of Mary Robinson in Rochester, New York.

At the time of her disappearance, Mary's life was tumultuous. She had been married and working as a telephone solicitor and waitress until her husband left the marriage to take up with her sister. Both Mary and her sister then began working in the sex trades. In June of 1976, Mary was seen going to work in a Rochester hotel. She was not seen again. Two days later, her sister and sort-of-ex-husband reported her missing. Mary's apartment was undisturbed, and nothing was missing except her purse and the clothing she had been last seen wearing. The missing person's investigation went nowhere.

Around the time Mary disappeared, the life of Leonard Lipsky came off its moorings. Lipsky was an accounting student and engaged to be married. At the time of Mary's disappearance, Lipsky's fiancé was on holiday. She returned to Rochester a few days after Mary's disappearance – an event that she had no knowledge of – to discover her boyfriend was extremely agitated. He announced he was dropping out of college and moving to Arizona. Lipsky asked his fiancé to come with him. She refused, but helped Lipsky clean out his apartment. She discovered a purse and some female socks and sandals. Inside the purse were glasses, some family pictures, and an identification card bearing the name and picture of Mary Robinson. The name meant nothing to Lipsky's fiancé. Lipsky said the purse belonged to a previous tenant. The fiancé kept the purse and asked friends if anyone knew the person it belonged to. Nobody did. Lipsky's fiancé put the items in her closet and soon forgot about them.

Lipsky moved to Arizona and then to Utah. He got married and started working for a distribution company. A little two years after he uprooted his life in Rochester, more tumultuous events occurred. Lipsky sexually assaulted and beat a woman on the campus of the University of Utah. He was charged with aggravated assault and pleaded guilty. The judge ordered a psychiatric examination prior to sentencing. Lipsky told the examining psychiatric social worker that he had another, more serious, crime to confess. After being warned about the possible legal consequences of confessing another crime, Lipsky said he had killed a woman named Mary Robinson in Rochester, New York.[13] Lipsky said he paid Mary for sexual services, but assaulted her when she was leaving. Lipsky said he feared retaliation from Mary's family so he strangled her, put her body in the trunk of his car, drove south for three hours, and threw her body in a gully. The police response to this detailed disclosure generated media attention, which in turn caused witnesses to come forward. Lipsky's ex-fiancé saw the newspaper coverage, remembered the purse she had in her closet, and gave it to the police. Two of Lipsky's co-workers reported he had disclosed murdering someone to them. One said when he threatened to tell police about the disclosure, Lipsky said, "well, go ahead and try to pin it on me, you can't because there isn't a body so there wouldn't be any evidence." Lipsky gave Utah police permission to search his apartment. They found a poem he'd written that read:

> To crush out a life with a hand or a heel;
> To be carelessly senseless and not even feel;
> To treat one as nothing and not even real;
> To be as a jackal, a thief who did steal.
> I was such a man, and it's a part of me now.
> I was such a fool and can't even tell how I did such a thing.
> Now, it weighs on my brow and I think of the peace such an act won't allow.
> But still I live on and remember it well.
> Yet still I must live to remember the hell.
> I can never let go of the body that fell, and it tears me to pieces where my thoughts on this dwell.
> I can never be free of this feeling inside.
> I will never be able to successfully hide.
> And there is no way to share the tears that I've cried.
> So I now live for two; by my hand one has died.[14]

Lipsky was taken back to Rochester and tried for murder. After hearing police describe their futile search for any indication that Mary was alive, Lipsky's voluntary confession, the disclosure to co-workers, and the ex-fiancé's report about his possession of Mary's purse, the jury convicted Lipsky of second-degree murder.

The trial judge overturned the jury decision, saying the prosecution had provided no evidence, independent of Lipsky's confession and disclosures, that Mary was dead or that Lipsky was the cause of her death. As a result, said the judge, there was no corpus delicti proving a crime had been committed.[15] Lipsky could not be convicted based on an uncorroborated confession alone. The prosecution appealed the judge's decision. The Court of Appeals for the State of New York reinstated the conviction, arguing that Lipsky's possession of Mary's purse combined with his suspicious post-event behavior was sufficient corroborated evidence to put the question of guilt to the jury. Their subsequent assessment of the veracity of his confessions should stand.[16] Two years later, in 1984, the Fourth Appellate Division of the Supreme Court of New York overturned the conviction, ruling that there was no evidence, independent of Lipsky's confession, that Mary had been murdered or that Lipsky was responsible.[17] In his closing arguments, the prosecutor had conceded Mary's work in the sex trades created doubt that disappearance meant death, let alone homicide. In the absence of the confessions and disclosures, it was possible she had left Rochester on her own, committed suicide, or been killed by another client. The judges went on to rule that Lipsky's confession was inadmissible because Utah officials had not given him a specific *Miranda* warning. It is likely Lipsky attempted to clear his conscience by confessing, but when faced with the prospect of serving decades in prison, he got a lawyer and fought for his freedom.[18]

There is a final postscript to the story. In 1988 – four years after Lipsky's conviction was overturned – the body of a woman believed to be Mary Robinson was discovered.[19] We will never know with certainty if this was her since the discovery preceded the introduction of DNA identification techniques. An attempt to identify using dental records was unsuccessful since Mary's dentist had retired and his records had been destroyed.

Sex Trade Clients and No-Body Homicides

Commercial sex is intrinsically risky for participants. The sellers of sexual services are at the most risk, but clients of sex trade workers also put themselves in danger. There have been four successful no-body prosecutions where the purchaser of sexual services was the victim. In each case, associates of the prostitute attempted to rob the customer. Violence escalated, the customer was killed, and his body disposed of. These cases all featured high levels of viciousness and stupidity. The killers were always stoned, drunk, or both. These killings were group affairs; upon arrest and prosecution, the participants all blamed their colleagues.

We will examine one of these cases.[20]

In 2003, Daniel Jamieson used a chat line to find a sex trade worker in Schenectady, New York. They agreed to meet. Daniel had no idea what he was getting himself into. The person he agreed to meet was part of an enterprise operated by 32-year-old Stacey Adamson, who used his 19-year-old wife and teenage girls as revenue earners. The person Daniel met was a 16-year-old girl kept in sexual servitude by beatings and the provision of illicit drugs. In addition to supplying virtual slaves to clients, Adamson enjoyed robbery. If a client appeared vulnerable, Adamson would rob them at gunpoint. On occasion, he forced clients to withdraw money from their bank account. Adamson exploited the fact the clients had engaged in sex with under-age girls to prevent complaints to police.

When Daniel arrived at the apartment, he discovered the woman he was meeting was still a girl. He attempted to leave without engaging in sex. Adamson emerged from his customary hiding place and robbed Daniel. He then demanded Daniel have sex with the girl to ensure he would not go to police. Terrorized, Daniel was unable to comply. His lack of ability to perform enraged Adamson. He tied up Daniel, punching and kicking him while demanding the production of semen. Adamson ordered the 16-year-old girl to perform oral sex on Daniel while he was being kicked and threatened with death for his lack of sexual performance. This violence did not have the desired aphrodisiac effect. In between beatings, Adamson used Daniel's vehicle to run errands, used Daniel's cell phone, and entertained guests in the apartment's living room. Twenty-four hours after Daniel entered the apartment, he died.

Adamson, his wife, and the 16-year-old girl used Daniel's car to transport his body to New York City. Daniel was thrown into a garbage dumpster. The three then returned to Schenectady.

Adamson ordered the girl to clean the room in which Daniel had been killed. His wife was ordered to entertain another client to raise money for their getaway. In the words of the New York Supreme Court, "Both complied, resulting in the accumulation of garbage bags full of bloodied evidence, a bleached-down apartment and additional cash, including money stolen from the customer's wallet."[21] They departed for Mexico in Daniel's car, leaving in such a hurry that they forgot to take the garbage bags containing Daniel's bloody clothing to a dumpster. They returned to New York City. Adamson had decided to disfigure Daniel's face in order to make identification more difficult. The garbage dumpster had been emptied, so the three continued heading south.

They got as far as Texas. Daniel's family had reported him missing. Police in Schenectady used the GPS tracker in Daniel's car to locate the vehicle. Texas police did the rest.

The two women were happy to see the police. Adamson's wife reported that he had decided the 16-year-old girl needed to be killed. The wife said she had been trying to talk Adamson out of this but was losing hope she would succeed. The logical conclusion of witness elimination had likely occurred to her.

The two women, promptly and independently, told the same incredible story. Adamson initially denied all knowledge of Daniel. When told the women had talked, Adamson changed his story to blame them for the killing. Adamson said he had been away when the women accidentally killed Daniel during rough sex; he had just helped with the cleanup.[22] The three were extradited back to New York. The two women pleaded guilty to second-degree murder.[23] Adamson was charged and convicted of murder in the first degree (three counts), kidnapping in the first degree (two counts), coercion in the first degree, assault in the first degree, sexual abuse in the first degree (two counts), robbery in the first degree (three counts), robbery in the second degree (two counts), grand larceny in the third degree, grand larceny in the fourth degree (two counts), tampering with physical evidence (two counts), rape in the third degree, promoting prostitution in the third degree (two counts), and endangering the welfare of a child. Adamson's defense was hindered by his lawyers withdrawing after he threatened them. While waiting for trial, Adamson was disciplined for sending "love letters" to his wife. She found them threatening, perhaps because he smeared them with blood before sending them.[24] After hearing the two women's testimony and viewing the extensive physical evidence, the jury convicted Adamson on all charges.

Notes

1 James Parise Guilty of Manslaughter in Beating Death of Catherine Todd," *Kitchener-Waterloo Record*, February 11, 2014.

2 Shypula, Brian, "Police Continue Search for Body of 48-Year-Old Catherine Todd," *Stratford Beacon-Herald*, May 27, 2013; "Police Stop Searching Landfill for Catherine Todd's Body," *CBC News*, May 17, 2013.

3 Butler, Colin, James Parise Pleads Guilty in Death of Catherine Todd," *CBC News*, February 14, 2014.

4 Ferrier, Melanie, "Catherine Todd Killer Sentenced to 9 Years," *CBC News*, February 19, 2014.

5 Salfati, C. Gabrielle, Allison R. James and Lynne Fergusson, "Prostitute Homicides: A Descriptive Study," *Journal of Interpersonal Violence* 23, No. 4 (April 2008): 505–543; Quinet, Kenna, "Prostitutes as Victims of Serial Homicide: Trends and Case Characteristics, 1970–2009," *Homicide Studies* 15, No. 1 (2011): 74–100; Potterat. John. J., Devon D. Brewer, Stephen Q. Muth, Richard B. Rothenberg, Donald E. Woodhouse, John B. Muth, Heather K. Stites, and Stuart Brody, "Mortality in a Long-term Open Cohort of Prostitute Women," *American Journal of Epidemiology* 169, No. 8 (2004): 778–785; Quinet, K. "The Missing Missing: Toward a Quantification of Serial Murder Victimization in the United States," *Homicide Studies* 11, No. 4 (2007)" 319–339; Beauregard, Eric and Melissa Martineau (2012) "A Descriptive Study of Sexual Homicide in Canada: Implications for Police Investigation," *International Journal of Offender Therapy and Comparative Criminology* 57(1): 1454–1476.

6 Beauregard, Eric and Melissa Martineau, *The Sexual Murderer: Offender Behavior and Implications for Practice* (New York, NY: Routledge, 2017): 154–156.
7 Oppel, Wally, *Forsaken: The Report of the Missing Women's Commission of Inquiry* (Victoria, BC: Government of British Columbia, 2012).
8 Quintet, *Missing missing.*
9 Keppel, Robert and William Birnes, *The Riverman: Ted Bundy and I Hunt for the Green River Killer* (New York, NY: Pocket Books, 1995); Rule, Ann, *Green River Running Red: The True Story of the Green River Killer* (New York, NY: Gallery Books, 2005); Reichart, David, *Chasing the Devil: My Twenty-Year Quest to Capture the Green River Killer* (New York, NY: St. Martins, 2005).
10 State of Washington v. Gary Leon Ridgeway, "Prosecutors Summary of the Evidence," Superior Court of Washington for Kings County, No. 01-1-10270-9 SEA.
11 Harvey, Marissa and Kirk Williams, "Cody Legebokoff Had Blood on Face, Legs When Arrested, Crown Says," *CBC News*, June 3, 2014.
12 Lavergne, Gary M., *Bad Boy from Rosebud: The Murderous Life of Kenneth Allen McDuff* (Denton, TX: University of North Texas Press, 1999); Stewart, Bob, *No Remorse: They Let Him Live; They Set Him Free to Kill and Kill Again* (New York, NY: Pinnacle, 1996).
13 State v. Lipsky, 639 P.2d 174 (1981).
14 People v. Lipsky, 57 N.Y.2d 560 (1982).
15 People v. Lipsky, 102 Misc. 2d 19 (April 24, 1980).
16 People v. Lipsky, 445 N.Y.S.2d 660; 84 A.D.2d 42 December 23, 1981.
17 People v. Lipsky, 103 A.D.2d 1033 (N.Y. App. Div. 1984).
18 State of Utah v. Leonard Lipsky, "Brief of the Appellant," Supreme Court of Utah Case No. Case No. 17,513 (1981).
19 Mills, Steve, "Irondequoit Bones May Solve '76 Murder Case," *Rochester Democrat and Chronicle*, August 12, 1988.
20 People v. Adamson, 47 A.D.3d 318 (2007).
21 People v. Adamson, 47 A.D.3d 318 (2007).
22 Suchowolec, Laura, "Adamson Denies Role in Sex-Scam Killing; Prosecutors: Victim Was Tortured," *The Daily Gazette*, July 1, 2003.
23 Suchowolec, Laura, "Lawyer Claims Suspect Made Deal with DA," *The Daily Gazette*, June 27, 2003.
24 Spagnoli, Victoria R., "Murder Suspect Faces New Charges: Blood-Stained Love Letters Alleged," *The Daily Gazette*, September 3, 2003.

7

KILLING IN VOLUME

Serial Killers and Body Disposal

John Haigh thought he was smarter than he was. As a child, Haigh won scholarships to attend prestigious grammar schools in England. As an adult, he had trouble maintaining employment because he stole from his employers. When Haigh was in his mid-20s, he became a conman. He was not very good at it. Haigh posed as a lawyer to sell fraudulent stock, claiming it came from the estates of deceased clients. Haigh got caught when his second potential victim noticed the name of their city was misspelled on Haigh's letterhead.

While in prison, Haigh studied legal texts. He learned a person could not be convicted of murder without a corpus delicti. Unfortunately, Haigh did not know enough Latin. He thought corpus delicti meant the body of a person rather than the body of the crime (evidence that the crime has been committed). Haigh also read about a French murder in which the victim was dissolved in a bathtub filled with sulfuric acid. Haigh devised a unique career plan. He would kill people, dissolve them in acid, and loot their estates.[1]

Haigh got out of prison during the Second World War. He rekindled an acquaintance with William McSwan, who collected rents for property owned by his parents. William kept a low profile to avoid being drafted. Haigh lured William into a basement, caved in his head with a lead pipe, placed his body in a barrel, and filled it up with sulfuric acid. Two days later, Haigh dumped the resulting sludge down the drain. He forged the documents necessary to get access to William's bank accounts. Haigh assumed William's rent collection and property management duties. The only people who missed William were his parents. Haigh told them William was hiding in Scotland to avoid the draft. It seemed plausible. William was never reported missing.

When the war ended, William's parents expected their son to emerge from hiding. Haigh said William was in London. The parents came to see their son. Haigh introduced them to the same lead pipe, barrel, acid, and drain as their son. Haigh used his forgery skills to sell their property and steal the £8,000 pounds it yielded. At the time, the average salary in Britain was £214 per year. Haigh supplemented his onetime gain by pocketing their pension checks. Nobody noticed the McSwans were gone.

Haigh lived well and gambled poorly. After two years, he ran out of money. New victims were needed. Haigh befriended Dr. Archibald Henderson and his wife Rose. He stole a revolver, rented a small workshop, shot the doctor, and put him in a barrel of acid. Haigh then summoned Rose, claiming her husband was ill. Her body went into the acid. When Archibald and Rose were sludge, they were dumped in the yard behind the workshop. Stealing their property was

DOI: 10.4324/9781003372134-7

complicated. Haigh fired a maid, who questioned his right to do so. Rose's brother was suspicious and threatened to call the police. Haigh claimed the couple were in South Africa under assumed names to avoid prosecution for performing illegal abortions; a police investigation would cause problems. Haigh emptied the Hendersons' bank accounts and sold their house, netting another £8,000. He kept the Hendersons' car and dog.

Haigh moved into a hotel in London and blew through his new fortune in one year. The manager threatened eviction. Haigh did not choose his next victim wisely, targeting a rich widow living in his hotel, Olive Durand-Deacon. Using the pretext of showing her an invention, he lured Olive to his workshop, shot her, and placed her body in a barrel of acid. Haigh sold Olive's jewelry in pawnshops and jewelry stores to raise the cash needed to prevent eviction. Olive wore a Persian lamb coat when she was shot. It got messy, so Haigh took it to a dry cleaner in preparation for sale.

Killing Olive was different from killing the McSwans and the Hendersons. Olive had friends. They wanted to know where she was. Haigh was the last person seen with her. One friend went to the police station to file a missing person's report. Haigh accompanied her to attempt damage control. It did not go well. The officer receiving the complaint checked to see if Haigh had a criminal record. When she learned of his theft and fraud convictions, the missing person's investigation transformed into a homicide case. The police found a dry-cleaning receipt in Haigh's attaché case. This led them to the Persian lamb coat – not yet cleaned. The clerk identified Haigh. The case made it to the newspapers, which caused a jeweler to report that Haigh sold him jewelry matching the description of Olive's best pieces. A search of Haigh's workshop revealed barrels, rubber protective clothing, a revolver, and empty acid containers. In the yard, police found 28 pounds of human fat, a foot, some gallstones, and Olivia's dentures. Police also found financial records and documentation for people unknown to them; three McSwans and two Hendersons. More incriminating documents were in Haigh's hotel room. Media coverage prompted Rose's brother to make a belated report of his sister's disappearance.

Haigh's legal prospects looked grim. He made them worse. When interrogated, Haigh promptly confessed to murdering and defrauding the McSwans, the Hendersons, and Olive. He also claimed three more killings that could not be corroborated. Haigh smugly announced he could not be convicted because of the corpus delicti rule. The police would never discover the bodies because they were dissolved. The interrogating officer gave Haigh a short Latin lesson. Haigh was disconcerted but rebounded quickly. He asked how long someone found not guilty by reason of insanity would be in a mental hospital. At trial, Haigh tried to convince the jury he was insane by telling stories of bizarre dreams and claiming he drank the blood of his victims. The jury convicted Haigh on six counts of murder.

Haigh had the false belief that destroying his victim's bodies made him immune from conviction. In this, he was wrong. His initial success as a serial killer came from victim selection rather than body disposal. Haigh's first victims were not missed, but his ideal potential victims are rare. People with money are usually promptly missed. When a disappearance was reported to police in a timely fashion, Haigh provided a wealth of forensic and circumstantial evidence. The police only needed to know they should be looking for it. Haigh was hanged only 172 days after Olive was reported missing.

Serial Killers, Motivation, and Body Disposal

John Haigh was a serial murderer. The FBI's operational definition for a serial murderer is someone who kills, in a criminally culpable way, two or more victims in separate events.[2] Of the 486 cases of successful American prosecutions examined for this book, 46 were serial killers.

In Canada 4 of the 31 were serial killers. These people killed at least two people in separate incidents and who hid or destroyed the body of at least one victim. This tally understates the number of victims since serial killers, by definition, kill more than once. We do not know how many victims were killed by these 50 serial killers. The numbers are imprecise. For example, Robert Pickton killed many people. We do not know how many. The *Commission of Inquiry* into the investigation identified 67 women who disappeared from the area where Pickton was operating and who were never found.[3] Pickton told an undercover police officer he killed 49. Traces of DNA from 33 were found on his property. He was charged with killing 27 and convicted of killing 6.[4] It is impossible to accurately quantify his toll but his impact is greater than implied by counting him as "one case."

There are numerous books, movies, podcasts, and magazine articles about serial killers. Most of these focus on sexually motivated serial killers. These tell only part of the story. As the FBI's Behavioral Analysis Unit notes, 'there are many other motivations for serial murders including anger, thrill, financial gain, and attention seeking."[5] We have seen how John Haigh killed repeatedly for financial gain. Harold Konigsberg killed because it was his job as "hit man" for organized criminal organizations.[6] After two divorces, Alejandro Ruiz decided homicide was more expedient when a wife got tired of his bad temper.[7] John Robinson killed to conceal other crimes. As with Haigh, Robinson was a conman who decided dead victims file no complaints to police.[8] Some serial killers have varied motives. Charles Schmidt killed his first victim for the thrill. The next two were killed to conceal the first murder.[9] H.H. Holmes killed for sexual gratification, theft, and concealment.[10] Some of his victims were killed for all three reasons. Kelly Cochrane partnered with her husband to kill her lover and then killed her husband to avenge her lover's death.[11] Robert Pickton, Kenneth McDuff, Cody Legebokoff, and many others were motivated by some sadistic sexual urge. Former child actor Skylar Deleon (a *Mighty Morphin' Power Ranger*) turned to fraud after his acting career hit the skids. Posing as a potential boat purchaser, he killed Tom and Jackie Hawks. After dumping their body into the ocean, he forged papers to claim ownership of the boat and loot their bank accounts. Their bodies were never recovered, but the body of another victim was found dumped in the desert in Mexico.[12]

The FBI is right. Serial killers have a lot of different motives.

To achieve serial killer status, a person must be competent enough at their first murder to have the opportunity to commit a second. Intent is not enough. Let us look at the short homicidal career of a wannabe no-body serial killer who failed to reach his goal.

Mark Twitchell was an unsuccessful salesman, an aspiring filmmaker, and a mediocre conman from Edmonton, Alberta.[13] He was obsessed with the television show *Dexter* in which a crime forensic examiner turns serial killer to eliminate bad guys. Twitchell started by making a short film depicting a murder. He then moved on to the real thing. Twitchell pretended to be a woman on an internet dating site, lured a man to a garage transformed into a murder set, killed, and dismembered him. Twitchell cut his victim into smaller pieces a few days later and dumped him down a storm sewer. Despite his aspiration to be a serial killer, he was too incompetent. He e-mailed his victim detailed instructions to the murder site. Police followed these instructions to the crime scene. Once there, they found a wealth of forensic evidence. More was in Twitchell's car and home. The victim's car was in Twitchell driveway. He told police a random stranger sold it to him for $40. Twitchell wrote a 200-page description of the crime, an unsuccessful earlier attempt, and his plans for future homicide. As police closed in, Twitchell deleted the document but did not override the automatic backup features on his computer. After the case was reported in the media, Twitchell's first intended victim came forward to verify the description of the attempted murder.

Twitchell was arrested and charged. It started as a no-body case. Given the evidence, any defense strategy would have probably been unsuccessful. However, Twitchell's defense was even more bizarrely incompetent than his crime. Twitchell told police where he dumped the remains of his victim. These were recovered. Twitchell attempted to plead guilty only to committing an indignity on a dead body. He claimed that the written description of the murder was an outline for a film script. Twitchell claimed he recreated Dexter's laboratory and lured people there to scare people and create a rumor that a serial killer was operating. This, Twitchell said, was intended to help get financing for the film. Twitchell said his victim took offense at the ruse and attacked. Death resulted from a combination of self-defense and an accident. Twitchell claimed he panicked and dismembered his victim – twice – before dumping him in a storm sewer. Twitchell acknowledged this had the unfortunate side effect of making it impossible for the coroner to confirm his story, but said the jury should see it was self-evidently true. The jury disagreed.

Every serial killer is better at murder than was Mark Twitchell, even though most are not as detailed in their planning. Most start with one killing before planning more. The first killing is sometimes unplanned; an escalation of a quarrel, robbery, or rape. After that, future murders are a matter of circumstance, taste, concealment, or habit. For Charles Schmidt, the path to becoming a serial killer was a bit like the old lady who swallowed the fly. He killed once because, well, just because. Two more murders were committed to prevent being caught for the first. One thing led to another.

To become a serial killer, the killer must create an investigative space between himself and his victims. If the same person keeps popping up in homicide or missing persons investigations, they become a suspect. For example, Alejandro Ruiz faced little scrutiny after his third wife, Tanya, disappeared. After Tanya's mother reported her daughter's disappearance to the police, Ruiz told police his wife left taking her clothes and money. This effectively ended the missing person's investigation. Ruiz remarried and divorced. He then married a fifth time. When this wife and her son disappeared, a friend filed a missing person's report. The police response was desultory until they discovered this was the second missing wife in three years. The intensity of the investigation suddenly increased. A search of Ruiz's property resulted in the discovery of two buried bodies – his last wife and her son. Both had been shot in the head. Ruiz was charged with committing three murders. The prosecution of two charges was based on autopsy reports and forensic evidence. Tanya's case was different. Her body was never recovered. There was no forensic evidence. Prosecutors argued she was dead by documenting her unexplained absence; this, combined with another wife's homicide, showed that Ruiz killed Tanya. The jury agreed.[14]

An ongoing connection between the serial killer and his victims helps police focus on the investigation. John Haigh created the connection by looting the property of his victims. Once police realized people had disappeared, Haigh left them ample circumstantial evidence. In the case of Alejandro Ruiz, the multiple disappearances of wives triggered a serious investigation. The disappearance of one missing wife was dismissed. When another disappeared, police started digging. Only two bodies were found, but three convictions were obtained.

When the motive for killing is some evil combination of sadistic sexual desire and joy of killing, the investigation is more difficult for police. Sexually motivated serial killers are usually opportunistic in their choice of victim. There is often no preexisting connection between killer and victims. Police need to see a pattern of deaths before they can move from individual investigations to a search for a serial killer. Establishing patterns requires the accumulation of cases, which in the case of homicide means numerous deaths. The investigative difficulties presented by serial killers are accentuated when the killer hides or destroys the bodies of his victims. Police must first realize that missing persons cases are homicides before looking for patterns in the accumulation of disappearances. If the killer preys on people who are not reported missing, police will remain oblivious to even the deadliest of serial killers.

Sexual Serial Killers and Body Disposal

On November 27, 2010, a police officer driving along a remote highway near Prince George, British Columbia, saw vehicle headlights coming down a logging road. A pickup truck swerved onto the highway, almost lost control, recovered, and sped away. The officer pulled the truck over. Inside was 20-year-old Cody Legebokoff.[15]

Legebokoff appeared to have bloodstains on his face and legs, and there was a pool of blood in the truck. Legebokoff claimed he and a friend were poaching deer, explaining the blood with a claim he beat a deer to death after it was wounded. He explained his actions by saying, "I'm a redneck, that's what we do for fun."[16] The officer did not buy this story. A search of the truck revealed a bloody knife, a bloody wrench, and a small "monkey" backpack containing identification from a 15-year-old girl, Loren Leslie. A conservation officer was dispatched to look for a poached deer. Following Legebokoff's tracks through the snow, he found body of a young woman who had been raped, stabbed, beaten with a blunt object, and stomped on. It was Loren.

For obvious reasons, Legebokoff was the prime suspect for Loren's murder. He also became the suspect for the murder of Cynthia Maas, whose body had been found dumped in a Prince George park nine weeks earlier. Cynthia had also been raped, stabbed, beat with a blunt object, and stomped on.

A forensic search of Legebokoff's home revealed splatters and DNA from two women. One was Jill Stuchenko. Her body had been found dumped in a gravel pit a year earlier Jill's. The cases had not been linked by police since Jill's body was moved after her death while Cynthia was killed where she was found. DNA was also linked to Natasha Montgomery, who disappeared about 11 weeks before the police caught Legebokoff. Natasha's body has never been recovered.

Legebokoff was charged with four counts of first-degree murder. At trial, he blamed unidentified drug dealers for the murders, saying they used his house for the Jill and Natasha's killings. He claimed the same drug dealers kidnapped Cynthia from his house. Legebokoff refused to identify these putative drug dealers, saying he did not want to enter prison labeled as a snitch. If these stories were implausible, his description of Loren's death was bizarre. Legebokoff claimed he took the young girl into the bush for consensual sex. Legebokoff claimed when they were finished, Loren "went psycho" and started hitting herself over the head with a pipe wrench and stabbing herself in the neck. She then got out of the truck to die. Legebokoff said he was too stunned to attempt first aid, but did have the presence of mind to drag her body into the trees. Legebokoff was quickly convicted on all four murder counts.[17]

Legebokoff's serial killing spree ended abruptly because of chance and coincidence. If the police officer had driven down the highway one minute earlier or later, he would not have seen Legebokoff. Loren would have been reported missing by her parents, but without the opportunistic traffic stop her body would not have been found until spring at the earliest. Perhaps it would never have been discovered.

Legebokoff was a prolific serial killer for his age, murdering four women during the span of just over a year. The pace of his killing was escalating. Despite this, police had no idea that a deadly serial killer was operating in their community. The crimes did not appear similar. Jill was the first to be murdered. When her body was found, it was obvious she had been murdered elsewhere and her body dumped. Natasha was next. Her body was never found. Police were not certain she was dead. When Cynthia disappeared, her body was found quickly, but the modus operandi was different from Jill's death. Her body was abandoned where she was murdered. The difference came from Legebokoff's learning process. Killing at home was messy and cleanup difficult. He had three roommates, which made things awkward. Legebokoff learned that bodies are heavy and awkward to move. It was easier if the victim walked to the disposal site than to carry her corpse. This process of learning confused the police. Jill appeared to have a different murderer than did Cynthia – and they did not know Natasha was dead.

The linkage between Loren's killing and Cynthia's was easy. They looked identical. However, this linkage was possible because both bodies were discovered. Had that not occurred – had the police officer stopped for a donut before patrolling the highway – no linkage would have been made between the two. Cynthia, like Jill and Natasha, was a sex trade worker. Legebokoff posed as a customer to lure them to their deaths. Loren was different. She was a teenage girl using an internet dating site to look for a potential boyfriend. She agreed to meet Legebokoff for a first face-to-face date. If Loren's body had not been discovered, police would be puzzling over two disappearances and two homicides that did not, on the surface, appear related.

Legebokoff's strategy for creating investigative space between himself and his victims was to dump them in different locations so discovery would be delayed or prevented. The discovery of a body was a matter of luck. Legebokoff's prosecution was a mixture of body-found and no-body cases. This is not uncommon.

Another strategy for serial killers is to collect bodies in one location where they can be hidden or destroyed. In these cases, a police investigation can suddenly transform from a no-body investigation to one with a plethora of bodies, often badly decomposed and mixed together. In Toronto, an investigation into disappearing gay men transformed into homicide cases when eight bodies were discovered buried in large planters at a home serviced by Bruce McArthur's landscaping company (the home owners were oblivious their yard doubling as a secret cemetery).[18] This was reminiscent of the time police found the remains of 26 young men and boys buried in the crawl space under John Gacy's house in Chicago and another three buried in his yard.[19] The key to a victim-storage strategy is controlling access to a suitable piece of property. For the killer, the benefits of this approach are transformed into an insurmountable legal liability if the police were to search the property. It is really, really, hard for a defense lawyer to explain away multiple bodies buried under the house of the accused. Gacy claimed that employees possessing keys to his house were responsible for burying the bodies under it. He received a lethal injection.

As we saw with John Haigh, a serial killer can use control of their disposal site to destroy the bodies rather than store them. With improvements in forensic techniques, complete disposal has become more difficult. In the 1940s, the sheriff described a small, charred bone fragment as the "the body of Wilson Turner." Today, microscopic blood splatters can produce the same effect.

Robert Pickton preyed on marginalized women, primarily those working in the sex trade in Vancouver's Downtown Eastside. He used promises of money and drugs to lure victims to his pig farm where he murdered them. The bodies were disposed of by feeding them to pigs, taking parts to a rendering plant, and, quite probably, grinding up their flesh and selling it mixed with ground pork. For some reason, he stored the bodies of three victims in freezers.

Pickton's murder spree presented to police as a series of disappearances. Vancouver police treated the disappearances as a series of unrelated missing persons cases.[20] They spent years denying that a serial killer was at work, ignoring both the opinions of the victim's family members and a statistical analysis from an internationally renowned geographical profiler on their own force. Pickton should have been caught long before he was. He was a known, regular visitor to the area from which women were disappearing. Several victims were known to have been going to his farm when they disappeared. Tips were ignored. One woman even escaped from his farm – stabbed, naked, near death, with a handcuff clamped to one wrist. Pickton had the key in his pocket. He was charged with attempted murder, but the charges were stayed. Police did see a connection between this attack and their multiple missing persons cases. Eventually a task force led by the RCMP took over the missing persons investigations and flipped the focus. Rather than focusing on the women as individual missing persons, the RCMP task force started with the assumption there was a serial killer and looked for potential suspects. This transformed Pickton from an almost-invisible component of the street scenery into a leading suspect.

The breakthrough came when a friend of Pickton's needed rent money. He offered to turn in drug dealers in exchange for enough money to pay his rent. Police rejected the offer since the cocaine dealers were already known to police. An offer to sell police the locations of marijuana grow-ops was rejected since police already had a backlog of sites to raid and did not want to add more to the list. In desperation, the snitch told police that Pickton had illegal handguns hidden on his property. Police used this information to get a search warrant to search Pickton's trailer. Because of Pickton's status as a suspect in the missing women's investigation, members of the RCMP task force participated in the search. They immediately found evidence linking two missing women to Pickton's property. With this, police obtained new, more expansive, search warrants for the entire farm.

The 14-acre Pickton farm site was used by Robert Pickton for raising and killing hogs and as an illegal dumping ground for contaminated soil and stolen vehicles. There were manure sewage lagoons, piles of earth 40 feet high, and 10 buildings.[21] Some were falling and infested with rats. The search took ten months and cost $70 million. One hundred twenty-five forensic technicians came from across Canada. They were supported by 110 anthropology and archeology students who visually inspected 383,495 cubic yards of soil. Another 600,000 meters were mechanically sifted. Over 500,000 DNA swabs were collected – 108,222 were processed. Over 76,000 exhibits were collected and logged, along with 543 fingerprint impressions. The search was documented with 132,125 photographs. The phrase "leaving no stone left unturned" is often used as a cliché. In the search of the Pickton farm, it was a statement of fact.[22]

This search found biological evidence of 33 women. Most could be identified through DNA matches with relatives of women reported missing, but one DNA profile was never matched. Police and prosecutors ended up referring to her as "Jane Doe." The amount of biological evidence varied. Three relatively complete bodies were found in freezers. Enough of these victims were left for a coroner to establish they were shot in the head. For the rest, not enough was recovered to determine *how* Pickton killed them. The case for murder rested on the fact of their disappearance combined with DNA evidence showing they visited Pickton's farm. No trace of 34 missing women was found. If Pickton's own count, as revealed to an undercover officer posing as a cellmate, was accurate, 16 women were murdered and their bodies disposed of without leaving a trace. Pickton was never charged for these deaths. Hale's dictum about needing a body to convict for murder was followed in spirit, even if the amount of the body required had become microscopic. Pickton was only charged for murdering 27 women for whom DNA evidence was found.

The trial judge took this further by reducing the number of charges Pickton faced at trial to six. First, the judge dismissed the charge for the murder of "Jane Doe." The judge said that a victim needed to be identified for a charge to be valid.[23] That left Pickton facing 26 murder charges.

The judge then reduced this to six cases. Citing a concern about trial length and the prejudicial effect of so many charges, he separated 6 charges from the other 20. The criterion for the separation was the amount of the victim's body found.[24] Of the six allowed to proceed to trial; three were for the bodies found in freezers. A portion of the jaw (along with five teeth) of another woman had been found in the soil. Her DNA was found on handcuff keys in Pickton's workshop and a jacket in his trailer. The hand bones of a fifth victim were found near Pickton's slaughterhouse. A portion of the jaw containing three teeth was found for a sixth woman. Pickton's lawyers conceded enough remained of these women to establish death. For the remaining 20 women, all that remained was small traces of DNA from blood, hair, or small pieces of tissue. The defense lawyers argued this showed the woman visited the property, but not was sufficient to establish they were dead. The prosecution planned to call multiple witnesses to establish a circumstantial case for death – namely that there had been no sign of their existence since their disappearance. The judge estimated it would take about 300 witnesses to establish death for these 20 women, and said this would make the trial too long and unwieldy. The judge limited the trial to the six women the defense conceded were dead based on the recovery of a "long bone." Among the excluded cases were three women whose flesh, ground up and packaged, was found in the freezers along with the three heads of other victims.

Creating this distinction based on how much, or, more accurately, what part of a body remained undermined the prosecution's case. It caused the judge to rule direct witness testimony inadmissible. One woman had escaped from Pickton's trailer, naked, covered with blood, badly wounded, and with a handcuff attached to one wrist. The judge ruled her testimony inadmissible because her ordeal occurred a few years before any of the six cases before the jury and because she had not been shot. The temporal disconnect was artificially created because of the excluded cases.[25] Another witness told police that Pickton described how he sometimes handcuffed and strangled his victims while engaged in sex. This testimony was ruled inadmissible because it did not match the forensic evidence of the three who had been shot – even though it did match the experience of the one who escaped.[26] The somewhat bizarre chain of evidentiary exclusions all stemmed from the limitation of cases to those for which a "long bone" had been recovered.

The limitation of the number of murders considered made the defense's argument for acquittal possible. The Pickton property covered 17 acres. Lots of people were coming and going. Most were disreputable. There was a steady stream of prostitutes, drug dealers, bike gang members, patrons of cockfights, partiers, deadbeats, and employees of Pickton's brother. The defense lawyers conceded the undeniable – six people had been killed, dismembered, and (mostly) disposed of on the property – but argued it was possible someone else committed the murders. Pickton, they said, could have been oblivious to what was going on. With a single case, this might have been credible. The jury did not buy it with 6. It would have been laughable with 27.

The exclusion of charges affected the question of premeditation. The prosecution argued that one killing was evidence of premeditation for the next. It is inherently inconceivable that a person would lure a prostitute to his home, kill them without premeditation, and then dispose of their body 27 times in a row. Volume creates an inference of premeditation. By restricting the number of cases being considered to six, the judge undermined this argument. In the end, the jury acquitted Pickton on the first-degree (premeditated) murder charges but convicted him on six charges of second-degree (unpremeditated) murder. The judge sentenced Pickton to life imprisonment with no possibility of parole for 25 years – the mandatory sentence for conviction on first-degree counts.[27]

Both sides appealed. The defense argued the convictions should be overturned because the judge instructed the jury they had to acquit unless it was proven Pickton pulled the trigger but corrected this after the jury requested clarification. The corrected instructions were that the jury could convict if Pickton played a substantial role in the killings. With this, the jury came back with the guilty verdicts. The defense argued this exchange created prejudice against Pickton. The prosecution filed a conditional appeal. If the second-degree convictions were overturned, the prosecution wanted to appeal the acquittal on the first-degree charges on the grounds the artificial separation of the charges based on the amount and nature of body parts recovered was legally wrong. On the other hand, life in prison was life in prison. If the appeal courts upheld second-degree convictions, the prosecutors had no desire to repeat the 11-month trial. The appeal court upheld Pickton's convictions and said the trial judge erred by separating the charges. Murder, said the appeal court, was murder. A sustained pattern of murder by a serial killer was more instructive than a distinction based on a killer's capacity to dispose bodies.[28]

We will leave the last words on Robert Pickton to Pickton himself. When he was arrested, the police placed an undercover officer in his police cell. The cell was wired for both audio- and video-recording. This is how part of their conversation went:

Robert PICKTON: They got you for murder charges? Or attempted murder?
Cpl. X: Well, they got, they got the attempt, they got, I talked to my lawyer there and there's some more pending, some more, a couple more fucking things they've got on me.
Robert PICKTON: But you're nothing like mine.
Cpl. X: Well, fuckin I'm fucking looking at some serious time if fuckin they put things together. Do you know what I mean? (PICKTON MADE A HAND GESTURE INDICATING "5" AND "0'.) What's that? Five, zero, fifty. (PICKTON NODS HIS HEAD.) Ha, ha, fuck you. (PICKTON PUTS A FINGER TO HIS LIPS TO INDICATE SILENCE.) You, you're full a, shitting me. (PICKTON POINTS AT THE CAMERA.)
Robert PICKTON: Camera.
Cpl. X: You yourself? I've fucking done a few of these.
Robert PICKTON: Um, hum. …
Robert PICKTON: I, I fuckin buried myself now.
Cpl. X: Hey.
Robert PICKTON: I buried myself.
Cpl. X: How?
Robert PICKTON: Got me. They got me on this one.
Cpl. X: No, no shit.
Robert PICKTON: (WHISPERING) (INDECIPHERABLE). ...
Cpl. X: Fucking guy does it right. I find the best way to fucking dispose of something is fucking take it to the ocean.
Robert PICKTON: Oh, really?
Cpl. X: Oh, fuck, do you know what the fucking ocean does to things, there ain't much left.
Robert PICKTON: I did better than that.
Cpl. X: Who?
Robert PICKTON: Me.
Cpl. X: No. Huh.
Robert PICKTON: (PICKTON MOVES AND SITS NEXT TO CPL. X)
Robert PICKTON: A rendering plant.
Cpl. X: Hey?
Robert PICKTON: A rendering plant.
Cpl. X: Ha, ha. No shit. Ha, ha, that's gotta be fucking ah, pretty good hey.
Robert PICKTON: Mm, hmm.
Cpl. X: Can't be much fuckin' left?
Robert PICKTON: Oh, no only ah, I was kinda sloppy at the end, too, getting too sloppy.
Cpl. X: Really.
Robert PICKTON: They got me, oh, fuck, gettin' too sloppy.
Cpl. X: See fucking you gotta be fucking meticulous you gotta be fucking.
Robert PICKTON: (INDECIPHERABLE). …

Robert PICKTON: I was gonna do one more, make it an even fifty.
Cpl. X: (LAUGHING)
Robert PICKTON: That's why, that's why I was sloppy about (INDECIPHERABLE).
Cpl. X: Yeah.
Robert PICKTON: I wanted one more, make, make the big five O.
Cpl. X: Make the big five zero (LAUGHING) fuck. That's fucked. Fuckin' five, zero. Fuckin' half a hundred. (PICKTON LAUGHING, NODDING.)
Robert PICKTON: Mmm Hmm.
Cpl. X: Yeah. Like you say that's the best part. That fuckin' the one.
Robert PICKTON: Everybody says (POUNDING). How many of those? Wouldn't tell em
Cpl. X: (LAUGHING)
Robert PICKTON: I wouldn't tell 'em.
Cpl. X: Yeah.
Robert PICKTON: Talk about half, about one quarter. Talking about all of them. I says no.
Cpl. X: (LAUGHING)
Robert PICKTON: You know they got forty-eight on the list.
Cpl. X: Yeah.
Robert PICKTON: You know the list has only got like, only got half the people in there. The other half might, might (INDECIPHERABLE). …
Robert PICKTON: Forty-nine.
Cpl. X: Almost made it.
Robert PICKTON: Hum.
Cpl. X: Almost made it.
Robert PICKTON: I'm worried about it.
Cpl. X: Hee hee.
Robert PICKTON: All the way up to fifty.
Cpl. X: Hey?
Robert PICKTON: I haven't done fifty yet.[29]

Pickton appears to have used different methods to dispose of the bodies of his victims. He told the undercover police officer he used a rendering plant – and, indeed, he regularly took loads of pig waste to this plant. Nobody but him saw what was in the barrels. There's evidence that parts of Pickton's victims were fed to his pigs. Some were probably ground up and mixed with pork for sale. A few bodies, or parts of them, appear to have been dumped in the surrounding area. Some were frozen and stored. If we accept Pickton's own tally of his killing, he murdered 49 women. He was convicted for only six. None were no-body cases.

Serial Killers and No-Body Prosecutions

Sometimes serial killers are unlucky or incompetent enough that police can build a homicide case tied to an individual victim. Mark Twitchell never became a serial killer because he created detailed instructions for police to follow to the scene of his first murder. Incompetence. Legebokoff was caught driving from the scene of his fourth murder. Bad luck. John Haigh had successfully murdered five people without enduring so much as questioning by police. Then he killed someone whose absence was noticed immediately. Both arrogance and incompetence. When this kind of close connection to a specific homicide or disappearance is established by police, the investigation can expand as connections and cases are discovered.

In other cases, killers are captured or caught because a pattern is noticed. Alejandro Ruiz successfully murdered one wife by converting homicide into a missing person's investigation. Twice was not a charm. An alert police officer saw the pattern the second time out.

With Robert Pickton, pattern identification took much longer. In part, this was because there was no ongoing connection between Pickton and his victims. He came, he lured, he killed, he disposed. Pickton also chose people unlikely to have their absence noticed promptly or their disappearance treated as potential homicides by police. As women from the Vancouver slum were reported missing, police believed they probably just moved on. If they were the victim of foul play, it was likely to be a random, onetime occurrence. Pickton specialized in killing drug-addicted sex trade workers. These people often live unstable lives, and their work exposes them to significant risk. It is not uncommon for them to suddenly be absent – but they usually show up again, either dead or alive. Permanent disappearances occurred in this part of Vancouver, but prior to Pickton's killing spree these numbered one or two per year. Suddenly there were a dozen or more every year. The volume was the pattern, but senior leadership at the Vancouver Police Service refused to accept this idea. Pickton's strategies for body disposal played a role. If his victim's corpses were found, it would have been impossible for the police to convince themselves there was no serial killer operating.

It is instructive to compare the prosecution of Pickton and Ruiz. In Ruiz's case, police noticed the pattern with the second disappearance. When they found two bodies in his yard, Ruiz was also charged and convicted for Tanya's murder. The disappearance, combined with the pattern, was deemed sufficient for the police, prosecutor, judge, and jury. It was different with Pickton. Many women disappeared before a pattern was seen. Unlike Ruiz, identification of the pattern did not automatically produce a primary (only) suspect. Pickton was placed on the list of potential killers, but he was one of many until physical evidence tied him to some of the disappearances. Even then, the pattern was not enough for him to be charged. Police believed he was responsible for all the disappearances, but he was not charged with specific murders until forensic evidence was found for each missing woman. The inductive conclusions about disappearing wives were different than for disappearing prostitutes. Unlike Ruiz, Pickton was never convicted for a murder where death had to be deduced from the circumstantial evidence of absence.

In many cases involving serial killers, the presence or absence of a body is largely a matter of chance. Bodies are dumped in isolated areas. Sometimes they are found. Sometimes they are not. As Pickton so graphically demonstrated, even when the serial killer is caught, no-body cases are sometimes treated differently from partial body cases. Police charged Pickton only for the murders where some DNA evidence of a victim could be tied to his property. Police strongly believed that Pickton killed more women than he was charged for – but he was never charged for killing those whose bodies he disposed of without leaving a trace. For the trial judge, even this difference was not enough. He eliminated the "trace-of-body" cases and only proceeded with those where a "long-bone" was found. Appeal courts ruled that this was an error, but the result was Pickton was only convicted of six murders when, according to his own admission, he killed at least 49 – and he was probably undercounting.

Notes

1 Dunboyne, Lord (ed), *The Trial of John George Haigh* (Glasgow, UK: William and Hodge, 1953); Oates, Jonathan, *John George Haigh the Acid-Bath Murderer: A Portrait of a Serial Killer and His Victims* (Barnsley, UK: Pen and Sword Books, 2014); Lefebure Molly, *Murder with a difference: The cases of Haigh and Christie* (London, UK: Heinemann, 1958).

2 Federal Bureau of Investigation, *Serial Murder: Multi-Disciplinary Perspectives for Investigators* (Washington, DC: FBI, 2005): 9.

3 Oppal, Wally, *Forsaken: The Report of the Missing Women Commission of Inquiry* (Victoria, BC: BC Ministry of Justice, 2012).
4 R v. Pickton, 2009 BCCA 300.
5 FBI, Serial Murder, 11.
6 Konigsberg, Eric (2009) *Blood Relation* (New York, NY: Harper Collins).
7 People v. Ruiz, 44 Cal. 3d 590 (1988).
8 Douglas, John and Stephen Singular, *Anyone You Want Me to Be* (New York, NY: Scribner, 2003).
9 Gilmore, John, *Cold-Blooded: The saga of Charles Schmid, the Notorious "Pied Piper of Tucson"* (Portland, OR: Feral House, 1996); Moser, Don, *The Pied Piper of Tucson* (New York, NY: Signet, 1967).
10 Larson, Erik, *The Devil in the White City: Murder, Magic, and Madness at the Fair That Changed America* (New York, NY: Vintage, 2004).
11 Phelps, M. William (2019) *Where Monsters Hide: Sex, Murder, and Madness in the Midwest* (New York, NY: Pinnacle Books).
12 Rother, Caitlin, *Dead Reckoning* (New York, NY: Kensington, 2011). Dirmann, Tina, *Vanished at Sea: The True Story of a Child TV Actor and a Double Murder* (New York, NY: St. Martins, 2008).
13 Lillebuen, Steve, *The Devil's Cinema: The Untold Story Behind Mark Twitchell's Kill Room* (Toronto, ON: McClelland and Stewart, 2012).
14 People v. Ruiz, 44 Cal. 3d 590 (1988).
15 Hunter, J.T., *The Country Boy Killer: The True Story of Cody Legebokoff - Canada's Teenage Serial Killer* (Self-Published, 2015).
16 Hunter, *Country Boy Killer*, 43.
17 R. v. Legebokoff, 2014 BCSC 1746.
18 Ling, Justin, *Missing from the Village: The Story of Serial Killer Bruce McArthur, the Search for Justice, and the System that Failed Toronto's Queer Community* (Toronto, ON: McClelland and Stewart, 2020).
19 Linedecker, Chris, *The Man Who Killed Boys* (New York, NY: St. Martins, 1980); Cahill, Tim, *Buried Dreams: Inside the Mind of a Serial Killer* (New York, NY: Bantam, 1986).
20 Cameron, Stevie, *The Pickton File* (Toronto, ON: Knopf Canada, 2007); Cameron, Stevie, *On the Farm: Robert William Pickton and the Tragic Story of Vancouver's Missing Women* (Toronto, ON: Knopf Canada, 2011); Shenher, Lorimer, *That Lonely Section of Hell: The Botched Investigation of a Serial Killer Who Almost Got Away* (Vancouver, BC: Greystone, 2015).
21 Cameron, *On the Farm*, 410–422.
22 Cameron, *On the Farm*, 556–564.
23 R. v. Pickton, 2006 BCSC 1477.
24 R. v. Pickton, 2006 BCSC 1212.
25 R. v. Pickton, 2006 BCSC 1447.
26 R. v. Pickton, 2006 BCSC 1448.
27 R v. Pickton, 2007 BCSC 2039.
28 R. v. Pickton, 2009 BCCA 300.
29 R. v. Pickton, 2009 BCCA 300.

8

MURDER INCORPORATED AND ITS IMITATORS

Criminal Gangs and Body Disposal

On July 30, 1975, Jimmy Hoffa loitered in a Detroit restaurant parking lot. Then he disappeared. It was big news. *Time* magazine ranked Hoffa third on a list of the most mysterious disappearances of all time.[1] The *History Channel*[2] and *Britanica.com*[3] put the Hoffa disappearance on lists that include pilot Amelia Earhart, the 115 members of the "lost colony" at Roanoke Island and airplane hijacker D.B. Cooper. The Hoffa case was the largest individual investigation in FBI history. It spawned books,[4] movies, and hundreds of magazine articles. Hoffa's fate officially remains a mystery, but everyone who has looked at the case agrees that Hoffa did not voluntarily disappear, commit suicide, get lost, or get abducted by aliens. "What happened to Jimmy Hoffa?" He was murdered.

Six months after Hoffa disappeared, the FBI identified 12 likely suspects.[5] All had extensive affiliations with "La Cosa Nostra" – the Mafia. The problem was proving which individual mobster did the dirty deed. The FBI was in the position of Agatha Christie's fictional detective, Hercule Poirot, attempting to identify the killer on the Orient Express. So many had motive and opportunity it was impossible to narrow the field.

Police have looked long and hard for Hoffa's body. Thirty-seven years after Hoffa disappeared, a homeowner in a Detroit suburb was shocked when hordes of police dug up his driveway.[6] Nothing was found. Hoffa has been rumored to be part of the foundation of Giants Stadium in New Jersey, lodged in a 55-gallon drum in a New Jersey landfill, being part of a Ford automobile, incinerated in a funeral crematorium, buried in the foundation of the General Motors head office building, and feeding the fishes in Lake Michigan. Police have paid for a swimming pool, a driveway, and a barn destroyed while digging for Hoffa. We will not mention the damage done to a cornfield and a golf course.[7]

Jimmy Hoffa had been the president of the International Brotherhood of Teamsters, the union representing truckers and warehousemen. After starting as an organizer in Detroit in the 1930s, by the 1940s, Hoffa became the dominant Teamster leader in the Midwest. After the Teamster's president was indicted for fraud, Hoffa was elected to the top job in 1957. He followed his predecessor to prison in 1967 after being convicted on bribery, fraud, and obstruction of justice charges.

During his rise to the top of the Teamsters, Hoffa forged a symbiotic relationship with the Mafia. The mob provided muscle to intimidate both employers opposed to the union and truckers opposed to Hoffa's leadership. In turn, Mafia members were given positions in the union

DOI: 10.4324/9781003372134-8

where they enriched themselves through extortion, kickbacks, and fraud. The union pension fund provided loans to build mob-owned casinos, primarily in Las Vegas. Under Hoffa, the Teamsters were corrupt but also a tough, strong union delivering good wages and benefits to its members. In 1964, Hoffa negotiated a first National Master Freight Agreement covering almost every trucker in the United States. In order to get the national agreement, Hoffa ruled as an iron-fisted dictator.[8]

When Hoffa went to jail in 1967, he named one of his allies acting-president. Hoffa wanted to run the Teamsters from his jail cell. Problems emerged. The acting-president decided he liked the top job. The Mafia found the new guy a softer touch than Hoffa. Hoffa tolerated – and used – corruption to get benefits for union members. After he went to prison, Teamster's corruption lost whatever "noble" purpose it had served. It became just corruption. Many local and regional leaders did not miss Hoffa's iron fist, even though most members wanted Hoffa back in charge.

In 1971, Hoffa got sprung from prison after President Richard Nixon granted a pardon. But there was a catch. The pardon was conditional on Hoffa resigning as Teamster president and barred him from participating in union activities. Hoffa accepted these terms, got released from prison, and immediately set out to regain control of "his" union. He threatened to expose the illegal activities of his opponents and geared up for a run for the Teamster presidency. All of this led to Hoffa standing around in the restaurant parking lot. A meeting had been scheduled with two of his most bitter opponents. Unknown to Hoffa, the people he expected to meet were hundreds of miles away. Someone else met Hoffa, killed him, and disposed of his body. Immediate suspicion focused on Hoffa's foster son[9] and on a longtime trusted union associate.[10] Police believed they were the only people Hoffa would voluntarily get into a car with. No real evidence was found against them. The flaw in the police theory was that Hoffa may not have left the parking lot voluntarily.

So where does all this leave us?

There is no doubt that Hoffa died on or soon after July 30, 1975; he was declared dead as soon as this was legally possible.[11] There is little doubt that he was murdered and that the killers were working on behalf of senior members of the Mafia. But Hoffa's body was never found. He disappeared without a trace. Nobody has ever been charged with killing Hoffa. Such are the benefits of body disposal after a murder is committed by a criminal organization.

Organized Crime and No-Body Murder Cases

People making their living through drug dealing, bootlegging, robbery, extortion, racketeering, kidnapping, illegal gambling, and so on have disputes with each other. In this they are no different from people in more legitimate occupations, although disputes are probably more frequent and intense. People attracted to illegal activities can be hard to get along with. They have added pressure created by the need to conceal their activities. Police are always trying to send them to prison. Anyone suspected being a "rat" must be silenced. The need for secrecy generates more disputes since written contracts can send people to jail. Agreements are necessarily verbal and often negotiated in coded language. This increases the frequency of misunderstandings. Finally, contract enforcement must be handled personally rather than through the courts. A nonpaying customer in a drug deal cannot be sued, so they are intimidated, beaten, or murdered. One sociologist calls it "self-help justice."[12] It can get rough. Being engaged in criminal activities or working with criminals creates risk. Just ask Jimmy Hoffa, if you can find him. When murder becomes an accepted business practice, murders become more common. Transforming murder into a missing person's case is but one strategy to avoid getting caught by police and convicted by the courts.

Murders in which the relationship between killer and victim is some sort of criminal activity – either competitive or cooperative – account for many no-body homicide cases. Of the 488 cases examined in the United States, 44 involved killing as a dispute settlement between people engaged in criminal activity. In Canada, a criminal relationship accounted for 3 of 33 cases. These tallies underrepresent the total death toll since mob killers are often serial killers. Calculating the number of no-body homicides committed by one killer can be impossible.[13] For example, the New Jersey–based Richard Kuklinski was convicted for five homicides. One was a true no-body case. Paul Hoffman disappeared while meeting with Kuklinski to purchase stolen prescription drugs. Other homicides committed by Kuklinski would have remained no-body cases but for the accidental discovery of the corpses. George Malliband was found stuffed in a 55-gallon drum. Gary Smith was strangled in a hotel room. Kuklinski hid his corpse between the mattress and box springs. It remained undiscovered until guests staying in the room complained about the smell. Kuklinski also intentionally delayed body discovery to create difficulties for the police. He shot Louis Masgay in the head in 1981 – then kept him in a freezer for 19 months. Kuklinski dumped Louis's body where it could be found. The freezing was designed to create confusion about the date of Louis's death. Kuklinski was a serial killer motivated by criminal commercial reasons. He also claims to have killed because of road rage and for entertainment. After being convicted of five homicides, he told book authors and television producers that he killed another 200. Kuklinski claimed he left some bodies where they fell but disposed of other corpses by a variety of means, including feeding them to hungry rats at a cave. Some of his claims are implausible (he claimed to be the killer of Jimmy Hoffa despite having no connection with the case). Kuklinski had incentive to exaggerate since his wife received a share of book and movie profits, but he probably killed more than the five he was convicted for.[14]

Kuklinski was a real-life example of that popular fictional character, the criminal contract killer. The reality is usually more murderously mundane. Let us look at several cases that cover a range in the sophistication and deadliness of the criminal gang killers.

In 1998, Gregory Chrysler was part of a group selling marijuana around Newburgh, New York. Chrysler and his wife got busted. Chrysler correctly believed one of his criminal associates was an informer, but suspected the wrong person. Six months after Chrysler was busted, fellow gang-member Dominick Pendino left for his day-job as a cook. He never arrived. Dominick's wife discovered his car still in the driveway. The door was open, and the keys were in the ignition. She called police, who quickly discovered blood. Forensic experts said Dominick was hit over the head with a baseball bat and dragged through his backyard to the driveway next-door. Dominick's eyeglasses and pager were also discovered. They were bloody. After Dominick disappeared, Chrysler phoned another gang member to brag he had disposed of the "rat." Unfortunately for Chrysler, this person was the actual police informant. He had a tape recorder. The conversation made Chrysler the primary suspect in a homicide investigation. Police soon learned Chrysler had borrowed a car (a Ford Crown Victoria, not a Chrysler) the day Dominick disappeared. The car had been seen on Dominick's street. Dominick's blood was found on the back seat and in the trunk. Police learned Chrysler borrowed a shovel the day before Dominick's disappearance. Police dug for Dominick's body in several locations, but it was never found.[15] Nonetheless, Chrysler and another gang member of the gang were charged and convicted.[16] Chrysler appealed, claiming his lawyer had been incompetent. The appeal court ruled that bad facts, rather than bad lawyering, caused the conviction.[17]

As gangland murderers go, Chrysler was incompetent. He killed the wrong person. He told a police informant he committed the crime. He generated damning forensic evidence tying him to the crime and circumstantial evidence that was impossible to explain away. His accomplice testified. From the purposes of getting away with murder, the only thing Chrysler did right was dispose of Dominick's body. This was not enough.

While Chrysler was a murderous drug dealer, the criminal gang he belonged to was low-level and local. Let us now move to a case involving more organized criminals.

In 1978, Joseph "Joe Onions" Scanlon was a member of the Rhode Island mafia. Joseph's colleagues believed he had become a police informer. It is unclear whether he was a "rat" or not, but the belief had consequences. The task of getting rid of Joseph was assigned to Nicholas Pari and Andrew Merola.[18] They lured him to a bar/social club operated by Merola. Pari provoked a fight and punched Joseph. This served as a distraction while Merola shot Joseph in the head. The two bundled their victim in a rug, took him to a construction site, and dumped him in a 13-foot-deep hole. They returned to the club to clean up. Bloodstained carpeting was ripped up and burned in a garbage-dump incinerator. "Joe Onions" disappeared without a trace.

But Peri and Merola were not as competent as this description makes them sound. They made two mistakes.

Their first goof was timing. Merola shot Joseph in the head while Pari was still in the act of punching him in the face. In addition to killing Joseph, the bullet mangled Peri's finger. Before cleaning up the crime scene, Peri had to get medical treatment.[19]

The second goof had greater consequences for the two killers. When Joseph came to the social club, he brought his girlfriend and his year-old child. She saw the killing. Pari and Merola were unconcerned, describing her as a "stand-up girl" who would keep her mouth shut. Joseph's girlfriend was given the $200 Joseph had in his wallet and his jewelry. She was told to go home in silence but was unhappy about the murder of her boyfriend and the father of her child. Instead of remaining silent, she told her story to the police. Pari and Merola were charged and convicted of murder. The girlfriend's testimony was corroborated by Pari's sore finger and bloodstains in the trunk of Merola's Cadillac.

There was a weird element to the trial. During her cross-examination, Joseph's girlfriend testified she gave only one version of events to the police. Defense lawyers produced a memo written by a state trooper saying he had interviewed the girlfriend and that she denied all knowledge of what happened to her boyfriend. During cross-examination, the girlfriend denied making such a statement, saying she never met or talked to this police officer. The officer was subpoenaed. He invoked his Fifth Amendment right to remain silent. The officer even refused to provide his place of residence or confirm he was employed by the state police. The judge ruled the officer could not be a defense witness. The Supreme Court of Rhode Island said this was an error and overturned the convictions of Pari and Merola.[20]

The apparent dereliction of duty by the police officer, combined with the disposal of Joseph's body, worked to the advantage of Pari and Merola. On the eve of their second trial, the two negotiated a plea bargain. In exchange for admitting guilt and telling police what they had done with Joseph's body, they were allowed to plead guilty to manslaughter rather than risk another murder conviction. With this, the two accepted a few years in prison rather than face a possible life sentence. Pari and Merola told police they dumped Joseph's body into Narragansett Bay.

Of course, being career criminals, they lied. In 2008 – 30 years after Joseph was murdered and 26 years after claiming his body had been dumped in the ocean – Pari was arrested for selling drugs and stolen goods. By this time, he was 71 years old and dying of throat cancer. Merola had died a few months earlier. Out of the blue, Pari told the arresting officer that "I've got something for you. I can tell you where the body of Joey Onions Scanlon is."[21] With that, Pari took police to Joseph's burial site. Digging confirmed that, this time, he was telling the truth.[22]

Nicholas Pari and Andrew Merola were good at hiding bodies but not particularly good at the trade of contract killers. Because they killed with their victim's girlfriend as a spectator, their killing career did not last long. To examine the relationship between body disposal and a longer career as a mafia murderer, we will turn to Roy DeMeo and his "crew."[23]

After starting out as a butcher's apprentice, DeMeo turned to crime in the early 1960s. He became part of the Gambino crime family operating in Brooklyn.[24] DeMeo started out as a loan shark and branched out into organizing a car theft ring which shipped hundreds of stolen cars to Kuwait.[25] DeMeo also took control of a credit union which he used as a front for money-laundering. His loan-sharking activities got him involved with drug dealing, pornography, and businesses, including an abortion clinic, a dentist's office, restaurants, and flea markets. DeMeo also organized hijacking delivery trucks near the Kennedy airport.[26]

DeMeo's first known foray into homicide occurred in 1972 when he and his boss shot a gang member suspected of cooperating with law enforcement. There was nothing fancy about this killing. The victim was shot on the street. His body was abandoned where it fell. DeMeo began to experiment with no-body homicide two years later after an associate in his car theft ring testified before a grand jury. A former girlfriend lured the victim onto the street.[27] He was kidnapped, taken to a supermarket (closed for the evening), and stabbed. The store's butcher shop was used to dismember and wrap the body. The pieces were thrown into a dumpster. DeMeo and his three murderous colleagues were good at killing, but not yet accomplished at body disposal. There was no garbage collection on weekends. The body was found by a pedestrian and his dog. Despite the discovery of the body, DeMeo was not charged.[28]

By the late 1970s, DeMeo and his crew operated a high-volume murder and body disposal contract-killing service.[29] The number of victims is unknown, but motives for confirmed killings include robbery, elimination of possible informants, and settling scores.[30] For example, one man was killed after he raped a woman. Her family hired DeMeo to exact revenge. Another was shot, stabbed, beaten, and sodomized because he molested a young boy known to a mafia boss. Most of these killings were no-body homicides. DeMeo's standard operating practice was luring the victim to an apartment behind a bar. Gang members would shoot the victim in the head and then stab him in the heart to minimize blood loss. The body would be hung above the bathtub until its blood congealed. The killers would then dismember the body, wrap the pieces, and dump them in a landfill.

The key to this method of making people disappear was luring them to the murder site. Sometimes this was difficult. It could go wrong. In 1979, DeMeo and his mafia boss, Anthony Gaggi, tried luring two intended victims to the backroom murder site to have a dispute resolution meeting. Both intended victims were mafia members. While on their way to the meeting, one realized they were heading for a trap. He ordered the other to stop the car. DeMeo and Gaggi shot the pair while in the car. The shootings were witnessed by a passing motorist, who called police. DeMeo escaped but Gaggi was shot and arrested while fleeing the scene. Gaggi was charged with murdering the two gangsters and attempted murder of the police officer who arrested him. After bribing a juror, Gaggi was acquitted on the murder charges and only convicted on a charge of assaulting the police officer.[31]

While some of DeMeo's murders became body-present homicides because of incompetence or bad luck, in other cases bodies were intentionally left to be found. A car thief working for DeMeo was suspected of talking to police. He and his girlfriend were shot. Their bodies were dumped in public locations to warn others about the dangers of being a snitch.

The balance between making people disappear and committing public murders was highlighted by a dispute with Cuban drug dealers from Miami. DeMeo and his associate, Chris Rosenberg, arranged to purchase 12 kilograms of cocaine from the Miami group. The sellers delivered the cocaine to Brooklyn. Instead of being paid, they were murdered, dismembered, and sent to the landfill. The son of one victim traveled north to search for his father. He met the same fate. This made the Miami-based drug dealers very unhappy and resulted in two highly public murders. The first was the killing of an innocent. An 18-year-old college student selling vacuum cleaners parked outside DeMeo's house. DeMeo mistook him for a hit man sent by the Miami drug dealers. The unfortunate young man attempted to flee. DeMeo and a friend followed. After a seven-mile high-speed auto chase, DeMeo shot the man seven times. Given the hubbub, there was no opportunity to destroy the body. A month after this highly public fiasco, DeMeo shot and killed Rosenberg to appease the unhappy Miami drug dealers. In order to ensure the Miami gang knew "justice" had been done, the killing had to be reported in the media. To ensure it received prominent notice, Rosenberg's car and corpse were machine-gunned.[32]

DeMeo's career as a mafia killer came to an end in January 1983. His frozen body was found in the trunk of his Cadillac. He had been shot in the head several times. At the time of his death, police were on the verge of arresting him. Three colleagues had been arrested and agreed to become witnesses. It is believed DeMeo was murdered by other gang members to keep him from talking.

DeMeo's killing career lasted just over a decade. It is not known how many people he killed, although an FBI wiretap recorded the head of his crime family putting the number at 49.[33] DeMeo's son claims the death toll could reach as high as 200.[34] Efficient body disposal contributed to DeMeo's ability to run up this score. Many killings were treated as missing persons' cases rather than homicides. Some were never reported to police. When a criminal disappears when making a major drug deal, survivors do not want police digging around. In other cases, murder is mistaken for flight from the law. One of DeMeo's victims disappeared after getting busted with 23 tons of marijuana. DeMeo killed him to prevent a plea bargain and finger-pointing. Police believed the victim fled to avoid prison.[35]

The most common method of body disposal used by DeMeo was dismemberment and disposal into a landfill. This presented a challenge. The victim had to be lured to a secure location where this messy and time-consuming task could be conducted. When DeMeo and Gaggi set out to kill two gangsters, the plan to have the two "disappear" unraveled because the victims realized it was not a good idea to attend the proposed meeting. This necessitated murder in a public location complete with a witness. Repetitive use of the same secure location to commit murder creates the risk of pattern identification.[36] Potential victims become reluctant to visit a place known to be the final destination of others.

Criminal Enterprise and No-Body Homicides

Members of organized criminal groups sometimes kill each other or their competitors. One side or the other in a drug deal can be tempted to complete the transaction with a bullet rather than cash or merchandise. Competitors can be eliminated. Real or potential informers need to have their lips sealed. People are killed to settle scores or maintain an image. When murder is used as a problem-solving solution, many reasons for killing can be found. At the same time, to stay in business, the killers must avoid arrest and conviction. Many strategies for achieving this have been utilized. Witnesses are to be eliminated. The confusion created by a shooting facilitates escape. Disguises or the use of contract killers prevents identification. Police are bribed and jury members tampered with. Disposing the victim's body is just one additional strategy to avoid capture.[37] It removes evidence, delays investigations, and creates uncertainty about whether the person is dead – and many victims also have valid reasons for going into hiding.

There are drawbacks and limitations to body elimination as a strategy. It is a lot of work. The process of disposal creates its own kind of evidence and generates additional opportunities for detection. Getting a speeding ticket when you have a dismembered body in the trunk of your car results in more than a small fine. The killing must occur in a private spot. The victim-to-be must be lured or forced to the location. Both processes can go wrong and generate their own evidence trail. If the criminally motivated killer is dealing with an alert enemy, setting up a homicide in a private location can be impossible. The killers of Jimmy Hoffa accomplished this difficult feat, but Jimmy Hoffa was a union leader, not a gangster. He did not carry a gun and was not accompanied by bodyguards.

There is another problem for criminal gang members using body disposal to avoid detection for their murders. These no-body murders tend to be a group activity. It takes a conspiracy to get someone to a secure, private location, kill them, and dispose of the body. When someone is part of a group that kills, they become a hostage to their colleagues. Gregory Chrysler's murderous colleague testified at the grand jury hearing. Nicholas Pari and Andrew Merola went to jail after trusting Joseph Scanlon's girlfriend would keep her mouth shut. Three of Roy DeMeo's colleagues became police informants and witnesses. With the exception of the aggrieved girlfriend, all were arrested for other crimes. Their participatory knowledge of numerous homicides gave them a "Get Out of Jail Free" card. One problem with having criminals as colleagues is that they get caught committing crimes and, once caught, they often behave in a self-interested way. This behavior comes with becoming a criminal. The truly amazing feature of Jimmy Hoffa's murder is not that he was killed or that his killers successfully disposed of his body. The real surprise is that the people involved in the conspiracy managed to keep their mouths shut. That is the reason we do not know what, precisely, happened to Jimmy Hoffa.

Let us turn to fiction for our final observations on body disposal. At the beginning of Mario Puzo's novel *The Godfather*, three murders and one attempted murder were committed.[38] After being rebuffed in a request for assistance in drug trafficking, the leader of the other gang sent hit men to kill Don Vito Corleone. They gunned him down on the street and ran. At about the same time, Corleone's favorite hit man was lured into a bar and strangled. His body was dumped into the ocean, where he "slept with the fishes." Corleone's son met with the drug dealer responsible for his father's shooting. He shot the drug dealer and a corrupt police captain and fled to Sicily. Three killings and an attempt. Only one was a no-body case. It was possible to lure that victim into a private place for an unobserved murder. This is the precondition for a criminal gang's no-body homicide. As a rule, it is a technique that can be used on "friends" rather than on known enemies.

Notes

1 Chan, Melissa, "The 5 Most Mysterious Unsolved Disappearances of All Time," *Time*, March 14, 2019. https://time.com/5532711/mysterious-unsolved-disappearances/.

2 Cohen, Jennie, "Six Mysterious Disappearances in U.S. History," *History.com*, March 10, 2021. https://www.history.com/news/6-mysterious-disappearances-in-u-s-history.

3 Blumberg, Naomi, n.d. "9 Mysterious Disappearances of People Other Than Amelia Earhart," *Britanica.com*. https://www.britannica.com/list/9-mysterious-disappearances-of-people-other-than-amelia-earhart. Downloaded August 12, 2022.

4 Brandt, Charles, *I Heard You Paint Houses: Frank "The Irishman" Sheeran and Closing the Case on Jimmy Hoffa* (New York, NY: Steerforth Press, 2016); Goldsmith, Jack, *In Hoffa's Shadow: A Stepfather, A Disappearance in Detroit, and My Search for the Truth* (New York, NY: Farrar Straus & Giroux, 2019); Moldea, Dan, *The Hoffa Wars: Teamsters, Rebels, Politicians and the Mob* (New York, NY: Paddington Press, 1978.); Russell, Haddeus, *Out of the Jungle: Jimmy Hoffa and The Remaking of the American Working Class* (Philadelphia, PA: Temple University Press, 2001); Hoffa, James, *Hoffa: The Real Story* (New York, NY: Stein and Day, 1975).

5 Federal Bureau of Investigation, "Hoffex Conference: FBI Headquarters," January 27 & 28, 1976. https://www.scribd.com/document/273002052/The-Hoffex-Memo.

6 Memmot, Mark, "Search for Jimmy Hoffa Leads to Driveway Near Detroit," *National Public Radio*, September 27, 2012.
7 Wilson, Michael, "Search for Jimmy Hoffa Under Jersey City Bridge Came Up Empty, FBI Says," *New York Times*, July 21, 2022.
8 Moldea, *Hoffa Wars.*
9 Goldsmith, *In Hoffa's Shadow.*
10 Brandt, *I Heard You Paint Houses.*
11 Treaster, Joseph B. "Hoffa Ruled 'presumed' Dead," *New York Times*, December 10, 1982.
12 Black, Donald, "Crime as Social Control," *American Sociological Review* 48, No. 1 (February 1983): 34–45.
13 Martin, Douglas, "Richard Kuklinski, 70, a Killer of Many People and Many Ways, Dies," *New York Times,* March 9, 2006.
14 Carlo, Philip, *The Ice Man: Confessions of a Mafia Killer* (New York, NY: St. Martins, 2006).
15 Mackson, Oliver, "Tip, Search Fail to Turn Up Body of Murder Victim Dominick Pendino," *The Times Herald-Record*, May 4, 2007.
16 O'Connor, Timothy, "No Body. No Weapon. No Problem: Guilty," *The Times Herald-Record*, July 14, 2000.
17 Chrysler v. Guiney, United States Court of Appeal, Second Circuit, No. 14-1485-pr. Decided November 19, 2015.
18 State v. Nicholas Pari and Andrew F. Merola, 420 A.2d 429 (1981), Supreme Court of Rhode Island, No. 79-486-C.A.
19 White, Tim, "State Police Recording Sheds Light on Infamous RI Gangland Slaying," *Tim White News Archive,* November 21, 2016. https://timwhitenewsarchive.wordpress.com/2016/11/21/state-police-recording-sheds-light-on-infamous-ri-gangland-slaying/#content.
20 State v. Nicholas Pari and Andrew F. Merola, 420 A.2d 429 (1981), Supreme Court of Rhode Island, No. 79-486-C.A.
21 Berry, Dan, "In Rhode Island, An Old Mobster Lets Go of a Long-Kept Secret," *New York Times*, December 21, 2008.
22 Russ, Hilary, "Remains Found During Mafia Victim Search," *Worcester Telegram*, November 19, 2008.
23 Mustain, Gene and Jerry Capeci, *Murder Machine* (New York, NY: New American Library, 1993); DeMeo, Albert, *For the Sins of My Father: A Mafia Killer, His Son, and a Legacy of Mob Life* (New York, NY: Crown, 2003).
24 Davis, John H. *Mafia Dynasty: The Rise and Fall of the Gambino Crime Family* (New York, NY: HarperPaperbacks, 1993).
25 Smothers, Ronald, "Castellano Named at Car-Theft Trial," *New York Times*, November 5, 1985.
26 United States v. Castellano, 610 F. Supp. 1359 (S.D.N.Y. 1985).
27 "2 Held in Murder of Auto Mechanic," *New York Times*, July 6, 1975.
28 Mustain and Capeci, *Murder Machine.*
29 Mustain and Capeci, *Murder Machine.*
30 Glaberson, William, "After 15 Months, Mob Trial Nears End," *New York Times*, May 28, 1989.
31 Freid, Joseph, "Jurors' Conduct at Murder Trial to be Studied," *New York Times*, November 8, 1981.
32 Mustain and Capeci, *Murder Machine.*
33 Mustain and Capeci, *Murder Machine.*
34 Laurence, Charles, "My Dad, the Family Man, Who Murdered 200 for the Mafia," *Dublin Independent*, October 21, 2002.
35 Mustain and Capeci, *Murder Machine.*
36 Rashbaum, William K., "Sometimes, Mob Victims Have Plenty of Company," *New York Times*, October 6, 2004.
37 Fernandez, Manny, "Densely Populated, But No Shortage of Dumping Sites," *New York Times*, April 13, 2011.
38 Puzo, Mario, The *Godfather* (New York, NY: Putmans, 1969).

9

MIDLIFE CRISIS, MURDER, AND BODY DISPOSAL

In the early 1950s, life was good for Joseph A. Peel, Jr.[1] The Florida lawyer had a successful practice and the part-time position of municipal judge in West Palm Beach. The judicial salary was not large, but duties included authorizing police raids. This made the position lucrative. Peel gave rumrunners, bootleggers, and moonshiners advance notice of raids for a price. Peel's flexible ethics made him a favorite of mobsters in the state. They wanted Peel to become the state's attorney general. Campaign financing for higher office did not present as a problem.

In June of 1955, Peel's position and future ambitions were threatened by another judge, Curtis Chillingworth, who chaired the judicial disciplinary committee. Peel was scheduled to appear before it. He faced disbarment – not for bribes, but for a combination of sloth, incompetence, and deceit in his private practice. Peel represented a woman in a divorce. Rather than do the work, Peel just told the woman her divorce had been granted. She remarried. According to Florida State Section 826.01, this made her guilty of the felony of bigamy. It carried a punishment of a fine of up to $5,000 and up to five years in prison. Peel's client was not happy. She complained to the judicial disciplinary committee. Judge Chillingworth was legendary for his rectitude and toughness; he had already given Peel one break but made it clear leniency was a onetime deal.

To avoid facing Judge Chillingworth, Peel turned to murder. He recruited two criminal associates, Floyd Holzapfel and Bobby Lincoln, to do the dirty work.

Judge Chillingworth and his wife, Marjorie, had a beachside home. The night before Peel's disciplinary hearing, the two hired killers took a boat to the Chillingworth home. Dressed as a yacht captain, Holzapfel knocked on the door and told the judge their motor had broken. Holzapfel asked to use the telephone to call the coast guard. Once inside, Holzapfel produced a gun. He and Lincoln bound and gagged their victims. Lincoln smashed the back porch light so they could leave in darkness. While being led to the boat, Marjorie worked out her gag and screamed. She was pistol-whipped. Curtis and Marjorie assumed they were being kidnapped for ransom. Save for the single scream, they went without a struggle, assuring the pair of intruders they would pay up to $200,000 for their safety.

Holzapfel and Lincoln took the Chillingworths two miles out to sea. The killers strapped lead weights to their victims. Marjorie was thrown overboard first. Lincoln later testified she went down with just "a few bubbles." Killing Curtis was harder. Despite having his hands tied and lead weights strapped around his waist, the judge managed to stay on the surface and started

DOI: 10.4324/9781003372134-9

swimming toward shore. Lincoln proposed shooting but Holzapfel pointed to the need for silence and used his shotgun as a club. The two tied an anchor around the judge's neck. With that, Curtis joined Marjorie in the briny deep. Holzapfel and Lincoln returned home.

In the morning, workmen arrived at the Chillingworth home. Nobody answered the door. This was peculiar; the Chillingworths were legendary for their punctuality. The workmen noticed the broken porch light and blood on the steps. They called the police. There was no sign of either Curtis or Marjorie. The police ruled out accidental drowning since the couple's bathing suits were still in the house. This left murder as the likely explanation for their disappearance. Robbery as a motive was ruled out since nothing was missing. The police correctly surmised the cause of the murders lay in Curtis's judicial activity, but believed the motive was revenge. They looked at the judge's past criminal cases for suspects. Despite a massive police effort and the posting of a $100,000 reward, the investigation went nowhere. Peel's plan worked. Instead of the permanent disbarment expected from Judge Chillingworth, Peel received a 90-day suspension from a more lenient judge.

Despite the successful murder, all did not go well for Peel, Holzapfel, and Lincoln. Their lives were intertwined in a series of criminal endeavors. It is a long and complicated story best told by journalist Jim Bishop.[2] The abridged version is that:

- Peel used a crooked insurance broker to place a life insurance policy on a fellow lawyer, naming himself beneficiary. He lured the lawyer to a bar, where Holzapfel attempted to murder him in a staged robbery. The lawyer survived. Holzapfel, Peel, and the insurance broker were all charged. They were acquitted when Holzapfel convinced a jury the attack was a crime of passion, claiming the lawyer tried to seduce his wife;
- Peel, Holzapfel, and a third man created a construction company to defraud investors. It was the classical Florida scheme involving swamp land, widows, and orphans;
- Holzapfel and Lincoln went into the moonshining and bootlegging business. After officers from the Florida Sheriffs Bureau intervened, the pair decided that a bootlegger named Lew Harvey was an informant. Holzapfel and Lincoln took Harvey into the swamps, shot him in the head, tied cement blocks to his body, and threw him in a creek.

This attempt to get rid of Harvey's body was unsuccessful. It bloated, rose to the surface, and was discovered. An officer from the Florida Sheriffs Bureau investigating this murder questioned the crooked insurance broker. Instead of talking about Lew's murder, the broker wanted to talk about the Chillingworth case. There was no reward for information about the dead bootlegger, but information on the missing judge was worth $100,000. The broker signed on as a paid informant and cultivated a relationship with Holzapfel. They hijacked a shipment of weapons intended for Nicaraguan rebels. Unknown to Holzapfel, the operation was staged by police. Holzapfel was arrested while the broker "escaped" and used a bail bondsman to post Holzapfel's bail to build trust. Holzapfel fled to Brazil. The bail bondsman became a second police informant, incentivized by the bail money he had posted and the prospect of a share of the reward.

Thus, four years after killing Curtis and Marjorie Chillingworth, Lincoln was in prison for bootlegging and Holzapfel was in hiding in Brazil. Only Peel was prospering, happily swindling investors. Holzapfel nursed the strongest sense of grievance. He discovered that existing broke and alone in Brazil was not much better than being in prison. Holzapfel wanted his share of the land swindle profits. Peel refused to share the money with Holzapfel. Instead, he took advantage of the situation to share the favors of Holzapfel's wife. This prompted Holzapfel to return to Florida to kill Peel. For his part, Peel wanted to kill Holzapfel. Both Peel and Holzapfel enlisted the aid of the crooked insurance broker to help with their murderous plans. The result was meetings in a hotel room wired for recording by police. Holzapfel drank heavily and described, in detail, how the Chillingworths had been killed. Both Peel and Holzapfel were arrested.

The arrests created incentives to talk. Lincoln, from his prison cell, negotiated an immunity agreement for his role in the murders of Curtis, Marjorie, and Lew in exchange for testimony against Peel and Holzapfel. Peel attempted to get an immunity agreement in exchange for his testimony against Holzapfel and Lincoln, but the prosecutor viewed him as the main prize. Holzapfel, perhaps realizing he was doomed, concentrated on getting revenge. He pleaded guilty to three counts of first-degree murder and agreed to testify against Peel.

At Peel's trial for the murder of Judge Curtis Chillingworth, both Lincoln and Holzapfel testified about Peel's instigating role. Peel made things worse by smuggling poison into the jail and attempting to bribe a trustee to put it in Holzapfel's food. The trustee informed police. Holzapfel, Lincoln, the crooked insurance broker/police informant, the bail bondsman, and another partner in the real estate swindle all testified. Peel took the stand to call them all crooked, conniving liars. Peel denied attempting to negotiate an immunity agreement, but the prosecutor produced two rebuttal witnesses who had been in hiding to witness the conversation. Peel was convicted of conspiracy to commit murder. The jury recommended mercy, so Peel was spared the electric chair.[3] Observers speculated the mercy recommendation arose from the immunity agreement given to Lincoln, who was black. Florida in 1960 was not the time or place for an all-white jury to send a white man to the electric chair while a black man admitting guilt walked free. Peel ended up serving 18 years of a life sentence for his instigation of the Chillingworth murders. After being paroled by Florida, he was turned over to the federal corrections system to serve a sentence for fraud convictions arising from his real estate swindle.

In 1982, Joseph Peel was released from prison on compassionate grounds and died of cancer nine days later.[4] Between his release and death, Peel was busy. He remarried and, after 22 years of denial and appeals, confessed he had arranged the murders of Curtis and Marjorie Chillingworth.[5]

Non-Shareable Secrets and Midlife Crisis Killers

Cases involving intimate partners, dependent children, and sex trade workers were defined by the relationship between killer and victim. Cases involving sexual serial killers and criminal organization killers were defined by motive. (Ex-)Judge Joseph Peel introduces a new typology of no-body homicides. It is defined by personality type and stage of life. The killers are pathological narcissists undergoing a midlife crisis.

These killers are well educated and articulate. They experience success as young adults, but there are warning signs something is a little "off." They are guided more by expediency than by ethics. As they reach middle age, they have a crisis. The proximate causes of these crises vary, but have one feature in common. Secrets must be kept. In his study of professional people who committed fraud, criminologist Donald Cressey argued that normally respectable people turned to fraud when they had a "non-shareable secret" – some failure or crisis threatening to ruin both their position and reputation if disclosed. They turned to fraud and embezzlement to keep their secret a secret.[6] The killers we look at also had secret problems, but turned to murder rather than fraud. The dynamic is the same.

We have seen that Joseph Peel faced a legal disciplinary hearing and turned to murder. In this chapter, we will look at more cases. Perry March was a lawyer with cash flow problems, a secret, and an unhappy wife.[7] Thomas Capano was a lawyer having two secret affairs. One mistress no longer wanted him.[8] William Bradfield, Jr. was a teacher with a dream of buying a sailboat to circumnavigate the world, no money, and several mistresses.[9] These cases are representative samples about which books have been written. There are more, albeit less, notorious. Abraham Cooper was embroiled in an endless series of disputes with other doctors in the hospital at which he worked.[10] Everett Drew Clark was a conman who coveted his victim's money and wife.[11] Carlton Foley lost a civil court case in a dispute over where his yard ended and his neighbors began.[12] Freddie Hall owned a business repairing high-end sports cars; a customer accused him of accepting payment without performing the work.[13] Alan Mackerley's school bus company lost a major contract to a hated competitor.[14] Gary Shawkey was an investment advisor; more than a quarter million dollars of a clients' money disappeared.[15] The retirement services company run by Eric Bechler and his wife was investigated for Medicare fraud.[16] Jeweler Werner Lippe was getting divorced but did not want to share his wealth in a property settlement.[17] Frank Schilt spent an inheritance received by his wife; she was unhappy when she found out.[18] The victims in these cases included wives, lovers, co-workers, business partners, clients, and neighbors. The immediate motives included concealment, jealousy, and greed. Despite the seeming diversity, these cases all have an eerie similarity. Hitherto successful people attempted to resolve a crisis in their lives with murder and body disposal.

Homicidal Lawyers: Perry March and Thomas Capano

On June 27, 1996, Thomas Capano murdered his former lover, Anne Marie Fahey in Wilmington, Delaware. Fifty days later and 773 miles away, Perry March murdered his wife, Janet March, in Nashville, Tennessee. The bodies of Anne Marie and Janet were never recovered. Both murders generated multiple books. In one of them, Michael Glasgow and Phyllis Gobbell noted the two killers "were both attorneys ostensibly living the 'perfect life' and moving in the right circles. Both were also arrogantly convinced they were smarter than those around them, and that regardless of their situation, they would always come out on top."[19] After long investigations, gaudy trials, and extensive media coverage, both Capano and March were convicted of murder.

Let us start by looking at Capano.[20]

Thomas Capano was part of a prominent Delaware family that made its fortune in construction and real estate development. Capano went into law and politics. He worked as Wilmington's city attorney, state prosecutor, and legal advisor to Delaware's governor. With his political connections established, Capano became a partner in a large law firm. He was married and had four daughters. In 1994, Capano began a secret affair with a woman 21 years his junior. Anne Marie Fahay worked as the appointment secretary for Delaware's governor. This was not Capano's only secret affair; he had secretly been seeing another woman for years. In 1995, Capano left his wife. Capano and Anne Marie became "on again – off again" lovers. The relationship settled into the uncomfortable dynamic of Anne Marie vowing to leave while Capano attempted to control and dominate. By the spring of 1996, Anne Marie decided she could remain "friends" with Capano while ending the sexual relationship. Capano responded by telling his brothers he was the victim of an extortion attempt and asked if he could borrow a boat to dispose of a body. He bought a picnic cooler big enough to serve as a coffin and got his other lover to buy a gun on his behalf.

On Thursday, June 27, 1996, Capano and Anne Marie dined in Philadelphia. The waiter later testified it was a silent meal. He was the last person other than Capano to see Anne Marie alive. At about 5:30 the next morning, Capano arrived at a brother's house asking to use his boat. Capano borrowed a vehicle big enough to hold the massive cooler from his ex-wife. Capano's brother helped load the cooler into the vehicle and then into the boat. They set off to sea. When the Capano brothers were about 60 miles offshore, they tossed the cooler into the ocean. It did not sink. Capano used a shotgun to shoot holes in it. It still did not sink. The two brothers retrieved the cooler, weighted Anne Marie's body with two anchors, and let her sink.

They rinsed out the cooler, discarded it, and returned home. The brothers threw a blood-soaked love seat into a garbage dumpster at a construction site run by the family construction company. Capano then spent the evening watching movies with his daughters and the night with his other lover. The next day, he bought a new rug for his great room and asked his second brother to ensure the dumpster was emptied immediately. Capano explained the blood on the love seat by saying Anne Marie had slit her wrists, but that she was "okay."

Because she worked for the governor, the investigation into Anne Marie's disappearance was immediate and vigorous. Anne Marie's diary and e-mail records quickly made Capano the prime suspect. Capano was the last person known to have been with the missing woman. He claimed his relationship with Anne Marie had become platonic and that he dropped her off at home after their dinner date. A few days after the disappearance, Capano allowed police an escorted "walk through" of his home. Everything appeared normal. Police returned with a warrant a day later. The forensics team found small spots of blood on a wall in the great room. The DNA profile matched Anne Marie's.

The police broke the case by applying pressure. They started with Capano's helpful boat-owning brother. He was charged with drug and firearm offenses. This induced him to talk about the disposal of Anne Marie's body. The police moved on to the brother who arranged for the premature garbage pickup. He was also convinced that his interests were best served by cooperating with police. From there, the police moved onto Capano's remaining mistress, who eventually admitted to buying Capano a gun.

When Capano was arrested 16 months after Anne Marie disappeared, police had Anne Marie's diary and e-mails providing evidence about a secret, troubled relationship. There were blood splatters on his great-room wall. Both of Capano's brothers described the disposal of Anne Marie's body and the bloody love seat. Capano's mistress provided testimony about his secret acquisition of a gun. There was also circumstantial evidence. Capano was the last person seen with Anne Marie. He had purchased the giant cooler and a new rug. He had borrowed his ex-wife's SUV the morning after Anne Marie disappeared. After Capano was arrested, more corroborating evidence came in. The cooler never did sink. A few days after Anne Marie disappeared, a fisherman found the floating cooler, patched up the holes, and claimed it as his own. After the publicity accompanying Capano's arrest, the fisherman realized the significance of his find and called police. The cooler corroborated the story told by Capano's brother. Capano's position was that his brothers were lying. "You going to believe them?" he asked police after his arrest.

Capano's bad judgment continued while he was in jail awaiting his trial. He placed several phone calls to his surviving lover to influence her testimony. The calls were recorded by police. When persuasion failed, he hired another inmate to burglarize and vandalize her house; writing out six pages of instructions, including floor plans and alarm codes. The burglar passed this on to the police. Another inmate claimed Capano offered him $90,000 to kill both his lover and the prosecutor.

Capano's ego was displayed when jury selection began. In quick succession, three attractive women in their 20s were summoned. Normally, the defense would object to a juror so like the victim. Capano, however, wanted these women on the jury. Capano's lawyers told the judge they advised Capano to exclude these jurors, but he overruled them. The lawyers wanted to put their advice on record to protect against an accusation of incompetence at appeal. One told the judge, "The dumb son of a bitch thinks they are going to fall in love with him."[21]

At trial, the evidence Capano dumped Anne Marie's body into the ocean was overwhelming. Both brothers testified about the disposal and cleanup; one had seen Anne Marie disappear below the waves. Their testimony was corroborated by circumstantial evidence, including the cooler riddled with holes and the purchase of a new rug. The case for murder was slightly weaker. Motive was established using Anne Marie's diary and e-mails. Anne Marie wanted it to end the relationship; Capano did not. Forensic experts testified about finding Anne Marie's blood in Capano's home. The living lover explained how she had secretly purchased a gun for Capano. Finally, there were awkward facts such as Capano being the last person seen with Anne Marie and his attempt to hire an inmate to terrorize his other lover.

The trial was marked by discord between Capano and his lawyers. One quit. Capano announced he wanted to fire the other four, but changed his mind. One lawyer described his client by saying, "he's an asshole." Another lawyer went further. Pointing to a mafia gangster he had once represented, the lawyer said, "I always thought he was the vilest man I ever met. He no longer has that distinction."[22]

Capano took the stand to concede the obvious. He was guilty of disposing of Anne Marie's body. But Capano denied killing her. He claimed Anne Marie was at his house for a friendly visit but was interrupted by the unexpected and unwanted arrival of his other lover. Capano claimed this lover was hysterical with jealousy, pulled out the gun, and threatened suicide. Capano said he was attempting to disarm her when the gun went off and accidently killed Anne Marie. Capano said he dumped Anne Marie's body in the ocean to avoid an embarrassing scandal. The prosecutor began his four-day cross-examination by asking about a murder trial Capano prosecuted to show he knew body disposal and cleanup would prevent an accurate crime reconstruction.

Capano's lover denied the story that she accidently killed Anne Marie, saying she did not know she had a rival until after Anne Marie's death. Capano was convicted of premeditated murder.

Under Delaware law at the time, a sentencing phase followed the determination of guilt. Evidence about extenuating or aggravating circumstances could be presented. The person convicted was allowed to speak (the right of allocution), but not allowed to contest the guilty verdict. It was an opportunity to demonstrate remorse and ask for mercy. The jury would then make a nonbinding recommendation about the imposition of the death penalty.

Capano turned this phase of his trial into a circus. He tried to re-litigate the trial by proclaiming his innocence, attacked the witnesses against him, and insulted the intelligence of the jury. After several warnings, the judge ended Capano's allocution address. This was likely Capano's objective, since the judge's decision to silence him formed the basis of his subsequent appeal. By a vote of 10 to 2, the jury members recommended Capano be executed. The judge agreed, saying:

> There is nothing in defendant's life which would call for the imposition of a life sentence. Defendant will not adjust well in prison; he will constantly scheme to by-pass prison rules; he will defy prison authority; he will continue to manipulate those who love him from within the prison walls. He poses a threat of harm even while incarcerated. He committed a horrific crime. That crime and his antisocial behavior outweigh any mitigating circumstances. The sentence of death is warranted in this case … He is a malignant force from whom no one he deems disloyal or adversarial can be secure, even if he is incarcerated for the rest of his life.[23]

Capano lost a series of appeals.[24] He managed to delay execution long enough to be alive in 2006 when the U.S. Supreme Court ruled that unanimity was required for jury recommendations for the death penalty.[25] Capano's sentence was converted into life in prison.[26] He died behind bars in 2011.[27]

The summer of 1996 was a season for lawyers responding to midlife crisis by killing intimate partners and body disposal. While Thomas Capano was murdering Anne Marie Fahey, another lawyer, Perry March, was doing the same to his wife, Janet March.[28]

Perry March was the son of an Army pharmacist. He met Janet Levine at college and married "above himself." The Levine family was far more affluent than the March's. Her father was the managing partner of a successful Nashville law firm. Janet's parents paid for March's law school at Vanderbilt University. After graduation, March was hired by Nashville's largest and most prestigious law firm. Janet pursued an art career, looked after the couple's two children, and designed a massive custom-built house. Her parents put up the money for construction.

March's path to murder began when he developed a fixation with an attractive paralegal. His courtship technique was unusual and unsuccessful. He composed long, anonymous, obscene messages describing his sexual fantasies involving the woman and left them in her work files. The paralegal alerted the management of the law firm. Hidden video cameras were installed in the firm's law library. March was revealed as the author of the notes. He was given a choice: resign or be fired. He opted to resign and joined his father-in-law's firm claiming he wanted to be part of the family business. March agreed to pay the paralegal $25,000 for damages. Half was paid in monthly installments. The other $12,500 was due in August 1996.

March had kept his sexual harassment a secret, but he had a problem arising from the monetary settlement. The problem was not the amount needed, but the need to keep the payments hidden from his wife. March managed to maintain secrecy for the monthly payments, but as the deadline for the lump sum payment approached, the secrecy challenge became acute. March responded by writing a letter to the paralegal asking for an extension – with interest.

Police believe Janet's murder was precipitated by her discovery of this letter. Whether or not this theory is true, Janet abruptly disappeared on the evening of August 15, 1996. Late that night, March began phoning relatives to report Janet had left. He claimed they quarreled and Janet declared she was going on a 12-day holiday. March showed his in-laws a 20-point, typed, "to-do" list she had left for him. He had signed it (purportedly at her insistence), but she had not.

This story delayed the filing of a missing-person's report to the police. Janet's parents did not want to cause embarrassment to their daughter. As time went on, they became increasingly worried. Janet was normally in daily contact with them and was an attentive parent. It did not make sense that she would go on a holiday without telling her parents or calling her children. Fears crystallized when Janet did not appear for her son's birthday party. A missing person's report was filed two weeks after the disappearance. The resulting publicity quickly resulted in the discovery of Janet's car a few miles from the March home, backed into a parking lot at a large apartment complex. The car contained a hastily packed suitcase. By common female consensus, it did not contain the items a woman would pack. Further, Janet's money, identification, and credit cards were still at her home. The police and Janet's parents were convinced that March killed Janet and disposed of her body.[29] Massive searches of the area were conducted without success.

Nine years of legal "trench warfare" between March and Janet's parents followed.[30] March first moved the two children to Illinois. He and his in-laws battled over the control and use of Janet's property, custody, and access to the children and who was entitled to billings made while March was at his father-in-law's legal firm. March then fled with the children to Mexico. Janet's parents obtained a court order to get visitation access. They used the temporary order to spirit the children out of Mexico and refused to return them. A year later, a court ordered the children's return to their father. Janet's parents filed a civil action suing March for causing the wrongful death of their daughter. They were awarded a default judgment of $113.5 million. When this decision was overturned on appeal, they launched another action. While all this was going on, March remarried in Mexico. He started an investment business catering to retired Americans living in Mexico. Complaints about fraud and misappropriated funds quickly followed.[31]

In 2005, prosecutors in Nashville secured a murder indictment against March. He was arrested by Mexican authorities and extradited to Los Angeles. From there, police escorted him back to Nashville. While on the flight, March asked the police officer to talk to the prosecutor about a plea bargain; March offered to plead guilty to manslaughter in exchange for a seven-year sentence.

At the time of March's arrest, the case was both circumstantial and weak. It rested on the fact of Janet's inexplicable disappearance and March's suspicious behavior. March's lawyers were confident they could obtain an acquittal. March put an end to their optimism. While in jail, he recruited another prisoner to murder Janet's parents. This, he believed, would remove the prosecutor's will to proceed. March offered to help the would-be killer obtain bail. The man would kill Janet's parents, flee to Mexico, and stay with March's father. March said the two could go into the kidnap-for-extortion business in Mexico after his own acquittal. March's recruit initially planned to accept the assistance in getting out of jail and then disappear without killing Janet's parents. His mother and lawyer pointed out a more promising possibility. The inmate struck a deal with the prosecutor to get legal release in exchange for helping police build the case against March. This led to the arrest of March's father in Mexico for conspiracy to commit murder. He was extradited to the United States.

March's father was 79 years old and in poor health. He had done a lot for his murderous son, but it was over. He negotiated a plea bargain and became a witness. The father said March killed Janet and temporarily buried her on property owned by one of clients. March called his father for help. The father arrived in Nashville from Mexico, ostensibly to help with childcare. The real purpose of his visit was body disposal. March had his father dig up Janet's body. The two drove north to Kentucky. While March rested in a motel, his father was dispatched to dump the body in a river. The father noticed a huge pile of brush drying after a farmer had cleared some land. March's father knew the pile would be burned, so he hid Janet's body in the brush pile.

The prosecution opted to conduct a series of three trials, starting with the least serious charge against March. It was for misappropriation of funds from his father-in-law's law firm. March was then tried for the conspiracy to murder Janet's parents. Finally, he was tried for murdering Janet.[32] March's defense attacked the credibility of both the father and the would-be hit man. According to March, every witness against him was a self-serving liar. He was convicted on all counts at every trial and sentenced to 56 years in prison. Numerous appeals were unsuccessful. March also launched lawsuits against prison officials over issues such as complaints about prison food.[33] After the U.S. Supreme Court refused to hear his case, March turned to other means to get out of jail. In 2015, he was abruptly moved to another prison amid reports he was organizing an escape attempt.[34]

Midlife Crisis: Not Just Lawyers

The cases of Joseph Peel, Thomas Capano, and Perry March are representative of midlife crisis no-body murder cases. Immediate motives, means of killing, and the extent of premeditation varied, but there were common features. In each case, the killer's desire to hide some earlier misbehavior turned the person from a respectable member of the community into a murderer. The killers were attracted to using bodies of water to hide bodies. The victims of both Peel and Capano were weighted down and dumped in the ocean. March told his father to dump Janet into a river. The investigations were long, complex, expensive, and frustrating for authorities. Each killer enlisted others to do much of their dirty work; Peel for both murder and disposal of bodies, Capano and March for disposal. These accomplices ended up being key witnesses for the prosecution. While waiting for trial, all three attempted to recruit another inmate to kill witnesses or the prosecutor. Their trials were all long and gaudy. In every case, the accused attempted to run their own defense. Conflicts with their lawyers were endemic.

There is something else. These guys were all lawyers. They were supposed to be intelligent, but behaved very stupidly. They used homicide to resolve a problem. Setting aside the moral and ethical issues, this was stupid. It escalated problems. Peel could have faced his disciplinary hearing. March could have got a divorce. Capano could have allowed his lover to leave. For all three, the consequence of homicide as a life-improvement tool was making their lives much worse. Their stupidity did not end with the murder. They all attempted to recruit another inmate to kill witnesses or the prosecutor. The inmates being recruited were not educated or particularly intelligent, but they were smarter than the murderous lawyers attempting to manipulate them. They saw the benefit of cooperating with law enforcement rather than carrying out an ill-conceived contract killing.

Thus far, we have focused on cases involving lawyers. We will now turn to school teachers to show that the problem of midlife crisis and murder is not confined to members of the bar.

In the late 1970s, the prestigious Upper Merion Area High School in an affluent suburb outside of Philadelphia had the most dysfunctional teaching staff of any school in North America – at least one hopes none are worse. We will focus on the school's principal, Dr. Jay Smith, and an English teacher, William Bradfield.[35]

Smith was an idiosyncratic administrator known for his long, bizarre announcements over the school's public address system and his fondness for keeping teachers off balance. He was also an active member of the U.S. Army Reserves. He rose to the rank of Colonel. Smith's idiosyncrasies turned into a full-blown midlife crisis in 1978 when his adult daughter and her husband abruptly disappeared. Both had severe addictions problems. Rumors circulated that Smith murdered the couple, but there was no evidence of this. Later that year Smith was arrested in a parking lot – masked, armed, and lurking around a van belonging to a local supermarket owner. A search of Smith's vehicle and home resulted in surprising discoveries; drugs, weapons, and a large cache of pornographic material. The resulting investigation revealed Smith had been the perpetrator in a series of armed robberies of Sears stores.

This brought William Bradfield to the attention of authorities. Bradfield was an English teacher at Smith's school. He was living with one female English teacher and was having an affair with another. Bradfield had at least two more mistresses along with two ex-wives from whom he was not legally divorced. Bradfield also had young male English teachers as devoted acolytes. His complicated life created financial problems. Bradfield, a mistress, and an acolyte were partners in a money-losing craft store. Bradfield's stated goal was to buy a sailboat and sail around the world, but his financial ability to fulfill this dream was nonexistent. Bradfield was a man with a lot of secrets – lovers were kept ignorant of the other's existence and of his financial woes. Even his dream of buying a sailboat to sail around the world was kept secret from some of his lovers. They had different understandings of the future.

Smith's arrest seems to have propelled Bradfield toward a homicidal midlife crisis. Bradfield had never gotten along with his principal, but after Smith was charged with the Sears robberies, Bradfield emerged as an alibi witness. He concocted a long, convoluted story purporting to prove he was out of state with Smith on the day of one robbery. The jury did not buy Bradfield's story and convicted Smith on the robbery charges.

As Bradfield was attempting to get Smith acquitted on the robbery charges, he was telling his group of mistresses and acolytes that Smith was planning on murdering Susan Reinhard. She was a mother of two who left her husband for affair with Bradfield. Susan was convinced that

Bradfield was going to marry her – so convinced that she gave him $25,000 to invest and took out $730,000 in life insurance. Bradfield was the beneficiary.

June 22, 1979, was Smith's last night of freedom before sentencing on the robbery convictions. Bradfield told a mistress and two of his male acolytes that Smith was going to kill Susan that night. Bradfield and his group traveled to a beach resort in New Jersey to establish an alibi. That evening, Susan and her two children drove away from their home. Susan's body was found the next morning in the trunk of her car. It was in a hotel parking lot; the hatch was up and an anonymous call directed police to the scene. Susan's killer wanted her body to be quickly discovered. Susan's children disappeared. Their bodies have never been found.

Bradfield was the obvious suspect for Susan's murder and her children's disappearance, but he had his alibi. He and his followers pointed at Smith, who was sent to prison on the robbery charges the morning Susan's body was discovered. To make a long and complicated story short, Bradfield was charged and convicted of defrauding Susan of $25,000. The police eventually put enough pressure on Bradfield's cult-like group to turn two mistresses and two acolytes into witnesses on murder charges. A third mistress remained loyal and closemouthed. Bradfield was convicted on three counts of murder, but how the homicides were committed remained murky. The police theorized that Smith did the actual killing in exchange for Bradfield's alibi testimony during his robbery trial and a split of the insurance money. Smith, still serving his sentence for robbery, proceeded to dig himself into deeper trouble by making a "sort-of/kind-of" confession to an inmate. More seriously, he conspired with another inmate to have the police investigators murdered.

With this, Smith was charged with murdering Susan and her children. The primary evidence was the testimony of Bradfield's mistresses and acolytes along with his attempt to have the police investigators murdered. There was a little physical evidence. A pin from the Philadelphia Museum of Art was found in Smith's car; it was like one belonging to Susan's daughter. A comb bearing the inscription of Smith's army reserve unit was found in Susan's car – along with a few fibers matching those from a rug in Smith's basement. A hair "similar" to Susan's was found in Smith's home, but in this pre-DNA era no definitive match could be made. Finally, there was the fact that Smith was just plain weird. In 1987, Smith was convicted and sentenced to death. Two books[36] and a made-for-TV movie[37] quickly followed. It was, after all, stranger than fiction.

In 1989, the Supreme Court of Pennsylvania overturned Smith's convictions. The testimony of Bradfield's mistresses and acolytes had been central in Smith's trial, but none of these witnesses had any actual direct knowledge. Their testimony was based on what Bradfield told them. It was all hearsay and should not have been admitted as evidence. A new trial was ordered.[38] Given his documented attempt to have detectives murdered, Smith remained in prison pending the new trial.

Then the wheels really came off the prosecution. At Smith's trial, a forensics expert testified there had been beach sand on Susan's feet. This police officer said he collected samples of this sand using sticky "lifters." Since Bradfield had taken great pains to be at the beach to establish an alibi, Smith's defense lawyers were interested in this testimony. The prosecution responded by accusing the forensics' expert of lying and claimed the lifters did not exist. Following the trial, the forensics officer was charged with professional misconduct. The investigation revealed the lifters existed and the prosecutors had intentionally concealed this evidence from the defense lawyers.

There was also the matter of perjury by one of the key prosecution witnesses. The inmate that Smith recruited to murder the police detectives testified he had not received any benefit for his cooperation and testimony. This was perjury. The prosecutor did not correct the record.

Things soon got worse for the police and prosecutor. Contrary to police policies, the lead detective stored boxes of evidence in his home. This evidence had not been disclosed to the defense as legally required. A few years after the trial, the officer was cleaning up his house and gave the contents of his attic to a junk collector who, in turn, gave them to Smith's defense lawyer. Among other things, the evidence boxes revealed the investigator had a secret contract with author Joseph Waumbaugh. He was paid $50,000 for inside case information for the book *Echoes in the Darkness*. A made-for-TV movie with the same name was based on this book. Payment in exchange for providing case information was bad, but another provision in the contract was even worse. The contract was signed while the investigation was ongoing and contained a provision that the officer would only be paid if Smith was charged. Only then would the story be interesting enough to justify payment.

It was too much for the Supreme Court of Pennsylvania. In 1992, three years after overturning Smith's conviction and ordering a new trial, the court ruled that "we now hold that the prosecutorial misconduct during appellant's first trial was not only impermissible, but had constitutional implications under the double jeopardy clause which prohibit retrial."[39] Smith was acquitted and released from prison that afternoon. The judges said, "the record establishes the bad faith of the prosecution beyond any possibility of doubt; indeed, it would be hard to imagine more egregious prosecutorial tactics."[40]

By this time, Smith's prosecutor was in prison on unrelated cocaine distribution charges?[41]

The fiasco of Smith's prosecution did not change anything for Bradfield. He died in prison in 1998. The differential treatment of the bodies of Susan and her children provides compelling circumstantial evidence of Bradfield's guilt. He was the beneficiary of $730,000 in life insurance from Susan. She needed to be declared dead before he could claim the money. Her body was dumped in a hotel parking lot and someone called the police to direct them to her. On the other hand, alive or dead, her children were a complication impeding a quick insurance payout. Their bodies were never found. Susan's children were legally declared dead in 1987 – two years after Bradfield was convicted of their murder. Because of a combination at Bradfield's scheming, police incompetence/corruption, and Smith's own actions, it remains a mystery whether Bradfield did the killing personally or whether he convinced someone else to do the dirty deed. Smith may have been an accomplice, but it is far more likely Bradfield took advantage of his principal's midlife crisis for an attempted frame. Lawyers are not the only ones susceptible to having midlife crisis generating no-body homicides.

The Nature of Midlife Crisis Killings

Earlier in the chapter, we noted the peculiar nature of midlife crisis murderers. These individuals are male and successful; albeit with an undertone of questionable moral and ethical standards behind their apparent success. When confronted with a problem that must be kept secret, they choose a remarkably stupid approach to solving their problem – murder. They do not seem to understand they will almost always become the prime suspects in the police investigation (Peel was an exception to this). Motive speaks to police. Perhaps because these guys always believe they are the smartest person in the room, these killers do not understand the relentless pressure that police can apply. Peel, Campano, March, and Bradfield all thought they were smart enough to get away with their dumb decision.

There is more. One characteristic of this kind of murderer is that they get others to do the actual killing or help with the heavy lifting inherent in body disposal. Inevitably, these assistants become prosecution witnesses. The midlife crisis killers denounce these witnesses as unsavory liars out to save their own skins. They are so self-centered as to be incapable of understanding that their assistants see no reason to go to jail in order to cover up another person's homicide. Once in jail and awaiting trial, the midlife crisis killers often attempt to recruit other inmates to murder witnesses, police, or prosecutors. Once they have used murder to solve their problems, it seems to be a hard habit to break. They seem incapable of understanding that the other inmates have their own interests which are best served by becoming a prosecution witness rather than a contract killer.

The two things midlife crisis killers are good at are body disposal and denial. The victims of Peel and Capano went to the bottom of the ocean. Janet March's body was incinerated by a farmer burning a brush pile. We still have no idea how Bradfield got rid of the bodies of Susan Reinert's two children. All four vigorously and persistently denied their guilt for years. Upon conviction their appeals were endless. Peel relented a few weeks before he died and admitted to the proven. Skill at body disposal combined with the pathological ability to deny means the investigation and prosecution of this type of killer is long, complex, and expensive. They have the resources to hire excellent defense attorneys (even though they tend to ignore the advice they receive). In the end, they go to prison. The transparency of their motives, their recruitment of accomplices, and the murderous post-arrest behavior means that, at the end of the day, juries convict and appeal courts uphold.

Notes

1 Bishop, Jim, *The Murder Trial of Judge Peel* (New York, NY: Papamoa Press, 2017).
2 Bishop, *Murder Trial.*
3 Peel v. State, 154 So. 2d 910 (Fla. Dist. Ct. App. 1963).
4 "Joseph Peel, Jr.; Had Murder Role," *New York Times*, July 5, 1982.
5 Palleson, Tim, "Sixty Years on, Chillingworth Murders Still Shocking," *The Coastal Star*, June 2015.
6 Cressey, Donald, *Other People's Money: A Study in the Sociology of Embezzlement* (New York, NY: Free Press, 1953).
7 Glasgow, Michael and Phyllis Gobbell (2007) *An Unfinished Canvas: A True Story of Love, Family and Murder in Nashville* (New York, NY: Berkley, 2007); King, Jeanne, *Never Seen Again: A Ruthless Lawyer, His Beautiful Wife, and the Murder that Tore a Family Apart* (New York, NY: St. Martins, 2008); King, Gary, *Love, Lies and Murder* (New York, NY: Pinnacle Books, 2014).
8 Barrish, Cris and Peter Meyer, *Fatal Embrace: The Inside Story of the Thomas Capano/Anne Marie Fahey Murder Case* (New York, NY: St. Martins, 1999); Rule, Ann, *And Never Let Her Go – Thomas Capano: The Deadly Seducer* (New York, NY: Simon and Schuster, 2000); Karem, Brian J., *Above the Law: The Sensational Murder Case That Stunned the Nation* (New York, NY: Pinnacle-Kennsington, 1999); Anastasia, George, *The Summer Wind: Thomas Capano and the Murder of Anne Marie Fahey* (Philadelphia, PA: Camino Books, 2018).
9 Costopoulos, William, *Principal Suspect: The True Story of Dr. Jay Smith and the Main Line Murders* (Philadelphia, PA: Camino Books, 1996); Schwartz-Nobel, Loretta, *Engaged to Murder: The Inside Story of the Main Line Murders* (New York, NY: Viking, 1987); Smith, Jay Charles, *Joseph Wambaugh and the Jay Smith Case* (Philadelphia, PA: Xlibris, 2008); Wambaugh, Joseph, *Echoes in the Darkness* (New York, NY: Bantam, 1987).
10 Magnussen, Hazel, "After Violence Strikes," *MacLean's Magazine*, September 1, 2003; Bergman, Brian, "Stranger than Fiction," *MacLean's Magazine*, October 9, 2000.
11 "Mrs. Schick Confesses: Involves E.D. Clark in Murder of Husband; Admits Theft of Property by Forged Documents," *San Diego Union*, October 20, 1923.
12 Petke, Fred, "Convicted Murderer Will Stay Behind Bars," *Tri-County Times-Tribune*, June 16, 2006.
13 Freddie Lee Hall v. Commonwealth of Virginia, Court of Appeals of Virginia, Record No. 1623-13-1 (2014).
14 MacKerley *v.* State, 754 So. 2d 132 (Fla. Dist. Ct. App. 2000).
15 People v. Shawkey G045698 (Cal. Ct. App. Sep. 6, 2013).
16 Pfeifer, Stuart and Jack Leonard, "First Degree Murder Verdict for Bechler," *Los Angeles Times*, February 2, 2001.
17 People v. Lippe, Supreme Court of the State of New York, Appellant Division, 2nd District, Ind. No. 08-01605 (2016).

18 Pankratz, Howard, "Attorney: Fight Over Money Led to Murder," *Denver Post*, September 25, 2006.
19 Glasgow and Gobbell, *Unfinished Canvas.*
20 Barrish and Meyer, *Fatal Embrace*; Rule, *And Never Let Her*; Karem, *Above the Law;* Anastasia, *The Summer.*
21 Talorico, Patricia and Esteban Parra, "20 Years Later: 12 Details about the Capano Trial," *The News Journal*, January 16, 2019.
22 Anastasia, *Summer Wind*, 281.
23 Cited in Capano v. State, 781 A.2d 556, 582, 2001 WL 980939 (Del. 2001).
24 Capano v. State, 781 A.2d 556, 582, 2001 WL 980939 (Del. 2001); Capano v. Delaware, 536 U.S. 958, 122 S.Ct. 2660, 153 L.Ed.2d 835 (2002); State v.Capano, 2005 Del.Super. Lexis 69 (March 9, 2005).
25 Ring v. Arizona, 536 U. S. 584 (2002).
26 *Capano v. State*, 889 A.2d 968 (Del. 2006).
27 Fowser, Mark, "Notorious Convicted Killer Thomas Capano Found Dead in Delaware Prison Cell," *WHYY-PBS*, September 19, 2011.
28 Glasgow and Gobbell, *Unfinished Canvas*; King, *Never Seen Again*; King, Gary, *Love, Lies and Murder.*
29 Stern, Willy, "A Good Thing Gone Bad: What the Police Know – And Don't Know – About the Janet March Case," *Nashville Scene*, January 16, 1997.
30 March v. Levine, 115 S.W.3d 892 (2003).
31 Glasgow and Gobbell, *Unfinished Canvas.*
32 Emery, Theo, "After 10 Years and Many Turns, Murder Trial Starts in Nashville," *New York Times*, August 7, 2006.
33 Barchenger, Stacy, "Notorious Nashvillian Perry March Sues Over Prison Food," *Tennessean,* February 15, 2017.
34 Beres, Nick, "Perry March Moved to New Prison After Rumors of Alleged Escape Plot," *NewChannel5 Nashville*, August 13, 2016.
35 Costopoulos, *Principal Suspect*; Schwartz-Nobel, Loretta, *Engaged to Murder*; Smith, *Joseph Wambaugh and the Jay Smith Case*; Wambaugh, *Echoes in the Darkness.*
36 Schwartz-Nobel, Loretta, *Engaged to Murder*; Wambaugh, *Echoes in the Darkness.*
37 Jordan, Glenn, director, *Echoes in the Darkness*, CBS-TV (1987).
38 Com. *v.* Smith, 568 A.2d 600 (Pa. 1989).
39 Com. v. Smith, 532 Pa. 177 (1992).
40 Com. v. Smith, 532 Pa. 177 (1992).
41 Lewis, Neil A., "How Cocaine Brought Low a Soaring Law Career," *New York Times*, February 24, 1991.

10

DEADLY SYNERGIES

Combinations Causing Homicide and Body Disposal

On September 22, 2007, a charter boat operator named Jake Branham agreed to take two men, Kirby Archer and Guillermo Zarabozo, to the Bahamas.[1] The two said they were meeting holidaying girlfriends on the islands. In addition to Jake, there were two crew members on the boat. It was a beautiful day, so Jake's wife decided to come for the ride. Jake, his crew members, and his wife were never seen again.

The voyage was expected to be a day trip. When the boat ("Joe Cool") did not return, Jake's family notified the Coast Guard. The next day, the boat was located; drifting, out of gas, about 30 miles from Cuba. It was 160 miles off course. The only sign of people were bloodstains and shell casings. A short time later, the Coast Guard located a lifeboat containing Archer and Zarabozo.[2] They claimed the boat was attacked by Cuban pirates who forced them onto the lifeboat after killing everyone else on board.

This story was greeted with skepticism. Why was the boat so far off course? Why would pirates kill four and spare two? Why would pirates leave their victims' money, credit cards, electronic equipment, and $70,000 worth of fishing equipment on the boat? FBI agents and Coast Guard officials took a jet to the Florida Keys, a helicopter to a Coast Guard cutter, and a "fast boat" to the *Joe Cool.* They launched an intensive forensic examination of the boat. Police learned Archer was under investigation for child molestation and wanted in Arkansas for stealing $92,000 from the Walmart store he worked for. Less than three weeks after the crew went missing, Archer and Zarabozo were charged with a host of charges. The most serious were four counts of first-degree murder.

After claiming innocence for ten months, Archer pleaded guilty and agreed to testify against Zarabozo.[3] Archer said he and Zarabozo each killed two, tossed the bodies overboard, and headed for Cuba – only to run out of gas. After Archer confessed, Zarabozo recanted the discredited pirate story. Zarabozo now claimed he was an innocent bystander. In his new version, Zarabozo claimed Archer duped him into going on the trip and had, without warning, killed everyone else on the boat. Archer's version was buttressed by a jailhouse informant who claimed Zarabozo told him a version of the story like that being told by Archer.[4] Zarabozo was convicted on weapons charges, but the jury could not reach a decision on the murder charges. At a second trial, he was convicted on all charges and sentenced to life.[5]

It is a weird story. Given the previous history of both Archer and Zarabozo, it seems inexplicable. At the time of the killings, Archer was 37. He had served in the U.S. Marines. While

DOI: 10.4324/9781003372134-10

stationed in Guantanamo Bay, he made friends in Cuba. After an honorable discharge from the Marines, Archer worked as an assistant manager at a Walmart store in Arkansas. He was accused of molesting a child. He responded by stealing all available cash from the store and fleeing to Miami. Archer intended to flee to Cuba and settle beyond the reach of American justice.[6] Archer was undergoing a midlife crisis, but his initial response was flight rather than homicide. While hiding in Miami, Archer met Zarabozo. He was an even more unlikely candidate to become a mass murderer. He was 19, working as a security guard, and applying to join Miami's police force.

It appears the four murders happened because Archer wanted to get to Cuba but faced obstacles arising from his fugitive status and travel embargos to the island. Archer decided to hijack a boat, but needed a helper. Journalist Carol Cope describes how Archer stumbled across Zarabozo.[7] The teen had a rich fantasy life and wanted to be a hero. Archer convinced Zarabozo he was being recruited for a secret CIA mission to Cuba. Hijacking a boat was a means to secretly enter the country. The two loaded up on weapons and chartered a boat under false pretenses. Archer was seeking a future outside of an Arkansas prison and Zarabozo was seeking adventure. When explaining the transition from boat hijacking to mass murder, both killers blamed the other. Archer claimed Zarabozo suddenly started to shoot people. Once the shooting started, he felt compelled to help. For his part, Zarabozo claimed Archer killed the crew members when they refused to change course. Both denied premeditation. Perhaps one of these self-serving stories is true, but then again, perhaps not. FBI crime scene reconstruction experts believe there were two active shooters.

Synergistic Killers and No-Body Homicides

On their own, neither Archer nor Zarabozo appeared to be violent, let alone being a mass murderer. Indeed, after the two were charged, Archer's ex-wife told reporters that she had not thought Archer was capable of murder. She believed that Archer was capable of many vile acts, but was shocked when he murdered.[8] This statement came from an ex-spouse fresh off an acrimonious divorce and child-custody dispute.[9] However, when Archer linked up with Zarabozo – who had no criminal record – four innocent people were killed and thrown into the ocean.

The word "synergy" is used to describe a mutually reinforcing interaction between things which produces an effect that is greater than the sum of each individual part. According to the *Oxford English Dictionary*, the first known use of the word came in 1632. Edward Reynolds, the bishop of Norwich, used it to describe the increase in virtue arising when people partnered with Christ and God.[10] In the interaction between Archer and Zarabozo, the interactive effect was the magnification of evil. On their own, each was a bit off. Together, they committed an act of unspeakable evil.

There is not a good word for this interactive magnification of evil; perhaps dyssynergy might work. However, the purpose of this book is to study no-body homicides rather than invent new words, so we will call people like Kirby Archer and Guillermo Zarabozo synergistic killers. They are not defined by their relationship with the victim or motivation. Instead, murders committed by the pathological interaction between two or more individuals were not lethal on their own.

Synergistic killers account for a surprising number of no-body homicides.

Perhaps the weirdest team was Diazien Hossencofft and Linda Henning. On their own, each was at least four standard deviations from normal. The word "weird" does not do them justice; neither do bizarre, outlandish, disturbing, grotesque, or creepy. Better words are needed. On her own, Henning was a couple of tin-foil hat-liners away from reality, but basically harmless.

She was fond of conspiracy theories, and believed the American government was controlled by alien shape-shifters disguised in human form. Hossencofft was more profoundly evil. He was a lying, manipulative conman. Hossencofft claimed to be a physician and a CIA agent who had invented a combination of youth serum and cancer cure. In addition to being married, he was engaged to at least three women and bilked hundreds of thousands of dollars from women looking for the secret of eternal youth. This came in the form of shots of mislabeled Vitamin B-6.[11] Unlike Henning, Hossencofft damaged the lives of people on his own, but he had never killed anyone before the two met in 1999 at a discussion group about UFO's. Hossencofft convinced Henning he was a reptilian shape-shifter. She was smitten.[12]

Hossencofft was married to a bank-teller named Girly Chow Hossencofft, who was originally from Malaysia. The two met while she was in the United States on a holiday. A long-distance romance developed by correspondence. Hossencofft told some lies and convinced Girly Chow to marry him in 1992. In 1996, Hossencofft arrived home with a son; the product of a deceit-filled relationship with a Japanese woman living in Canada. Despite the surprise arrival, Girly Chow provided maternal care to the child. Early in 1999, about the time Hossencofft met Henning, Girly Chow left Hossencofft and filed for divorce citing physical assault and death threats. She attempted to keep her address a secret from her husband. They fought for custody of the three-year-old child, even though Hossencofft put the child up for adoption while fighting for custody.

On September 10, 1999, Girly Chow did not arrive at work. Her co-workers immediately called police. When the police entered her apartment, they smelled bleach. Forensics technicians used Luminal to discover that blood had been shed in the apartment – a lot of blood. Subsequent DNA testing showed matches to both Girly Chow and Henning. Hossencofft disappeared. He was driving to South Carolina with a new fiancé who was unaware her husband-to-be was either still legally married or a newly minted widower. The search for Hossencofft quickly led to Henning. She told police she did not know Hossencofft was married and that she had never met Girly Chow. Bank surveillance video showed this to be untrue. Henning had been checking out Girly Chow. In Henning's attic, police found a Ninja sword purchased just before Girly Chow's disappearance. A few days later, Girly Chow's clothing was found along a highway wrapped in a tarpaulin. A piece of duct tape had a few of Henning's hairs stuck to it.

Both Hossencofft and Henning were charged with murder.

Hossencofft pleaded guilty after negotiating a deal allowing him to serve his sentence in Wyoming rather than New Mexico. Hossencofft said he allowed a third member of the UFO discussion group to kill Girly Chow to practice killing human beings in preparation for a "final showdown." The man Hossencofft fingered managed to convince police of his innocence, pleaded guilty to an evidence-tampering charge, and received a year's probation.

Henning went on trial for the actual killing and body disposal. Hossencofft appeared as a defense witness. He admitted arranging the murder, but claimed Henning had not been part of the plan. Hossencofft claimed he inspected the crime scene after the killing and realized blood had been spilled. He returned home, got a vial of Henning's blood (he stored vials of people's blood in his refrigerator), mixed it with bleach and dumped it in Girly Chow's apartment. Hossencofft claimed the bleach was intended to destroy the DNA sequence to make identification impossible but confuse police by showing two women shed blood in the apartment. The jury did not buy this convoluted story, and Henning was convicted. Girly Chow's body has never been found. The prosecutor said Henning told at least four people she had eaten parts of Girly Chow's body, but he had not called them as witnesses because he did not want the trial to become even more bizarre and sensationalistic.[13]

Hossencofft and Henning are probably the most bizarre of a bizarre batch of synergistic killers. The largest and most complicated synergistic effect came with a group popularly known as the Billionaire Boys Club. The complexities of their murderous interactions have been described in books,[14] a television mini-series,[15] and a movie.[16]

Joseph Henry Gamsky was a scholarship student at the exclusive Los Angeles private high school, Harvard School for Boys (no connection to Harvard University and now called Harvard-Westlake). Gamsky was a (relatively) poor boy surrounded by the progeny of the rich, famous, and powerful. The experience left a chip on his shoulder. Upon graduation from high school, he briefly attended university and worked for an investment brokerage. He changed his last name to Hunt to create the impression he was related to the Texas oil billionaires, moved to Chicago, and became a trader on the Chicago Commodities Exchange. He quickly lost all his client's money and was kicked off the exchange. After returning to Los Angeles, Hunt became the leader of a group of high school classmates whose parents were considerably more successful than their children. Hunt created a scheme in which he funded the ill-conceived business schemes of his deadbeat high school friends out of profits from commodity trading. He used his friend's family and social connections to generate investors. It was a Ponzi scheme, in which money from incoming investors was used to create the illusion of profits for earlier investors. All Ponzi schemes are inherently unstable and eventually collapse; the Billionaire Boys Club was more unstable than most because of the high overhead costs of supporting the ill-conceived schemes of a bunch of high-born, incompetent, and shiftless wannabe titans of industry. Hunt added to this mixture a martial arts instructor and bodyguard named Jim Patterson who received the title of security director. It was a tottering tower of conceit, dreams, and deception.

In 1984, Hunt attempted to bring financial stability to the organization by convincing a conman named Ron Levin to invest $5 million in the club. Hunt was getting conned by the more experienced conman Ron. Amid the resulting acrimony, Ron abruptly disappeared. Neither he nor his body has ever been discovered. In his apartment, police found several sheets of paper in which Hunt had written out a detailed, step-by-step plan for the murder, body disposal, and robbery. For example, a portion of the list read:

- Closed blinds
- scan for tape recorder
- tape mouth, handcuff
- put gloves on
- explain situation
- kill dog.[17]

It was a bad thing for a murderer to leave at the crime scene. Hunt also told a dozen members of the group that he and Patterson murdered Ron and buried his body in the desert. Hunt said the plan had been to coerce Ron into signing a check for $1.5 million, make him disappear, and cash the check before the victim's absence was noticed.

Ron's murder failed to bring financial stability to Hunt's club, so he turned his attention to Hedayat Eslaminia. He was the father of a member of Hunt's group who had been a high-ranking official in the shah of Iran's regime. According to some members of the group, the plan was to kidnap Hedayat in San Francisco and use torture to obtain the banking information needed to access hidden funds. This plan, if it was the plan, went awry when Hedayat died of suffocation and heat stroke while being transported to Los Angeles. Hedayat's body was dumped in the desert. As police pressure mounted, members of the group started pointing fingers at each other. One led police to Hedayat's skeleton. Police had two murders to deal with – one a no-body case and one for which remains had been found.

It was a legal mess. Hunt first went to trial for Ron Levin's murder. He argued Ron was alive and hiding from authorities to avoid prosecution for fraud. A few witnesses were produced to claim they had seen the missing man. None were particularly credible. For example, one was a young woman from Tucson, New Mexico. She had read a magazine article about the case, and decided she had seen a man matching the description at a service station two months earlier. Hunt claimed the notes found in Ron's apartment were an outline for a movie script. Members of the Billionaire Boys Club testified about Hunt's disclosures and activities. Hunt was convicted. Patterson was then tried for the same murder. Two trials resulted in hung juries. Patterson pleaded guilty to being an accessory after the fact and was sentenced to time served, which had amounted to three and a half years.

The trials for Hedayat Eslaminia's death were more convoluted. Two members of the group were convicted on the testimony of a third member who had immunity. At a separate trial, Hunt defended himself. His trial turned into a circus. Hunt claimed he and his colleagues had been hired by Hedayat to smuggle him out of his apartment to evade hit men sent by the Ayatollah Khomeini. Hunt claimed that Hedayat reached Los Angeles alive, but was killed by the key prosecution witness – the member of the club granted immunity in exchange for his testimony. After a trial lasting months and costing millions, the jury split. A mistrial was declared. In part because Hunt was already serving a life's sentence for Ron's murder, the prosecution abandoned further efforts. A murder charge against Patterson was withdrawn. The murky result of Hunt's trial formed the basis of an appeal for the two already convicted. After serving a decade in prison, their convictions were overturned. Protected from further prosecution by the double jeopardy rule, Patterson gave a television interview admitting guilt for both Ron Levin and Hedayat Eslaminia. Hunt remains in prison for Ron's murder. His numerous appeals dragged on until 2016 when the United States Court of Appeals (Ninth Circuit) issued a terse, four-page, decision saying that "in light of the 'overwhelming evidence' of Hunt's guilty and the state court's factual findings" the conviction was "reasonable."[18] Hunt then turned his attention to attempting to obtain a grant of parole eligibility from California's governor.[19] He and his supporters have an online petition on Change.Org which (as of September 2022) had gathered over 28,000 signatures.[20]

Joe Hunt took a lot of ethical shortcuts in attempts to get rich. There were two synergistic effects that led to murder. The first came when he made himself the leader of a group distinguished by the privilege of their upbringing rather than talent or a work ethic. This created a situation fraught with ethical quagmires and desperation. The next synergistic component was the addition of Jim Patterson to the group. On his own, Patterson was a harmless security guard. When combined with Hunt and the Billionaire Boys Club, he admitted becoming the triggerman in Ron Levin's murder and a participant in the quasi-accidental death of Hedayat Eslaminia.

The prosecution's case for these murders was based on circumstantial evidence and finger-pointing testimony from members of the Billionaire Boys Club. Rats do flee sinking ships. The presence or absence of the victim's body was irrelevant. Hunt was convicted of murder in the case where the body was never found, but avoided conviction in the case where an accomplice led police to the victim's remains.

Synergistic Killers and Body Disposal

We have examined three synergistic no-body cases in detail in order to illustrate the flavor of kinds of killings. They are weird. Synergy can produce strange and evil outcomes. Homicidally synergistic groupings are rare, but they are well represented in no-body cases.

Richard Ford and Robert Von Villas were decorated Vietnam War veterans and well-regarded officers in the Los Angeles Police Department. They became friends. Journalist Jan Golab tells how they then launched a criminal career that included insurance fraud, armed robbery of a jewelry store, and operating a dial-a-prostitute service called "Classy Ladies."[21] Within a few years of coming together, Ford and Von Villas graduated to homicide when Janie Ogilvie paid the pair $20,000 to get rid of her estranged husband, Thomas Weed.[22] Thomas disappeared in February 1983. He has never been seen again, and his remains have never been found.

Von Villas took out a $100,000 life insurance policy on an exotic dancer. On July 7, 1983, he established an alibi while Ford set off to kidnap and murder the dancer. The plan was to dump her body in an area where the bodies of sex trade workers were often found. Von Villas and Ford knew police would assume their victim had been killed by a client. Fortunately for the dancer, Ford recruited a friend to help with the heavy lifting. The friend went to police. As Ford waited for his opportunity to kill, he was under surveillance and his conversation with his helper was being recorded.[23] The resulting audio recording resulted in an avalanche of criminal charges, including a murder charge for the disappearance of Thomas Weed. Von Villas and Ford were convicted in this no-body homicide case based on testimony from Ogilvie and an intermediary who had put her in touch with the two police officers, large deposits of cash into Ford's bank account, circumstantial evidence about preparations and, in Ford's case, a recording of a conversation held with his wife while he was in jail waiting for trial. The two had separate juries, but, for the most part, heard the same evidence. Only Ford's jury heard his taped conversation with his wife. This process generated a long series of unsuccessful appeals by Von Villas after one of his jurors admitted that, during deliberations, she had seen a newspaper headline announcing Ford's conviction.[24]

Sante Singhres[25] was a con artist, kleptomaniac, and part-time prostitute who managed to snare, for her third husband, a millionaire hotel developer a few decades her senior. With this marriage, she became Stante Kimes and achieved her goal of financial security. In 1975, the two had a son, Kenneth. Marriage, motherhood, and financial security did not change Kimes. She continued practicing theft and arson, with a specialty in insurance fraud. In 1985, Kimes was arrested and convicted for "involuntary servitude" – that is, slavery – for her treatment of household servants.[26] Kimes promised young Mexican women jobs and illegally smuggled them into the United States. Instead of paying them, Kimes kept them imprisoned behind locked doors and beat them into submission with wire coat hangers. She got five years in a federal prison. Kimes was twisted and dishonest her entire adult life. It took her husband's death and her son's graduation from college to turn Sante Kimes homicidal.

Kimes's husband died of a heart attack in 1994. Because she feared his children from a previous marriage would inherit, Sante Kimes hid his death from family members and authorities while using her forgery skills to loot the estate. Her dead husband had been secretive, paranoid, and duplicitous. Locating and accessing his wealth was not easy. While Sante Kimes was working on this task, Kenneth Kimes finished college. He partnered with his mother for fraud, murder, and incest. The first person probably murdered was a bank official in the Bahamas. He disappeared in 1996 while investigating Kimes's suspicious financial transactions. Kenneth Kimes later told police he and his mother drugged the banker, drowned him in a bathtub, and dumped his body into the ocean. Sante Kimes denied this story. No charges were ever filed. The next homicide came in March 1998. Sante Kimes forged David Kazdin's name to obtain and appropriate a $280,000 loan. When the bank wanted repayment from Kazdin, he was unhappy. Kenneth Kimes shot Kazdin in the head. Mother and son forced a homeless man they enslaved to help with body disposal. Kazdin's body was discovered in a garbage dumpster, which provoked a prompt investigation focusing on the Kimes duo. They fled to Florida, committing a series of frauds along the way. While in Florida, the two looked for promising targets and identified Irene Silverman, an elderly wealthy ex-ballet dancer who operated a small, expensive residential hotel in Manhattan. Kenneth Kimes paid $6,000 to rent a room for a month. A few days later, Kimes used a stun gun on Irene, strangled her, transported the body to Hoboken, New Jersey, and used a garbage dumpster for disposal. The dumpster was emptied before the body was discovered, so Irene's remains have never been recovered.

Irene's disappearance was quickly noticed and immediately treated as a homicide investigation.[27] Irene had been suspicious of her new tenant, so friends and staff at her hotel pointed police at a prime suspect.[28] Police had difficulty in finding him. Kenneth Kimes was already in jail. On the same day Irene was murdered, police pursuing the Kimes for David Kazdin's murder caught up with them and made an arrest. The two investigations had their own synergistic effect. The pursuit for David's murder resulted in police finding Sante Kimes's notebooks documenting her preparations for Irene's death. The murderous mother-and-son team was tried and convicted in New York for Irene's murder – and 117 other charges, including robbery, burglary, conspiracy, forgery, and grand larceny. Jury members told the media that the case was so overwhelming they voted for conviction on the first poll; no discussion was needed to achieve unanimity. Then California had its turn for David's murder. Sante and Kenneth Kimes presented a common front against the prosecution for the New York trial, but California had the death sentence. Kenneth Kimes agreed to confess, plead guilty, and testify against his mother in exchange for the prosecution not seeking the death penalty against either of them. Sante Kimes proclaimed her innocence until her death in 2014. By her version, she was the victim of a vast conspiracy by police, prosecutors, judges, her defense lawyers, and, ultimately, her own son.[29] Left unexplained was the motive all these people would have to persecute her. The case generated four books,[30] and two made-for-television movies[31], including one with the counterintuitive casting of Mary Tyler Moore playing Sante Kimes.

Synergistic no-body cases are fodder for book publishers and movie makers.

In 2000, Jerry Williams was murdered by his best friend, Brian Winchester, as part of a conspiracy with Jerry's wife, Denise. Winchester attempted to drown Jerry while duck hunting on Lake Seminole, Florida. When the attempt failed, Winchester used a shotgun. Winchester transported Jerry's body and buried it miles away. Authorities concluded Jerry drowned and his body eaten by alligators. Winchester and Denise Williams married and split a million-dollar insurance payout. The case generated a book[32] and became an episode of the cable television show *Disappeared* on the *Investigation Discovery* channel.

Another book was generated in Canada when spoiled rich kid Dellen Millard and his sidekick Mark Smich graduated from thrill-seeking robberies to thrill-seeking murders.[33] Millard prepared for their murders by buying a portable crematorium designed for disposing of road-killed deer. This case will be examined in more detail in chapter 12.

Understanding Synergistic No-Body Homicides

The psychology of synergistic killers was first captured by Truman Capote in his "non-fiction novel" *In Cold Blood.* While in jail, Richard Hickok was told a fanciful story of a farmer keeping large amounts of cash in his home. Upon his release, Hickok recruited another former inmate, Perry Smith, to rob the farmer. The plan called for killing all potential witnesses to avoid discovery. It was only partially successful. The story of hidden wealth was a lie; as a robbery, the venture was unsuccessful. The plan for mass murder was more successful. The four members of the Clutter family were killed. Hickok and Perry were captured, convicted, and hanged. The investigation was the exact opposite of a no-body case; it began when four dead bodies were discovered in their home. However, Capote captured the essential nature of most homicidal synergistic combinations. A somewhat twisted person with a dominant personality finds someone who is submissive, manipulatable, and willing to do the actual killing.[34]

Synergistic killings frequently become no-body cases. In part, this is because they are often the subject of detailed planning. We have seen that both Joe Hunt and Sante Kimes even committed their planning to paper. Their detailed "to-do" lists did not have "destroy list" as the last item; their notes helped prosecutors get convictions. In addition to planning and preparation, synergistic killings are likely to include body disposal for operational reasons. With synergistic killings, there are two murderers involved. It is easier for two people to handle the dead-weight of a body than it is for someone acting alone.

By definition, synergistic killings involve more than one person. This means that as legal pressure mounts, team unity is placed under great strain. A classical "prisoner's dilemma" situation arises. If the killers remain united in their denial, chances of any conviction are lessened. When conviction appears likely, the established legal principle is "he who talks first gets the best deal." The first to confess can shape the prosecutorial theory of the crime and the narrative told to the jury. Finger-pointing testimony creates both opportunities and challenges for prosecutors. They get confirmation of collective guilt, but disputes over individual culpability. Kirby Archer and Guillermo Zarabozo agreed they had intended to hijack the boat. Each blamed the other for murdering the crew. Joe Hunt recruited a crowd of accomplices for the kidnapping of Hedayat Eslaminia. When kidnapping turned to homicide, a program was needed to try to make sense of the finger pointing. Sante and Kenneth Kimes remained united in denial during their trial for the murder of Irene Silverman, but son blamed mother for instigating the murder of David Kazdin. Darren Hossencofft departed from the standard script. At Linda Henning's trial, he attempted to protect her by assuming the blame (and pointing to someone else as the actual killer). However, his testimony was so bizarre it probably helped convict Henning. Sometimes rupture of the pair of killers is the cause, rather than the result, of arrests. After getting away with killing Jerry Williams for a dozen years, Brian Winchester and Denise Williams got divorced. Winchester did not deal with this well. He kidnapped Williams – possibly with the intention of killing her. After he was sentenced to 20 years for this kidnapping, Winchester aired his grievances about the fate of their homicidal partnership. Denise Williams joined him in prison.

Synergistic killings are rare, but are disproportionately represented in no-body cases. The personality mixtures producing the lethal reaction are interesting, if not outright bizarre. As a result, these kinds of no-body cases receive a lot of media attention. In almost every case, at least one book gets written. Often there are several. Made-for-television movies and true-crime podcasts of these cases abound. This media attention has shaped people's perception of no-body cases. As we saw in Chapters 4–6, most no-body cases are more banal, but a man strangling his wife and burying her body or a parent throwing the corpse of a beaten child into the garbage is just not as interesting.

Notes

1 Cope, Carol Soret, *Murder on the High Seas: The True Story of the Joe Cool's Tragic Final Voyage* (New York, NY: Berkley, 2011).

2 Federal Bureau of Investigation, "Murder on the High Seas: The Strange, Sad Tale of Joe Cool," February 22, 2009. https://archives.fbi.gov/archives/news/stories/2009/february/joecool_022609.

3 "Hearing Scheduled for Arkansas Man Accused in Boat Killing," *Arkansas Democrat-Gazette*, July 17, 2008.

4 Anderson, Curt, "Inmate Says Suspect Told of Role on Boat," *Miami Herald-Tribune*, December 22, 2007.

5 Weaver, Joe, "Man Convicted in Killings," *South Florida Sun Sentinel*, February 20, 2009.

6 USA v. Kirby Archer, "Criminal Complaint," USDC Southern District of Florida, Case No. 07-3200RLD, September 26, 2007.
7 Cope, *Murder on the High Seas.*
8 Anderson, Curt, "Boat Suspect's Ex-wife Speaks Out," *Miami Herald-Tribune*, September 28, 2007.
9 Archer v. Archer, Arkansas Court of Appeals, Division III, Case CA06-486. July 31. 2007.
10 "Synergy," *Oxford English Dictionary* (Oxford, UK: Clarendon Press, 1989).
11 Horner, Mark, *September Sacrifice* (New York, NY: Kensington, 2004).
12 Springer, John, "Reptilian Queens, UFOs, a Cancer Cure: New Mexico Murder Trial Begins," *CNN Justice*, September 26, 2002.
13 "Prosecutor: N.M. Defendant Claimed She Ate Victims Flesh," *CNN Justice*, January 7, 2003.
14 Horton, Sue, *The Billionaire Boys Club: Rich Kids, Money and Murder* (New York, NY: St. Martin's Press, 1989). Sullivan, Randall, *The Price of Experience: Money, Power, Image and Murder in Los Angeles* (New York, NY: Atlantic Monthly Press, 1996).
15 *Billionaire Boys Club* directed by Marvin J. Chomsky (NBC, 1987).
16 *Billionaire Boys Club* directed by James Cox (Vertical Entertainment, 2018).
17 Gray, Malcolm and Ann Gregor, "Murder and Intrigue, California Style," *MacLean's Magazine*, February 16, 1987.
18 Hunt v. Virga, United States Court of Appeal, Ninth Circuit, No. 13-56207 (2016).
19 Zabrecky, George, "Billionaire Boys Club Joe Hunt Seeks Cut in Life Sentence," *WTVQ-DT*, October 22, 2018.
20 "Free Joe Hunt," Change.Org. https://www.change.org/p/to-the-governor-of-california-free-joe-hunt. Accessed September 28, 2022.
21 Golab, Jan, *The Dark Side of the Force: A True Story of Corruption and Murder in the LAPD* (New York, NY: The Atlantic Monthly Press. 1993).
22 Harris, Michael, "Woman Confesses to Hiring Two Policemen to Kill Husband," *United Press International*, July 18, 1984.
23 Golab, *Dark Side*, 158–168.
24 People v. Von Villas, Court of Appeal, Second District, Division 7, California, No. BO33751 (October 9, 1992); People v. Von Villas, Court of Appeal, Second District, Division 7, California, No. B041110 (November 16, 1992); People v. Von Villas, 36 Cal.App.4th 1425 (Cal. Ct. App. 1995); Robert Von Villas *v.* Kathleen Allison, 11-56396 (9th Cir. 2014).
25 Havill, Adrian, *The Mother, The Son, and the Socialite: A True Story of a Mother-Son Crime Spree* (New York, NY: St. Martins, 1999); King, Jeanne, *Dead End: The Crime Story of the Decade – Murder, Incest and High-Tech Thievery* (New York, NY: M. Evans and Company, 2002); McQuillan, Alice, *They Call Them Grifters: The True Story of Sante and Kenneth Kimes* (New York, NY: Onyx, 2000); Walker, Kent and Mark Schone, *Song of a Grifter: The Twisted Tale of Sante and Kenny Kimes, the Most Notorious Con Artists in America* (New York, NY: William Morrow, 2001); Andrews, Suzanna, "The Story of Sante Kimes: Mother, Murderer and Criminal Mastermind, *Vanity Fair*, March 2000; McFadden, Robert D. and Frank Bruni, "A FAMILY PORTRAIT: A Special Report: A Twisted Tale of Deceit, Fraud and Violence," *New York Times*, July 14, 1998.
26 Walsh, Elsa, "Woman Convicted of Taking Furs Arrested on Slavery Charge," *Washington Post*, August 7, 1985.
27 McFadden, Robert D., "Search Fins No Trace of Missing Widow," *New York Times*, August 28 1998.
28 Barnes, Julian, "Police Say Socialite and a Suspect Argued," *New York Times*, July 11, 1998.
29 Feuer, Alan, "Sante Kimes Dies in Prison at 79; Killed and Swindled With Her Son," *New York Times*, May 22, 2014.
30 Havill, *The Mother, The Son, and the Socialite;* King, *Dead End;* McQuillan, *They Call Them Grifter;* Walker and Schone, *Song of a Grifter.*
31 *Like Mother, Like Son: The Strange Story of Sante and Kenny Kimes.* Arthur Allan Seidelman, director (New York, NY: CBS, 2001); *A Little Thing Called Murder*, Richard Benjamin, director (New York, NY: Lifetime TV, 2006).
32 Epstein, Steven B. (2020) *Evil at Lake Seminole: The Shocking True Story Surrounding the Disappearance of Mike Williams* (Baker City, OR: Black Lyon Publishing).
33 Brocklehurst, Ann (2019) *Dark Ambition: The Twisted Pact of Serial Killers Dellen Millard and Mark Smich* (Toronto, ON: Penguin).
34 Capote, Truman, *In Cold Blood* (New York, NY: Random House, 1966).

11

BLACK BOX EXPLANATIONS AND PROSECUTING NO-BODY HOMICIDES

The previous seven chapters examined different types of no-body homicides. Three were based on the nature of the relationship between killer and victim: intimate partner homicides, homicides of children by guardians, and people engaged in commercial sex. The next two typologies were defined by motive. Members of criminal organizations kill for greed, to maintain secrecy, to get revenge, and to eliminate competition. Sexually motivated serial killers murder for pleasure. The final two typologies of no-body cases are situational killings. Someone responds to a midlife crisis by turning to homicide, or a deadly synergistic effect is created by the intermingling of different types of pathological personalities.

Categorization is a good first step, but does not complete the journey to understanding. Swedish biologist Carl Linnaeus created a foundation for modern biology by developing a taxonomy system for plants and animals, but it took another century before Charles Darwin provided an explanation for the process by which each type of living thing came into being. In this chapter, we move from categorization and description to understanding processes.

Homicide Prosecution as Narratives and Black Boxes

In homicide trials, the prosecutor uses testimony from witnesses to construct a narrative. Each witness tells a fragment of the story. The more seamless the narrative, the more compelling the story. The more compelling the story, the more likely a conviction.

The best-selling author of western novels Louis L'Amour always started his stories in the middle of the action. This gets the readers' attention. From there, past and future are filled in to create a narrative. Most prosecutors take the same approach when presenting a homicide case to a jury.[1] The first witness in most homicide trials is the person who discovered the body or the first police officer to respond to the call. From there, the prosecutor establishes how a living person became a corpse. This is based on medical evidence from an autopsy. A pathologist or coroner explains the physical trauma that snuffed out life; how the victim was shot through the heart, or raped and strangled, or stabbed twenty-three times, or beaten over the head with a blunt object. Evidence from the body describes the last moments of the victim's life. It conveys the horror of the event. Cuts on the hands or skin under the fingernails tell a story of struggle and resistance. Semen tells a story of sexual assault. Multiple wounds tell a story of savage rage. Once this chapter describing the physical act of killing has been told, the prosecutor calls other witnesses

DOI: 10.4324/9781003372134-11

to establish what happened leading up to the killing and what the accused did afterward. The investigation of "self-solver" homicides is labor intensive for police because of the need to fill in this narrative. Police might know immediately who committed the crime, but they need to provide the prosecutor with enough evidence to construct a narrative. What was the motive? How was the weapon obtained? What did the suspect do afterward? A good narrative does more than allow a jury to deliver a verdict. It determines what charges are laid. The story determines the legally appropriate charge and the legally appropriate punishment after conviction. The narrative establishes whether there was intentionality, premeditation, and aggravating or extenuating circumstances. A hole in the story can result in acquittal. So too can the full story. What first looks like murder can look like non-culpable self-defense once the full story is told.

This narrative does not work in no-body cases. There is no body to mutely tell a story of pain, struggle, despair, and death. The prosecutor must use a different approach in a no-body case. The lack of a body to open the narrative of the victim's death necessitates starting with a "black box."

A "black box" explanation shows that a known input creates a predictable output. The mechanism creating the transformation remains unknown – hence the term "black box." We cannot see what happened inside the box, but for practical purposes this is irrelevant. What matters is the certainty with which output follows input. Think of a light switch. The function of a light switch is to complete or disrupt the flow of electricity to a light bulb which then turns "on" or "off." The mechanism for a light switch is encased and remains invisible to the user. It is a black box. There are several kinds of mechanisms used in light switches. The first effective mechanism was a "quick-break" system developed in 1884. In 1916, a "toggle switch" was invented. About four decades later, a "mercury switch" appeared on the market. In the 1970s, electronic switches began to replace earlier types.[2] For someone wanting to turn on a light, this variation is irrelevant. Unless we work as electricians, we just need to know whether the light turns on or off when we flick the switch.

In the absence of a body, prosecutors in no-body homicide cases must use a black box explanation for the crime. A person was present – the light was on. The suspect flicked the switch. The person was gone – the light was off. The story of homicide can be told even if the chapter describing the killing is missing. A conviction can be obtained without proving whether the victim was shot, strangled, stabbed, smothered, beaten, poisoned, or killed in some other way. The same applies to body disposal. It is not necessary to prove whether the body was burned, buried, dumped in the ocean, thrown into a garbage dumpster, or dissolved in acid. The core of a no-body case is the black box mechanism of "There. Not there."

An important early legal case establishing the use of black box analysis came in England in 1854. A man named Burton was found in a spice warehouse with a pocket full of pepper. He argued he could not be convicted of theft since nobody had seen him steal the pepper. The judge disagreed, saying,

> if a man go into London Docks sober … and comes out of one of the cellars very drunk, wherein are a million gallons of wine, I think that would be reasonable evidence that he had stolen some of the wine in that cellar, though you could not prove that any wine was stolen or any wine missed.[3]

Let us make this abstract discussion more concrete by looking at the disappearance of Gail Bierenbaum from New York in 1985.[4] Her husband, Dr. Robert Bierenbaum, told police he and his wife quarreled. Gail left their apartment and was never seen again. The police were suspicious of Bierenbaum. Despite this, for almost 15 years their suspicions did not result in criminal charges. Even if Gail's absence demonstrated death, police could not build a narrative for a murder. There were no signs of struggle in the Bierenbaums' apartment. Gail had a history of mental health and substance abuse problems. Suicide was one possibility. Misadventure on the then-mean streets of New York was another. If Bierenbaum was the killer, there was no clue as to how he disposed of her body. Bierenbaum had motive and opportunity to kill his wife, but police could not tell a story.

After a decade and a half, Bierenbaum was charged.[5] What changed?

The passage of time increased the certainty Gail was dead. In most criminal cases, the passage of time degrades and weakens evidence. In no-body cases, it has the opposite effect on the question of death. It was plausible to argue that Gail was alive after a disappearance of a week. Or a month. Maybe even a year. After a decade and a half, absence almost certainly meant she was dead. The light had been turned off in 1985.

Bierenbaum was shown to have his hand near the light switch. A person not in the room cannot plausibly be accused of flicking the light switch. In this case, establishing Bierenbaum's proximity was easy. He was the last person known to be with Gail. By his own statement, they had been quarreling.[6]

One significant new piece of evidence was discovered before charges were laid. Bierenbaum, an enthusiastic amateur pilot, rented a plane the day Gail disappeared. He had not filed a flight plan or told the police about it. He lied to them about his activities that day. The obvious conclusion was that Bierenbaum used his unreported plane trip to dispose of Gail's body. Police and prosecutorial theorized he dumped her in the ocean.[7] Perhaps. Journalist Kieren Crowley made a plausible argument she was dumped into a water reservoir. In 2020, the prosecution theory was verified – Bierenbaum told a parole board that Gail's body went into the Atlantic Ocean.[8] For the purposes of obtaining a conviction, it did not matter. Because of black box reasoning, the location did not have to be proven. There. Secret plane rental. Not there. Go to prison.

The discovery that Bierenbaum surreptitiously rented a plane the day Gail disappeared formed the evidentiary justification for charges after 15 years. That alone was not enough. Learning about the secret plane flight allowed prosecutors to infer Bierenbaum was responsible for disposing of Gail's body. It did not establish her death or show how she died. To overcome this hurdle, prosecutors in New York City needed to change their orientation. For decades, they believed a body and a relatively complete narrative was necessary to prosecute for homicide. With the successful prosecution of Sante and Kenneth Kimes (discussed in Chapter 10), this changed.[9] The Kimes case seems to have convinced this prosecutorial office of the utility of black box reasoning. Bierenbaum was charged without any new evidence about how he killed his wife. Police and prosecutors theorized Bierenbaum strangled her, but this was just an informed guess. With black box reasoning, it did not matter HOW he killed her, just that she was gone.

We will discuss changes to technology that contributed to the increase in the number of no-body homicide prosecutions in Chapter 12, but the adoption of black box reasoning was central. The slow, halting, hesitant acceptance that a seamless narrative is unnecessary for a conviction means fewer people get away with murder. It also has dangers. The black box can contain unexpected surprises and hidden processes. Police must shrink the scope of the black box as much as possible. If possible, they also want to fill in what happened within the black box.

One reason police and prosecutors want to fill in the black box mechanism is that there are degrees of culpability. The transformation of "there" to "not there" is absolute, but criminal culpability is not. Dead is dead, but guilt is more nuanced. Canadian and American criminal codes all recognize a range of culpability stretching from almost-accidental manslaughters to premeditated murders. A black box is not good at distinguishing these graduations.

Let us look at the case of Darin Randle.[10] In 2008, Randle partnered with Dennis Cornish in a marijuana grow operation in British Columbia. Dennis abruptly disappeared. Randle was the last person seen with him. Prior to the disappearance, Randle texted and phoned Dennis several times per day, but stopped the day of the disappearance, before anyone else knew that Dennis was gone. Randle assumed sole operation of the grow op and started using Dennis's property. Randle bragged to his girlfriend about new affluence. As a black box case, it seemed straightforward. Randle was standing beside the light switch. The light went out. Randle appeared to know about Dennis's disappearance before anyone else and profited from the knowledge. Many juries would convict Randle of murder in this circumstantial case. This would have been a mistake. Dennis was indeed dead – he was shot – but when police opened the black box, they discovered Dennis's death was not due to murder.

Police used the Mr. Big technique to open the black box of Dennis's disappearance. In a Mr. Big operation (discussed in detail in Chapter 14) undercover police officers trick a suspect into believing he is being recruited into a powerful criminal gang. At a job interview with the gang's boss ("Mr. Big"), the suspect is told the gang's police contacts revealed the suspect is under police investigation. The resulting "heat" precludes membership until the problem is cleaned up. Mr. Big offers to help, but says he needs full details to ensure a successful cover-up. In several hundred cases, Mr. Big operations have generated video-taped, detailed disclosures that juries find fascinating.[11] In this case, Randle told Mr. Big the two partners were arguing. Dennis produced a gun to threaten Randle. The two struggled; the gun went off; Dennis died. As described, the death was a combination of self-defense and accident, but Randle saw an opportunity to profit from his friend's misfortune. He burned Dennis's body, threw the ashes in a garbage dumpster, and threw the gun into a lake. With Dennis gone, his property was available for appropriation. Randle was guilty of many unsavory acts following his friend's death, but does not appear to have been a murderer. He was convicted of committing an indignity to a body,[12] but never charged with murder.

In this case, the Mr. Big operation acted as a different kind of black box. In most airplanes, an (almost) indestructible flight recorder ("black box") stores data about the plane's operation. If the plane crashes, the flight recorder allows investigators to determine whether the crash was caused by engine failure, pilot error, or some combination. The Mr. Big operation served as a flight recorder. It got Randle off an impending murder charge.

Eyewitness testimony can serve as the airplane flight recorder to fill in the narrative between "there" and "not there," but reliable eyewitnesses are rare in homicide cases. Murder, like sexual intercourse, is usually conducted in private. Most potential eyewitnesses are the killer(s) and accomplices. They tend to be profoundly unreliable eyewitnesses. During police interrogation or court-room testimony, they will lie to shift blame or minimize their guilt. One interesting feature of Randle's case is that if he told the same story while being interrogated or at trial, he probably would not have been believed.[13] His story was implausible and destruction of the body made verification impossible. We saw how John Wallace and Thomas Capano claimed the death of their victim was accidental. Juries dismissed these claims, inferring that the effort required to burn a body or dump it into the ocean probably indicated guilt. The difference for Randle was the circumstances of his disclosure. In talking to Mr. Big, there was no reason for him to minimize his culpability. If anything, he had reason to exaggerate. Tough guys are more likely to be accepted into criminal gangs. If Randle had been arrested before telling his story, he may have joined John Wallace and Thomas Capano in being convicted of murder.

In most no-body cases some things will remain unknown. Deductive logic can fill in gaps to a degree, but this remains a bit speculative. Wrong conclusions can be drawn. If there is a gathering and the lights in the room suddenly go out, people assume someone turned off the light. This inference is usually correct, but sometimes there is a power outage.

Deductive inferences can be drawn from actions associated with body disposal. Robert Bierenbaum's secret charter of an airplane caused police, prosecutors, and, ultimately, a jury to conclude he dumped his wife's body in the ocean. It was a reasonable inference, but not an inevitable conclusion. He could have buried her somewhere or put her in a garbage dumpster.

Gary Rawlings also rented a plane the day his ex-wife, Sally Rawlings disappeared in Oklahoma City. He disconnected the instrument recording flight time and twice purchased fuel in Texas. Police inferred from this that Rawlings dumped Sally's body in the Gulf of Mexico. The inference was supported by blood in the plane. This was in 1982, before DNA testing was available. However, the blood type was the same as Sally's and different from Rawling's.[14] This evidence combined with black box reasoning resulted in a quick charging decision and a conviction.[15]

Kristina Sandoval disappeared in 1995. Over a decade passed before her estranged husband, John Sandoval, was charged.[16] How Sandoval killed his ex-wife and where he disposed of her body remained unknown. When questioned by police following Kristina's disappearance, Sandoval had muddy shoes and there was a muddy shovel in the trunk of his car. The jury accepted the prosecution's inference that this likely meant he buried Kristina.[17] Sandoval was convicted in 2010. Six years later, Sandoval won an appeal because the trial judge inappropriately allowed hearsay and similar-fact evidence. However, the appeal court ruled the muddy shovel was admissible as evidence from which inferences could be drawn.[18] In 2017, rather than face another trial, Sandoval confessed and led police to Kristina's body.[19] He had taken her corpse to a cemetery, deepened an open grave, and deposited Kristina. Cemetery workers later put a coffin on top of Kristina and filled in the grave. The deductive inference from the muddy shovel was correct.

Bierenbaum, Rawling, and Sandoval were convicted in large part because evidence created a logical inference that they disposed of the body of the missing person. This made the transition from "there" to "not there" sinister.

While police and prosecutors attempt to fill in the black box of disappearance, a challenge can be linking the suspect to the case. Let us return to our analogy of a light being turned off. Usually, but not always, this means someone flicked the switch. If there is only one other person in the room and they were beside the switch, deduction is easy and probably accurate. If there are more people in the room, it gets complicated. To assign blame, we must know who was close to the switch. If lighting was bad to begin with or there was movement in and out of the room, it can be difficult to determine who was near the switch. The light can be wired to multiple switches. Deciding at whom to yell "turn on the damn light, you idiot" can be complicated. One way of narrowing the field is to look at past behavior. Chronic practical jokers are most likely to be blamed.

In some no-body cases, murderers make it easy for police. When Kenneth Kimes murdered Irene Silverman, it took police only hours to identify him as the primary suspect. He had rented a room under false pretenses, behaved suspiciously, left a record of his activities, and was being pursued by police for another homicide. Detectives in New York did not need to be the reincarnation of Sherlock Holmes. It was similar when Abraham Cooper murdered Douglas Snider. The two had been quarreling. Cooper invited Douglas to a meeting. Douglas never returned. There was blood in Cooper's office and in the trunk of his car. From the time of Douglas's disappearance, police needed only three weeks to build a case sufficient to arrest, charge, and convict Cooper.

But sometimes placing the right suspect beside the light switch can be difficult.

Let us go back to the case of Etan Patz discussed in Chapter 5. Etan disappeared while walking to the bus stop. It was correctly assumed he had been killed. But who was standing beside the light switch? Who changed Etan from a living boy to a missing corpse?

The first suspect was Etan's father. The second suspect was a handyman contractor working in the neighborhood. There was no evidence against them other than proximity. The next suspect was a known pedophile dating a woman previously hired to walk Etan to school. The pedophile made a great suspect. He had both proximity and a history of bad behavior. Etan's parents even won a wrongful death civil suit against him, but there was another person present when the switch on Etan's life was flicked. Someone nobody knew was there. Thirty-two years after Etan disappeared, Pedro Hernandez explained how and where he killed Etan.

When the absence of a corpse precludes telling how the killing occurred, good documentation of pre-death activity makes it easier to obtain a conviction. Kimes put himself in Irene's presence for a few weeks before the killing and behaved suspiciously. Cooper had a long history of conflict with Douglas and had summoned him to a meeting. When police learned of this history, they had no difficulty surmising what happened next. They did not know whether Irene or Douglas had been shot, stabbed, strangled, suffocated, or beaten to death, but they did not need to know.

The more precisely police determine the moment of disappearance (and the sooner they do so), the easier it is to identify the most likely suspect. Killers of intimate partners such as Edward Rulloff, Leonard Scott, David Woods, John Bayerl, Michael Clark, Eugene Zapata, Paul Calnen, Perry March, Robert Bierenbaum, and so many others worked to delay the filing of any missing persons' report. This creates time for crime scene cleanup and transfer of financial assets. The passage of time causes evidences to decay; a witness is more likely to remember something they saw yesterday than something three weeks earlier. Delay in filing a missing person's report creates a window during which the victim could have met other potential killers. Robert Bierenbaum delayed filing a missing person's report and told police his wife left the apartment. In the 1980s, the streets of New York were not celebrated for their safety. Police had to consider the possibility Gail was killed somewhere other than her apartment by someone other than her husband.

Pre-killing events and relationships are one way for police to make sense of what happened and who was responsible. Post-offence behavior can create another for police to create a narrative after the black box disappearance. In Chapter 4 we saw how the reactivation of a police investigation a quarter century after Jeanette Zapata's disappearance caused her husband to create an evidence trail by permanently disposing of a body that he had, for a quarter century, merely stored.

The trail of circumstantial evidence back to the killing usually does not take that long for police to gather.

In 2012, a 77-year-old Alberta man named Otto Loose disappeared. Three days later, his car was found in a casino parking lot. There was blood inside. The disappearance was treated as a probable homicide but nothing in Otto's life pointed to a suspect. Despite this, police quickly solved the case. Timmy Engel cashed a $10,000 check drawn on Otto's account and used Otto's ATM card to withdraw more cash. Engel claimed that a mysterious and unidentified "Mike" did the actual killing, but soon gave a detailed confession and was convicted. Engel's efforts to profit from his killing left a clear trail for the police.[20]

Killers who destroy or hide the body of their victims are determined to avoid being punished for their crime. It can backfire on them. Disposing an adult body is hard work. The process of disposal itself takes time and leaves an evidence trail. The additional time needed complicates efforts to construct an alibi. In most cases, proving the suspect destroyed or hid a body is enough to convince a jury the suspect should be convicted of murder.

Let us consider the forensic evidence created by body disposal in some of the cases we have touched on so far in this book.

Adam Strong was caught because his body disposal strategy drew attention. As he flushed pieces of his second victim down the toilet, he plugged the sewer line. His neighbors called a plumber. When police investigated, they found bloodstains from an earlier killing.

John Wallace left the brain of Wilson Turner in the bottom of a dried well. A charred bone fragment was found in the creek near the site of Wilson's incineration.

When the body of Dorothy Woods was eventually found, she was wrapped in polyethylene secured with green tape. Her husband purchased both the day Dorothy disappeared and police had found the leftovers in Woods's garage.

After DonaMae Bayerl disappeared, police found blood in the garage and in her husband's car. When DNA testing techniques were developed, Bayerl was arrested and convicted.

Police found gallstones and undissolved human fat in the gravel behind John Haigh's workshop. Inside, they found acid-stained protective gear and a large barrel.

After Dominick Pendino disappeared, police found his blood in the trunk and backseat of a car used by Gregory Chrysler. Police also learned Chrysler had borrowed a shovel the day of the disappearance.

The recovery of the large picnic cooler, complete with bullet holes in it, contributed to the conviction of Thomas Capano.

After Girly Chow Hossencofft disappeared, police found her clothing wrapped in a tarpaulin – along with some of Linda Henning's hair.

Forensic evidence generated by body disposal and found away from the initial crime scene was significant in 37 percent of the successful prosecutions examined for this book. In other cases, body disposal made the original crime scene a lot messier, creating forensic evidence for investigators.

Timothy Shephard strangled his girlfriend, Tynesha Stewart, in his apartment. This is a "clean" way to kill; it usually does not generate significant amounts of forensic evidence. To avoid detection, Shephard went to a hardware store and bought a jig saw. He dismembered Tynesha's body in the bathtub and burned parts of her in a balcony BBQ. He sent other parts down the garburator in the kitchen sink. Other pieces of Tynesha were bagged and tossed in a garbage dumpster. Shephard's body disposal efforts generated far more forensic evidence than did the actual killing. It also undermined his attempt to claim self-defense at trial. After hearing graphic testimony about Tynesha's dismemberment, the jury was in no mood to give Shephard any benefit of doubt; indeed, the trial judge refused to even instruct the jury about the law governing claims of self-defense.[21]

Adult bodies are tough to move. They are heavy and awkward to carry. In 12 percent of the cases examined, the killer killed alone but sought help for body disposal. We have already seen how John Wallace demanded that two of his sharecroppers help pull Wilson Turner's body from the well and burn it. Thomas Capano got his brother to help dispose of the body of his victim while Perry March pressed his father into service. In all these cases, police turned helpers into prosecution witnesses. Loyalty crumbles when confronted with the possibility of prison. In other cases, the helper volunteers the information.

Killers who obtain assistance for body disposal face a long-term problem. They have asked people who are willing to help them. Criminologist Edwin Sutherland noted that people who become "career" criminals learn the technical skills needed to commit crime. As importantly, they acquire an orientation. If someone walks by a jewelry store at night and notices the owner has left the door open, they have several options. They can walk on by. They can close the door. They can call police or try to locate the owner. People who have a criminal orientation will walk into the empty store and fill their pockets.[22]

Let us apply this insight into the killer's choice of a helper for body disposal. Wallace asked people he was accustomed to ordering around; people who were dependent upon him. They were not orientated toward murder. Horrified by what they helped do, Wallace's helpers told police the full story.

Capano and March appealed to family loyalties. Again, the relatives were not orientated to murder. They were willing to testify.

In other cases, the killer chooses an acquaintance he believes will be willing to help – just because. Consider the hypothetical situation. A friend shows up at your house with a body in the trunk of his car. Do you tell him to go away? Do you call the police? Or do you find a shovel and help him bury it? The people who help share a common characteristic. They are prone to getting into trouble with the law. If (when) they get arrested for something else, their knowledge of the murder gives them a "get-out-of-jail-free" card. Police and prosecutors would rather put a murderer in prison than a burglar, thief, or drug dealer. This creates opportunities to make a deal.

In 2016, Bernadine Montgomery disappeared. Police found forensic evidence that the body of the 84-year-old woman lay on her couch for several days before being dragged away. Suspicion focused on David Mariotti, who tried to pawn some of Bernadine's belongings. Mariotti's girlfriend was arrested on credit card fraud charges. She told police that Mariotti enlisted her assistance to drag Bernadine's body from her house and dump it in the Ocala National Forest.[23] Bernadine's body was never found, but Mariotti was convicted of murder.[24] The fraud charges against his girlfriend were dropped.

If the helper participated because of fear, disclosure can occur when it seems safe to do so. In 1982, William Wickline and his girlfriend went to the home of Peggy and Christopher Lerch to collect a debt arising from a drug deal. They collected the money, but Wickline was not satisfied. He handcuffed Christopher, beat him, and cut his throat. Wickline then strangled a sleeping Peggy to eliminate her as a witness. Wickline ordered his girlfriend to help cut up the two bodies and put the pieces in garbage bags. Terrified, she complied.[25] Wickline distributed the body parts to several dumpsters while his girlfriend cleaned up the crime scene. The two murders remained unsolved until Wickline was arrested on an unrelated charge. Once he was behind bars, his girlfriend became talkative with police. She showed them the bloodstained handcuffs, knife, and boots used in the murders. She also showed where Wickline hid Peggy's jewelry. Blood around the edge of the bathtub in Peggy and Christopher's house and body tissue on Wickline's provided more corroboration for the girlfriend's story.[26] Wickstrom was executed in 2004.[27]

Sometimes accomplices are actively involved in the murder as well as the body disposal. In 1992, Elmon Davidson was released from prison in North Carolina. Less than two weeks later, he disappeared. Police received a tip that there was a body in a garbage dumpster. By the time they got to the dumpster, it had been emptied. Police searched through 10,000 tons of garbage, but were unable to find a body. This concluded the matter until Antonio Wrenn was arrested on an unrelated charge. As part of a plea bargain, he told police that Charles Walker killed Elmon in retaliation for an attempted burglary. According to Wrenn, Elmon's murder and body disposal had been a group effort. Walker's girlfriend lured Elmon to her apartment where Walker and two friends tied him up, beat him, and cut his throat. When this failed to kill Elmon, Davidson shot him. Wrenn said he participated in the cleanup. Elmon's body was stuffed in garbage bags and tossed in a dumpster. Everyone named by Wrenn were arrested. All except Walker told the same story and pleaded guilty to charges reflecting different levels of culpability. Walker's girlfriend got off the lightest; she pleaded guilty to an accessory charge and was sentenced to the two years already served. Walker refused to plead guilty to second-degree murder, but the testimony of his girlfriend and his three former friends resulted in a first-degree murder conviction.

Walker was sentenced to death in 1995.[28] He had been convicted solely based on testimony from his accomplices.[29]

There is a long, continuing postscript to this story. Over ten years after being sentenced to death, Walker's conviction was overturned. The prosecutor had failed to disclose the legal difficulties that caused Wrenn's decision to start bargaining with police. Walker's conviction was overturned. Rather than face a new trial, in 2007 he pleaded no-contest and received a 30-year sentence. After receiving credit for time served, Walker was released on parole in 2009. In 2010, Walker was convicted of attempting to murder his ex-girlfriend. After serving over two years for this offense, he was convicted for obtaining property under false pretenses.[30] Release from prison was followed by arrest and conviction for participating in the armed robbery of two jewelry stores.[31]

When a killer gets assistance for murder itself or disposal, he makes himself hostage to the nerves of his accomplice.[32] In 2006, Colorado rancher Patrick Frazee had an affair with a nurse from Idaho. The woman became pregnant. Frazee convinced her to get an abortion and the affair ended. A decade later, Frazee contacted his old lover. She had married and divorced. They resumed the affair. Frazee was engaged to Kelsey Barreth, with whom he had a young daughter. Frazee wanted to get rid of Kelsey. He (untruthfully) told his past-and-present-again lover that Kelsey was abusing the baby. He wanted his girlfriend to kill his fiancé. According to the girlfriend, she agreed but did not follow through. For example, she backed out of commitment to poison Kelsey's coffee.

On Thanksgiving Day, 2018, Frazee phoned his girlfriend to ask for cleanup assistance. He had beaten Kelsey to death with a baseball bat, and her apartment was now messy. Frazee's girlfriend concocted a cover story, drove from Idaho to Colorado, spent four hours cleaning up the gory mess, and helped Frazee burn the body on his ranch. Frazee bought time by using Kelsey's phone to send texts to her mother and her employer to create the impression she was still alive. Cleanup and body disposal completed, the girlfriend took Kelsey's cell phone back to Idaho and sent a text to another man asking, "do you even love me" and a text to Kelsey's boss saying she would not be into work. The purpose was to create an electronic evidence trail away from the scene of the crime.[33]

Frazee's plan worked right up till the moment Kelsey was reported missing. After Kelsey did not return phone calls, her mother and brother flew to Colorado to investigate. They found a deserted apartment and filed a missing person's report. Police began to glower suspiciously at Frazee. They used the record of his cell phone calls to identify the girlfriend in Idaho. Tracking data showed Kelsey's and the girlfriend's cell phones traveled together to Idaho. Kelsey's phone then sent the two strange messages and went black. FBI agents visited the girlfriend, who denied knowing anything. They returned a few days later to accuse her of lying. The girlfriend crumbled and gave a detailed confession, including taking police on a show-and-tell tour of Kelsey's apartment and Frazee's ranch.[34] There were spots of blood in the apartment and fragments of female teeth at the body disposal site. Frazee was arrested and charged.[35] While waiting for trial, he attempted to hire another inmate to kill eight people, including his talkative girlfriend, the lead investigator on the case, and a forensics technician.[36] It is unclear why Frazee recruited his old girlfriend as an accomplice to the murder of his fiancé, but in so doing he made his conviction a certainty.

People who know where bodies are buried can decide to talk to police for very idiosyncratic reasons. After Charles Schmid killed three people in Tucson, New Mexico, and hid their bodies in the desert, he showed the bodies to a friend. Braggers need to brag. Braggees need to talk.[37] The friend was sent to Ohio to live with his grandparents after attempts to get a date crossed into harassment. The friend got homesick and went to police to reveal Schmid's secrets in order to be sent back to Tucson. Schmid's mother hired F. Lee Bailey to get Schmid off the resulting murder charges, but the most famous lawyer of the period struck a plea bargain.[38]

Testimony from accomplices was a key part of 28 percent of the successful prosecutions examined in this study. Testimony from nonparticipating eyewitnesses was presented in 20 percent of these cases. In 4 percent of successful prosecutions, both nonparticipating eyewitnesses and accomplices testified. When a killer involves someone else in the killing or the cleanup, it allows police to pry open the black box.

Conceptualizing the Investigation and Prosecution of No-Body Homicides

Most homicide investigations start with the discovery of a body. When the case comes to trial, the mute story told by the body starts the narrative told to the jury in the middle of the action. It is a great narrative technique, and good narratives get convictions. Police and prosecutors in no-body cases do not have this advantage. To get convictions, they must use a different approach. Unless the killer confesses or brags, they use a black box approach. The person was there. Then they were not. Even if the precise mechanism of this transition is not known, someone flipped a switch. Someone was responsible for the disappearance. The prosecutor then presents evidence placing the suspect in temporal, geographical, and situational proximity to the disappearance. They document events leading up to the disappearance or the evidence trail created by body disposal. Ideally, they do both. Sometimes prosecutors can also use witnesses to fill in the mechanism of the disappearance. Usually, these witnesses will have involvement in the killing or the disposal of the victim's body. Because body disposal is hard work, the killer often recruits helpers. These assistants often become the means by which juries can be told how the victim was killed and how the body was hidden or destroyed. These assistants often convert a "no-body" investigation into a more traditional homicide prosecution by leading investigators to the disposal site, but even when this is not possible their testimony can be crucial.

Notes

1 Ambrose Jr., Charles E., Michael D. Wims, and Jack B. Rubin, *How to Try a Murder Case: Pretrial and Trial Guidelines for Prosecution and Defence* (Washington, DC: American Bar Association, 2012).
2 "Light Switch", *Wikipedia*, August 14, 2022. https://en.wikipedia.org/wiki/Light_switch#:~:text=The%20first%20light%20switch%20employing,circuit%20was%20opened%20or%20closed.
3 R. v. Burton, Dears. C.C. 282.
4 Crowley, Kieren, *The Surgeon's Wife: A True Story of Obsession, Rage and Murder* (New York, NY: St. Martins, 2007); DePaulo, Lisa, "Intimations of Murder," *Vanity Fair*, September, 2000.
5 Roane, Kit R., "Police Charge A Surgeon Murdered Wife in '85," *New York Times*, December 9, 1999.
6 People v. Bierenbaum, 301 A.D.2d 119, 748 N.Y.S.2d 563 (N.Y. App. Div. 2002).
7 Finkelstein, Katherine, "In Trial Without a Body, Prosecutors Put a Theory on Video," *New York Times*, October 17, 2000.
8 Gilbert, Asha C., "Report: Man Confesses He Was 'immature' After Throwing Wife's Body Out of Plane, into the Ocean," *USA Today*, October 21, 2021.
9 Finkelstein, Katherine E., "No Corpse, But Plenty of Precedent," *New York Times*, October 13, 2000.
10 R. v. Randle, 2014 BCSC 1990; R. v. Randle, 2016 BCCA 125.
11 Stobbe, Mark, *The 'Mr. Big' Sting: The Cases, The Killers, The Controversial Confessions* (Toronto, ON: ECW, 2021).
12 R. v. Randle, 2014 BCSC 1990.
13 R. v. Randle, 2014 BCSC 1990.
14 Donovan, Kevin, "Bloodstains Linked to Missing Woman," *The Oklahoman*, June 25, 1983.
15 Rawlings v. State, 740 P.2d 153 (1987.

16 Dunn, Sharon R., *In Tina's Shadow: The True Story of a Murder, a Husband's Guilt, and a Family's 14-Year Vigil for Justice*, 2nd Edition (Greely, CO: CreateSpace Independent Publishing, 2015)

17 Mitchell, Kirk, "Sandoval Found Guilty in Wife's Death," *Denver Post*, August 15, 2010.

18 Dunn, Sharon, "Colorado Court of Appeals ruling on John Sandoval Murder Conviction," *Greeley Tribune*, March 20, 2016.

19 Schladebeck, Jessica, "Colorado Man Pleads Guilty to Killing Wife in 1995, Leads Cops to Remains Hidden Under WWII Vet's Grave," *New York Daily News*, April 1, 2017.

20 R. v. Engel, 2016 ABCA 58.

21 SHEPHERD v. STATE, 14-08-00970-CR (Tex.App.-Houston [14th Dist.] 1-11-2011)

22 Sutherland, Edwin, *Principles of Criminology*, 4th edition (New York, NY: Lippincott, 1947).

23 Stanfield, Frank, "Mariotti's Girlfriend to Testify Against Him in Leesburg Murder," *Ocala Star-Banner*, March 21, 2018.

24 Stanfield, Frank, "David Mariotti Guilty in Murder of Bernadine Montgomery," *Leesburg Daily Commercial*, April 11, 2018.

25 Spencer, Carrie, "Man to Be Put to Death for Murdering People; His Girlfriend Testified They Were Killed over $6,000 Drug Debt; Bodies Were Butchered, Stuffed in Trash," *Akron Beacon Journal*, March 28, 2004.

26 State v. Wickline, 50 Ohio St. 3d 114 (Ohio 1990).

27 Spencer, Carrie, "State Executes Man Involved in Dismemberment Slayings," *The News Herald*, March 31, 2004.

28 State v. Walker, 469 S.E.2d 919 (1996)

29 Amnesty International, "Death Penalty/Legal Concern: Charles Anthony Walker" AI Index: AMR 51/165/2004, November 25,4, 2004.

30 The Charley Project, "Elmon Tito Davidson Jr." https://charleyproject.org/case/elmon-tito-davidson-jr. March 4, 2010.

31 Fowler, Hayley, "$600,000 Armed Heist of Two Kay Jewellers Nets Guilty Verdict for NC Man, Feds Say," *The News & Observer*, December 15 2020.

32 Kackley, Rod (2020) *The Murder of Kelsey Berreth: A Shocking True Crime Story* (Grand Rapids, MI: Lyons Circle Publishing).

33 Kackley, *Murder of Kelsey Berreth*.

34 Fieldstadt, Elisha, "Patrick Frazee Girlfriend Who Testified Against Him in Kelsey Barreth Murder Sentenced to Three Years," *NBC News*, January 28, 2020.

35 Hannah, Jack and Darran Simon, "Patrick Frazee Convicted of Killing His Fiancée, Sentenced to Life without the Possibility of Parole," *CNN News*, November 18, 2019.

36 Maxouris, Christina, "A Former Inmate Testified Patrick Frazee Asked Him to Kill Witnesses in Murder Trial," *CNN News*, November 18, 2019.

37 Bruns, Richard, *I, a Squealer: The Insider's Account of the 'Pied Piper of Tucson Murders* (Ashland, OH: Twin Feather Publishing, 2018).

38 Schafer III, William J., "Murder in the Desert," *Arizona Attorney*, December 2008, pp. 28–34.

12

EXPLAINING SUCCESS

Why Have No-Body Convictions Become More Common?

For a long time, prosecutions and convictions for no-body homicides were extremely rare. This began to change in the 1960s, even though there is no reason to believe the number of no-body homicides suddenly started to increase. In the United States, there were three no-body convictions in the 1950s and 148 five decades later. Similar increases were seen in Canada. The increase in the number of successful no-body prosecutions occurred against a backdrop of declining homicide clearance rates. Marc Riedel and John Jarvis document a linear decline in clearance rates of almost a percentage point per year from 1960 to 1997. In 1960, 92 percent of known homicides resulted in an arrest. By 1997, this dropped to 66 percent.[1] In this century, clearance rates have stabilized but not increased.[2] Canada experienced a similar trend, although not quite as accentuated.[3] Killers remain unpunished for about a third of all known homicides in the United States and for about one quarter of cases in Canada. We have a paradox to explain. Police and prosecutors have gotten BETTER at catching killers who dispose of the body of their victim while they have gotten WORSE at catching killers whose victims' bodies are found.

In this chapter, we will focus on half this equation, namely, the improvement in the justice system's ability to punish killers in no-body cases.

This can be partially accounted for by changing laws and legal doctrine. Edward Rulloff was convicted of kidnapping his missing wife, but not of killing her. His conviction for the murder of his daughter was overturned on appeal. No body, no murder conviction. That simple. Courts began creating new precedents after the Second World War. John Wallace was convicted when police found a small, charred fragment of the body of his victim. L. Ewing Scott was convicted on circumstantial evidence and incriminating post-disappearance behavior. These cases created precedents for prosecutors in subsequent cases. Legislative changes occurred. For example, Section 1204 of the Texas Penal Code stated that "No person shall be convicted of any grade of homicide unless the body of the deceased, or portions of it, are found and sufficiently identified to establish the death of the person charged to have been killed." The Texas legislature abolished this provision in 1974.[4] Similar legislative changes in other jurisdictions made more prosecutions possible.

There is more. Success begets success. Convictions begat more charges. Prosecutors were encouraged by example. Perhaps the best example came in the person of Robert Morgenthau. He was elected as District Attorney for the County of New York (Manhattan) in 1975 after campaigning to crack down on violent crime.[5] In 1985, Robert Bierenbaum murdered his wife

DOI: 10.4324/9781003372134-12

and used a plane to dump her body into the Atlantic Ocean. Morgenthau refused to authorize charges on the belief that a successful prosecution needed a body.[6] In 1998, Kenneth and Sante Kimes murdered Irene Silverman. The case was a classic self-solver. Within hours of her disappearance, police knew Irene was murdered and that Kenneth Kimes was responsible. The overwhelming evidence of guilt caused Morgenthau to allow prosecutors to proceed with a no-body case. This was bad news for Bierenbaum. Almost immediately after the Kimes convictions, charges against Bierenbaum were authorized.[7] Morgenthau learned that successful no-body prosecutions were possible. One conviction can inspire many prosecutors. In predicting the future of no-body prosecutions, Thomas DiBiase concludes,

> As more cases are brought to a close by a guilty plea or conviction, police and prosecutors are becoming more aggressive not only bringing more cases to trial but going through their cold cases to see if they have older no-body cases that can be reinvestigated and closed.[8]

New precedents, legislative change, and increased prosecutorial confidence all contributed to the increased volume of no-body prosecutions. These changes were necessary, but not sufficient, conditions for reducing the ability of killers to get away with murder by disposing the body of their victim. New investigative tools also emerged. The three most important are the growth of bureaucracies, improvements in forensic techniques, and the creation of new communications technologies such as the internet, social media, and cell phones.

Bureaucracy as a Crime-fighting Tool

A century ago, an impediment to prosecuting no-body homicide cases was ease of benign disappearance. Gone did not mean dead. As we saw in Chapter 2, prosecutors bold enough to proceed with charges in no-body cases could be embarrassed by the putative victim returning to life. Juries had good reason to be cautious about convicting for homicide unless someone credible had seen a corpse.

Let us look at changes to the life of the average person. We will focus on the United States, but a similar process unfolded in Canada.

At the beginning of the 20th century, it was difficult to establish that a person had been born. In the United States, the federal government did not begin to establish a standardized birth certificate until 1902. Progress was slow and uneven.[9] In 1943 – when Congress made service in the armed forces and working in many weapons-production industries contingent on proving citizenship – 46 million Americans could not produce a birth certificate.[10] More than a third of all Americans could not document their birth.

In a 1921 report of a payroll robbery, the *New York Times* opined that

> one of the commonest sites in a bank is a young person, sometimes a girl, filling a bag at the paying teller's window with rolls of notes and gold pieces, the 'payroll' of a careless employer and walking out the door and down the street with the utmost unconcern.[11]

This method of paying workers presented opportunities for armed robber. Cash payrolls also made wage payments anonymous and undocumented. A person could work without leaving a financial paper trail. Relatively few people had bank accounts. Not only were wages paid in cash, but most people had little disposable or savable income. According to a study by the United States Bureau of Labor Statistics, the average household spent 80 percent of their household income on food, shelter, and clothing in 1901, compared with 50 percent a century later. Most households lived a hand-to-mouth existence. They did not need a bank account. Another reason for avoiding documented financial transactions was that putting money in a bank was risky. Even during the prosperous 1920s, an average of 634 banks failed annually. Bank failure meant depositors' money evaporated. Banks then got riskier. In 1929, there were 25,733 banks in the United States. By March of 1933, 9,000 had abruptly gone out of business. Keeping one's savings hidden in a mattress was a rational decision. This changed with the 1934 introduction of deposit insurance. A few decades later, only cranks and cantankerous old people trusted mattresses more than banks.[12] This had the effect of documenting people's financial activity.

People did not need as much permitting from government to go about their business. For example, in 1918 New York became the first state to require a mandatory driver's license to operate an automobile. The rest of the country followed slowly. South Dakota did not start issuing driver's licenses until 1954.[13] There was no government documentation of employment until the Social Security Administration created the first (almost) universal unique identifier in the form of the Social Security Number.[14]

Cash wage payments were replaced by paper pay checks, which then had to be cashed. For this, identification was needed. In the 1920s, department stores and gasoline companies started regularizing credit purchases. In 1928, the "Charga-plate" was introduced as the template for a modern credit card. Their format became standardized after 1938 when wallet manufacturers started including a holder for the new Social Security card. People started using this feature to carry credit cards. In 1949, Diner's Club introduced the first general credit card which could be used at more than one retailer. Carte Blanche and American Express soon followed. Use remained confined to the affluent until the Bank of America got into the credit card business in 1958.[15]

Over the course of the 20th Century, people became more identified and trackable. By the 1980s, over 90 percent of American adults had a driver's license, complete with picture. Businesses began to ask to see it when someone checked into a hotel, boarded an airplane, or used a check or credit card to purchase a can of beans. Payment with cash all but disappeared from many activities. Most hotel operators are suspicious of anyone attempting to rent a room without a credit card.

The process of government and corporate documentation of people's activities took a giant step forward with computerization of records and the ability to link data files. As the 20th century ended, it became possible to conduct quick, inexpensive searches on a national or international basis. Linkage of databases increased reliability. For example, it used to be easy to fraudulently obtain a birth certificate. A dead baby's obituary provided enough information for the application. The birth certificate could, in turn, be used to get a Social Security Number. These allowed someone to obtain driver's licenses, credit cards – all the identification needed to live under a new name. Computer linkages and policy changes ended this. Birth records were linked with death records. Social Security Numbers were assigned at birth. People's identity within bureaucracies was established earlier and became almost immutable. It is still possible for a person to disappear by living under a new name, but it has become much more difficult. Just ask Johnny Wright. He avoided arrest for the murder of Rebecca Doisy for two decades until a linkage between Social Security and driver's license computer systems resulted in his arrest.

The increased bureaucratic documentation of people's lives made it easier for prosecutors to argue that absence means death. By the time Evelyn Scott disappeared in 1956, prosecutors were able to convince a jury that, because of the sudden termination of financial transactions, her absence meant death. Evelyn's case was a harbinger. She was a wealthy woman whose life was better documented than that of the average waged worker, but the rest of America was catching up. Prosecutors can now present evidence to show that, following the disappearance, the missing person never held a job, spent any money, drove a car, boarded an airplane, had a phone, and so on. It meets a common-sense, "nod-test" for a juror. A little over a century ago, rumors that Judge Fountain had been sighted in other states helped get an acquittal. The prosecution could not demonstrate that the judge and his son were dead.[16] Today, this task is easy enough that DiBiase argues that any defense claims a victim is still alive "actually benefits the prosecution."[17]

Governments created a system of licensing drivers to make automobile travel safer. The Social Insurance Number was created to administer pensions. Employers stopped paying their workers in cash to eliminate payroll robberies. Stores invented the credit card to get people to spend more money and to generate interest-bearing debt. Banks collected financial information to lower the risk of lending. Collectively, these measures had the serendipitous effect of helping police and prosecutors convict murderers in no-body cases. It creates a modern version of the Sherlock Holmes observation about the dog that did not bark.[18] Silence has meaning.

The Locard Exchange Principle and No-Body Homicide

Forensics is the application of scientific principles and techniques to criminal investigations. A careful examination of the body of a homicide victim and the surrounding crime scene is conducted to find physical clues. The findings are analyzed to determine whether one fingerprint matches another; whether blood, saliva, or semen comes from a suspect; or whether a footprint narrows the range of possible suspects by identifying gender, foot size, or fashion sensibilities. The cornerstone of forensic analysis is known as the Locard Exchange Principle named after Dr. Edmond Locard, a French scientist known as the "French Sherlock Holmes." Locard argued "every contact leaves a trace" or "with contact between two items, there will be an exchange."[19] In a traditional homicide investigation, forensics is used to place the killer at the crime scene. Police forensics technicians look for fingerprints, footprints, fiber, hair, skin, saliva, semen, and blood of someone other than the victim. These traces are used to identify who was with the victim at the time of their death.[20] If this effort is successful, this individual becomes a suspect with hard questions to answer.

The direction of proof shifts in no-body cases. Instead of being used to place the killer at the scene where the body was found, forensics is used to place the body in the presence or custody of a suspect. If it can be shown that the missing person was in the trunk of a car driven by a suspect, some fancy explaining is needed. Forensic evidence generated by the killer transporting the body was featured in 39 percent of the successful prosecutions examined during research for this book.

In 1991, William Thomas was getting divorced from his wife, Rachel Thomas, and was known to be unhappy about the impending property settlement. Rachel disappeared. The same day, an acquaintance saw Thomas parking Rachel's car in a shopping mall parking lot. The acquaintance thought it odd that Thomas was driving his ex-wife's car; odder still that he wiped it down with towel. After Rachel was reported missing, forensics technicians found Thomas's palm print on the hood of the car and Rachel's blood in the trunk. Thomas was convicted of his wife's murder. He pleaded guilty to murdering his mother as well. Elsie Thomas learned her son had killed his wife and was murdered to ensure her silence.[21]

In cases of intimate partner homicide, the implications of the forensic evidence depend on circumstances. Finding Rachel's DNA in her own car meant nothing. DNA coming from blood was more suggestive of foul play, but the amount and freshness of the blood matters. Exculpatory explanations for the presence of significant amounts of a missing person's blood in the trunk of the car are going to be greeted with skepticism by police.

The presence of a missing person's blood becomes more compelling when found in the vehicle of a stranger. In 2007, Masumi Watanabe was visiting a relative in Hawaii. She disappeared while walking home from her volunteer work.[22] A witness reported seeing a man guiding her into a pickup truck owned by a pest-extermination company. Masumi appeared either confused or resistant. Publicity about Masumi's disappearance generated another witness who reported seeing a man digging a hole in a beach. When confronted, the man drove away in a truck bearing the logo of the same extermination company. Blood matching Masumi's DNA profile was found inside the truck assigned to Kirk Lankford, who told police he had never encountered Masumi. At Lankford's trial, he changed his story. According to Lankford's new version of events, he accidentally sideswiped Masumi. She was not seriously injured, so he gave her a ride home. Lankford claimed she became agitated and jumped out of the moving truck, killing herself instantly. Lankford said he feared being fired over the unfortunate accident, so he continued working his assigned extermination visits; purchased a shovel, plastic bags, a flashlight, and duct tape; and made an interrupted attempt to bury Masumi's body. Lankford said he ended up throwing Masumi into the ocean. The jury found this story unconvincing[23] after an accident reconstruction expert pointed out that events as described would have produced damage to the truck.

Forensic evidence can reveal the circumstances of a disappearance. This is often key in no-body intimate partner homicides. The husband or boyfriend typically tells police that "she just left."

In Chapter 4, we saw how John Bayerl's description of his wife's departure was undermined by the discovery of blood in the garage, his car, and on a rug inside their home. This trail of forensic evidence cast doubt on Beyerl's veracity. But DonaMae Bayerl disappeared in 1979. Her murderous husband was not arrested until 2019. The 14,530-day delay between disappearance and arrest highlights a key reason for the increasing number of forensically based no-body prosecutions. When DonaMae disappeared in 1979, forensic DNA testing techniques did not exist.[24] Police could not prove that the blood belonged to DonaMae. In 2019, when a cold case reinvestigation of the disappearance was conducted, they could.

Forensic evidence left at the scene of the killing helped ensure that missing persons' reports turned into homicide investigations in 36 percent of the successful prosecutions examined for this book.

Forensic evidence can also be found where a body is destroyed. It is hard to destroy a body. Traces are left. In Chapter 3 we saw how a charred bone fragment helped convicted John Wallace after he murdered and cremated Wilson Tucker. In Chapter 6 we saw how fat and gallstones from John Haigh's last victim did not get dissolved along with the rest of her body. Residue from body destruction contributed to convictions in 15 percent of the successful convictions examined in this book.

Let us look at a few examples.

In 2002, housing was scarce in the oil-patch boom town of Fort McMurray, Alberta. Robert rented a room from Dax Mack. Robert disappeared. A month later, a man overheard Mack telling a friend he killed Robert because his tenant stole a piggybank belonging to Mack's son. Rather than evicting Robert, Mack shot him five times and burned his body. Police used a Mr. Big operation to trick Mack into taking undercover officers to a firepit where he'd cremated his sticky-fingered tenant. Mack told the undercover officer there was "nothing left" of Robert. Mack was wrong. Forensic investigators found small charred bone fragments along with shell casings fired by a rifle found in Mack's closet. The combination of Mack's disclosure to Mr. Big and the corroborating forensic evidence in the fire-pit resulted in a first-degree murder conviction.[25]

Efforts to avoid detection through body destruction can create another kind of evidence trail. In 2012, Dellen Millard shot his father in the head and arranged the crime scene to suggest suicide. He fooled police; Millard's prize was ownership of an aircraft charter and repair company. Journalist Ann Brocklehurst tells how Millard company employees were directed to build an incinerator capable of cremating bodies.[26] When they were unsuccessful, Millard purchased a portable, propane-fired incinerator (brand name – "ELIMINATOR") designed to cremate road-killed deer. It had a 500-pound capacity and cost $13,440 (tax and shipping extra). Millard used a credit card to pay for the machine.[27] A short time later, his ex-girlfriend disappeared. Millard and a friend, Mark Smich, moved on to random thrill killing. They located a person selling a pick-up truck, booked a test ride, killed the owner, and used the ELIMINATOR to dispose of the body. By tracking cell phones and accessing business surveillance cameras, police quickly closed in on Millard and Smich. Forensics investigators found bone fragments in the machine, but the machine worked well enough to destroy all DNA. Nonetheless, the methodical preparations for body disposal contributed circumstantial evidence that led to convictions.[28]

Forensic evidence created by killing, transportation, or bodily destruction has long played a role in prosecuting no-body homicides. In the past five decades, the forensic techniques available to investigators have gotten better. We will look at two examples: blood and odor.

Blood can tell compelling stories in homicide cases. It is liquid, so the Locard exchange principle very much applies. Blood spills. The most common methods of homicide – shooting, stabbing, beating – spill blood. Once spilled, blood is remarkably hard to clean up. It seeps into cloth, soil, and cracks in flooring. The patterns of distribution tell a story. Drops that fall straight down have a different shape than those that are flung or sprayed.[29] For blood to tell its story in a no-body homicide investigation, it must first be located; then it must be tied to the missing person. When Albert and Henry Fountain disappeared in 1896, there was blood in their buckboard. It probably came from the missing people, but this could not be proven. This has changed.

In most no-body cases, the killer or a helper cleans up the crime scene and means of transportation. Killers who attempt to avoid detection by body disposal have some degree of forensic awareness. Many go to great lengths to destroy forensic evidence – up to and including burning down buildings. In less extreme cases, killers use soap, water, and elbow-grease to clean up the blood of their victim. For a long time, cleaned-up blood told no stories. This began to change in the 1930s. German scientists found that a chemical called luminol enhanced the luminescence of blood. In 1939, two San Francisco pathologists found a pragmatic, crime-fighting application to the German scientific discovery. If luminal was mixed with hydrogen peroxide, it could be sprayed over a suspected crime scene. In the dark, a combination of luminol spray and ultraviolet light caused blood to glow. The process could be repeated, making photographic documentation possible. The process worked on dried blood, so older crime scenes could be quickly and effectively examined. Luminol testing could detect blood in extremely small amounts and document cleanup activity since the luminescence shows smearing. Luminol testing revolutionized the ability of forensic technicians to detect places where blood had been spilled and cleaned up.[30]

But there was a catch with using luminol. It detected more than blood. Bleaches, urine, fecal matter, and even smoke residue produced the same luminescent effect. Luminol is called a presumptive test. It allows investigators to presume blood has been spilled. It does not allow them to prove it. It serves as a stepping stone to investigative follow-up. Luminol has another shortcoming. It does not tell investigators whose blood has been spilled.

Throughout the 20th century, scientists and forensic investigators worked to improve their ability to translate blood into convictions. In 1901, a scientist named Paul Uhlenhoff discovered that blood from different species contained different proteins. This allowed forensic investigators to determine whether blood found in the back of a hunter's truck likely came from a deer or his missing wife. The same year, Karl Lansteiner discovered there were different types of blood. The medical benefit was making blood transfusions possible by ensuring compatibility between donor and donee, but forensic investigators saw the crime-detection potential almost immediately. Blood typing was a crude sorting mechanism since the most common type of blood ("O") is shared by 44 percent of the population, but could still be useful. If a suspect claimed blood was his own, the claim could be disproved if he had a different blood type. By the late 1930s, the basic blood typing categories were enhanced by the identification of about 100 antigens. These allowed for a more detailed analysis based on the presence or absence of specific antigens. However, blood analysis remained exclusionary. The tests could often prove that blood was NOT spilled by a specific person, but it could not prove who it WAS spilled by.[31]

While scientific discoveries early in the 20th century made blood-based forensics more useful to investigators, the revolutionary breakthrough came in the century's last decade. DNA technology was the Rosetta Stone that allowed blood (and other bodily substances) found at a crime scene to be translated into convictions. We do not need to go through the detailed history of the remarkable science behind DNA testing. We just need to know that scientific breakthroughs in the mid-1980s began to significantly impact criminal investigations in the 1990s. One impact was a wave of exonerations as DNA showed that persons convicted of the crime were not the ones who left blood, semen, or skin at the crime scene.[32] Another was a dramatic increase in the ability of police and prosecutors to obtain convictions for no-body homicides. In 1979, police could not prove whose blood was on the rug in John Bayerl's home. Three decades later, they could. As a result, Bayerl went to prison.

Blood is a key piece of evidence in many no-body homicide investigations. Particularly since the development of DNA technology, it often provides compelling evidence that the body of a missing person was stored or transported by the suspect. Properly conducted DNA testing is considered definitive by the courts. More controversial is improvements to an ancient technology – a dog's nose.

Dogs have a much better sense of smell than do humans. They have more olfactory receptors; the receptors are better positioned for smelling and they draw more air through their nose. Humans have long used dog's scent-detecting abilities. In the United States, bloodhounds became emblematic of efforts to recapture escaped slaves prior to the Civil War and convicts escaping from chain gangs.[33] Partly as a result of the Vietnam War, in the 1970s people began an organized effort to improve the utility of the dog's nose to fight crime. Dogs were trained to locate illicit drugs or explosives. Others were trained to find human corpses. Known as "Human Remains Detection Dogs" or "Cadaver Dogs," these animals were selected and trained to identify the unique smell of decaying human flesh. Cadaver dogs have become a common forensic tool in no-body investigations in the United States[34] but have not been utilized as frequently in Canada.[35]

In many cases, cadaver dogs have transformed a no-body investigation into a more traditional prosecution by helping investigators find a body, or at least part of it. Sometimes it does not take much. In 1986, Helle Crafts disappeared from her Connecticut home. The day before Helle's disappearance, her husband, Richard Crafts, bought a large freezer. A few days after Helle was last seen, Crafts rented a wood chipper. Crafts was seen operating the chipper near a river in a snowstorm. A cadaver dog narrowed the search area. Police found a few blond hairs, skin, and a fingernail. Crafts was convicted of murdering his wife in 1990.[36]

Use of cadaver dog evidence in a homicide trial is more controversial when no portion of the body of the missing person is found.

Late one Saturday night in February of 2009, Lyle Herring was seen moving a large, rolled-up rug from his apartment. The witness later described Herring as looking "aggravated, dishevelled" – even a bit "crazy." Herring's wife, Lesley Herring, failed to arrive at her workplace the following Monday morning. She was never seen again. As Lesley's family members and police launched a search, Herring behaved erratically. He redid his will and stayed in hotels under an assumed name. Herring told a cousin that he (Herring) was going to "burn in hell." Less than two weeks after Lesley's disappearance, Herring was detained while trying to enter Mexico. He claimed Lesley had gone to Mexico and that he was following to locate her. Police were skeptical. They became more skeptical when a cadaver dog signaled that a human body had been in Herring's vehicle. The dog's handler testified at Herring's trial. After his conviction for second-degree murder, Herring argued at appeal that the cadaver dog evidence should not have been admitted because it was prejudicial and unreliable. His conviction was upheld, with the California Court of Appeal saying cadaver dog evidence was admissible if the dog was well trained and the handler properly certified – and if there was other independent evidence linking the accused to the crime.[37]

In Herring's case, the cadaver dog was looking for a fresh scent. In other cases the dog's nose created forensic evidence in cold cases. In 1990, Aurelio Montano flew into a jealous rage and strangled his wife, Gaudalupe. Montano recruited his sister to help wrap Gaudalupe's body in a rug and his brother to help bury her. Whether from sibling loyalty or fear (the sister later testified that Montano promised "he would send me and my children to hell" if she talked), Montano's siblings kept their brother's secret. A few years later, Montano asked his nephew to help dig up the body. The nephew refused. A short time later, Montano got an acquaintance to help dump some garbage bags along a highway. A long-dormant investigation into Gaudalupe's disappearance was reactivated in 2006 after Montano's daughter (ten at the time of her mother's disappearance) reached adulthood and told police about disturbing memories.[38] Perhaps emboldened by the fact Montano was in prison for two other murders, his family members became more helpful to investigators. Seventeen years after Gaudalupe disappeared, three different cadaver dogs zeroed in on the location Montano's brother said her body had been buried. The rug was still there.[39] After Montano was convicted, an Illinois Appeal Court ruled it did not need to deal with whether the cadaver dog evidence was admissible since there was enough other evidence to justify conviction.[40]

When cadaver dogs convert a no-body investigation into a body-present (in whole or in part) homicide case, the evidence is uncontroversial. The accuracy of the dog's nose is confirmed by the discovery. If the body is gone, the dog cannot tell whose body was once there. Sometimes circumstances make this clear, but ambiguity is possible. There is also the question of accuracy. Cadaver dogs and their handlers are tested and certified, but even the best teams report a success rate of around 95 percent.[41] That is an impressive accomplishment, but it does leave room for reasonable doubt in a criminal case.

One principle of the criminal justice system in both the United States and Canada is that an accused has the right to confront and cross-examine witnesses. Cadaver dogs have remarkable skills, but they cannot speak any known human language. They cannot be cross-examined. Their handlers interpret the dog's behavior to reach an evidentiary conclusion. It is a form of hearsay (actsay?) evidence. As a result, cadaver dog evidence will always be vigorously challenged by any competent defense attorney. Judges usually admit evidence generated by the dog's nose but, as in the trials of Herring and Montano, only if there is significant independent evidence pointing toward guilt.[42]

In some cases, the dog's nose helps generate a conviction even if the evidence itself is flawed. The most illustrative case comes from a tracking dog rather than a cadaver dog.[43] In 1980, a young Virginian college student named Gina Hall went to a nightclub. She met and danced with Stephen Epperly. A group of Epperly's friends decided to meet at a cabin to go swimming;

Gina agreed to go along. She and Epperly left in her car and arrived at the cabin before the others. When Epperly's friends arrived, they saw him but not her. Epperly (and they assumed) Gina departed while they were swimming. Gina's car was found the next morning parked beside a railroad trestle bridge a few miles from Epperly's home. Police found Gina's ankle bracelet and some bloodstains in the cabin. Her clothes and a towel were found in the woods near her car. The day after Gina disappeared, Epperly asked a friend, whose brother was a lawyer, to find out "if there was anything that they could do to him if they didn't find a body." Epperly became the prime suspect in a homicide investigation. Almost two weeks after Gina disappeared, police brought in a renowned tracking dog and his handler. Police let the dog sniff some of Epperly's clothing where Gina's car had been abandoned. Without hesitation, the dog crossed the trestle bridge and went straight to Epperly's home. Police then took the dog to the police station. Epperly was inside being interrogated. The dog identified Epperly's car in the parking lot and followed his scent into the interrogation room. After being told what the dog had done, Epperly put his head in his hands and said, four times, "That's a damn good dog." The statement triggered Epperly's arrest and later became the title of a book by his defense attorney.[44]

At trial, Epperly's lawyers argued that the story of the dog's accomplishments should not be admitted because the trail was too stale to be reliable. The judge and jury disagreed, as did the appeal court judges who said:

> We hold that dog-tracking evidence is admissible in a criminal case after a proper foundation has been laid to show that the handler was qualified to work with the dog and to interpret its responses, that the dog was a sufficiently trained and proven tracker of human scent, that the dog was placed on the trial where circumstances indicated that the guilty party had been, and that the trial had not become so stale or contaminated as to be beyond the dog's tracking capabilities.[45]

These conditions, said the appeal court judges, had been met. They had not been. As journalist Rod Peterson later showed,[46] too much time had passed for any tracking dog to follow the scent of Epperly walking from the abandoned car to his home. A reputable dog handler would have known this. However, the handler in this case was later described by an Arizona judge as "a liar, a charlatan and a fraud." The dog had not been following Epperly's scent; it had followed the scent of the police officer who had walked the route to bring Epperly's clothing to the site of the abandoned car.[47] For Epperly, it did not matter. His 1993 federal habeas corpus petition to have his conviction overturned was rejected since "the dog-tracking provided a merely cumulative link between Epperly and Hall's death." Another, stronger, link was his response to being told about the dog's accomplishment. The repeated words, "that's a damn good dog," were the exact opposite of a denial.[48]

The idea that dogs could be taught to identify the scent of decaying human flesh occurred in the 1970s. The ability to look at people's genetic codes and use this information for forensic investigations came a decade later. Both techniques have been refined and improved. Both have allowed investigators in no-body homicide investigations to apply the Locard Exchange Principle in ways that would have been inconceivable to Dr. Edmond Locard. They have contributed to the ability of police and prosecutors to get convictions in no-body homicide cases.

Cell Phones and Solving No-Body Homicides

The first handheld, cellular, mobile phone call took place in 1973. The first automated cellular network was launched in Japan in 1981. Two years later, the first cell phone became available for purchase by the general public in North America. It weighed over two pounds and cost $4,000. Sales were slow, but increased after 1989 when Motorola introduced the MicroTAC, which could fit into a shirt pocket. A big shirt pocket; it was 9 inches long when opened and weighed over 12 ounces. It also cost over $2,500. Over the next two decades, cellular coverage areas expanded; the size, weight, and cost of phones plummeted; and new features were added. Cell phone usage became ubiquitous.[49] By 2000, 28 percent of North American adults had a cell phone. Usage reached 50 percent in 2003 and 70 percent in 2005. By 2020, 93 percent of American adults had a cell phone;[50] Canadians lagged a little behind with "only" 89 percent having one.[51]

Some no-body killers saw a use for cell phones. The victim's cell phone could be used to convince friends and family the victim was still alive. An investigation could be delayed or prevented.

In 2012, Allan Shyback put software on his girlfriend's cell phone to allow him to monitor her communication. He discovered evidence of infidelity, posting of nude photos, and texts planning for paid sexual acts. In the resulting quarrel, Lisa Mitchell ended up dead. Shyback later claimed his memory was murky about how she died; a coroner said she was strangled. Shyback put Lisa's body in the basement and covered her with kitty litter to mask the smell of decomposition. He dug a hole in the basement, buried her, and poured a new concrete floor. To buy the time for this labor-intensive body disposal, Shyback used Lisa's phone to generate texts, e-mails, and voice mail messages to her family and friends. He managed to delay any police investigation for two years. Shyback was eventually caught with a Mr. Big operation. While he was with an undercover officer posing as the boss of a powerful criminal gang, police phoned Shyback to say they had a warrant to search his basement. This was a ruse; police did not yet have enough evidence to obtain a search warrant. Shyback provided this by telling Mr. Big about the killing, body disposal, and cover-up. Lisa's body was recovered and Shyback went to prison.[52]

George Delacruz was another intimate-partner killer who used a cell phone to create misdirection.[53] The Texas man separated from his wife, Julie. She renewed a romance with her old high-school sweetheart; the two planned on moving in together. Then Julie disappeared. Her boyfriend received text messages, sent from Julie's phone, saying she was ending the relationship. Julie's phone was also used to post messages on social media platforms that she was disillusioned with her life, had met a new man, and was running away to Austin. The messages were not particularly effective at creating a diversion. For one thing, the grammar and spelling were worse than Julie normally used. For another, Julie averaged 25 to 30 phone calls, 40 to 50 texts, and 60 to 70 data connections every day. Concurrent with her disappearance, this pattern of usage shrunk to a few texts to her boyfriend and the social media posts saying she had left her life. Finally, Julie's phone was in Delacruz's house when the messages were sent. Police noted another suspicious electronic indicator. Delacruz was a compulsive online video game player. The day Julie disappeared was the only day Delacruz did not spend at least six hours playing video games. They suspected he was busy doing something else. Police found a freshly dug hole in Delacruz's backyard containing ashes and clothing fragments. Cadaver dogs indicated a corpse had been in both Delacruz's house and on the ground near the hole. Delacruz got life, with the Texas Court of Appeal noting, "it need not necessarily be known what caused the victim's death" to uphold the conviction.[54]

Cell phones and video games also came together in the prosecution of Douglas Stewart. Instead of using modern electronic technology to create the impression the victim still lived, Stewart used it to create an alibi. He lived in Virginia; his ex-wife, Venus Stewart, lived in Michigan. Stewart was a compulsive online video game (X-Box Live) player. He convinced another player to stay in his apartment to create an electronic record of constant video game playing. Stewart drove to Michigan and pretended to be a letter carrier delivering a package. When Venus opened the door, Stewart put her in a headlock, dragged her away, and strangled her. He buried Venus in a secluded wooded area and marked her grave with two tree stumps. Stewart returned home thinking he had committed the perfect murder. Stewart forgot about cell phone tracking. After he killed and buried Venus, Stewart phoned the friend in his apartment to say, "Okay, dude, it's done."[55] Police noted the anomaly of Stewart's phone being in Michigan while he was supposed to be in Virginia. This led them to the friend, who focused on staying out of prison. Stewart got two concurrent life sentences.[56] Seven years after his conviction, Stewart's father and sister convinced him to show police where Venus's body was hidden. He also traded his knowledge of body location for a few "perks" from prison officials, such as a video gaming system in his cell. "The story is going to make me look bad," Stewart told reporters from a Kalamazoo television statement. "I was wretched, cold and calculated."[57]

Perhaps the most intense effort to use cell phone technology to misdirect an investigation was done by Shanna Golyar in and around Omaha, Nebraska. Golyar had an affair; her lover moved on. Cari Farver was staying with Golyar's ex for a few days. She disappeared. Leslie Rule[58] documents how Golyar used Cari's cell phone for the next three years to leave messages with Cari's parents. Golyar also used the phone to drive her ex-lover back into her arms by sending over 12,000 threatening, abusive text messages and e-mails to the once-and-current lover – and to herself. Golyar used this apparent cyberstalking campaign to make the guy feel guilty enough to feel responsible for protecting her. Golyar used a time-delay app so she and the lover would simultaneously start to receive threatening texts while they were together – all apparently being sent by Cari. After three years, the cyber-harassment campaign moved past text messages. Golyar set her own house on fire to force the lover to take her into his own home. The campaign began to unravel when Golyar shot herself in the thigh in order to blame Cari. Like the "hate-crime" attack staged by Jussie Smollett,[59] police found the facts did not match the story being told. When Golyar was eventually arrested, evidence against her included photographs in her phone's memory of distinctive tattoos identical to those possessed by the missing Cari Farver.[60]

Just as killers saw the potential of cellphones as a tool to hide disappearance caused by death, police saw their potential in bringing killers to justice. In using Julie's cell phone to create a false trail, George Delacruz created evidence used to convict him. In Chapter 11, we saw how Patrick Frazee's use of Kelsey Barreth's cell phone to misdirect investigators backfired. Frazee's girlfriend and cleanup helper sent misleading messages. Police tracked the side-by-side travel of two phones – one belonging to Kelsey and the other to the girlfriend – from Colorado to the girlfriend's home in Idaho. Police discovered the existence of the girlfriend by looking at Frazee's phone records. Frazee's attempt at digital deception backfired badly.

Police use cell phone records to demonstrate that disappearance means death. If a person regularly uses their phone, a sudden termination of communication allows inferences to be made.

A sudden termination of attempts to contact the missing person can point police toward a suspect. In Chapter 11, we saw how police looked at Dennis Cornish's phone records. His friend and drug-dealing partner communicated with Dennis several times a day up till the moment Dennis disappeared. Breaking the pattern made Daren Randle the prime suspect.

The content of messages can generate useful evidence. In 2010, 24-year-old Charise Ragins disappeared. Police noted that her boyfriend, Travis Elleby, called Charise more than ten times per day prior to Charise's disappearances. There were no attempted calls after Charise disappeared. Elleby said the couple broke up; he no longer had a reason to call. Elleby had turned off his phone the day Charise disappeared, making it impossible for police to track his movements. However, police found a text message from Elleby saying, "No, I'm ready to permanently get away from her, nothing, I just want to kill this bitch." It was sent the day Charise disappeared. Elleby was convicted after a three-day judge-alone trial.[61]

Cell phones have become a bodily appendage for most people. This, combined with the architecture of cell phone networks, has enabled police to catch several no-body killers. The networks consist of towers receiving and transmitting signals over a prescribed geographical area. To ensure constant coverage, the systems are designed so every phone is within reach of three towers. Triangulation establishes location. This tracking capacity was enhanced when cell phone manufactures installed GPS trackers to allow phones to giving people real-time directions. This feature allows police to track the movements of any person they are interested in – or at least the movements of their phone.

The crime fighting power of cell phone tracking was demonstrated by the conviction of Jason Gross in Maryland after the disappearance of 16-year-old Rochelle Battle in 2009. The teenager used her cell phone to tell her mother she was going to visit a shopping mall before returning home. With that, Rochelle disappeared. Police used the GPS tracking feature of Rochelle's cell phone to track her to the Gross' home. Gross told police he talked to Rochelle on an internet chat room and arranged to meet her at the shopping mall, but that she never arrived.[62] Circumstances and the cell phones told a different, more sinister story. Gross had a record of sexual offenses and kept an incinerator in his backyard. The cell phone records showed Rochelle's phone traveled to Gross's house. Later, the phones belonging to both Rochelle and Gross left the house together and traveled to the local landfill. Rochelle's electronic trail ended there while Gross's phone returned home. Gross was convicted by the cell phone records. He did not confess, no human witnesses saw the two together, nothing belonging to Rochelle was found at Gross's house, and there was no forensic evidence in the form of blood or body parts. The cell phone records and the inference created by the incinerator in the backyard were enough for the jury to convict.[63] One can imagine jury members wondering how many people keep industrial-capacity incinerators in their backyard.

Bringing the Developments Together: The Conviction of Cid Torrez

The increase in successful prosecutions for no-body homicides started with a change in attitude by police and prosecutors. These authorities became convinced it was possible to obtain convictions without the presence of a body. As the great NHL hockey player Wayne Gretsky said, "you miss 100% of the shots you don't take."[64] Success in obtaining convictions in no-body homicide cases begat more prosecutions, which generated more convictions. A virtuous circle began. This increased success in bringing these killers to justice also rested on improvements in the evidence available to investigators. The growth of bureaucratic systems made it easier to argue that disappearance meant death. New forensic technologies made it possible for identity to be determined from droplets of blood. Dogs were trained to identify the scents of human decomposition. Cell phones allowed police to track people's communication and movement. As prosecutors adopted a more aggressive approach to prosecuting no-body cases, police got new tools to provide new kinds of evidence.

Let us put the impact of bureaucratic systems, DNA, cadaver dogs, and cell-phones (and other surveillance technology) together by looking at the successful Florida prosecution of Cid Torrez for the murder his wife, Vilet Torrez.[65]

In 2011, Torrez assaulted Vilet. Although they remained married, the two separated. Torrez moved to an apartment of his own. The couple entered counseling while deciding whether to remain married or get a divorce. Two months later, after spending the night with a boyfriend, Vilet disappeared. She did not show up for work, and her minivan was found near her home.

Torrez moved back into the family home to care for the couple's children and filed a missing person's report, saying he was mystified by his wife's abrupt departure. A visual inspection revealed no visible signs of violence in the home.

Contra-factual analysis is popular with some historians. It involves creating an alternative narrative for history had a single event come out differently. For example, on June 28, 1914, a Serbian nationalist named Gavrilo Princip shot and killed Archduke Franz Ferdinand, heir to the Austro-Hungarian throne. The resulting kerfuffle activated what Henry Kissinger once called a "diplomatic doomsday machine" network of treaties and alliances; by the beginning of August, the First World War was underway.[66] A contra-factual historian poses questions such as: "What would the history of the 20th century have looked like if Princip was a bad shot?" The *Back to the Future* movies are premised on contra-factual analysis.

Contra-factual history is always speculative; unlike in the movies, we cannot create two chains of events. However, if Cid Torrez killed Vilet in 1971 rather than in 2011, there is every reason to believe he would have gotten away with her murder. If the killing occurred in 1951, it would have been a certainty. As Torrez's defense lawyer told the jury,[67] there was no body, no murder weapon, and no witnesses. Torrez had a (dubious) alibi that could not have been disproven. Claims that Vilet was alive could not have been challenged. Police might have been suspicious, but unless Torrez confessed there would have been no charges. Things were different in 2011. Eight months after Vilet disappeared, Cid Torrez was arrested. The evidence not available to police in past decades included:

- Vilet paid for her all purchases with a credit card. Financial transactions ended the night before she disappeared. This allowed the prosecutor to argue she died when she disappeared.
- The Torrez family lived in a housing development with a security video camera at the entrance. This showed that Vilet returned home the morning of her disappearance. She did not leave the subdivision. The first public security camera of this nature was installed in Olean, New York, in 1968. Without the security video camera, police could not have proven Vilet returned home before disappearing.
- An examination of Vilet's cell phone revealed Torrez had installed spyware allowing him to listen to his wife's conversations and view her texts and photos. This allowed the prosecutor to establish motive and demonstrate Torrez's jealous, possessive personality.
- Torrez told police he did not speak to Vilet the day of her disappearance. Cell phone records showed he had.
- Although there was no sign of violence visible in the Torrez home, forensic investigators found traces of blood containing DNA from both Torrez and Vilet in three places in the house.
- A cadaver dog indicated a corpse had been on the grass beside the front door. Later, two different cadaver dogs picked out Torrez's car from vehicles in an impound parking lot. Both dogs indicated the scent came from the trunk.[68]

Torrez was convicted of second-degree murder based on evidence that police could not have gathered a half-century earlier. This evidence could not establish premeditation, but was enough to convince a jury that Torrez murdered his wife.[69] At his trial, prosecutors said Torrez probably buried Vilet's body in the Everglades swamp, but it did not matter whether this guess was correct. Nor did prosecutors have to show how Vilet was killed. New forms of evidence and the new approach to prosecuting no-body cases made knowing how Torrez killed and what he did with the body legally irrelevant.

Notes

1 Riedel, Marc and John Jarvis, "The Decline of Arrest Clearances For Criminal Homicide: Causes, Correlates, and Third Parties," *Criminal Justice Policy Review* 9, No. 3 &4 (1999): 279–306.
2 Farrandino, Joseph, "Getting Away With Murder: Homicide Clearance by Arrest in Chicago and Its Community Areas," *Homicide Studies* 25, No. 2 (2020): 164–188; Jarvis, John P. and Wendy C. Regoeczi, "Homicides Clearances An Analysis of Arrest Versus Exceptional Outcomes," *Homicide Studies* 13, No. 2 (2009): 174–188; Litwin, Kenneth and Yili Xu, "The Dynamic Nature of Homicide Clearances: A Multilevel Model Comparison of Three Time Periods," *Homicide Studies* 11, No. 2 (2007): 94–114; Ousey, Graham C. and Mathew R. Lee, "To Know the Unknown: The Decline in Homicide Clearance Rates, 1980–2000" *Criminal Justice Review* 35, No. 2 (2010): 141–158; Roberts, Aki, "Adjusting Rates of Homicide Clearance by Arrest for Investigation Difficulty: Modeling Incident- and Jurisdiction-Level Obstacles," *Homicide Studies* 19, No. 3 (2015): 273–300.
3 Pastia, Christina, Garth Davies and Edith Wu, "Factors Influencing the Probability of Clearance and Time to Clearance of Canadian Homicide Cases, 1991–2011," *Homicide Studies* 21, No. 3 (2017): 199–218. Trussler, Tanya, "Explaining the Changing Nature of Homicide Clearance in Canada," *International Criminal Justice Review* 20, No. 4 (2010): 336–383.
4 Bubany, Charles P., "Texas Penal Code of 1974, The," *SMU Law Review* 18, No. 1 (January 1974): 294.
5 Chambers, Marcia, "Morgenthau is Sworn In; Vows Fight on Violence," *New York Times*, January 3, 1975.
6 Crowley, *Surgeon's Wife*.
7 Roane, Kit R., "Police Charge A Surgeon; Murdered Wife in '85," *New York Times*, December 9, 1999.
8 DiBiase, *No-Body Homicide Cases*, 43.
9 Brumberg, H.L., D. Dozer and S.G. Golombeck, "History of the Birth Certificate: From Its Inception to the Future of Electronic Data," *Journal of Perinatology* 32 (2012): 407–411.
10 Blakemore, Erin, "The History of Birth Certificates is Shorter Than You Might Think," *History.com* , August 22, 2018. https://www.history.com/news/the-history-of-birth-certificates-is-shorter-than -you-might-think.
11 "Payroll Robberies," *New York Times,* December 17, 1921.
12 Richardson, Gary. "Categories and Causes of Bank Distress during the Great Depression, 1929—1933: The Illiquidity versus Insolvency Debate Revisited." *Explorations in Economic History* 44, no. 4 (October 2007): 586–607.
13 Nix, Elizabeth, "When Was the First U.S. Driver's License Issued?" *History.com*, August 30, 2018.
14 Puckett, Carolyn, "The Story of the Social Security Number," *Social Security Bulletin* 69, No. 2 (2009).
15 Frankel, Robin Saks, "When Were Credit Cards Invented: The History of the Credit Card," *Forbes Advisor*, July 27, 2021.
16 Sonnichsen, *Tularosa,* 173–190.
17 DiBiase, *No-Body Homicide Cases*, 35.
18 Doyle, Arthur Conan, "The Adventure of Silver Blaze," *Strand Magazine*, December 1892.
19 Kirk, P.L., *Crime Investigation: Physical Evidence and the Police Laboratory* (New York, NY: John Wiley and Sons, 1953).
20 McDermid, Val, *Forensics: What Bugs, Burns, Prints, DNA, and More Tell Us About Crime* (New York, NY: Grove Press, 2014); U.S. Department of Justice, *Crime Scene Investigation: A Guide for Law Enforcement* (Washington, DC: National Institute of Justice, 2000).
21 William Gregory Thomas v. State of Florida, Supreme Court of Florida, No. 84,256 (March 20, 1997).
22 Hawaii v. Lankford, Intermediate Court of Appeals for State of Hawaii, No. 29287, May 13, 2011.
23 Daranciang, Nelson, "Victim's Murderer Gets Life in prison: The Watanabe Family Pleads with Kirk Lankford to Reveal the Location of the Body," *Honolulu Star-Bulletin*, August 1, 2008.
24 Aronson, J.D., "DNA Fingerprinting on Trial: The Dramatic Early History of a New Forensic Technique," *Endeavour* 29, No. 3 (September 2005): 126–131.
25 R. v. Mack, 2012 ABCA 42; R. v. Mack, 2014 SCC 58.
26 Brocklehurst, Ann, *Dark Ambition: The Twisted Pact of Serial Killers Dellen Millard and Mark Smich* (Toronto, ON: Penguin, 2019).
27 R. v. Millard, 2018 ONSC 1299.
28 R. v. Millard, 2017 ONSC 5275.
29 Bevel, Tom; Gardner, Ross M. *Bloodstain Pattern Analysis with an Introduction to Crime Scene Reconstruction*, 3rd Ed. (Boca Raton, FL: CRC Press 2008).
30 Hesskew, D. "Luminol," *Law and Order* 39, No. 1 (November 1991): 31–33.

31 Nordby, Jon J. *Dead Reckoning: The Art of Forensic Detection* (Boca Raton, FL: CRC Press, 2000)
32 National Registry of Exonerations, n.d., https://www.law.umich.edu/special/exoneration/. Accessed September 14, 2022.
33 Tyler D Parry, Charlton W Yingling, "Slave Hounds and Abolition in the Americas," *Past & Present* 246, No. 1 (February 2020): 69–108; Campbell, John, "The Seminoles, the 'Bloodhound War,' and Abolitionism, 1796–1865." *The Journal of Southern History* 72, no. 2 (2006): 259–302.
34 Smith, Peter Andrey, "The Sniff Test," *Science* 3474, Issue No. 6565 (October 14, 2022): 251–255; Riezzo I., Neri M., Rendine M., Bellifemina A., Cantatore S., Fiore C., Turillazzi E., "Cadaver Dogs: Unscientific Myth or Reliable Biological Devices?" *Forensic Science International 244 (*2014): 213–221.
35 Pace, Natasha, "Meet Doc: The First RCMP Cadaver Dog in Canada," *Global News*, March 4, 2016.
36 Herzog, Arthur, *The Wood-Chipper Murder* (Wainscott, NY: Leslie Mandel, 2012); Scinto, Rich, "Richard Crafts, 'Wood-Chip Killer', Released From Prison," *Newtown Patch*, February 3, 2020.
37 P. v. Herring, 2015 CA 2/3 No. B249468.
38 Ward, Clifford, "Daughter's Quest Leads to Charges for Father," *Chicago Tribune*, July 27, 2008.
39 Neil, Martha, "Cadaver-Dog Evidence Helps Convict Husband of Murdering His Wife in 1990," *ABA Journal,* October 31, 2013.
40 P v. Montano, 2017 Appeal Court of Illinois 2d No. 2-13-0236.
41 Warren, Cat, *What the Dog Knows: The Science and Wonder of Working Dogs* (New York, NY: Touchstone, 2013).
42 Ensminger, John J., *Police and Military Dogs: Criminal Detection, Forensic Evidence, and Judicial Admissibility* (Boca Raton, FL, CRC Press, 2012).
43 Lookabill, Royce Glennwood, *That's a Damn Good Dog': Commonwealth of Virginia vs. Stephen Metteson Epperly (1980) A Retrospective* (Ararat, VA: Laurel Hill Publishing, 2016); Peterson, Rod, *Under the Trestle: The 1980 Disappearance of Gina Renee Hall & Virginia's First "No-Body" Murder* (Bloomington, IN: IUniverse, 2018).
44 Lookabill, *Damn Good Dog.*
45 Epperly v. Commonwealth **294 S.E.2d 882 (1982).**
46 Pederson, *Under the Trestle.*
47 Pederson, *Under the Trestle.*
48 Epperly v. Booker, 997 F.2d 1 (1993).
49 Dryoff, Charlee, "Here's How Much Cell Phones Have Actually Changed over the Years," *Business Insider,* July 25, 2018.
50 O'Dea, S., "Smartphones in the U.S. – Statistics & Facts," *Statistica.com,* May 31, 2022.
51 Statistics Canada, *Smartphone Use and Smartphone Habits by Gender and Age Group,* Table 22-10-0115-01, June 22, 2021.
52 R. v. Shyback, 2017 ABQB 332; R. v. Shyback, 2018 ABCA 331.
53 Cobb, Gary and Monica Flores, "A Murder Case with No Body," *The Texas Prosecutor,* July/August 2015.
54 Nisbett and DeLacruz v. Texas, Court of Criminal Appeals of Texas, NOS. PD-0041-17 & PD-0503-17 (2018).
55 People v. Stewart, Michigan Court of Appeals, St. Joseph's Circuit Court, LC No. 10-016574-FC (2012).
56 People v. Stewart, Michigan Court of Appeals, St. Joseph's Circuit Court, LC No. 10-016574-FC (2012).
57 Dominianni, Andy and Michael Krafcik, "Venus Stewart's Killer Details Her Death While Police Excavate Her Remains," *WWMT Kalamazoo TV News,* October 22, 2018; "Estranged Husband Leads Police to Body of Venus Stewart Eight Years After She Disappeared," *WWMT Kalamazoo TV News,* October 22, 2018.
58 Rule, Leslie, *A Tangled Web: A Cyberstalker, A Deadly Obsession, and The Twisting Path to Justice* (New York, NY: Citadel Press, 2020).
59 Shivaram, Deepa and Jonathan Franklin, "Jussie Smollett Will Serve 150 Days for Lying about an Attack on Him," *NPR News,* March 10, 2022.
60 Orti, Camila, "Shanna Golyar Sentenced to Life for First Degree Murder," *KETV Omaha,* August 15, 2017; Baker, K.C., "Woman Gets Live for Killing Love Rival and Posing as Her Online To Make it Seem Like She Was Still Alive," *People,* August 17, 2017.
61 Elleby v. State, Court of Special Appeals of Maryland, Baltimore County, Case No. 03-K-16-004625 (September 4, 2019).
62 "Jury Hears from Teen's Suspected Killer," *WBAL-TV,* October 13, 2011.
63 Schuh, Mike, "Man Gets 40 Years in Death of Teen," *WJZ-13 TV News,* January 6, 2012.

64 Brown, Paul, "'You miss 100% of the shots you don't take.' You Need to Start Shooting at Your Own Goals," *Forbes*, January 12, 2014.
65 Torrez v. Florida, Florida District Court of Appeal, Fourth District, No. 4D18-1277 (April 22, 2020).
66 Kissinger, Henry, *Diplomacy* (New York, NY: Simon and Schuster, 1994).
67 Murray, Joan, "Defense: No Definitive Proof Cid Torrez Killed Wife, Dumped Boy," *CBS4 Miami TV News*, July 13, 2017.
68 Torrez v. Florida, Florida District Court of Appeal, Fourth District, No. 4D18-1277 (April 22, 2020).
69 Olmeda, Rafael, "Convicted Killer's Strange Statement Invoking Trump Halts Sentencing Hearing," *Fort Lauderdale Sun Sentinel*, October 5, 2017.

13

BODILY SECRETS

Negotiating over Disclosure of Body Location

Clifford Olson knew the value of information. The strategic revealing of secrets gave him the freedom needed to launch a killing spree that claimed at least 11 victims. In 1976, Olson was in prison. He was a career criminal – 94 total convictions – who had been behind bars almost continuously since 1959. Olson received a "get-out-of-jail-free" card when he became a cellmate of Gary Marcoux, who was waiting for trial for raping a nine-year-old girl and leaving her tied to a tree to die. Marcoux wanted Olson to help fabricate an alibi. Olson tricked Marcoux into describing, in writing, how he committed the crime. Olson's treachery ensured a conviction. A short time later, Olson was released from prison. He got married, had a child, and, in November 1980, began to kill.[1]

Olson's method was to approach teenagers posing as a real estate manager and offer them jobs cleaning apartments. He plied them with alcohol spiked with chloral hydrate and took them to isolated locations. He then tortured, raped, and killed. Bodies were hidden with minimal effort or abandoned. Four were found by chance; seven were not. It took time for a serious police investigation to be mounted. Olson had a smooth con approach so there were no witnesses providing reports of struggling children being forced into cars. The disappearances took place in different police jurisdictions. Some victims had a history of being runaways; missing persons' reports were filed tardily and treated with a lack of urgency. Olson preyed on both boys and girls. This slowed pattern recognition by police who believed that sexually motivated serial killers were consistent in their sexual orientation. Body discovery was belated. Despite these difficulties and delays, police began a massive investigation. At its peak, over 200 police officers were involved. Media coverage intensified pressure on police.[2]

After his release from prison, Olson had intermittently acted as a police informant. When asked if he could generate information about the disappearing children, Olson asked for $3,000 per month. Despite his apparent willingness to be helpful, Olson became a prime suspect. On July 15, 1981, he was placed under intermittent surveillance. Police observed him committing several burglaries but missed three murders. On July 29, Olson was arrested after picking up two girls and getting them intoxicated. He was released that night without surveillance. A few days later, Olson killed his last victim. By early August, Olson was under continuous surveillance. Police made an arrest after he picked up two girls hitchhiking. The charge was impaired driving. Two burglary charges were added to prevent him from getting bail. The police surveillance team had watched him commit these crimes. A few days later, one murder charge was added

DOI: 10.4324/9781003372134-13

after the name of one victim was found written in Olson's address book. Police and prosecutors were skeptical this was enough to get a conviction. Olson did not appear to understand how weak the case against him was but knew a prison stay would be unpleasant if he went to prison as a child-killer. He offered to plead guilty in exchange for an assurance he could serve his sentence in a psychiatric hospital. Olson's lawyer told him the police and prosecutor could not determine the sentencing outcome.

With this, Olson shifted strategies. Four bodies of his victims had been found; seven were still missing. Olson said to the interrogating police officer:

> Tell you what, Fred, I'll give you eleven bodies for $100,000.00 …
>
> I'll give you a freebie. I'll give you a body and a statement, you have $100,000.00 in cash, or one of your guys. When we are finished at the scene, I'll phone, or you'll phone your man, who will hand over $10,000.00 to Joan [Olson's wife]. Then, you can talk to your man, and I'll talk to Joan to make sure she has the money. Then, we'll go onto the next.[3]

Olson's lawyer had been hired to represent Olson on burglary charges, but found himself working out the mechanism for the body-for-money exchange. There was, after all, a high level of mutual distrust between Olson and the police. British Columbia's attorney general "stipulated that under no circumstances was money to go to Olson or to be used for his benefit."[4] The solution was a trust fund for Olson's wife administered by another lawyer. The fund would hold the $100,000. As Olson led police to the bodies, money would be released at a rate of $10,000 per body. It was transferred to blind accounts in the Cayman Islands to prevent seizure after all the bodies were located. The money was ultimately used for a variety of purposes. A sum of $10,000 was used to pay expenses incurred by Olson's defense lawyer. Debts Olson owed to his father-in-law and brother-in-law were repaid, and a $10,000 down-payment was put on a condo purchased by Olson's wife. Other expenditures included paying for trips by Olson's lawyers to visit him in an Ontario prison and legal expenses associated with drawing up a contract for a book deal.[5] Olson believed his new notoriety would make his autobiography a bestseller. He even had a working title: *Kiss Daddy Goodbye*.[6]

The deal was negotiated at a lawyer's office. Present were Olson, his wife, three lawyers, and four police officers. One lawyer described the meeting as "extremely bizarre and distasteful." He said Olson's wife was hysterical and oblivious to the arrangements being made. The lawyer said, "it is impossible to describe the sadness visited on that woman" when she learned her husband was a serial killer. The police were described as functioning under "visible stress." Olson was having fun. The lawyer described "how Olson moved about his office that afternoon smoking White Owl cigars and directing him to be sure the police were served more coffee." Another lawyer later said "he felt like an errand boy" and that "all of us were under the thumb of that man." The police delivered $100,000 in used bills carried in an old black briefcase. Olson watched, smoking a cigar while a lawyer counted out the money. Such is the power of knowing a secret. The lawyer handling the trust fund later said the scene was so bizarre he half-expected Satan to appear.[7]

Olson then guided police on a body-finding tour. A cavalcade of cars carrying forensics technicians and police dogs went to each body disposal site. Olson re-enacted each killing and bragged. Between stops, the killer and police dined at local steakhouses. Radio stations provided hourly updates on the number of bodies recovered. Four months later, Olson pleaded guilty to 11 counts of first-degree murder and was sentenced to life. Media in British Columbia had learned about the payments, but the province's attorney general personally called editors and news directors to ask that secrecy be maintained until after Olson's guilty pleas were accepted by the court. Meanwhile, Olson was calling reporters to brag about his deal. When the payments were reported, public outrage exploded. Politicians ran for cover. The attorney general claimed he had merely been informed of the deal rather than authorizing it. The deal and quasi-denial ended his political career. Canada's solicitor general, responsible for overseeing the RCMP, said he was informed only after the money was paid. The groundswell of outrage was generalized. Inmates in Olson's jail Olson threw garbage and lit cigarettes at him. Many criminal defense lawyers condemned the deal, including Olson's own, who said, "I think it was politically insane and I do not approve it ... We know police pay informants, but I don't think they should pay the culprit."[8]

There were calls for the government to recover the money. The Canadian solicitor general refused, saying police need to make deals to get information. Deals, no matter how controversial or distasteful, had to be honored to keep future deals possible. Families of Olson's victims sued for the money. A trial court judge ruled in their favor but was overturned by the British Columbia Court of Appeal which said,

> It is clear on the facts of this case that the payment by the R.C.M.P. to McNeney [the lawyer administering the trust fund] was not made as compensation for the deaths of the children. As I have indicated, it was authorized by the Attorney General primarily to obtain evidence to convict Olson of the murders of the children.[9]

Olson's directions for the distribution of the money remained sacrosanct. Olson was not done. He soon claimed his list of victims was incomplete and offered to lead police to hidden bodies. This time cash was off the table. Olson demanded, and received, a visit with his wife and child. He was flown on a RCMP aircraft from prison in Ontario to British Columbia,[10] but the media learned about the trip while Olson was in the air.[11] Reporters and television cameras were waiting at the airport. The police found themselves pursued in a car chase. When they could not shake off the television crews, Olson was returned to prison in Ontario before he could reveal more bodies – if any existed. With that, further efforts to pry secrets from Olson ended. British Columbia's attorney general told the media that "I'm not going to make any more deals with Olson. There is no consideration being given to bringing Olson from the Kingston penitentiary again." Olson claimed to have killed another 30 people, but provided no detail. Until dying of cancer in 2011, he delighted in tormenting people by sending greeting cards to the parents describing how he tortured their children[12] but was never again able to use knowledge about the location of the bodies as a bargaining tool.

The Power of Secrets and No-Body Homicides

How can we explain the strange and disturbing saga of Clifford Olson's cash-for-bodies deal?

In 1906, German sociologist Georg Simmel explained that a secret is a possession providing its owner with power over those who know a secret exists but who do not know the content. You can test this proposition yourself by telling someone you know a secret. Almost invariably, they will implore, threaten, bribe, or cajole you into sharing the secret. As soon as the secret is revealed, it becomes valueless. Simmel argued that:

> Secrecy involves a tension which, at the moment of revelation, finds its release. This constitutes the climax in the development of the secret; in it the whole charm of secrecy concentrates and rises to its highest pitch - just as the moment of the disappearance of an

> object brings out the feeling of its value in the most intense degree. The sense of power connected with possession of money is most completely and greedily concentrated for the soul of the spendthrift at the moment at which this power slips from his hands. Secrecy also is sustained by the consciousness that it might be exploited, and therefore confers power to modify fortunes, to produce surprises, joys, and calamities, even if the latter be only misfortunes to ourselves.[13]

A secret gives its holder power, but creates a psychological pressure to disclose. As others learn the secret, its value is diminished. When a secret is transformed into common knowledge, it becomes valueless. This helps explain Olson's behavior and the response by law enforcement officials. Olson knew revealing the location of his victims would remove any chance of acquittal. As a seasoned veteran of the legal system, he understood that the desperation of the police for a confession meant the case against him was weak. Silence brought a chance of acquittal; disclosure meant dying in prison. Despite knowing the consequences, Olson couldn't help himself. He had to use his power. The days and hours before disclosure were likely the high point of his life. In the words of the lawyer handling the trust fund arrangement, "all of us were under the thumb of that man."[14] Olson had lawyers, police, and politicians submitting to him. Making it sweeter was the public spectacle. As the authorities frantically tried to keep their submission a secret, Olson phoned reporters to brag. He reveled in the notoriety. Even the hostility of other prison inmates was a form of homage. Once the bodies of his victims were recovered by police, the power of the secret was gone. He was strip-searched, handcuffed, and bundled off to a prison in another province. Olson relived his great moment by reminding the families of his victims of the power he once exercised, but the power itself was gone. Olson tried to recreate it by claiming to have more hidden bodies to reveal. His currency was devalued. Cash payments were no longer being offered. The most he could get was a break from the monotony of protective custody in prison and a brief meeting with his wife and child. Even this was contingent upon his potential revelations remaining a secret. When the media reported what was happening, the authorities decided Olson's secrets were not worth the price. Another indicator of the devaluation of value of his secrets was an inflation of the body count. Olson initially claimed 11 victims and promised to lead police to 7 undiscovered bodies. Less than a year later, he was claiming to have killed and hidden another 30.[15] This was implausible, if for no other reason than he had spent most of his adult life in prison. He may have killed during a brief period of freedom in 1973, but he may not have. In 1906, Simmel pointed out that a unique feature of a secret as a possession is that you do not have to know a secret to enjoy the benefits of possession; others just have to believe you have a secret for its powers to take hold. Authorities did not believe Olson had 30 more secrets.

Most killers who hide or destroy the bodies of their victims do so for the pragmatic reason of avoiding detection and punishment. In so doing, they create a secret. They know what happened to the missing person's body. Others want to know. It is a very powerful secret. The desire to mark the transition between life and death with respectful, spiritual treatment of the body is hardwired into humans. It helps separate us from other animals. The form of this farewell to the body is culturally specific and varies but the desire is universal.[16] Archeological evidence suggests that decorating the bodies of the dead goes back at least 60,000 years. Some of the most magnificent and enduring architecture – ranging from the Egyptian Pyramids, the Taj Mahal, the Terra Cotta warriors in China, the Roman catacombs – were created as mausoleums. Bodies are often destroyed by fire, but this destruction is part of a ritual of respect. The ashes are ceremonially dispersed or carefully saved. The thousands killed in war without their bodies being memorialized are symbolically, collectively, housed in tombs dedicated to unknown soldiers. We have a special horror for the mass crematoriums of the Nazi concentration camps and the unmarked graveyards of residential schools for indigenous children in Canada.

When a killer buries the body of their victim in a hidden, unmarked grave, dumps it in the wilderness to decompose or be eaten by animals, throws it in a garbage dumpster, secretly burns it, or dissolves it in acid, he has done more than commit murder. He has denied the family and friends of the victim the ability to commemorate life by treating the body with respect. It creates a special kind of horror. When John Wallace burned the body of Nelson Turner, people in Georgia were horrified. Cremation was not the problem. It was the secret, disrespectful, unceremonious cremation that revulsed enough to send Wallace to the electric chair. Because of the configuration of race and class privilege in that time and place, simple murder would have been treated more leniently. Wallace was executed while his accomplices only served a few years in prison. He desecrated and destroyed Nelson's body while they did not.[17]

There is more. No-body homicide cases begin with a missing person. Someone is gone. Family and friends are tormented by the combination of the unknown and our capacity for imagination. Scenarios and possibilities are conjured up, each more terrible than the last. The community, media, and police attempt to make sense of the situation by proposing theories which become transformed in a maelstrom of rumor. These rumors inevitably point an accusatory finger at the missing person's loved ones. As family members struggle with their loss and grief, they must deal with others looking at them with suspicion. Some try to convince the world they are innocent, but find themselves in the position of the peasant described by Guy de Maupassant who saw a piece of string on the road and picked it up. As fate would have it, a rich person lost his wallet that day. The peasant was accused of finding and keeping it. The more he protested his innocence, the more he was disbelieved.[18] Making the suspicion worse is that family members usually feel in some way "responsible" for the disappearance even if, objectively, they did nothing wrong. "If only they had locked the gate…."

When police make an arrest and a prosecutor successfully builds a no-body case, much uncertainty is removed. Family members might know their loved one was murdered and by whom, but the killer keeps the secret of the body.

Our need to acknowledge life with respectful treatment of the body and our preference for the horror of knowledge over the torments of the imagination gives the killer in a no-body homicide a very powerful secret. Clifford Olson used his secret to extract $100,000 from the governments of Canada and British Columbia and to inflict considerable discomfort to those putting him in prison. Other killers have used their secret to bargain for reduced charges, earlier release from prison, avoidance of the death penalty, or things as mundane as a view from their prison cell window.

But possession of the secret of body location is a two-edged sword. Before looking at some of the ways killers have used their secret for their own benefit, we will look at how the possession of the secret rebound against them.

There are few innocent explanations for knowing where a murdered person's body is buried. In the best-case scenario, the person revealing where the body is located can blame someone else for the killing. They still stand revealed as someone willing to help cover up a heinous crime. For most, revealing the secret of the body location means acknowledging guilt for the killing. Disclosure is tantamount to conviction. Even after a killer has been convicted and sentenced, there are negative consequences to disclosure. Any hope of a successful appeal disappears. As a result, the secret is often kept until after the appeal process has run its course.

In 1994, 19-year-old Shannon Melenda served as a scorekeeper at a softball game. After the game, she was seen talking to the umpire, Colvin Hinton III. Police learned Hinton had a history of assaulting women and had abducted and molested a young girl. Searches of Hinton's property found women's clothing and a softball scorecard buried in the back yard. Police also found a black tote back matching the one Shannon carried when she disappeared. A friend reported Hinton borrowed a butcher's saw the day Shannon disappeared and neighbors reported a lot of burning in the back yard.[19] Hinton responded to the police pressure by burning down his house. Police believed he committed the arson to destroy evidence, but Hinton tried to claim insurance.[20] This resulted in conviction and a ten-year sentence for fraud and arson. Six inmates reported Hinton made incriminating statements. A decade after Shannon disappeared, Hinton was charged with her murder and convicted with the combination of circumstantial and jailhouse informant evidence. Hinton continued to deny any knowledge of what happened to Shannon until his appeal was denied by the Supreme Court of Georgia.[21] A month later, Hinton confessed. As police and prosecutors had theorized, Hinton said he dismembered Shannon and burned her remains in a bonfire.[22]

In 1999, a neighbor of Lori Kirkley saw a man on a bicycle enter her garage. A short time later, Lori arrived home in her Ford Explorer. Twenty minutes later, Lori's vehicle left. Lori was never seen again. When Lori's husband arrived home from work, he discovered the lights on, the garage door open, and a note saying, "There's a gun pointed at your head" taped to the wall. An earring was under the fridge and the lens from Lori's glasses were under the oven. The only thing missing – besides Lori and her vehicle – was the contents of her underwear drawer. There was blood on the floor. Police immediately treated her disappearance as a homicide investigation. Two days later, a boy found a plastic bag. A note in the bag said: "Please give this letter to Mr. Kirkley [*sic*]. His wife is missing." Inside the bag was a set of Lori's keys and a letter saying,

> I'm sorry about your wife. She wouldn't cooperate, even with a .44 Magnum pointed at her head … I tackled her and attempted to cover her mouth. She bit the tip of my finger off … I had no plans to kill her, but unfortunately I had to. You will never find the body.

The next day, Lori's Ford Explorer was found, burned, in a cornfield. There were bullets on the floor.

It did not take police long to find a suspect. A co-worker of Lori's named David Malinski had a draft of the letter to Lori's husband on his workplace computer. Malinski's index finger was injured. A dentist said the wound was caused by a human bite. On Malinski's home computer, police found a document outlining a surveillance of Lori, a detailed plan of her house, and a plan to obtain a key and override her alarm system. The document outlined possible alibis, a list of property Malinski intended to take from the house, and a list of evidence he planned to plant to mislead police. After being in jail for a month, Malinski told a cellmate (about to be released) where to find incriminating Polaroid photographs and asked him to destroy them. The cellmate told police, who located pictures showing a naked Lori in a bed. She was bound. In some photographs, a vibrator was inserted into her vagina. She appeared to be alive in some pictures; in others, she appeared dead. Bruising and signs of struggle could be seen. Police later found a hidden "porn room" in Malinski's house with photos of Lori pinned to the wall.

Malinski admitted burglarizing Lori's house, but denied involvement with her disappearance. The next day, Malinski changed his story. He claimed to have had a consensual sexual relationship with Lori and said they planned to run away together. Malinski claimed that, at the last minute, he decided to stay with his wife. This, he said, caused Lori to grab a map of the United States and leave. Police were skeptical of this story, as was the jury.[23] Malinski's unsuccessful appeal centered on a claim his *Miranda* rights were violated. Malinski stuck with his second story for two more years before telling a prison chaplain Lori's body was buried under his father's driveway.[24]

Some killers wait even longer. We have seen how Joseph Peel and Leonard Ewing Scott spent decades in prison launching endless appeals. As death approached, they confessed. Nicholas Pari and his partner, Andrew Merola, got an advantageous plea bargain conditional upon disclosure of what they did with the body of Joseph (Joey Onions) Scanlon. Peri and Merola lied, claiming they dumped Joseph's body in the ocean. Three decades later, facing unrelated charges and dying of cancer, Peri suddenly gave up his secret. The motivation for these belated admissions and disclosures is usually murky. Some argue they show the existence of a conscience even in the most conscienceless. More likely, it is gloating and psychic release. As Simmel noted, possessing a secret creates a psychic pressure. Just as money begs to be spent, a secret begs to be disclosed. These killers were convicted and spent decades behind bars, but they took pride in their cleverness. Nobody found the body. They kept the secret. They defeated their tormentors. Ultimately, disclosure was the only way their victory could be acknowledged.

The Secret of Body Location and Instrumentalist Disclosure

In Chapter 11, we saw how accomplice testimony contributed to the prosecution's case in 28 percent of the cases examined for this book. In most cases, these accomplices received leniency in exchange for their testimony. Thomas Capano's two brothers were granted immunity for their role in disposing of the body of Anne Marie Fahey in exchange for their testimony. Sometimes the accomplices got away with murder. Robert Lincoln helped kill three people, but got immunity from prosecution for his testimony against (former) Judge Joseph Peel. Accomplices are in an excellent position to maximize the value of a shared secret.

Killers make strategic pretrial disclosures to make plea bargains. When a body has been hidden, it is not uncommon for the killer to lead police to the disposal site. This transforms the case from a no-body to a body-present prosecution, often resolved with a guilty plea on a lesser charge. Murder will be transformed into manslaughter or capital punishment will be taken off the table. There is a different dynamic when the body was destroyed or dumped where it cannot be recovered.

Faced with overwhelming evidence that he dumped Anne Marie Fahey's body into the Atlantic Ocean, Thomas Capano told the jury he tried to cover up an unfortunate accident. This strategy was profoundly unsuccessful. William Horman was also unsuccessful with this approach. Horman worked for Robert Dowd at a carwash. For reasons not made clear in court documents, Harman believed he deserved to become a partner in the business. Horman's bargaining strategy was based on death threats. In 2015, Harman and a friend went to the car wash. The friend later testified that Horman asked him to kill Robert. The friend said when he refused, Horman grabbed a club and entered the carwash office where his boss was sleeping. The sound of 10 to 15 thuds followed. The friend was called in to help with cleanup. As they wrapped Robert's body in a tarp, Horman gave his boss's head another three whacks. The two burned Robert's body, scooped up the ashes and bone fragments, and threw them in a river. Police later located the site of the fire. There were bone fragments remaining, but they were too badly damaged for DNA analysis. Horman's friend decided he would rather be a witness than a defendant while Horman told police he knew nothing. After his friend testified, Horman confirmed the destruction of Robert's body but claimed Robert died accidentally after slipping and hitting his head. If this version of events was true, Robert would have had one skull fracture rather than many. Burning his body made counting fractures impossible. Horman was convicted and sentenced to 40 years.[25]

In January 1992, Eric Humbert left a pickup basketball game with a co-worker, Jonathan Whitesides. He was never seen again. Whitesides told police Eric dropped him off at home.

Three months later, Eric's car was discovered containing blood in the trunk. DNA testing showed it was Eric's. When police visited Eric's widow to report the car had been found, they discovered Whitesides had taken up residence with her. After some prodding, Whitesides said he had thrown Eric's body in the Ohio River, but had not murdered him. Whitesides claimed the two had car trouble after leaving the basketball game. As they examined the engine, Eric accused Whitesides of having an affair with his wife and attempted to stab him. In the ensuing struggle, Eric accidentally stabbed himself. Whitesides said he panicked and disposed of Eric's body and car.[26] The story was implausible, but if true, Whitesides was guilty of committing an indignity to a body and obstruction of justice, but not of murder. Crime scene reconstructionists found problems with the story. There was a pattern of tiny blood drops on the inside of the car's engine hood consistent with a gunshot wound. Bright green threads were embedded in the blood. When last seen, Eric wore a green wool cap. A bullet was embedded in the vehicle's firewall; there was a fragment of a green thread in the lead core of the bullet. There was brain tissue and skull fragments on the radiator cover. Eric had been shot, not stabbed. Whitesides's own truck contained a handgun with bloody blowback on the barrel.[27] There was not enough DNA material to confirm was Eric's, scientists said it came from a "higher primate." At Whitesides's trial, one expert said, "Jonathan Whitesides either went to a zoo and shot a chimp or gorilla or he shot a human being with that gun."[28] Whitesides got 40 years.

Others had more success with disclosing body disposal while denying murder. In 1993, five-year-old Andrea Gonzalez disappeared from the home where she lived with her father, Paul Gonzales, and stepmother, Kim Gonzales. The two adults claimed Andrea had been kidnapped by her birthmother. This was disproven. A year after Andrea disappeared, her stepmother disclosed that she and her husband threw Andrea's body in a lake. Death, she said, came from an accidental scalding. Divers and hundreds of volunteers searched the lake and shoreline for 13 days without success.[29] The two were charged with first-degree murder, but Paul Gonzales pled guilty to manslaughter and testified against his wife. She was convicted of manslaughter as well. Both were sentenced to ten years and served slightly over four.[30] Capano, Horman, and Whitesides all told unlikely, self-serving stories about the destruction of body that could not be verified. The Gonzales told a more plausible story that could not be challenged because of body disposal. For the Gonzales, pretrial disclosure of body disposal while claiming innocence of murder was a successful strategy for the accused.

Other killers hoard the secret of what they did with the body for bargaining purposes post-conviction. This allows them to maintain denial of guilt through the trial and appeal process. If unsuccessful at trial, they use their secret to influence sentencing, disposition of other charges, parole eligibility, or treatment when in prison. We will look at representative cases for these types of bargains.

In 1987, Anton Myers lured 14-year-old Kathy Engels out to drink some beer. Kathy disappeared. Myers told police he was talking to two other girls while Kathy used a payphone. He said when he looked back, she was gone. Although there was a strong circumstantial case against Myers, he was not charged until 1992. He was in prison for another rape when he told several inmates he killed Kathy after she rebuffed his sexual advances. Myers was convicted in 1994 and sentenced to death.[31] Myers stuck with denial until his appeals were exhausted.[32] He then agreed to draw a map showing where he buried Kathy to exchange the electric chair for a life sentence.[33] Kathy's body was recovered 14 years after she disappeared.

Shakara Dickens waited until conviction before revealing her secret. As we saw in Chapter 5, Dickens's nine-month-old daughter, Lauryn Dickens, disappeared. After conviction for killing her daughter, Dickens confessed in exchange for a recommended sentence of 19 years. She had been facing close to 60 years without the deal.[34] Dickens said she smothered her baby because it was crying. She threw Lauryn into a garbage dumpster. From there, the girl ended up in the Memphis municipal landfill. Dickens was unable to produce Lauryn's body, but was able to provide a credible explanation of what happened to it.

In 1990, Brad Brisbin met his friend and hunting partner, Larry Moore, at a Montana truck stop. Moore believed Brad was having an affair with his estranged wife and said he wanted to clear the air. Brad was never seen again. Moore told police that Brad announced he was "fed up" with his life, hopped in a red sports car driven by a woman, and disappeared. Moore claimed the bullet holes in his trailer were the result of shooting at rats and that blood found in the trailer came from a deer. When police established there were no rats present and the blood came from Brad, Moore changed his story. In his new version of events, Moore said he arrived at his trailer to find a despondent Brad holding a gun contemplating suicide. The two struggled for the gun. It went off, wounding Brad. Moore says he left the trailer to get a pail of water to clean up. When he returned, Brad had disappeared. Moore was charged[35] and convicted of murder, but stuck with his story even after being sentenced to 60 years in prison and losing his appeal.[36] Five years later, Moore was charged with conspiring to plant a bomb in the prison warden's office. Prosecutors agreed to drop the bomb-conspiracy charges in exchange for Brad's body.[37] Moore took police to a gravel pit where he used a backhoe to bury his ex-friend. Moore also showed police where he hid the gun used in the murder. Moore was paroled in 2020 after serving 28 years.[38] If convicted on the bomb conspiracy charges, he would have been ineligible for this consideration.

In 1995, Lawrence Gaudenzi said he dropped his wife, Lisa Gaudenzi, off at the bus depot. She was supposed to report for an army officer training course. Lisa never arrived and was never seen again. While the county sheriff's department conducted a missing person's investigation, the army gave Lisa a dishonorable discharge for desertion. Two years later, the Virginia State Police Bureau of Criminal Investigation took over the case. Gaudenzi responded by disappearing, along with the couple's daughter. In 2002, a true-crime television show broadcast an episode on the case. A viewer recognized Gaudenzi. He was living under the name of Randy Evans, a homeless man not seen since Gaudenzi fled from police.[39] Even with this, Gaudenzi was not charged until 2008.[40] Gaudenzi pleaded not-guilty, but the strength of the prosecution's case caused him to plead guilty during the trial. He claimed Lisa's death was semi-accidental, saying she fell during a fight and broke her neck. Gaudenzi refused to disclose what he did with Lisa's body.[41] Sentenced to 25 years, Gaudenzi attempted to use his knowledge of what he did with Lisa's body to negotiate special treatment from prison officials. When this was rebuffed, Gaudenzi started thinking about parole eligibility. Refusal to disclose what he did with Lisa's body made it unlikely a parole board would grant parole. The longer he kept the secret, the more it would be held against him. A year after being convicted, Gaudenzi told police he wrapped Lisa in a sleeping bag, dissolved her in a barrel of acid, and dumped what remained on the ground. Gaudenzi told police where this occurred. Police found several empty acid bottles and Lisa's ceramic dental bridge. Everything else was gone.[42] Gaudenzi was careful to only reveal secrets that would improve his legal position. For obvious reasons, police believe Gaudenzi killed Randy Evans. Gaudenzi refused to disclose what happened or reveal where Randy's body was hidden or dissolved.

In Chapter 12, we looked at the case of Douglas Stewart, who used a friend playing his X-Box Live video game system to create an alibi while he drove to Michigan to strangle his ex-wife and bury her body in an isolated wood. Ten years after he was convicted, Stewart admitted guilt but would not reveal where he hid the body of Venus Stewart. He saved this secret for bargaining purposes. Five years after admitting guilt, Stewart told police where Venus's body was hidden in exchange for a video game system in his cell. Prison authorities said it was not connected to the internet.[43]

Killers who hoard their secret or those who retain it for strategic disclosure in the future can wait too long. If someone else finds the body, their secret is no longer a secret. Its value instantly evaporates. Craig Anderson killed his ex-fiancé, Denise Redlick and dumped her body in the Santa Clara Hills. Anderson was convicted in 1986 on a circumstantial case, but continued to insist he was innocent.[44] A year after Anderson's conviction, hikers found Denise's body. This left Anderson without bargaining power.[45] Despite subsequent admissions of guilt and statements of remorse, five requests for parole were denied. He served 33 years before being successful with a sixth application.[46]

Secrets, Denial and No-Body Killers

In our criminal justice system, a confession is generally regarded as the highest form of evidence. Common sense tells us that if a person confesses to something which results in severe negative consequences, they would not lie. This common-sense understanding is wrong. It is a well-documented fact that some people falsely confess to committing major crimes. Sometimes the reasons are thoughtful and considered; they believe conviction is inevitable and confess as part of a plea bargain. In other cases, the reasons for a false confession might be as trivial as needing to go to the bathroom during an interrogation.

We also know people falsely deny committing crimes when they are guilty. False denial is more common than false confession, but less studied, likely because reasons for false denial make sense. Confessing to a major crime means going to prison for a long period of time. Post-conviction confession destroys any hope of a successful appeal. The reasons for persistent denial run deeper than the legal process. Most killers, no matter how overwhelming the evidence against them, still have people who believe in them. Confession, particularly after long denial, shatters these relationships. In the end, however, most guilty people confess. Over 90 percent of people in prison in North America are there because they pleaded guilty. Even when the person continues to deny after the prison doors slam shut, the workings of parole boards create a powerful incentive for eventual confession.

Killers who hide or destroy the body of their victim are, as a group, more determined to avoid detection and punishment than your average murderer. They put in the work needed for body disposal and are indifferent to the anguish of uncertainty inflicted on the family and friends of their victim. They have possession of a powerful secret that can be used either for instrumentalist, bargaining purposes or just to savor. Make no mistake about it. Continued denial can bring benefits, even when in prison. Joe Hunt, the conman who organized the Billionaire Boys Club before turning to murder, was sentenced to life in prison for killing Ron Levin. Decades later, he persists in denial with remarkable persistence and energy. There is a "Free Joe Hunt" website, Twitter feed, and YouTube channel. A "Free Joe Hunt" group on Facebook has over 1,200 followers.[47] He has an online petition to California Gavin Newsome demanding clemency. By the end of 2021, it collected 28,000 signatures. Hunt's crimes generated two books and two movies. The 1987 NBC version was nominated for four Emmy and two Golden Globe awards.[48] The poster in the 2018 film described him as "Young, Handsome, and Cunning." Dominick Dunne and the Discovery Channel did programs on him. The case inspired an episode of *Law and Order.*[49] He has a steady stream of visitors and has packaged himself as a prison reform guru.[50] Hunt was a conman motivated by a quest for recognition and adulation as much as by a quest for cash; he used most of his ill-gotten gains to support a group of adoring acolytes. The combination of murder, conviction, and sustained denial gave him a level of recognition that would have otherwise been impossible. If he revealed the secret of where Ron Levin's body was hidden, this attention goes away. He would become just another convicted murderer in a country that has too many of those.

For those convicted of no-body homicides, revelation becomes a tool available to negotiate special treatment or help establish parole eligibility. Most parole boards treat demonstration of remorse as a condition of release. Remorse cannot be expressed without an acknowledgment of guilt; guilt can best be acknowledged through disclosure of where the victim's body is. This adjudicative orientation can be buttressed legislatively. In 2020, the British Parliament passed the Prisoners (Disclosure of Information About Victims) Bill,[51] or more popularly described as "Helen's Bill." The legislation arose from a lobbying campaign by Mary McCourt, whose daughter Helen McCourt was abducted and murdered by Ian Simms in 1988. Simms was released on parole in 2019.[52] Public outcry led to the legislation directing the Parole Board in England and Wales to "take into account" the nondisclosure of body location when making parole decisions. Helen's Law was soon cited as a reason for two denials of parole requests. Glyn Razzell was convicted of murder following the disappearance of his estranged wife. Razzell denies guilt and knowledge of where his victim's body was hidden.[53] David's Harker's case was gaudier. Harker was convicted of murdering Julie Paterson in 1998. He admitted killing Julie and eating her thigh as part of a pasta and cheese dish, but refused to disclose how he disposed the rest of her body.[54]

Helen's Law was criticized as being "a law with no teeth." Some family member of missing homicide victims called for an absolute "no body, no parole" provision.[55] This was rejected by the British Parliament because some killers could never be considered for parole, even if they acknowledged guilt. Killers who dumped the bodies of their victims in the ocean, burned them, or dissolved them in acid would automatically be perpetually ineligible. Those who buried or dumped their victims would have their parole eligibility held hostage to the number of carnivorous animals in the area, construction activity, or the vagaries of memory. When John Wallace threw the body of Nelson Turner down an abandoned well, he had trouble locating the right well; he even consulted a psychic for assistance. Wallace faced these difficulties, even though he was in an area he was intimately familiar with, operated in daytime, and was looking only a few days afterward. Even a motivated killer can have trouble finding a body dumped in a strange area, at night, years later. Eduard Baranec buried the body of Katelyn Noble in rural Saskatchewan. Three years later, he was unable to lead undercover police officers to the site, despite several days of frantic search. An absolute "no body, no parole" provision would mean a ban on parole for most parents convicted of infanticide in no-body cases since garbage dumpsters are the most common means of body disposal for these homicides. Once the dumpster has been emptied into a large landfill, the body is well and truly gone. On several occasions, police have conducted massive searches of landfills looking for a body. These searches are expensive, dangerous, and almost always futile.

A bigger problem with making release from prison conditional on disclosing the body of the victim is that it increases the punishment of those who have been wrongfully convicted. This can affect the legal process as well. In Chapter 15, we will look at the conviction and subsequent acquittal of Robert Baltovich. After Elizabeth Bain disappeared, her parents believed in Robert's innocence but, over time, police certainty convinced them of his guilt. After Robert's conviction was overturned. *Toronto Star* reporter Rosie DeManno reported that Elizabeth's parents asked the prosecutor to retry the case unless Robert disclosed where Elizabeth's body was hidden. It was a condition impossible for Robert to fulfill. As DeManno concluded, "but Baltovich is not guilty of murder and that's no mere technicality. This, of course, means he can't possibly know where that poor girl's rotting body lies."[56]

Notes

1 Broderick, *Beast of British Columbia;* Mulgrew, *Final Payoff*; Worthington, *Predator;* Holmes, *Where Shadows Linger.*
2 Worthington, *Predator.*
3 Mulgrew, Ian, "Clifford Olson – Canada's National Monster – Dead at 71" *Vancouver Sun*, October 3, 2011.
4 Grey, Malcolm, $100,000 Soaked in Blood," *MacLeans Mazazine*, January 25, 1982.
5 Rosenfeldt v. Olson, 1984 CANLII 384 (BC SC).
6 Worthington, *Predator.*
7 Mulgrew, *Final Payoff.*
8 Mulgrew, Ian, "Clifford Olson – Canada's National Monster – Dead at 71" *Vancouver Sun*, October 3, 2011.
9 Rosenfeldt v. Olson, 1986 CANLII 997 (BC CA).
10 Martins, Monisha, "'I was Clifford Olson's Lawyer'," *Maple Ridge-Pitt Meadows News*, October 7, 2011.
11 Grey, Malcolm, "Olson's Fast Trip to the Coast," *MacLean's Magazine*, December 13, 2982.
12 Carton, Sharon F. "Making Room for a Serial Killer Within Canada's Faint-Hope Statute: Clifford Olson, Master Manipulator in Canada's Criminal Justice System," *Global Business and Development Law Journal* 13, No. 1 (2000): 37–74.
13 Simmel, Georg, "The Sociology of Secrecy and of Secret Societies," *American Journal of Sociology* 11, No. 4 (January 1906): 465.
14 Mulgrew, Ian, "Clifford Olson – Canada's National Monster – Dead at 71" *Vancouver Sun*, October 3, 2011.
15 Worthington, *Predator.*
16 Laqueur, Thomas W., *The Work of the Dead: A Cultural History of Mortal Remains* (Princeton, NJ: Princeton University Press, 2015).
17 Moore, *No Remorse.*
18 "He began to tell anew of his adventures, lengthening his recital every day, each time adding new proofs, more energetic protestations, and more solemn oaths which he thought of, which he prepared during his hours of solitude, his mind being entirely occupied by the story of the string. The more complicated his defence, the more artful his arguments, the less he was believed."
19 Spencer, Marcie and Ira Sutow, "The Phone Call," *48 Hours, CBS News*, January 21, 2006.
20 "Figure in Melendi Case Charged with Arson," *United Press International*, June 22, 1995.
21 Hinton v. State, 631 S.E.2d 365 (2006).
22 "Convicted Killer Admits Melendi Murder," *Dalton Daily Citizen*, July 17, 2006.
23 Malinski v. State, Supreme Court of Indiana, No. 64S00-0004-CR-287 (September 3, 2003).
24 Tomlinson, Amber L., "Kirkley Family Gets Closure," *Rensselaer Republican*, October 5, 2005.
25 People v. Horman, 2018 IL App (3d) 160423.
26 Cazares, David, "Murder Suspect Portrayed as Passive, Calculating," *Louisville Courier-Journal*, January 28, 1993.
27 Englert, Rod and Kathy Passero, *Blood Secrets: Chronicles of a Crime Scene Reconstructionist* (New York, NY: Thomas Dunne, 2010): 99–104.
28 Englert and Passero, *Blood Secrets*, 104.
29 "Outgoing Franklin County Sheriff Haunted by Missing Girl 17 Years Later," *The Birmingham News*, January 17, 2011.
30 Smith, Tom, "Gonzales Completes Sentence, Leaves Jail," *The Times-Daily*, October 27, 2001.
31 "Jury Convicts Anton Myers of Killing Girl," *Orlando Sentinel*, June 17, 1994.
32 Myers v. State, Supreme Court of Florida No. 85617 (March 13, 1997).
33 "Directed by Murderer, Team Finds Remains," *Tampa Bay Times*, September 23, 2001.
34 Brown, George and Sabrina Hall, "Shakara Dickins Admits to Killing Daughter," *WREG Memphis News Channel 3*, June 22, 2012.
35 "Arrest stuns West Yellowstone," *Deseret News*, December 6, 1990.
36 State v. Moore, 250 Mont. 254 (Mont. 1991).
37 Lutey, Tim, "Moore's Bombing Partner Convicted," *Bozeman Daily Chronicle*, November 6, 1996.
38 Ehli, Nick, "Infamous Gallaton County Murderer Larry Moore Wins Parole," *Bozeman Daily Chronicle*, May 4, 2020.
39 Glod, Mary, "Police Led to Remains of VA Woman," *Washington Post*, June 14, 2010.
40 Williams, Reed, "Man Charged in Wife's 1995 Caroline County Death," *Richmond Times-Dispatch*, May 17, 2008.

41 Bitz, Ellen, "Angry Family Blasts Killer," *Fredricksburg Free-Lance Star,* May 8, 2009.
42 Smith, Portsia, "15 Years Later: Gaudenzi Remains Found in Spotsy," *Fredricksburg Free-Lance Star,* June 14, 2010.
43 "Michigan Inmate's Deal to Reveal Remains Included X-Box," *WBNS Channel 10 News*, October 23, 2018.
44 Beck, Janet Parker, *Too Good To Be True* (New York, NY: Penguin, 1992).
45 Anderson v. Sisto Civ S-08-1751 KJM CHS P (E.D. Cal. Feb. 17, 2011).
46 "Parole Granted for Man Convicted of Killing Fiancée," *San Mateo Daily Journal*, May 13, 2019.
47 https://www.facebook.com/FreeJoeHunt. Accessed October 3, 2022.
48 "Billionaire Boys Club: Awards," IMDb, https://m.imdb.com/title/tt0092659/awards/?ref_=tt_awd. Accessed October 3, 2022.
49 "American Dream (1993)" IMDb, https://m.imdb.com/title/tt0629155/trivia/?ref_=tt_ql_trv. Accessed October 3, 2022.
50 "Criminal Justice Reform," https://freejoehunt.com/tag/criminal-justice-reform/. Accessed October 3, 2022.
51 United Kingdom, Prisoners (Disclosure of Information About Victims) Act 2020, c. 19. https://www.legislation.gov.uk/ukpga/2020/19/contents/enacted.
52 "Helen McCourt Murderer Ian Simms Released from Prison," *BBC News*, February 6, 2020.
53 "Helen's Law: Killer Refused Parole for Failing to Disclose Where Body Hidden," *The Guardian*, October 27, 2021.
54 "Helen's Law: Self-Proclaimed Cannibal Killer David Harker Denied Parole," *BBC News*, October 28, 2021.
55 Hull, Liz, "Betrayal of Helen's Law: Killers Who Won't Say Where Victim's Body Is Still Hidden Could STILL Get Parole Despite Promise of Rule Change after Helen McCourt Case," *Daily Mail*, December 22, 2020.
56 DiManno, Rosie, "Where's Miscarriage of Justice on Baltovich," *Toronto Star*, January 15, 2010.

14

"ONLY IN CANADA, EH?"

Mr. Big and No-Body Investigations

Police in Canada developed an interesting way to get convictions in no-body cases. An officer politely asks the suspect detailed questions about the crime. The suspect answers the questions. It is all very simple.

Of course, context matters. The suspect believes the police officer is the all-powerful boss of a mysterious criminal gang. "Mr. Big" offers to have a terminally ill cancer patient or someone already serving a life sentence in prison confess to the crime. In no-body cases, Mr. Big says that knowledge of body location is needed to make the confession convincing. While a hidden video camera records captures the scene, the suspect tells how he killed the victim and disposed of the body. The police corroborate the disclosure by recovering the body if that is possible. Even when the body cannot be recovered, the suspect is arrested. The prosecutor plays the videotape to a jury. The killer goes to prison.[1]

Let us look at a few no-body Mr. Big cases.

In 2003, Lyne Massicotte met Alain Perreault on an internet dating site.[2] The Quebec City woman left her daughter with a babysitter to meet Perreault in person. The babysitter phoned Perreault's apartment to talk to Lynn. Perreault answered the call. He said Lyne stepped out to buy cigarettes. Lyne was never seen or heard from again. Her abandoned car was found near the historic Château Frontenac hotel. There was mud on the undercarriage and the driver's side seat was pushed back as far as it would go.

The police questioned Perreault several times. He seemed cooperative. He said the two smoked some marijuana before preparing to go out for supper. Lyne asked Perreault to drive, but after getting behind the wheel he decided he was too stoned. Perreault said his refusal to drive impaired angered Lyne. She left. Perreault said he spent the rest of the evening alone in his apartment. It was a plausible story. Police did not initially view Perreault as a suspect, but one ugly fact was inescapable. Perreault was the last person known to have been with Lyne. He was in her presence; then she vanished. Police noticed that Perreault's story did not line up with that of the babysitter. There was something else. Lyne was short; Perreault was tall. Perreault's story accounted for why the driver's seat had been pushed back, but did not explain why Lyne did not move the seat forward before leaving – or, indeed, how she could have driven without being able to reach the gas pedal. A search of Perreault's apartment did not find any physical forensic evidence, but an examination of his computer showed he spent part of the evening searching for information on police procedures in investigating missing persons. He also looked at Canada's

DOI: 10.4324/9781003372134-14

Criminal Code; specifically, Section 229 (Murder) and Section 182 (Interference with a dead body).

Six years after Lyne's disappearance, the police called for Mr. Big. Perreault befriended an undercover officer. Over the next 107 days, Perreault had 41 interactions with his new friend. He ran errands, delivered packages, and counted money. He earned $15,000 for these tasks. Perreault's friend said this was just a start. Full membership in the gang was more lucrative, but was subject to approval by Mr. Big.

Perreault met Mr. Big in a luxury hotel room. Mr. Big was a great host, offering food and drink. He asked Perreault about his life and past employment. They looked at brochures for luxury condominiums and talked about the cars money could buy. Then Mr. Big got down to business. He told Perreault he was ideal for gang membership, but there was an issue. Members had to be "white as snow" in the eyes of the police. Mr. Big said he had "done some checking" and "learned certain things that were not good." Mr. Big told Perreault the gang did not care what he had done. Problems could be fixed and black marks erased. The gang had power. To exercise this power, they needed knowledge and absolute honesty from members.

Perreault introduced the issue of Lyne's disappearance. He told Mr. Big the version he told police. Mr. Big told Perreault he was free to go. In fact, since he was lying, he had to go. Goodbye. No hard feelings, but no membership in the gang. Perreault shifted gears. He told Mr. Big that "You'll be the first to know what really happened." Perreault said that everything "up to the pot" was true. He went on. The transcript of the conversation reads (in translation from French):

Alain: Then I wanted to snuggle up a bit, but she didn't want to, so . . .
Boss: Yeah, O.K., so what happened?
Alain: I strangled her.[3]

Perreault told a detailed story. After Lyne's refusal to snuggle up, he "picked her up" by the throat and held her against the wall for two or three minutes. When Lyne stopped moving, Perreault carried her into the bedroom, undressed her, and attempted to have sex without, he said, success.

Perreault explained he thought through his story before organizing the body disposal around it. The story of the abortive trip to the restaurant was designed to cover carelessness. It provided an excuse if his DNA or fingerprints were found in Lyne's car. Perreault said he used Lyne's registration to identify her car. It was parked down the block. He moved it to his apartment. After wrapping Lyne's body in a blanket, he moved her through his window to avoid the security camera in the apartment lobby. The trunk of Lyne's car was full, so he put her body in the back seat. Perreault said he drove to the St. Lawrence River and rolled Lyne's body into the water. He threw her clothes into a dumpster and left the car at the Château Frontenac, leaving it unlocked to encourage theft. The car keys and his gloves went into a storm sewer.

The Quebec Court of Appeal later observed that "The confession is rife with details and explanations. It is hard to imagine how a person who did not commit the murder could give them."[4] The police were able to verify many details. For example, the trunk of Lyne's car was full. Perreault's original story to police could not account for this knowledge. At trial, Perreault claimed Lyne put her purse in the trunk as they prepared to leave for the restaurant, but this recollection came nine years too late. Lyne's body was never recovered. An expert witness explained how spring tides would wash a body out to sea from the spot he described dumping her. Mud on the riverbank matched the mud on the undercarriage of the car.

At his trial, Perreault recanted his disclosure to Mr. Big. He claimed he was afraid of Mr. Big and told the putative crime boss what he wanted to hear. The jury watched the video of the session and evidently concluded that Perreault did not look afraid. He was convicted of second-degree murder. Perreault appealed. The Quebec Court of Appeal judges made it very clear they believed Perreault was guilty but overturned the conviction because of problems with the judge's instructions to the jury.[5] Perreault was convicted a second time at the do-over trial.[6]

Let us look at another case where Mr. Big obtained a conviction in a no-body case.

April 8, 1994 was going to be a big day for Jodi Franz.[7] She had an appointment with police to describe how her ex-husband, Glenn Franz, was stalking and threatening her. She anticipated receiving a restraining order. Jodi was also scheduled to meet with her lawyer to sign divorce papers. On the evening of April 7, Jodi had several emotional telephone conversations before telling her mother she was going out. Jodi's car was discovered the next day in the parking lot of the bus depot, but Jodi was never seen again.

Police suspected foul play; Franz was the primary suspect. Police learned Franz had been stalking Jodi in the hopes of catching her doing something that would undermine her in a custody dispute. Franz had threatened Jodi, but there were no reports of physical violence. Franz admitted talking to Jodi on the phone, but claimed they did not meet the evening she disappeared. He had an alibi of sorts. Franz's claim that he was home all evening was more or less confirmed by his father, his brother, and a woman renting a basement suite in his house, but none said they had seen Franz all evening. They had not seen him leave. No forensic evidence was found in the Franz home or vehicles. The police belief that Jody was dead and transformed hardened as time passed, but the investigation remained at an impasse for almost three years.

In 1997, Franz found a new friend – or, more accurately, the friend found him. The new friend said he was a drug dealer. Franz was interested in opportunities. He was put to work making deliveries of illegal cigarettes, bootlegged liquor, stolen property, and drugs. Franz was well paid and pressed his friend for more opportunities. The friend said a major cocaine deal was coming up. The friend took Franz to a bank to deposit $20,000 in a safety deposit box. This, he explained, was to pay the person selected to transport the cocaine from Montreal. Franz wanted the job. The friend conditionally agreed, but said the final decision was up to Mr. Big.

Franz met Mr. Big in a hotel room.[8] Mr. Big conducted a job interview. It went well, but as it was wrapping up, Mr. Big raised an issue. Sources in the police told him that Franz was under surveillance. Mr. Big said new DNA testing techniques had emerged, and police were waiting for test results. If these pointed toward Franz, he would be arrested for Jodi's disappearance. Franz protested that he was innocent. Mr. Big said guilt or innocence did not matter to him. All that mattered was the courier being free of heat from police. Mr. Big offered to help. He knew a guy in a Mexican prison looking for a Canadian murder to confess to in order to be extradited to Canada. After all, Canadian prisons were more pleasant than those in Mexico. Franz again said he was innocent, but offered to say he killed Jodi if this would help. Mr. Big replied that a false confession was useless. If the scheme was to work, he needed truthful details so his friend's false confession would be convincing.

With that, Franz told his story to Mr. Big.[9] Franz said he convinced Jodi to meet at the bus depot to resolve their differences. He knocked her out and strangled her. Franz said he wrapped Jodi in a tarp, drove to a dairy farm where he once worked, dragged her to the manure lagoon, and cut her body into six pieces. Franz said he threw the pieces into the lagoon where the aerating action dissolved her. Jodi's remains were liquefied and sprayed over nearby fields as fertilizer. Franz said he threw Jodi's head and the saw into a nearby river. With this, Jodi was well and truly gone.

Mr. Big asked what happened to the tarp. Franz said he washed it with bleach, and that it was around his home somewhere. The next day Franz produced a faded tarp. It had been covering his wood pile. After the bleaching and the passage of four years, no forensic evidence remained.

Franz took undercover officers on a tour of his route the night of the murder. They bought him a disposable camera. Franz took pictures of the key locations and explained their significance. With that completed, out came the handcuffs.

At trial, Franz claimed Jodi voluntarily ran away to avoid a custody battle. The judge ruled Jodi's abrupt and permanent disappearance was sufficient evidence she was dead. The case came down to Franz's video-taped disclosures. Franz claimed he lied to Mr. Big because he was afraid of him. Franz stuck to this claim through 12 days of cross-examination by the prosecutor, but to no avail. The simple fact of the matter was that Franz did not look afraid when telling Mr. Big about the murder. He looked eager. The judge ruled that Franz's revelation to Mr. Big was more compelling than his recantation.[10] When Franz appealed the resulting conviction for second-degree murder, the appeal court judges said, "it was not unreasonable to view the evidence in the way that he [the trial judge] did."[11]

The voluntary – indeed eager – confession to Mr. Big resulted in Franz getting a life sentence with no possibility of parole for 17 years. He killed Jodi without generating witnesses, forensic evidence, or any egregiously incriminating post-offence behavior. Jodi's body was gone without a trace. With his pre-disappearance harassment and threats, Franz ensured he was the primary suspect when Jodi disappeared, but he was a successful murderer – until he met Mr. Big.

Sometimes a Mr. Big operation yields an unexpected bonus for police.

Fifteen-year-old Katelyn Noble disappeared from a Saskatchewan farm/marijuana grow operation in August, 2008, but was not reported missing until the following January. Eduard Baranec told her boyfriend that Katelyn had decided to leave.[12] In 2010, police launched a Mr. Big operation against Baranec.[13] He was arrested for a parole violation and released a few days later. His cellmate during this short stay in jail was an undercover police officer. He recruited Baranec into a criminal gang engaged in loansharking and selling contraband goods such as stolen credit cards, explosives, and illegal firearms. When Baranec was being considered for full membership, he assured Mr. Big there was "no heat" on him, even though he "had four bodies on him."

One of the bodies was Katelyn. Mr. Big told Baranec they needed to permanently destroy Katelyn's body. Baranec and undercover officers traveled from British Columbia to Saskatchewan. Baranec showed where he killed Katelyn and left her near the farmhouse while he got help for body disposal. He took the undercover officer to another farmyard and showed where he and his assistant used a backhoe to bury her. Baranec explained that he did not trust his assistant to keep the secret, so he returned, dug up Katelyn, and reburied her in an isolated location. Despite spending a few days driving around with an undercover officer, Baranec was unable to locate Katelyn's grave. Her body was never recovered, although Baranec's assistant corroborated the story of the first burial. Baranec eventually pleaded guilty to manslaughter for killing Katelyn.[14]

While Baranec was trying to show the undercover police officer where he buried Katelyn, he was also telling about another murder. Baranec said he murdered an East Indian woman for $15,000, paid by the girlfriend of his victim's husband. His description of the killing matched the unsolved homicide of Amanpreet Bahia. Mr. Big said he needed to ensure Amanpreet's husband and his girlfriend had not told anyone about the murder. Baranec introduced an undercover officer to his clients. They assured the officer kept their mouths shut about arranging Amanpreet's murder. All three were convicted of first-degree murder.[15]

Baranec told Mr. Big he committed two earlier murders in Ontario while working in the illegal drug trade. Police could not obtain enough corroboration for these killings to support charges; besides Baranec was already serving two life sentences.

Another Mr. Big investigation linking British Columbia and Saskatchewan unexpectedly turned a stalled missing persons investigation into a successful murder conviction. In 2003, a

Mr. Big team was investigating Brian Casement for the death of a street person found in a garbage dumpster in British Columbia.[16] The Mr. Big operation was put on hold while Casement served time in prison on an unrelated offense. After his release in 2006, Casement participated in what he believed was the construction of an alibi for a murder suspect, smuggling explosives into Canada for sale to terrorists, and acquiring murder weapons. Casement met Mr. Big to be interviewed for full membership in the gang. The conversation began:

TM (Mr. Big): Let me ask you this, have you ever killed anybody else?
BC (Brian Casement): Yes.
TM: Please do not bullshit.
BC: I am not bullshitting.
TM: Why should I believe you?
BC: Um (scratching sound) you don't have to. Why should you believe me uh, because I uh, I have put what I believe, my life in your hands. There is no reason for me to lie to you, there is no reason for me to embellish anything that I do. This other death, I am not (scratching sound), I'm not extre- The, th-this one, as far as I'm concerned, the guy had it coming.
TM: Is this your first one or your second one?
BC: No the second.
TM: So how many have you done?
BC: Two.
TM: So the f-this is your second, I'm sorry, you said?
BC: Yeah.
TM: So when was the first one?
BC: Uh (cracking sound) about uh, six months before that.
TM: And where did that happen?
BC: Saskatoon.
TM: Tell me about that.
BC: I picked up a hooker. Uh, she didn't wanna come across, I took her out into uh, a back area of uh, Saskatoon. I was doin' a job for Kal Tire, I had a rental car uh, took her down, raped her, fucked her and strangled her.
TM: Did they ever find her body?
BC: I don't know.
TM: D'you know what her name is?
BC: Victoria. That's all, that's all I know . . .
TM: At what point did she realize she was in trouble?
BC: Um, probably when I kinda grabbed her and put my arm, arm around her uh, her neck and uh, I think she made a comment like uh, I've always wondered if this would happen and uh, and then she just sorta went uh, like, like acted as if she passed out. And uh, and I did my thing and then uh, and then she got up. Started to walk away. And said uh, can I go now? (Chuckles) I said, I don't think so. And that was when I decided to do what I did. Dead people don't talk.[17]

The surprised Mr. Big team now had two homicides to investigate. Casement gave a detailed description of how he had killed the homeless person over a $100 outstanding drug debt. Aspects of his disclosure did not match the medical examiner's report, so Casement was never charged in that case. Things were different in Saskatoon. Casement led undercover officers to an abandoned farm house about 20 miles from the city. Victoria's body was found where he left her in the root cellar. This time, his description of the murder matched the medical examiner's findings. At his trial, Casement claimed he lied to Mr. Big. His new story was that Victoria died accidentally during rough, but consensual, sex. After comparing both versions of her death with the medical evidence, the jury convicted Casement of first-degree murder.[18]

Mr. Big generates detailed disclosures. Mr. Big offers killers absolution for their past crimes and reward for their future ones – but only if they tell the truth, the whole truth and nothing but the truth. The resulting descriptions of the crime and cover-up are compelling. They can usually be verified. Perreault knew that the trunk of Lyne's car was full when, according to his original story to police, he had never seen the opened trunk. Franz said he wrapped Jody's body in an orange tarp that he bleached. He produced an old orange tarp that had been bleached. Baranec led the police around rural Saskatchewan looking for Katelyn's body. He also described Amanpreet's house, the clothes she was wearing when killed, and the type of knife used to kill her. Baranec described Amanpreet's children, saying he was surprised to find them home when he arrived to kill their mother.

Mr. Big and Finding Bodies

Mr. Big was responsible for obtaining convictions in at least seven no-body prosecutions. There are also at least 14 Mr. Big cases that were no-body investigations until the killer led the police to the body.[19] Willingly. Enthusiastically. If we include these cases in the tally of no-body cases, Mr. Big was responsible for almost half of all successful Canadian no-body prosecutions.

Mike Bridges strangled his girlfriend and buried her in another person's freshly dug grave. He took Mr. Big to the cemetery and spelled out the name of the tombstone marking her grave.[20] Allan Shyback strangled his common-law wife and buried her in his basement. After she was buried, he poured cement to create a new floor. He used her cell phone to send messages to her friends and mother to create the impression she was still alive. Three years later, he told Mr. Big where the body was buried.[21] Franjo Perovic robbed a drug dealer, murdering him with a hatchet. He buried his victim in an isolated area and planted grass over the grave. He took undercover police officers to the remote site and told them where to dig.[22] Police were able to verify Perovic's purchase of a hatchet, a shovel, and grass seed the day before his victim disappeared.[23] When a killer shows Mr. Big where the body is buried, he goes to prison.

Let us look at a Mr. Big case where the undercover officers were led to the body in a bit more detail. It is representative in that it involves the killing of an intimate partner. It is unusual for a no-body case in that a woman killed a man.[24]

Keith Black was a well-known and successful Taekwon-Do instructor in Kelowna, British Columbia. In 1992, he married one of his students, who became Rhonda Black. She helped run Keith's schools and worked as an instructor. The marriage did not go smoothly. They separated in 1994, but reconciled the following year. A year later, they had a child. The relationship went downhill again. There were public quarrels. Each was overheard wishing the other was dead. Keith started an affair with another Taekwon-Do instructor in a different city. The couple had financial difficulties. There was a downturn in the Taekwon-Do business so Keith started working at a truck manufacturing company in addition to running his schools. The quarrels escalated. Black asked at least two people to murder her husband. She started researching poisonous mushrooms. On July 21, 1998, Keith did not show up for work at the truck plant and was officially terminated a week later. At the same time, he stopped showing up for his Taekwon-Do classes without notifying students. A few days later, Black rented a rug cleaner. She took a couch and rug that had been in the basement of their home to the garbage dump. As people attempted to reach Keith, Black told them he went hunting and she had not seen him since. Despite this, she did not report Keith missing to police for 11 days. The same day she reported her husband missing, Black obtained a court order giving her exclusive interim custody of their child.

Police found Keith's car abandoned on an overgrown country road a few hours away from his home. There was an empty gun case in the car. Black responded to this news by telling a friend, "He would only need one bullet, he's suicidal." She told another friend, "He's gone, no more Keith."[25] Black told police that Keith was doing drugs, was addicted to pornography, and was suicidally depressed. Friends and other family members disputed this description. Less than a month after the disappearance, Black filed for divorce. She put the family home up for sale. A court order stipulated she would get half the proceeds with the balance held in trust for Keith. Black sometimes said Keith probably committed suicide. Other times she said that he was purposely hiding.

The investigation went nowhere. The police kept investigating while Black continued behaving strangely. For example, in 2000 police divers searched a local pond. After this was reported in the media, Black went to the police station to complain angrily, claiming Keith was hiding in the United States and planning to kidnap their child.

In November 2001 – a little over three years after Keith disappeared, Mr. Big was called in.

Black was taking classes at a college in Kelowna. A female undercover officer posed as a student. After establishing a nod-and-smile relationship, the officer pretended to lock her keys in her car. She asked Black for a ride to get a replacement set from her boyfriend, described as a powerful crime boss. The officer enlisted Black's help in moving around large amounts of cash as part of a money laundering operation. Black liked the pay. The officer introduced Black to her "brother." Black was smitten. Lust joined greed as a lure. Despite this, Black was suspicious. She heard trial coverage about another Mr. Big case and smelled a rat. Black consulted her lawyer, who warned it was a trap. Despite her suspicion and the lawyer's warning, Black still wanted to join the criminal gang. She had earned enough for a down payment on a new car and hoped to buy a house.

Black met Mr. Big in a hotel room wired for sound and containing a hidden video camera. While waiting for Mr. Big to arrive, Black told undercover officers she wanted protection from the police. They discussed producing a witness in the United States who would convincingly claim to have seen Keith. The officer said he was worried about the body being found. Black assured him this would not happen, saying a friend helped bury Keith in a different province. Then Mr. Big arrived. He told Black that he had a friend facing execution in Thailand who wanted to be extradited to Canada. Prison was unpleasant in Thailand[26] and execution a real threat; the previous year 11 people had been executed there. Thai execution technique had once been to wrap the condemned in oil-soaked cloth and set him on fire, but the modern method of lethal injection left one just as dead.[27] Mr. Big's imaginary friend was looking for a Canadian murder to confess to. It needed to be realistic, and he needed to know where the body was buried. Black told Mr. Big that she stabbed her husband while he was asleep on the couch in the basement. She dragged his body to her car and put him in the trunk. Then, with their two-year-old child in the car seat, she drove over 200 kilometers to get help from a friend. The friend came through for her. He cut off Keith's hands and head to make identification more difficult. They buried Keith in several locations. Black said her friend shot Keith's head with a shotgun to make identification through dental records impossible. After the body disposal was completed, the pair cleaned up the crime scene and moved Keith's car to an overgrown road.

This, said Mr. Big, was quite a story. His friend could confess, tell the police where the body parts were, and get a free flight back to Canada. He would dodge the needle of poison while Black would get the police off her back. Black said there was a problem. Although she was with her friend when pieces of Keith were buried, it has been dark. She was in a strange place and, after killing her husband, she had been distraught. She did not know where, exactly, the body parts were.[28]

In most investigations involving accomplices, the suspect making a disclosure to Mr. Big introduces him to others involved. Multiple disclosures are harvested. In this case, relations between Black and her friend were strained. It appears help was provided in anticipation of special benefits. When the benefits were not forthcoming, the friend felt used. Black now claimed to be afraid of him.

To make a long story shorter, the Mr. Big team kept the operation with Black on a "maintenance" basis while they launched a separate one against the friend. He independently told Mr. Big the same story and took the undercover officers to the various places that Keith was buried.[29] With that, both he and Black were arrested. Black was charged with murder; the friend was charged with being an accessory after the fact. She got a life sentence,[30] he got four years.[31]

The strength of the case made by Mr. Big caused Black's defense to become a farce. To explain away her statements to Mr. Big, Black claimed she knew Mr. Big and the other officers were police officers. Black said the real killer was her father, but that she cleaned up to protect him. Black told the judge that she did not want to point the finger at her father directly so she lied to Mr. Big in order to get charged. She said this was designed to cause her father to confess, thereby eliminating all suspicion against her. Black claimed her father was planning on making a dramatic confession at her trial but died of cancer before his plan could be implemented. The judge was not impressed, saying:

> In jury trials, judges instruct juries not to abandon their common sense, and to rely on their knowledge of human affairs. While judges are required to set out the path of their reasoning in writing and juries are not, the same basic instruction is applicable to judges as well. With respect, Ms. Black's evidence at trial as to why she confessed to J. makes no sense at all. As the Crown says, it is incoherent and illogical when considered in the context of the evidence as a whole. I am satisfied beyond a reasonable doubt that Ms. Black did not confess on the basis that she thought J. and K. were police officers and she was playing a double fake on the police.[32]

Black was not a particularly good murderer. Left to her own devices, she would have been caught quickly. She killed Keith in their home in a way that left blood. A prompt search would have produced damning results. She telegraphed the murder by trying to recruit killers. Her post-disappearance conduct was suspicious. She delayed reporting Keith's disappearance, offered contradictory theories for his absence, and quickly launched divorce action. The one good move she made was her choice as a helper for body disposal. He was willing to help and was resourceful. Separating the hands and head from the rest of the body and burying them separately in isolated areas made accidental discovery unlikely. Dumping Keith's car, complete with empty gun case, created a powerful reasonable doubt argument. The helper had a cool head and thought strategically. Until meeting Mr. Big, he kept his mouth shut. Despite his talent for covering up murder, the helper was just as susceptible to Mr. Big as Black was.

Using Mr. Big in No-Body Investigations

Mr. Big creates pre-arrest disclosures of guilt almost magical in their revelatory power. The suspect enthusiastically provides a video-taped explanation of the crime. If the body was hidden, police are taken to the location. If the body was destroyed, the killer explains how. The disclosures are so detailed that follow-up provides confirmation. For example, during an oil boom in the northern Alberta city of Fort McMurray, Dax Mack rented out a room in his house. When he discovered the tenant stealing his son's piggy bank, Mack shot him five times and burned his body. He described all of this to Mr. Big. Forensic examiners found charred bone fragments, zippers, and five shell casings in the ashes.[33] Earlier in the chapter, we saw how the credit card receipt for Franjo Perovic's purchase of grass seed became compelling evidence of premeditation.

Mr. Big is but one way for police to get a disclosure of guilt prior to arrest and interrogation. There are other types of disclosures. All have significant limitations.

Killers often tell friends, family members, criminal colleagues, and sometimes even random strangers about their crime. These are often crucial. In Chapter 5, we saw how Pedro Hernandez's murky disclosures to family members ultimately resulted in his arrest 42 years after he murdered Etan Patz. If he had kept his mouth shut, he would have never been a suspect. But secrets are hard to keep. Killers divulge and listeners betray. But for prosecutors, these disclosures can present problems. They are not electronically recorded. They can be misinterpreted, mis-remembered, and denied. The credibility of the witness determines how a jury will respond, and these witnesses are often discreditable characters. After all, killers talk about their crime with those they believe will not judge them harshly. The witness often has legal problems of their own. People often remember these disclosures only when facing criminal charges. The willingness to testify becomes a get-out-of-jail-free card. This often, and properly, raises doubts about veracity.

Another common type of disclosure comes from jailhouse informants. The suspect, upon arrest, tells a cellmate that he did the dirty deed. The cellmate passes on the information to authorities. At least, that is the theory. These disclosures are often worse than useless. They are often fabricated by the jailhouse "informant" to resolve their own legal difficulties. Even in cases where the disclosure is likely true, credibility in court will be low. After all, the witness was in jail for something. Prosecutor Thomas DeBiase notes that murderers often confess to cellmates "because of either guilt or pride" but "any half-decent defence attorney will shred an informant in court if his statements are not corroborated" and "jurors are predisposed not to like most cooperators."[34]

These difficulties can be overcome with a "plant" in the cell. An undercover police officer pretends to be another prisoner. Ideally, the cell is wired for audio recording and, if possible, for video. In Chapter 7, we saw how this technique was used to obtain damning statements from serial killer Robert Pickton. However, in both Canada and the United States, this approach walks a very fine legal line. The suspect is under arrest and has the right to be warned before interrogation. The cell plant cannot ask the suspect questions about the case. He can talk about other things, but primarily he must just listen. If the suspect makes something approaching a disclosure of guilt, follow-up questions can turn the session into an illegal interrogation. This makes the disclosure unusable in court and can threaten the entire prosecution. As a result, undercover officers working as cell plants must be very well trained and disciplined. There are also practical limitations on how long an undercover officer can pose as an inmate. It is unpleasant, and, if discovered, it can be dangerous. This approach is usually used when the suspect is still in police cells before being transferred to a remand facility.

There is also an ethical problem with reliance on jailhouse informants and cell plants as an investigative tool. They can only be used after a suspect has been arrested. Being arrested has a serious negative impact on a person's life. Someone should be arrested only after police have enough evidence such that there is already a reasonable chance of conviction. When the testimony of a jailhouse informant or cell plant forms the foundation of a case, it is a sign the person was arrested without adequate cause. When combined with the inherent unreliability of jailhouse informants, the possibility of a false conviction looms large.[35] Informants and plants also make jails more dangerous places. Snitches are often punished by other inmates, and the use of snitches creates more paranoia in an already paranoid place.[36]

Mr. Big eliminates these problems. Disclosures come before arrest. They are made to police officers. They are video-recorded. They provide details which can provide corroboration.

Despite these advantages, there are drawbacks to Mr. Big. The operations are time-consuming and expensive. Sending in Mr. Big involves a significant commitment of police resources. This sometimes creates a tendency to view an operation as a failure if the suspect does not admit guilt. This can cause police to push too hard. Almost every Mr. Big disclosure is followed by a recantation. Mr. Big provides a positive incentive to admit guilt. Handcuffs change the incentive structure. Once arrested, the suspect will switch to denial by claiming that he admitted guilt because of greed, desire to impress, or fear.

Mr. Big does not work for all types of no-body homicides. There must be a clear primary suspect who has an unfulfilled – often unknown – desire to join a criminal gang. Mr. Big cannot be used for the capture of sexual serial killers such as Robert Pickton. If someone was murdered by a suspect being cultivated by undercover officers, the legal and moral liability for the police would be too ugly to continence. Mr. Big does not work for suspects who are already a member of a real criminal gang. A member of Kiwanis will not want to join an imaginary Shriner's group. Mr. Big is very effective in dealing with two kinds of murderers. The first are those who have killed an intimate partner. The second are low-level criminals who have killed someone in a robbery or in a dispute over drug turf. These kinds of murderers seem incapable of keeping their mouth shut when approached by Mr. Big.

It is a little puzzling that Mr. Big has not been adopted in the United States. Disclosures generated by Mr. Big have been accepted in American courts. Two people were convicted for murder in Washington State after the RCMP conducted a Mr. Big operation on behalf of American police.[37] On a few occasions, inspired American police officers have independently created the technique.[38] However, Mr. Big does not appear to have ever been used in a no-body investigation in the United States. It is hard to see why. Let us look at just one case where Mr. Big would likely have served justice and saved lives.

In December 2009, Susan Powell disappeared from her home in Utah.[39] Her husband, Josh Powell, claimed he had taken their two young sons camping – notwithstanding a blizzard. The marriage was troubled. The couple had just declared bankruptcy but Susan's life insurance made her worth over a million dollars dead. Susan left a note in her safety deposit box saying that if she died, "it may not be an accident, even if it may look like one."

When Susan disappeared, police were understandably suspicious. Powell was questioned. Warrants were obtained to seize and search his van and house. While the police were searching, Powell rented a car and disappeared for two days. He put on 800 miles, but refused to say where he had gone. A month after Susan's disappearance, Powell liquidated her retirement savings and moved, along with his sons, to live with his father in Washington State. The investigation into Susan's disappearance was massive. Eight months after Susan disappeared, the police department in Utah revealed that it had devoted 6,850 person-hours to the search and investigation. All to no avail. Then things got weird. Powell said he planned to publish Susan's teenage diaries on the internet. His father was arrested for pornography and voyeurism. Police discovered he had taken thousands of surreptitious photos of naked young women and girls – including Susan. Powell lost custody of the two young children, who were placed in the care of Susan's parents. During a supervised visit, Powell murdered his two sons with a hatchet and committed suicide by burning himself alive. Police found evidence that Powell's brother may have helped dispose of Susan's body. The brother also committed suicide. In short, it was a tragic mess. Authorities in Utah and Washington State spent a lot of time pointing fingers at each other. Susan's parents sued Washington State officials for failing to protect their grandchildren. In July of 2020, a jury agreed and awarded them $98 million[40] – reduced by the presiding judge to $32 million.[41]

History is not a controlled experiment. It is impossible to predict results with accuracy. Although nothing is certain, this looks like a case that Mr. Big, sent in six months or a year after Susan's disappearance, could have gotten Powell to admit he killed Susan and tell how or where he disposed of her body. He was made to measure for Mr. Big; broke, with a history of looking for quick, easy money. He was under enormous pressure from the police investigation and publicity; just the type of guy susceptible to a promise to make it all go away. If a timely Mr. Big operation had been launched, it is likely that Powell would be in prison and his sons still alive. Not certainly, but likely. The investigation into Susan's disappearance was a profound failure; it generated no criminal charges, two suicides, and two additional murders. The suicides have generally been interpreted as tantamount to a confession of guilt, but the possibility, however remote, exists they were the result of innocent despair. Mr. Big could well have provided clarity.

Notes

1 Stobbe, Mark, *The "Mr. Big" Sting: The Cases, The Killers, The Controversial Confessions* (Toronto, ON: ECW Press, 2021).
2 Perreault c. R, 2115 QCCA 694.
3 Perreault c. R, 2115 QCCA 694.
4 Perreault c. R, 2115 QCCA 694.
5 Perreault c. R, 20015 QCCA 694.
6 "Perreault Found Guilty in Second Trial for Murder of Lyne Massicotte," *Montreal Gazette*, September 30, 2016.
7 R. v. Franz, 2000 BCSC 802.
8 R v. Franz, 2000 BCSC 0227.
9 R. v. Franz, 2000 BCSC 802.
10 R v. Franz, 2000 BCSC 802.
11 R v. Franz, 2003 BCCA 230.
12 R v. Baranec, "Agreed Statement of Facts," SKQB INFORMATION #24133877, September 21, 2021.
13 R. v. Baranec, 2020 BCCA 156.
14 Zakreski, Dan, "Hitman's Guilty Plea to Manslaughter Offers Small Comfort to Mother of Katelyn Noble," *CBC News*, June 3, 2021.
15 Lovegreen, Tina and Meera Bains, "Realtor Tanpreet Kaur Athwall Found Guilty in Surrey Mothers Murder," *CBC News*, November 25, 2017.
16 R. v. Casement, 2009 SKQB 105.
17 R. v. Casement, 2009 SKQB 105.
18 "Jury Finds B.C. Man Guilty of Saskatoon Woman's Murder," *CBC News*, January 21, 2009.
19 Stobbe, *"Mr. Big" Sting*, 12.
20 McIntyre, *To the Grave*.
21 R. v. Shyback, 2017 ABQB 332; R. v. Shyback, 2018 ABCA 331.
22 R. v. Perovic, 2004 BCSC 643.
23 R. v. Perovic, 2004 BCSC 1823.
24 R. v. Black, 2007 BCSC 1105.
25 R. v. Black, 2007 BCSC 1105.
26 Fellows, Warren, *4.000 Days: My Life and Survival in a Bangkok Prison* (Sydney, AU: St. Martins Griffin, 2000); Cole, Martin, *Welcome to Hell: One Man's Fight for Survival in the Bangkok Hilton* (London, UK: Maverick House, 2005).
27 "Death Penalty 'Here to Stay'" *Bangkok Post*, June 20, 2018; Morris, James and Son Nguyen, "Capital Punishment Is Back in Thailand: Cold Blooded Murderers and Drug Traffickers Are in a Spot," *Thai Examiner*, August 8, 2018.
28 R. v. Black, 2007 BCSC 1105.
29 R. v. Steadman, 2008 BCSC 1613.
30 R. v. Black, 2007 BCSC 1105.
31 R. v. Steadman, 210 BCCA 382.

32 R. v. Black, 2007 BCSC 1105, 288.
33 R. v. Mack, 2012 ABCA 42; R. v. Mack, 2014 SCC 48.
34 DiBiase, *No-Body Homicide Cases*, 23–25.
35 Covey, Russell D. "Abolishing Jailhouse Snitch Testimony," *Wake Forest Law Review* 49, No. 5 (2001): 1375–1430; Wetmore, S. A., Neuschatz, J. S., & Gronlund, S. D., "On the Power of Secondary Confession Evidence," *Psychology, Crime & Law*, 20, No. 4 (2014): 339–357; Neuschatz, Jeffery S., Danielle K. DeLoach, Megan A. Hillgartner, Melanie B. Fessinger, Stacy A. Whetmore, Amy B. Douglass, Brian H. Bornstein, and Alexis M. Le Grand, "The Truth about Snitches: An Archival Analysis of Informant Testimony," *Psychiatry, Psychology and Law* 28, No. 4 (2021): 508–530.
36 Stobbe, Mark, *Lessons from Remand* (New York, NY: Key Publishing, 2013), 45–66.
37 State v. Rafay, 168 Wn. App. 734 (Wash. Ct. App. 2012)
38 Stobbe, *The 'Mr. Big' Sting*.
39 Olson, Gregg and Rebecca Morris, *If I Can't Have You* (New York, NY: St. Martins, 2014); Rule, Ann, *Fatal Friends, Deadly Neighbors* (New York, NY: Gallery Books, 2012); Graves, Jennifer and Emily Clawson, *A Light in Dark Places* (Scotts Valley, CA: CreateSpace, 2013).
40 "Washington State Ordered to Pay Parents of Susan Powell $98 Million in Case of Her Murdered Sons," *KING 5-TV News*, July 31, 2020.
41 Stauffer, MacKenzie, "Judge Reduces $98.5M Award by Two-Thirds in Cox Family Wrongful Death Case," *2KUTV-News* (September 14, 2020).

15

PROSECUTORIAL MISFIRES

Unsuccessful Prosecutions in No-Body Cases

The criminal justice system has two basic tasks when confronted with a homicide. It must identify, convict, and administer the legally prescribed punishment to the person(s) who committed the crime. It must do this while operating within prescribed legal rules and norms. Police, prosecutors, and the courts must punish the right person in the right way. From these two mandates, different types of error are possible. In this chapter, we will look at error and failure in the investigation and prosecution of no-body cases.

The disappearances of Jimmy Hoffa and the Fountains resulted in one type of failure. No rational person could reach a conclusion but that they were murdered. The motives for these murders were known with a high degree of certainty. Jimmy Hoffa and Albert Fountain had dangerous enemies. Henry Fountain was killed because he was an inconvenient witness to the assassination of his father – nothing personal, but deadly nonetheless. Despite this, nobody was ever convicted. We can speculate in an informed way about which relatively small group contained these killers but the justice system failed to establish which individual(s) did the dirty deed. We can say with certainty there was a system failure; people got away with murder. Scientists call this type of error a Type 2 error, or a false negative.[1] Someone was murdered, but the killer was not convicted.

Jimmy, Albert, and Henry are unrepresentative of most Type 2 errors for no-body homicides. Their disappearances became famous. Massive amounts of time, money, and investigative effort were devoted to finding their killers. I have described their cases in detail because so much information is available. Most victims of no-body killers remain anonymous. Their disappearances remain officially classified as missing persons' cases. They are not included in official homicide statistics at the time of their murder. When Robert Pickton's killing spree in British Columbia was revealed, Statistics Canada made significant, retroactive adjustments to the province's official homicide rate.[2] The fate of people who permanently disappear remains unknown. Most remain obscure. On the anniversary dates of their disappearance, there is sometimes a small flurry of media coverage. Their names and faces might remain posted on yellowing posters in bus depots. For the most part they are only remembered and missed by family and friends.

We do not know how many of these victims there are and how many killers avoided punishment. The unknown is, by definition, unknown. We do know these cases exist. For decades, the prosecution of no-body homicide cases was effectively nonexistent. As police and prosecutorial attitudes began to change, as people's lives became enmeshed in bureaucracy, as new forensic

DOI: 10.4324/9781003372134-15

and cell phone technologies emerged, more no-body cases resulted in arrests, charges, and convictions. There have been over a dozen per year in the 21st century. There is no reason to believe that body disposal is a new strategy for killers. At a very minimum, current conviction rates provide a base-line for estimating how many people got away with murder in the past.

But this estimate just scratches the surface.

In the United States, the 2020 year-end report of the National Crime Information Centre (NCIC) reported 48,714 unresolved missing persons' cases.[3] The National Missing and Unidentified Persons System (NamUs) uses different methodologies to report 21,205 unresolved long-term missing persons' cases at the end of 2021.[4] The range in estimates by these two government agencies highlights a problem. There is a lot we do not know about what we do not know. Some long-term missing people are likely still alive, and some who are dead were not murdered, but the volume of long-term missing people suggests there are several thousand murderers who avoided punishment by disposing of the bodies of their victims.

In Canada, pressure from families of murdered and missing indigenous women slowly and painfully made homicides masquerading as missing persons cases a public issue. In 2013, the Royal Canadian Mounted Police reported there were 164 indigenous women who had been missing longer than 30 days (in some cases, for years) in circumstances deemed "suspicious."[5] Almost all these women were likely victims of no-body homicides. Public pressure mounted by families of victims helped create the National Centre for Missing Persons and Unidentified Remains (NCMPUR). In 2020, it reported that 18,329 adults and 6,964 children went missing for "unknown" reasons and were still missing by year's end.[6] If 1 percent of these people missing for unknown reasons were victims of homicide, another 252 people would be added to the Canada's homicide count; this would increase Canada's homicide rate by over 33 percent.

Some homicide victims are never even reported missing. Police do not – cannot – conduct even the most cursory of missing persons' investigations. In the words of former U.S. defense secretary Donald Rumsfeld, these victims are the unknown unknowns.[7] Criminologists call them the missing missing.[8] In Chapter 6 we got a glimpse of this problem. When police found the clusters of bodies dumped by Gary Ridgeway, 11 of 48 had no ongoing missing persons' investigation outstanding. Another five victims remain unidentified. In 2007, criminologist Kenna Quinet painstakingly examined multiple data sources to conclude that somewhere between 182 and 1,832 victims of serial killers disappear annually in the United States but are never reported missing.[9] The size of her estimate interval is a stark illustration of the difficulties inherent in researching unknown unknowns. These killers evaded even being investigated through a combination of astute victim selection and body disposal, but we cannot say how many.

As we saw in Chapter 1, most people who go missing eventually turn up alive. The longer a person is missing, the more likely it is they are to be dead, but not every no-body fatality is a no-body homicide. But still. The volume of unresolved, long-term missing persons cases means there are a lot of Type 2, false-negative, errors out there. We cannot say much more than that.

Let us turn our attention to Type 1, false-positive, error. These are cases where someone was charged, but not ultimately convicted or where a conviction was overturned. We will call these misfired prosecutions.

Misfired Prosecutions: When the Prosecution Does Not Prove Its Case

In researching this book, successful prosecutions in 487 no-body prosecutions in the United States and 32 in Canada were examined. Another 70 American and 4 Canadian cases were examined in which someone was arrested and charged but for which:

- Charges were withdrawn; or
- The accused was acquitted at trial; or
- The accused was convicted but the conviction was overturned on appeal, and not ultimately convicted again after a new trial. Many people who win appeals are later re-convicted or reach a plea bargain before a second trial. These cases were counted as successful prosecutions; or
- The accused was convicted and their conviction upheld on appeal, but were subsequently officially exonerated.

More misfires and successful prosecutions will emerge as current cases wind their way through the court system. This process can take a long time. For example, on August 15, 2015, Taylor Samson went to the apartment of William Sandeson to complete a drug deal. Closed circuit television (CCTV) cameras showed Taylor going in carrying a large duffel bag (known to be filled with $40,000 worth of marijuana), but not coming out. The people living across the hall from Sandeson testified they saw a body slumped in a chair, blood, drugs, and cash the night William disappeared. The apartment's CCTV system recorded Sandeson carrying garbage bags out of the apartment. The next morning, CCTV cameras in the apartment's parking lot recorded Sandeson cleaning the trunk of his car. Taylor's DNA was found in the trunk of Sandeson's car. Cell phone tracking showed Sandeson's cell phone traveled from the apartment to a farm owned by his family. Garbage bags containing material with William's DNA were found on the farm. A search of Sandeson's apartment showed signs it had been cleaned, but William's blood was found on the floor and walls. A gun was found with spots of William's blood on it, consistent with someone being shot from two to four feet away. A bullet with traces of William's DNA on it was found embedded in the windowsill.[10]

William Samson's murder was a self-solver. Sandeson was arrested three days after William disappeared. In 2017, Sandeson was convicted. In 2020 the conviction was overturned on appeal.[11] The two witnesses who testified seeing a body in Sandeson's apartment initially told police they had not seen anything, but changed their story after talking to a private investigator hired by the defense lawyer. This investigator, a recently retired police officer, convinced them to tell the truth. He then told police investigators the two should be reinterviewed. The defense lawyer did not know his investigator helped the police assemble the case against his client. When the lawyer found out, he was unhappy.[12] The Nova Scotia Court of Appeal judges agreed his distress was warranted and overturned the conviction. A second trial has been scheduled for 2023 – almost eight years after Sandeson was arrested and six years after he was first convicted.[13] When this book was completed, Sandeson remained in jail after being denied bail.[14]

Prosecutorial misfires occur for two basic reasons. Either the prosecution failed to convince a trial judge or jury that the case was proven beyond a reasonable doubt, or, as in the case of William Sandeson, appeal court judges found that the right of the accused to a fair trial was violated. Every homicide prosecution has the potential to misfire, but no-body prosecutions have unique features and thus present unique opportunities for things to go wrong.

In Chapter 5 we examined the case of A.S. who convinced her family she was pregnant when she was not. This resulted in a murder charge for killing a baby that never existed. Justice was served with an acquittal. Some misfired prosecutions mean the courts successfully did their job.

In 1928, four-year-old Melvin Horst played with friends in a small Ohio town. His mother called him for supper. Melvin never arrived home. Despite an intensive search, he was never found. Rewards totaling $2,900 were posted; this represented almost two years of income for the average American male. The reward drew interest from a private detective from Cincinnati. He found an eight-year-old boy willing to say he saw Melvin with a young man from a family of bootleggers.[15] Arthur Arnold and his father, Elias, were arrested and charged. Their house was searched. Ashes in the suspect's wood furnace contained bones, although the effect of this incriminating find was undermined when they were identified as coming from chickens, rabbits, pigs, and cows rather than from small humans. Nonetheless, the prosecution proceeded. The prosecutor's theory was Arthur and Elias killed the boy to get revenge on Melvin's uncle, the town's marshal, who had arrested them several times for bootlegging. The two admitted having a grudge against Melvin's uncle, but denied any involvement in the disappearance. Elias testified that "If I wanted to get even with Marshal Horst, I'd take it out of his skin."[16] The prosecution got a conviction for "child-stealing" (not homicide) based on the eight-year-old's testimony and the imputed motive. The conviction was overturned on appeal after it was learned the eight-year-old witness had provided five different, contradictory, statements. As a second trial, the prosecution attempted to keep the contradictory statements from the jury by claiming they were the personal property of the prosecutor. The ploy failed, and the accused were acquitted.[17] No sign of Melvin Horst has ever been found. He probably died about the time of his disappearance. He may have been murdered, but there is a possibility he died of exposure in some strange location. It was, after all, a cold day in December.

Defense lawyers are paid to create reasonable doubt. This is sometimes harder than it seems. The first trial of A.S. resulted in a hung jury, with 11 of 12 jurors voting to convict. Arthur and Elias Arnold were convicted at their first trial. These three people came close to spending a long time in prison, even though the evidence against them was about halfway between nonexistent and extremely sketchy. In most cases, prosecutors have more evidence to present, which makes creating reasonable doubt more difficult, but doubt can be created even when police have built a strong case.

Dead Alive Sightings and Misfires

A common feature in a homicide trial is the accused claiming they were elsewhere when the killing occurred. It is called an alibi. A good alibi is created when credible witnesses testify that the suspect was not at the crime scene. Two principles serve as indicators of an alibi witnesses' credibility. The first is the ability to make a strong identification. The witness must be definite about seeing the suspect at a specific place and time. Identification is more certain if the witness knows the accused than if they are identifying a stranger. The second factor impacting the credibility of an alibi witness is whether they have a reason to lie.[18] Jail guards testifying the suspect was locked up make good alibi witnesses. As a rule, mothers do not. In between are taxi-drivers, store clerks, co-workers, and people encountered on a semi-casual basis.

Police and prosecutors are usually skeptical about the credibility of alibi witnesses while defense lawyers embrace them, although credibility can be strained even for them. Cici McNair was a private investigator working for the lawyers defending Kenneth and Stante Kimes after the murder of Irene Silverman. She tells of being dispatched to track down dozens of people the Kimes claimed would give them an alibi. Most were waiters, store clerks, taxi drivers. The list was almost endless, groundless, and contradictory. When one person denied seeing the Kimes, another possibility was conjured up. Despite almost endless attempts, the Kimes were unable to find someone able to testify they were somewhere else when Irene Silverman disappeared.[19] If the private investigator had found one alibi witness among the dozens interviewed, that person would have become a defense witness. All those who refused to confirm the Kimes's story would have been ignored.

In most no-body cases, alibi witnesses serve a different function. As we saw in Chapter 10, prosecutors must convince jurors that the putative victim is, in fact, dead. It is the necessary, but not sufficient, condition for getting a conviction. Prosecutors prove death by proving absence. Although increased bureaucratization makes this task easier, one piece of evidence trumps the best documentation of absence. After Topsy Warren, Jenny Wilson, James Smith, and Mary Vickery were discovered alive, the case against their putative killers dissolved like a sugar cube in coffee. Abraham Lincoln got murder charges against his client dismissed when the victim was located. The reappearances of Russell Colvin and Connie Franklin were more contentious since their identity was disputed. Nonetheless, as soon as they were deemed to be the putative victim, the people accused of murder were set free. In these cases, reappearance preceded execution. The Perry family, Andrew Hudspeth and William Marion were more unfortunate in the timing of the reappearance of the people they were convicted of killing. Stretching the human neck is irrevocable.

If police have thoroughly documented a disappearance, defense lawyers are unlikely to produce a living homicide victim. As a result, defense lawyers must rely on a substitute – testimony from witnesses claiming to have seen the missing person. It is a form of alibi and a common tactic in no-body homicide trials. A railroad ticket seller claimed to have sold Evelyn Scott a train ticket to New York City.[20] Perry March produced a blurry picture purporting to show Janet Murch attending a World Cup soccer match in Italy.[21] Ron Hunt produced two people claiming to have seen the missing Ron Levin in Tucson, New Mexico and a man claiming to have seen Ron standing in a movie line-up.[22] Some defense lawyers are even more desperate. After Nina Reiser disappeared, Hans Reiser's lawyer adopted the "still-alive" argument based on language fluency rather than witnesses, saying, "the evidence hasn't excluded her from being in Europe. She speaks German, English and Russian. No one ever looked for her that we know of in any of the European countries."[23] After the jury convicted Reiser of first-degree murder, he was allowed to plead guilty to second-degree murder in exchange for showing where he hid Nina's body.[24]

Witnesses claiming to have seen the victim are almost inevitable in any no-body case receiving media attention. These witnesses usually fail every test developed to assess the credibility of eyewitness testimony. They often claim to have recognized a stranger based on a fleeting encounter occurring after seeing media coverage about the case. At Joe Hunt's trial, the Tucson witnesses said the person they saw at a gas station months earlier was absolutely and beyond a shadow of a doubt Ron Levin. If a prosecutor presented this kind of witness, any marginally competent defense attorney would explode with objections, and rightly so. When dubious witnesses claim they have seen the missing person, defense lawyers demand these reports be treated with absolute deference.

There is a paradoxical irony to all this. The more seriously police approach the disappearance with an open mind, the more false-reports of sightings are generated. Diligence by police manufactures reasonable doubt claims by defense lawyers. False sightings distract investigations. In 2002, Mike Bridges strangled his girlfriend, Erin Chorney. He buried her in someone else's grave. About two years later, Bridges told an undercover police officer what he did and where Erin's body was hidden. Police dug up her corpse. We know, with absolute certainty, that Erin was killed the night she disappeared and buried the next day. Despite this, police received over 160 "sightings" in the year following her disappearance.[25] Each one had to be investigated no matter regardless of credibility. Failure to follow up on a single sighting can create a prosecutorial misfire.

This brings us to the fiasco known as the Canadian justice system's response to the disappearance of Christine Jack from her Winnipeg, Manitoba, home.

Christine Jack was a speech pathologist, married with two children. Her husband, Brian Jack, had a four-year professional football career in the Canadian Football League culminating in two years with the Winnipeg Blue Bombers. After his football career ended, Brian divorced his first wife, met and married Christine, had two children, and opened four sporting goods stores. All went well until Brian's business went into receivership. Marital trouble followed financial setbacks. In November of 1988, Christine told Brian she wanted to end the marriage. The two took a brief stab at marital counseling before Christine consulted a lawyer about getting a divorce. She told family and friends she was ending the marriage. On the evening of December 17, 1988, she disappeared.[26]

Brian told friends, family, and police that the two quarreled before Christine drove away in the family vehicle, a yellow Ford Bronco. The search for Christine began the next morning. Police became suspicious of Brian because of his demeanor. He seemed too calm about his wife's disappearance. Their suspicions hardened when Brian opposed using a helicopter to search for his missing wife. Five days after Christine disappeared, police received an anonymous telephone tip directing them to a restaurant parking lot containing the Ford Bronco. Brian denied knowledge of the call, but after being told the call had been traced to his house, admitted to making it. He claimed friends told him they saw the vehicle. The friends said they had not. There was blood on the tailgate of the Bronco. Police got a warrant to search the Jacks' home and found blood on the couch and rug. Brian was arrested on Christmas Eve, questioned, released, and put under surveillance. Social workers placed Brian and Christine's children in a temporary receiving home.

Concurrent with Brian's first, temporary, arrest, police issued a public appeal for information that included a picture of the yellow Ford Bronco. It was a distinctive vehicle, and he was a distinctive man. The appeal caused a flurry of calls from the town of Ste. Anne, about 40 minutes east of Winnipeg. Hotel staff reported that, on the night of December 17, a man matching Brian's description arrived looking for a mechanic. His yellow Ford Bronco was overheating. Two local mechanics inspected the vehicle and found a leaking transmission seal. The man said he was in too much of a hurry to wait for parts, so the mechanics gave him two gallons of transmission fluid. The man left without paying; the mechanics took chase, caught up to the Bronco, and were given a $50 bill. The mechanics paid more attention to the vehicle than its driver. Both positively identified the Ford Bronco but were less certain whether Brian was the driver. One said yes; one said maybe. The hotel staff was positive in their identification of Brian. It was good enough for police. Seventeen days after Christine was reported missing, Brian was charged with murder. Even though the search for her body was unsuccessful, the case seemed like a classic self-solver.

But police left one thing uncovered. It led to a legal quagmire. In addition to the Ste. Anne's witnesses placing Brian and the Bronco in Ste. Anne's the night of the disappearance, the publicity caused two Winnipeg waitresses call police to report they served a woman matching Christine's description on the night of December 23rd. If their report was accurate, Christine was alive a week after Brian was alleged to have killed her. Police did not investigate. Prosecutors were not told of the report and so did not include it in disclosure material to defense lawyers. The existence of the call emerged months later when a police officer testified at a preliminary hearing. During cross-examination, police were blunt about the reason this sighting report was ignored:

Q. *And if you had a fact that somebody saw Christine Jack, you wouldn't bother to go and speak to that person and check that out? You wouldn't bother doing that? Is that your evidence?*

A. *No. Because in my mind what had transpired in the family room at 170 Alburg Drive on the night of the 17th of December had led to her death and her husband was involved in that.*[27]

In a book about the case, the lead prosecutor in Brian's first trial defended the police nonresponse to the call by arguing the officers believed, with "moral certainty," that Brian was guilty.[28] For a defense lawyer, a police officer's moral certainty has another name: tunnel vision. In and of itself, the failure to follow up with the waitresses did not threaten the case against Brian. There were lots of evidence pointing toward guilt. At trial, Brian was convicted of second-degree murder, but the moral certainty of the police was a bit like the fly swallowed by the old lady. One thing led to another.

The Manitoba Court of Appeal overturned the conviction, saying,

> In all of the circumstances of this complex and difficult case, I have come to the conclusion that the appeal must be allowed because of the error in the trial judge's charge with respect to the Charter House [waitress] witnesses. A new trial is ordered on the charge of second-degree murder.[29]

At the second trial, the jury asked for clarification on the distinction between second-degree murder and manslaughter. In a self-acknowledged slip of his tongue, the judge told them that unless they were convinced a homicide resulted from a "specific intent" to kill, they must acquit for both murder and manslaughter. This was legally correct for the murder but not manslaughter. Thirty-eight minutes later, the jury returned with an acquittal. The prosecution successfully appealed based on the incorrect judicial instruction. The Manitoba Court of Appeal ordered a new trial on a manslaughter charge.[30] During deliberations at the third trial, the jury asked for clarification on how to treat the conflict between the Ste. Anne and waitress testimony. The judge got a little testy with them, saying:

> Was this woman in the red coat, who looked like Christine Jack, in fact Christine Jack? Do not isolate and try to decide this issue as if there were no other material evidence to be considered.
>
> Consider it. Can you rationally, in the light of the other evidence you have heard, accept this proposition? If you accept it, as I've told you, you must acquit. If you have a reasonable doubt, you must acquit. But before deciding whether the doubt you have on this or any other aspect of the case is reasonable, do take the evidence and place it in the context of the whole case. Place it in the context of the other evidence which points to her disappearance being explained only by death on December 17th...
>
> I have said before, and I say again, that in their deliberations, jurors do not leave their common sense hanging on the peg along with their coat. Avoid trying to be amateur investigators, avoid being speculators. You're not called here to try and be Sherlock Holmes. Stick to the evidence that you have and, with good will, apply your common sense and debate the issues honestly and fairly...
>
> A reasonable doubt arises only from rational consideration, not from insecure, fanciful or unfounded musings.[31]

With this admonition ringing in their ears, the jury promptly returned with a guilty verdict. At appeal, the defense argued the judge openly exhorted the jury to convict. Although the Manitoba Court of Appeal upheld the conviction, it was a split decision.[32] This moved the case to the Supreme Court of Canada. On June 27, 1997 – 3,115 days after Christine Jack disappeared – the Supreme Court issued a terse, two-page opinion striking down Brian's conviction. It also ordered the charges be stayed "because of the numerous trials and appeals the accused has been subjected to."[33] It was not exactly an acquittal, but it served the same purpose.

In all three trials, problems stemmed from the judge's instructions. In both convictions, ultimately overturned on appeal, the problematic instructions attempted to untangle the original police decision to ignore the report that Christine had dinner in a restaurant a week after she disappeared. The trial judges were trying to explain how eyewitness testimony should be evaluated in different circumstances; one where the police followed up to corroborate and one where they did not.

The nine-and-a-half-year process left Brian Jack legally innocent, but this result came from some judges parsing the language of other judges rather than an evaluation of the evidence. The courts were trying to deal with an explicit acknowledgment by police that they failed to investigate all possibilities because of "moral certainty" of Brian's guilt. The result was a legal quagmire satisfactory to nobody. On the 13th anniversary of Christine's death, her daughter told a reporter, "We just want closure. We want to give her the proper burial that she deserves." She had no doubt about her father's guilt, saying, "There was just so much evidence that pointed in his direction. I wish he could find it in his heart to help us find her remains, or give us a clue, or tell somebody to tell somebody where she is."[34]

The investigation into the disappearance of Christine Jack was a self-solver, but the misfired prosecution of Brian Jack shows what can happen when police do not investigate every claimed sighting of the missing person, regardless of credibility. This can consume much police time and seem like a distraction from the "real" investigation. However, if the work is done, DiBiase argues that the prosecution's case is strengthened when the defense introduces witnesses claiming to have seen the victim still alive.[35] Police testimony about the follow-up for all leads bolsters the argument the victim is dead. The refutation of witness sightings also allows the presentation of character evidence about the victim to show they would not be the type of person to abandon, without notice, children, parents, friends, employers, and societal commitments.

Confessions Good and Bad

If a prosecutor cannot build a case around a body, they try to build it around a confession. If the killer admits guilt, juries tend to convict. Bruce McFarlane, a senior prosecutor from Manitoba, says, "Except in the rare situations where a perpetrator is actually caught in the act of committing a crime, a confession is regarded as the most powerful, persuasive, and demanding evidence of guilt that the state can adduce."[36] If a suspect confesses, the case is generally considered "closed" by investigators. If the accused later recants the confession (and most do at some point), juries almost always give more credence to the original confession than to the recantation.

In no-body cases, confessions fill in the black box by explaining what happened. The accused provides a narrative of how death occurred and how the body was disposed of. When one of the people hired to kill Judge Chillingworth told how the judge and his wife were weighted down and tossed into the ocean, the lack of bodies became explicable.

Police and prosecutors work hard to get confessions out of suspects in no-body cases. They can be imaginative. We saw how police in Canada create imaginary criminal gangs to trick a suspect into disclosure. On occasion, police work too hard to get a confession. Overly enthusiastic post-arrest interrogation or the use of jailhouse informants can produce confessions that create a misfired prosecution. In most of these cases, police arrest based on suspicion and hope a convictable case can be created post-arrest. Sometimes this works. In Chapter 8, we saw how Perry March made conviction a certainty by attempting to recruit another inmate to murder the parents of his dead wife. This inmate led police to March's father, who ultimately told police how he helped destroy the body of Janet March.

In other cases, using arrest as an investigative tool created prosecutorial misfires.

Not every confession is truthful. People confess to crimes they did not commit. There is a vast body of academic research exploring why people make false confessions.[37] For our purposes, we do not need to explore this research in detail. If you are skeptical that people falsely confess to serious crimes, consider that over a dozen people confessed to the murders committed by Ted Bundy.[38] Courts in both Canada and the United States are aware of the potential for false confessions and have placed limitations on police behavior during interrogations. Suspects cannot be tortured. They must be told of their right to remain silent and warned that anything they say will be used against them. They must be told they have the right to consult a lawyer. Despite these legal guardrails, suspects still confess. Some are lying. The courts examine police behavior in obtaining confessions. If legal standards are violated, the confession can be ruled inadmissible as evidence. Truthful confessions can be inadmissible on procedural grounds. The courts also attempt to evaluate veracity by comparing the confession against other evidence. For example, if a suspect confesses to shooting the victim when the medical evidence shows the victim was strangled, the validity of the confession is suspect. Both bad process and a lack of corroboration can create misfired prosecutions.

In 1972, a burned car was found beside Macy, Nebraska. It was not quite a full no-body case; there were human remains inside the car. However, the body was so badly burned that identification and cause of death could not be determined. Based on who was missing from the community, police concluded the body was Dennis Thomas. He was last seen passed out in the car after an evening of heavy drinking. After the car and body were discovered, police questioned Raymond Stabler, a teenager who had also been drinking heavily. Stabler told police that he robbed a person sleeping in a car, stabbed him, and set the car on fire. Stabler was still intoxicated when he gave this confession. A recantation accompanied sobriety. Stabler was convicted of second-degree murder. The conviction was overturned on appeal because it rested on an uncorroborated confession made when impaired.[39]

In 2000, Michael Lord of New Hampshire disappeared. In his home, police found bondage equipment and a contact list of dominatrix service providers. This led them to Massachusetts professional dominatrix Barbara Asher. Police reported that Barbara confessed she watched Michael die of a heart attack during a session but failed to call an ambulance because she was afraid of the impact on her business. Police said she watched Michael die, called a friend to help with body disposal, cut Michael into eight pieces, and dumped the bagged body parts into a garbage dumpster behind a Chinese restaurant in Maine.[40] Michael's body was never recovered, and no corroborating forensic evidence was found in Barbara's apartment. At her trial for involuntary manslaughter and dismemberment, Barbara denied both guilt and making the confession. Police recorded the interrogation for two hours, but claimed they turned off the tape recorder when Barbara began to confess. Police also said they destroyed their notes. Cutting a body into eight pieces is messy, but no forensic evidence was found in Barbara's studio. She was acquitted.[41]

Confessions can get murkier when made to people other than police officers. The credibility of the person claiming to have heard the confession becomes important.

In 1981, 12-year-old Brian Beyrl disappeared from Phoenix, Arizona, while collecting money from his paper route customers. In 1989, Stephen Wilson was charged with his murder after three people claimed he confessed. Stephen denied both killing and confession, alleging the witnesses against him were motivated by homophobia. There was no corroborating evidence. Stephen was acquitted.[42]

In 1986, Martin Gentry disappeared from Sacramento, California. In 1989, Martin's best friend, Joseph Stanley, was charged with murder. Joseph's ex-girlfriend triggered the arrest. At the time of the disappearance, she told police she knew nothing. Three years later, she said Joseph told her about shooting his friend. Two attempts at prosecution resulted in hung juries. After the second trial, the prosecutor gave up trying.[43]

In the prosecution of both Stephen Wilson and Joseph Stanley, the absence of a body – and indeed, of any corroborating evidence – made conviction dependent upon the credibility of the person testifying they heard a confession. Even when the person reporting the confession is credible, problems can emerge. In Chapter 6, we learned how Leonard Lipsky told a psychiatric social worker he murdered Mary Robinson. The New York Supreme Court ultimately ruled this confession was inadmissible since the social worker was an agent of the State of Utah. A *Miranda* warning should have been given.

The most questionable confessions are those alleged to have been made to "jailhouse snitches." When a person is charged with a homicide, they spend time in jail awaiting trial. Other prisoners view them as an opportunity. Testimony about a real or imagined confession can get favorable treatment on their own charges. In no-body cases, the desire of police and prosecutors to fill in the narrative of the crime creates a temptation to use jailhouse informants or "snitches." This can create prosecutorial misfires. In his advice to prosecutors in no-body cases, DiBiase recommends caution. If the informant is acting as an agent for the police when the suspect has a lawyer, any confession will likely be ruled inadmissible. There are also problems of credibility. In a report on a wrongful conviction in Manitoba, a retired Supreme Court judge said, "Jailhouse informants comprise the most deceitful and deceptive group of witnesses known to frequent the courts...They rush to testify like vultures to rotting flesh or sharks to blood. They are smooth and convincing liars...Jailhouse informers are a uniquely evil group."[44] Or, as DiBiase says, "Any half-decent defense attorney will shred an informant in court if his statements are not corroborated."[45] If the defense lawyers undermine the credibility of the informant, it undermines the credibility of the entire case and can result in a misfired prosecution.

An exception to the problems of using confessions made to jailhouse informants is when the suspect conspires with fellow inmates about future crimes. We have seen that midlife crisis killers seem prone to hiring other inmates to kill witnesses, police, or prosecutors. Killers such as Perry March, Thomas Capano, and Joseph Peel are just a few who attempted to recruit another inmate to kill on their behalf. These attempts are treated as being tantamount to a confession. However, there is a caution. There is really no doubt that Jay Smith attempted to recruit another inmate to kill the police officers leading his investigation. However, there was almost no evidence that he killed Susan Reinhart and her two children. His ill-conceived and ill-fated attempt to have his tormentors killed appears to have been generated by the anger of an innocent man rather than the desperation of a guilty one.

Accomplice Testimony and Misfires

No-body homicides are more likely to be a group activity than are body-present homicides. This stems from the practical problems of body disposal. Corpses are hard to move. Killers often recruit helpers who become accomplices. Twenty-eight percent of successful prosecutions featured accomplice testimony as a key part of the evidence. While this testimony can be compelling and lead to convictions, it can create problems. In Chapter 9, we saw how Judge Joseph Peel got his associates Floyd Holzapfel and Bobby Lincoln to do the actual killing. These accomplices both testified against Peel. While their testimony sent Peel to prison, it also presented problems for the prosecution. Holzapfel was a disreputable character whose credibility was subject to attack. Lincoln had an even bigger problem with credibility. He received immunity from prosecution for his active role in the murders. The prosecution had to convince the jury that a self-confessed murderer was not pointing the finger at an innocent person to evade punishment. A southern jury in 1960 had to believe a black criminal was telling the truth while a white judge was lying. Peel's late-life confession confirmed the jury's wisdom in believing the black criminal, but Lincoln's accomplice testimony had the potential to create a prosecutorial misfire.

In the Peel prosecution the accomplice was telling the truth, but people providing accomplice testimony often lie. They shift culpability by downplaying their role and accentuating the role of the person on trial. Sometimes a person will even lie about being an accomplice.

In 2002, 17-year-old Brian Carrick disappeared from a Chicago suburb. Brian was a high school student working part-time as a "stock-boy" at a local supermarket, which also appears to have been a hub for small-time drug dealing. The owner's son, Mario Casciaro, provided ounces of marijuana to the other stock-boys on credit. They paid Mario when it was sold. After Brian disappeared, police found his blood splattered in the produce cooler, smeared in a trail down the hallway to the back door, and on cardboard in the garbage dumpster. There was no body in the dumpster. It appears Brian was placed there for temporary storage and subsequently moved for permanent disposal. DNA tests showed Brian's blood was mixed with blood from another stock-boy, Robert Render. The handle on the produce cooler door had a bloody fingerprint belonging to Render. A few days after Brian disappeared, Render quit his job and ran away from home. Render was spotted and caught after a flight attempt. In addition to the forensic evidence and post-event behavior, a witness told police that Render owed Brian money. Render claimed he was innocent, saying his blood was at the crime scene because he chewed his fingernails. Render pointed an accusing finger at another stock-boy, Shane Lamb.

Shane was a great choice for Render to accuse. Most of the stock-boys were high school students. Shane was 28 years old. He had been charged with attempted murder when 14. As an adult, he had five convictions for a combination of aggravated assault and cocaine offenses. When Render identified him as the killer, Shane was in jail for parole violations and faced new drug charges carrying a potential for 30 years in prison. The prosecution had offered him a plea deal carrying a 12-year sentence. Normally, being accused of murder is a bad thing. For Shane it was an opportunity. He negotiated an agreement giving full immunity for anything to do with Brian's death and cut the proposed penalty on his drug charges in half. An accusation of murder caused his sentence on the drug charges to be cut from 12 years to 6.[46] Shane eventually served 3. In exchange, Shane implicated Mario. According to Shane, Brian was attempting to collect money owed by Brian when he (Shane) happened by and joined in. Shane said he hit Brian a few times and accidently killed him. Mario was charged with murder. The prosecution argued he used Shane to intimidate Brian and was therefore legally responsible for Brian's death. One trial resulted in a hung jury and mistrial. At a second, Mario was convicted and sentenced to 26 years in prison.

Judges on the Appellate Court of Illinois, Second District were not impressed. They noted that, even if Shane's story was true,

> Lamb's unequivocal testimony that the defendant did not ask or tell him to threaten Carrick simply cannot be twisted to support the inference that the defendant used Lamb to threaten Carrick. Accordingly, the State failed to prove that the defendant committed intimidation as a principal.

But there was more. "The physical evidence and the testimony of disinterested witnesses show that whatever happened to Carrick could not have been what Lamb portrayed." The blood evidence was "irreconcilable with Lamb's testimony" and the police acceptance of Render's fingernail-biding explanation was "outlandish."[47]

Mario Casciaro's conviction was overturned, and he was ordered acquitted. Brian Carrick's murder will always remain legally unsolved. The Appellate Court judges said the case against

Render "cannot so easily be dismissed" and summarized the evidence against him. However, Render died of a heroin overdose during the period between Mario's first and second trials, so this evidence will never be tested in court. The whole fiasco highlights the potential for a misfire arising from putative accomplice testimony. In the words of the Illinois Appellate Court:

> Lamb admitted that he lied whenever it suited him. He testified that he lied to the grand jury but was never charged with perjury. He testified that he lied to FBI agents. He said that he told prison authorities so many lies that he got confused.[48]

Testimony from such a person is a poor foundation upon which to build a prosecution. Shane later recanted his testimony,[49] providing one more reason to avoid relying on unreliable witnesses.

Immunity agreements are powerful chips the prosecutors play in order to obtain testimony. The problem is, these chips usually must be thrown on the table early in the game. Once a deal has been made, prosecutors defend them fiercely. Admitting to being conned by a criminal can be career ending. The dynamic can create misfired prosecutions.

No-Body Homicides and False Convictions

The most egregious error the criminal justice system can make is to convict the wrong person for murder. An innocent person is sent to prison or is executed. But there is more. With the false conviction, any official investigation ends. After all, the crime is "solved" and the perpetrator punished – or so it is believed. The inevitable result of a false conviction is that the real killer gets away with the crime. Once a conviction has been secured, prosecutors will defend it through the appeal process. That is, after all, part of their job. The guilty as well as the innocent appeal and protest their conviction.

In a (relatively) few cases, new evidence emerges indicating the person sitting in prison is factually innocent. This takes many forms. Sometimes there is a revelation of police misbehavior such as failure to reveal exculpatory evidence. Other times the police learn something new. A key witness changes their story or the real killer starts bragging. In the 1990s, an important source of new evidence was the emergence of DNA identification. The ability to make a definitive identification from trace samples of blood, skin, saliva, hair roots, or flesh transformed many cases. As we saw in Chapter 11, DNA testing helped win good convictions in a lot of no-body cases. A suspect could no longer argue that blood in the trunk of his car came from a leaking hamburger or a cut on his own hand once DNA identification tied it to the missing person.

The emergence of DNA testing also revealed many false convictions. In 1992, Peter Neufeld and Barry Scheck of the Cardozo School of Law began using DNA testing to revisit convictions of people claiming they were falsely convicted.[50] The logic was simple and compelling. If the presence of skin under the fingernails of the victim or semen in her vagina was treated as evidence of guilt at trial, proving this biological material came from someone else should be proof of innocence. In the United States, DNA testing resulted in over 300 exonerations for rape or murder.[51] In Canada, numbers were lower even after adjusting for a lower population and homicide rate, but false convictions were uncovered.[52] In both countries, the reaction from police and prosecutors was mixed. Some wanted to establish the truth, whatever that might be. Others defended the original convictions with a determination that sometimes became pathological.

To examine the issues raised by false convictions in a no-body case, we'll look at the murder of Elizabeth Bain and the conviction of her boyfriend, Robert Baltovich.

In June of 1990, a University of Toronto student named Elizabeth Bain disappeared.[53] Three days later, her car was discovered. There were bloodstains suggesting a body was carried in the passenger's seat and was then dragged out of the car. Police assumed that the blood came from

Elizabeth and began treating her disappearance as a homicide case. DNA testing later confirmed this assumption.

Police quickly concluded Elizabeth's boyfriend, Robert Baltovich, was the culprit. All investigative effort was directed at proving his guilt.[54] The relationship between Elizabeth and Robert had been a bit tumultuous. Elizabeth had recorded the ups and downs in a diary. Police focused on the entries suggesting strain to conclude Robert killed because Elizabeth wanted to end the relationship. Other parts of the diary appeared to be missing. Robert told police that Elizabeth had given him these pages three days before her disappearance, but that he had given them back to her father. Police and the father denied possession of these pages, so their absence was treated as a sign of Robert's guilt. In response to media appeals, three witnesses came forward. An acquaintance of Elizabeth said she had seen the missing woman talking to an unidentified man. A man said he saw Elizabeth's car being driven near a lake three days after the disappearance. This witness told police he only saw the driver for a "split second" and "I wasn't really paying attention to him." Both these eyewitnesses gave vague descriptions that did not particularly match what Robert looked like. A third witness said she had seen someone who looked like Elizabeth arguing with a man a few days before her disappearance. This witness had not seen the man; some trees obstructed her view. For all practical purposes, that was the case against Robert. Police theorized that Robert killed Elizabeth in a jealous rage, hid her body in a park before moving it in her car three days later and dumping her into a lake. Over time, the witnesses changed the descriptions to align more closely with the police theory. The two saying they had seen the man became certain of their identification after seeing photographs of Robert in the newspaper. Hypnosis was used to enhance the memories of one witness. Baltovich was convicted of second-degree murder.[55]

The Ontario Court of Appeal described the case against Robert as based on opportunity, motive, and after-the-fact conduct indicative of guilt.[56] The prosecution's theory of opportunity was anchored by the two eyewitnesses. If Robert was the man seen by Elizabeth's acquaintance, he was the last person seen with her. If he was the man seen driving her car three days later, no innocent explanation was possible. Evidence for motive came from a selective culling of Elizabeth's diary entries and the eyewitness who said she saw a woman arguing with an unidentified man. From this, the prosecutor argued Elizabeth broke off the relationship only to be murdered because of a jealous rage, even though numerous witnesses, including Elizabeth's mother and best friend, testified the relationship seemed loving and ongoing. The "suspicious" after-the-fact conduct consisted of Robert's denials. Robert said he was at home with family members when Elizabeth was last seen. His family members confirmed this story. This was treated as a fabrication and thus as an indicator of guilt. Other aspects of denial were also treated as indicators of guilt. Elizabeth's car had a standard transmission. Robert told police he did not know how to shift gears with a standard transmission. This was interpreted as over-protesting. No behavior was deemed innocent. Robert got a haircut while in remand custody. This was interpreted as an attempt to change his appearance before the preliminary hearing.

To make a long story short, Robert was convicted in 1992. His appeal dragged on for years; he was eventually released on bail pending the appeal hearing in 2000. In 2004, the Ontario Court of Appeal overturned the conviction, primarily because of the trial judge's charge to the jury which was described as "unfair and unbalanced. It also contained significant errors of law that were prejudicial to the appellant." A new trial was ordered.[57] The prosecution's case unraveled further. In another case, Canada's Supreme Court ruled eyewitness testimony obtained through hypnosis was too prone to be the result of suggestion to be admissible in court.[58] This rendered the testimony of a key witness inadmissible. Then the missing diary pages were discovered in a police investigative file. Robert had, in fact, returned the pages to

Elizabeth's father who had, in turn, given them to the police. The pages were exculpatory to Robert; Elizabeth was writing about reconciliation. This undermined the putative motive. The charitable explanation for the initial failure to provide these pages in disclosure was incompetence; a less charitable explanation also existed. The last straw for the prosecution came when, in a routine pre-trial interview, Elizabeth's father effectively told prosecutors he would testify any way they thought would increase the chances of conviction. The prosecutors took the position that made his testimony unreliable.[59] If the case against Robert had been weak in the first trial, it promised to be nonexistent in a second. When this trial began in 2008, the prosecution presented no evidence and asked the jury to acquit. The jury obliged. Sixteen years after Elizabeth disappeared – undoubtedly because she was murdered – Robert was acquitted on the charge of murdering her.[60]

This left Elizabeth's murder unsolved. There is a good suspect. In the two years prior to Elizabeth's disappearance, there were a series of violent rapes of women in parks in that part of Toronto. The last occurred three weeks before Elizabeth's disappearance. Media called the perpetrator "The Scarborough Rapist." Robert's lawyers suggested the real killer was this then-unidentified rapist. Police rejected this theory because it did not fit a pattern. There was, they said, no evidence that Elizabeth had been raped and that The Scarborough Rapist was just a rapist, not a killer. A year after Robert's trial, DNA testing put a real name and face to The Scarborough Rapist. He was Paul Bernardo. In the meantime, Bernardo had moved to St. Catherines, Ontario, got engaged, accidently killed his future sister-in-law while raping her, and got married. He and his wife then kidnapped, raped, and murdered two young women. They dumped the bodies in water.[61] Bernardo confessed to raping 14 women in his guise as The Scarborough Rapist. When asked whether he killed Elizabeth Bain, Bernardo told police that:

> Well, that's a loaded question. I mean, are we going to go back and go through the time sequence of what happened in my life? I mean I could just give a yes or no answer. But you know, there are a lot of issues about that.[62]

Bernardo later said he did not kill Elizabeth,[63] but many are skeptical.[64] He looks like more of a suspect than Robert Baltovich ever did.

At one level, the affair looks like a typical false conviction case. There was a high-profile homicide. Police were under tremendous pressure to solve the case. They focused on the "obvious suspect" – the intimate partner of the victim – with single-minded intensity. Exculpatory evidence was ignored or treated as evidence of guilt. The performance of the defense lawyers at trial was less than stellar. The judge joined the condemnatory rush to judgment. The jury convicted. A more careful examination of the case by the Court of Appeal led to the conviction being overturned. The real killer was never charged, tried, or convicted. In all of this the disposal of Elizabeth's body played a role. When police responded to the suggestion that The Scarborough Rapist was responsible, they replied that there was no evidence she had been raped. If it existed, this evidence disappeared with her body, as did any DNA evidence that could have pointed to her killer.[65] Whether Elizabeth's killer was Paul Bernardo or someone else, disposing of her body was a successful strategy for avoiding detection. It also directly contributed to the false conviction of Robert Baltovich.

Notes

1 Banerjee, Amitav, U.B. Chitnis, S.L. Jadhav, J.S. Bhawalker, and S. Chaudhury, "Hypothesis Testing: Type 1 and Type 2 Errors," *Industrial Psychiatry Journal* 18, No. 2 (July-December 2009): 127–131.

2 Walker, Nancy Ann (Canadian Centre for Justice Statistics), e-mail message to author, January 31, 2014.
3 National Crime Information Center, *2020 NCIC Missing Person and Unidentified Person Statistics,* https://www.fbi.gov/file-repository/2020-ncic-missing-person-and-unidentified-person-statistics.pdf/view.
4 US Department of Justice, *National Missing and Unidentified Persons System*, n.d. https://namus.nij.ojp.gov/.
5 Royal Canadian Mounted Police, *Murdered and Missing Aboriginal Women: An Operational Overview,* https://www.rcmp-grc.gc.ca/en/missing-and-murdered-aboriginal-women-national-operational-overview. Accessed July 11, 2022.
6 Government of Canada, n.d. "Canada's Missing," https://canadasmissing.ca. Accessed Jun 21, 2022.
7 Rumsfeld, Donald, *Known and Unknown: A Memoir* (New York, NY: Sentinel, 2011).
8 Quinet, Kenna, "The Missing Missing Toward a Quantification of Serial Murder Victimization in the United States," *Homicide Studies* 11, No. 4 (2007): 319–339; Weinberg, Steve, "Missing and Presumed Murdered," *American Bar Association Journal* 81, No. 9 (1995): 62–68; Newiss, Geoff, "Estimating the Risk Faced by Missing Persons: A Study of Homicide Victims as an Example of an Outcome-Based Approach," *International Journal of Police Science and Management* 6, No. 1 (2004): 27–36.
9 Quinet, "The Missing Missing."
10 R. v. Sandeson, 2017 NSSC 193.
11 R. v. Sandeson, 2020 NSCA 47.
12 R. v. Sandeson, 2017 NSSC 146.
13 R. v. Sandeson, 2020 NSCA 47.
14 "Former Nova Scotia Med Student Awaiting Second Trial Appeals Bail Denial," *Toronto Star,* October 26, 2021.
15 Turzillo, Jane Ann, *Unsolved Murders and Disappearances in Northeast Ohio* (Charleston, SC: History Press Library, 2015).
16 Turzillo, *Unsolved Murders.*
17 Turzillo, *Unsolved Murders.*
18 Bell, Joshua D. and Megan R. Kienzle (eds.), *Alibis and Corroborators: Psychological, Criminological and Legal Perspectives* (New York, NY: Springer, 2022); Olson, Elizabeth and Steve D. Charman, "'But Can You Prove It?': Examining the Quality of Innocent Suspects' Alibis," *Psychology, Crime & Law* 18, No. 5 (2012): 453–471; Burke, Tara M., John W. Turtle and Elizabeth Olson, "Alibis in Criminal Investigations and Trials," in *Handbook of Eyewitness Psychology (Vol. 1),* ed. Michael P. Toglia, J. Don Read, David F. Ross (New York, NY: Psychology Press, 2007): 157–174.
19 McNair, Cici, *Never Flirt with a Femme Fatale: Lust, Money and Murder on the Island of Manhattan* (New York, NY: Fedora Press, 2010).
20 Wagner, *Corpus Delecti.*
21 King, *Never Seen Again.*
22 Sullivan, *Price of Experience.*
23 Lee, Henry, *Presumed Dead: A True Life Murder Mystery* (New York, NY: Berkley, 2010).
24 Lee, Henry and Jaxon Van Derbeken, "Wife-Killer Leads Cops to Body in Deal with D.A." *San Francisco Chronicle,* July 7, 2008.
25 McIntyre, *To the Grave.*
26 Montgomery, John. D., *Trials & Errors* (Winnipeg, MB: Watson & Dwyer, 2001).
27 Montgomery, *Trials & Errors*, 105.
28 Montgomery, *Trials & Errors*, 104.
29 R. v. Jack, 1992 CanLII 2754 (MB CA).
30 R. v. Jack (B.), 1993 CanLII 15019 (MB CA).
31 R. v. Jack, 1996 CanLII 2351 (MB CA)
32 R. v. Jack, 1996 CanLII 2351 (MB CA).
33 R. v. Jack 1997 CanLII 356 (SCC).
34 Thorpe, Ryan, "An Open Wound, 30 Years Later," *Winnipeg Free Press*, December 14, 2018.
35 DiBiase, *No-Body Homicide Cases*, 35–36.
36 MacFarlane, Bruce, "Convicting the Innocent: A Triple Failure of the Justice System," *Manitoba Law Journal* 31, No. 3 (2006): 474.
37 Kassin, Saul, "The Psychology of Confession Evidence," *American Psychologist* 52, No. 1 (1997); Kassin, Saul, "On the Psychology of Confessions: Does Innocence Put Innocents At Risk" *American Psychologist* 60, No. 1 (2005); Kassing, Saul, "False Confessions: How Can Psychology So Basic Be So Counterintuitive?" *American Psychologist* 72, No. 9 (2017).

38 Dekle Sr., George R., *The Last Murder: The Investigation, Prosecution, and Execution of Ted Bundy* (New York, NY: Praeger, 2011).
39 United States v. Stabler, 490 F.2d 345 (1974).
40 "Dominatrix Describes Dead Client's Demise," *The Telegram & Gazette*, January 19, 2006.
41 Mishra, Raja, "Dominatrix Acquitted of Manslaughter," *The Boston Globe*, January 31, 2006
42 Rubin, Paul, "End of an Ordeal," *Phoenix New Times*, January 5, 1994.
43 The Charley Project, "Martin Alan Gentry," https://charleyproject.org/case/martin-alan-gentry, May 13, 2010.
44 Cory, Peter, *The Inquiry Regarding Thomas Sophanow* (Winnipeg, MB: Manitoba Justice, 2001).
45 DiBiase, *No-Body Homicide Cases*, 23.
46 People v. Casciaro, 2015 Ill. App. (2nd) 131291 (2015).
47 People v. Casciaro, 2015 Ill. App. (2nd) 131291 (2015).
48 People v. Casciaro, 2015 Ill. App. (2nd) 131291 (2015).
49 Marrazzo, Amanda, "Conviction Overturned in Infamous Johnsburg Grocery Store Murder," *Chicago Tribune*, September 18, 2015.
50 Innocence Project, n.d. https://innocenceproject.org/. Accessed October 2, 2022.
51 National Registry of Exonerations, "DNA," https://www.law.umich.edu/special/exoneration/Pages/DNA.aspx. Accessed October 8, 2022.
52 Innocence Canada, "Exonerations," https://www.innocencecanada.com/exonerations/. Accessed October 8, 2022.
53 Finkle, Derek, *No Claim to Mercy: Elizabeth Bain and Robert Baltovich*, A suburban mystery (New York, NY: Viking, 1998).
54 Baltovich v. Attorney General for Ontario, 2018 ONSC 1291.
55 Clawdge, Thomas, "Jury Convicts Baltovich of Murder: Girlfriend's Body Never Found; Couple Last Seen at Scarborough Campus," *Toronto Globe and Mail*, April 1, 1992.
56 R. v. Baltovich, 2004 CanLII 45031 (ON SC).
57 R. v. Baltovich, 2004 CanLII 45031 (ON SC).
58 R. v. Trochym, 2007 SCC 6.
59 Finkle, Derek, "New Twist in Baltovich Acquittal," *Toronto Star*, May 17, 2008.
60 Small, Peter, "Baltovich Acquitted of Murder," *Toronto Star*, April 22, 2008.
61 R. v. Bernardo, 2000 CanLII 5678 (ON CA).
62 *National Post*, "Paul Bernardo: Did You Kill Elizabeth Bain?" February 28, 2018, 3:29. https://youtu.be/A0PCeivaEkM.
63 Small, Peter, "Lawyer Rejects Bernardo Link," *Toronto Star*, April 26, 2008.
64 "Bernardo 'probably' Bain Killer, Lawyer Says," *Toronto Star*, April 22, 2008.
65 Small, Peter and Betsy Powell, "Bain's Body Wouldn't ID Killer," *Toronto Star*, April 24, 2008.

16

RESULTS AND PROSPECTS FOR NO-BODY HOMICIDE PROSECUTIONS

This book began with four cautionary tales. Jennifer Wilbanks, Eduardo Sanchez, Alicia Ross and Dennis Cornish all disappeared in circumstances strongly suggestive of murder. As it turns out, Jennifer was still alive. Eduardo died by accident. Alicia was murdered, but not by the prime suspect. Dennis was killed without criminal culpability. These cases should instill a bit of caution about assuming disappearance means murder. At the same time, some killers attempt to avoid detection and punishment by disposing of the bodies of their victims. Their efforts should not be rewarded.

There is an adage that bad cases make bad law. In 1660, William Harrison disappeared. Three members of the Perry family were convicted of murdering him and hanged. Harrison reappeared. Whether he was captured by pirates or absconded with his employer's money was irrelevant to the unfortunate members of the Perry family. A neck cannot be unstretched. This case led Lord Mathew Hale to opine that "I would never convict any person of murder or manslaughter, unless the facts were proved to be done, or at least the body found dead." For three centuries, this opinion (almost) had the force law in Great Britain, the United States, and Canada. In some jurisdictions, the principle was enshrined in legislation. In others, the absence of a body made prosecutors reluctant to prosecutors and courts hesitant to convict. Killers got away with murder by doing away with the bodies of their victims. Although it is impossible to quantify these miscarriages of justice, we can state with absolute certainty that it happened. It is a bit like frostbite on a very cold winter day. We cannot count the number of people who had frozen skin, but if the temperature drops below –30 for a few days, we know it happened to someone.

During the three centuries governed by Hale's opinion, a killer could almost guarantee getting a "get-out-of-jail-free" card with successful body disposal. Sometimes the line between immunity and the hangman was a matter of luck. Let us look at the case of John Colt, brother of Samuel Colt of six-shot revolver fame.

In 1841, John Colt was in a New York office preparing to ship a box of accounting texts he authored to Louisville, Kentucky. The crate of books needed to travel by ship to New Orleans and then up the Mississippi River. The journey would take about three months. When the printer arrived, he carried an invoice rather than the textbooks. Colt wanted the books. The printer wanted payment in advance. In the resulting argument, Colt whacked the printer over the head with an ax. After calming down, Colt cleaned up the blood and threw the printer's

DOI: 10.4324/9781003372134-16

belongings into an outhouse. He stuffed the printer's body into the waiting crate, nailed it shut, and called a delivery company to take the box to the waiting ship. Colt carried on as if nothing untoward had happened.[1]

The printer was missed by his family and employees. They went to the police and launched a public search. Colt's landlord saw a poster and realized the missing printer entered Colt's office the night of the disappearance but did come out. The landlord also remembered hearing loud noises from Colt's office. The landlord notified the police, who tracked the crate to the ship. Unfortunately for Colt, inclement weather and unfavorable winds prevented the ship from leaving New York as scheduled. The crate was in the hold. It did not smell like a box of accounting textbooks. When the lid was pried open, the rotting body of the printer was found.

At his trial, Colt's lawyers argued for an acquittal or a manslaughter verdict based on a mixture of self-defense, provocation, and momentary insanity. The prosecutor argued it was plain and simple murder. If Colt had not attempted to ship the body into the oblivion of Louisville, his defense might have succeeded. He had excellent lawyers and his family was well connected. However, his attempt to ship the body to Kentucky transformed a relatively mundane homicide into a public sensation. Daily newspapers were coming into being, and the case provided sensationalistic headlines. The papers claimed the unfortunate printer was cut up and salted to preserve him for the long voyage. Cannibalism was hinted at. Hundreds lined up to witness the trial. The jury found it difficult to reconcile Colt's claim of momentary insanity with the calculating actions to avoid discovery. As Jim Rasenberger observed in his biography of Sam Colt, "It was those hours *after* the killing, not the act of violence itself, that turned John Colt from a run-of-the-mill hothead into a psychopath."[2] Colt was found guilty of murder and sentenced to hang. Because of the notoriety of the case, New York's governor refused a plea for clemency. Colt committed suicide on the morning of his scheduled hanging.

If the weather had been a little better, the ship would have left New York as scheduled. Given the communications technology of the day, Colt would have gotten away with murder regardless of the circumstantial case against him. Reliance on this level of chance is not a hallmark of a properly functioning criminal justice system. The reluctance to prosecute no-body homicide cases undoubtedly led to many miscarriages of justice. Killers went free.

Juries have often been blamed for prosecutorial reluctance to proceed with no-body cases. Prosecutors justified inaction by claiming the ordinary people sitting on juries are unable to properly understand circumstantial evidence, and are thus unwilling to convict in no-body cases. My review of almost 600 cases found little evidence to support this contention. When juries have been presented with solid evidence to build a circumstantial case, they are perfectly willing to convict. For example, after Edward Rulloff murdered his wife and daughter in 1844, a jury was willing to convict him of murder. It was the more educated and sophisticated judges on New York's Court of Appeal who were incapable of inferring guilt from compelling circumstantial evidence. Over a hundred years later, juries in Georgia and California transformed the jurisprudence in no-body cases by convicting John Wallace and Leonard Ewing Scott. This time, appeal court judges caught up to the ability of jury members to engage in inferential logic. In Canada, the pivotal case came in 1946 when a jury convicted Sydney Chambers of murdering and burning Marion Rusnak. Judges on Ontario's Court of Appeal overturned the conviction, only to have a second jury re-convict.

The convictions of Wallace, Scott, and Chambers began the transformation of the legal framework for no-body prosecutions. Convictions became more common as prosecutors took inspiration from other successful prosecutions. The rise of bureaucratic systems, improved forensic techniques and the adoption of cell phones provided new tools police could use to generate evidence. DiBiase notes that conviction rates in no-body cases brought to trial are now higher than in body-present cases.[3] In part, this reflects prosecutorial caution in no-body cases; for the most part, only the stronger cases proceed to trial. But there is something more. Killers who hide or destroy the bodies of their victims understand they are eliminating a key piece of evidence. They fail to understand that their concealment activities create other evidence. Moving bodies creates more locations for police to find forensic evidence. Recruiting helpers for disposal creates accomplices who can become highly motivated witnesses. The time needed for disposal makes alibi construction more challenging. Post-disappearance behaviors such as delays in filing missing persons' reports become markers of guilt. Many killers created the evidence needed for conviction through their body disposal efforts – and, as John Colt learned in 1843 and John Wallace found just over a hundred years later, the shocking horror of body disposal increased their punishment. Both transformed what would have likely been a few years of imprisonment into execution by making the body of their victims disappear.

For police and prosecutors, much learning has occurred in the past half century. Law enforcement authorities have gotten better at dealing with killers who use body disposal to evade justice. More needs to be done. DiBiase argues that the biggest mistake police make in no-body cases is waiting too long before converting a missing person's investigation into a homicide investigation. There is truth to this, but, as we saw in Chapter 1, there are often good reasons for hesitation. Hindsight is easy, but effective triage during an investigation can be challenging. My own conclusion is like DiBiase's, but a little different. I believe that police and prosecutors sometimes spend too much time looking for the corporal presence of the missing person, whether believed alive or dead. "Have you seen this person?" appeals generate dozens or hundreds of well-meaning, but frivolous, reports that must be followed up. This effort can overwhelm an investigation while, as was shown by the prosecution of Brian Jack, failure to do so can scupper a conviction. Even if investigators believe the missing person has been killed, sometimes too much effort is wasted searching for the body. It is one thing to drag a lake; it is another to attempt to find a corpse in a big-city landfill. I have read descriptions of more than a dozen attempts to do so. All involved massive expenditure of resources and created risk for searchers. None were successful. In addition to being almost intrinsically futile, these searches can undermine a successful prosecution. Defense lawyers can use lack of success to argue that the evidence trail leading to the landfill should be discounted. On occasion, police are better off acknowledging that gone is gone while focusing investigative efforts on the evidence trail leading to disappearance. In many cases, the killer will lead police to the body after conviction or as part of a plea bargain.

The objectives of the criminal justice system should be to punish the guilty while avoiding punishing the innocent. There is a tension-laden balance between these two objectives. For police and prosecutors, investigating and prosecuting no-body cases require focus, determination, and persistence. The danger is that this can become transformed into a disease of certainty or tunnel vision. In most of cases described in this book, and in the hundreds of others I have reviewed, law enforcement officials achieved the required balance. In a few cases, they have failed. The result is that body disposal no longer provides a "get-out-of-jail-free" card to killers.

Notes

1 Rasenberger, Jim, Revolver: *Sam Colt and the Six-Shooter that Changed America* (New York, NY: Scribner, 2020), 158–163.
2 Rasenberger, *Revolver*, 175.
3 DiBiase, *No-Body Homicide Cases*, 43–44.

APPENDIX

"True Crime" Accounts of No-Body Homicide Cases

We are fascinated by homicide. It is a mainstay of fiction, television, and movies. "True Crime" accounts of homicide regularly reach the best-seller lists. Many cases have been turned into movies. In the last decade, "true crime" podcasts have become ubiquitous. If homicide fascinates, homicide accompanied by body disposal seems mesmerizing. Put simply, no-body cases generate many books. Here is a list of "true crime" books describing specific no-body homicide investigations and prosecutions.

Anastasia, George (2018) *The Summer Wind: Thomas Capano and the Murder of Anne Marie Fahey* (Philadelphia, PA: Camino Books).

Bailey, Richard W. (2003) *Rogue Scholar: The Sinister Life and Celebrated Death of Edward H. Rulloff* (Ann Arbor, MI: University of Michigan Press).

Barnes, Margaret Anne (1983) *Murder in Coweta County* (New York, NY: Pelican).

Barrish, Cris and Peter Meyer (1999) *Fatal Embrace: The Inside Story of the Thomas Capano/Anne Marie Fahey Murder Case* (New York, NY: St. Martins).

Beck, Janet Parker (1992) *Too Good To Be True* (New York, NY: Penguin).

Bishop, Jim (2017) *The Murder Trial of Judge Peel* (New York, NY: Papamoa Press).

Blevins, Brooks (2012) *Ghost of the Ozarks* (Champaign, IL: University of Illinois Press).

Bommersbach, Janice (2008) *Bones in the Desert: The True Story of a Mother's Murder and a Daughter's Search* (New York, NY: St. Martins).

Borchard, Edwin M. (1932) *Convicting the Innocent: Sixty-Five Actual Errors of Criminal Justice* (Garden City, NY: Garden City Publishing Company).

Brady, Steve and Frank Roderus (1996) *Murder Revisited: A True Story of Deadly Deception* (New York, NY: Avon).

Brandt, Charles (2016) *I Heard You Paint Houses: Frank "The Irishman" Sheeran and Closing the Case on Jimmy Hoffa* (New York, NY: Steerforth Press).

Brocklehurst, Ann (2019) *Dark Ambition: The Twisted Pact of Serial Killers Dellen Millard and Mark Smich* (Toronto, ON: Penguin).

Broderick, Elizabeth (2016) *Clifford Olson: The Beast of British Columbia* (Toronto: RJ Parker Publishing).

Bruns, Richard (2018) *I, a Squealer: The Insider's Account of the 'Pied Piper of Tucson Murders'* (Ashland, OH: Twin Feather Publishing).

Bugliosi, Vincent and Curt Gentry (1994) *Helter Skelter: The True Story of the Manson Murders* (New York, NY: W.W. Norton & Company).

Cameron, Stevie (2007) *The Pickton File* (Toronto, ON: Knopf Canada).

Cameron, Stevie (2011) *On the Farm: Robert William Pickton and the Tragic Story of Vancouver's Missing Women* (Toronto, ON: Knopf Canada).
Cannell, Michael (2020) *A Brotherhood Betrayed: The Man Behind the Rise and Fall of Murder, Inc.* (New York, NY: St. Martins).
Carlo, Philip (2006) *The Ice Man: Confessions of a Mafia Killer* (New York, NY: St. Martins).
Carlo, Philip (2009) *Gaspipe: Confessions of a Mafia Boss* (New York, NY: HarperCollins).
Carpenter, Teresa (1988) *Missing Beauty* (New York, NY: Kensington Publishing).
Clark, George (ed.) (1959) *The Campden Wonder* (London, UK: Oxford University Press).
Cohen, Lisa R. (2014) *After Etan: The Missing Child Case That Held America Captive* (New York, NY: Grand Central).
Cope, Carol Soret (2011) *Murder on the High Seas: The True Story of the Joe Cool's Tragic Final Voyage* (New York, NY: Berkley).
Costopoulos, William (1996) *Principal Suspect: The True Story of Dr. Jay Smith and the Main Line Murders* (Philadelphia, PA: Camino Books).
Crowley, Kieren (2007) *The Surgeon's Wife: A True Story of Obsession, Rage and Murder* (New York, NY: St. Martins).
Davis, John H. (1993) *Mafia Dynasty: The Rise and Fall of the Gambino Crime Family* (New York, NY: Harper Paperbacks).
DeMeo, Albert (2003) *For the Sins of My Father: A Mafia Killer, His Son, and a Legacy of Mob Life* (New York, NY: Crown).
Dirmann, Tina (2008) *Vanished at Sea: The True Story of a Child TV Actor and a Double Murder* (New York, NY: St. Martins).
Doneman, Paula (2006) *Things a Killer Would Know: The True Story of Leonard Fraser* (Crows Nest, NSW: Allen & Unwin).
Douglas, John and Stephen Singular (2003) *Anyone You Want Me To Be* (New York, NY: Scribner).
Dunboyne, Lord (ed.) (1953) *The Trial of John George Haigh* (Glasgow, UK: William and Hodge).
Dunn, Sharon R. (2015) *In Tina's Shadow: The True Story of a Murder, a Husband's Guilt, and a Family's 14-Year Vigil for Justice, 2nd Edition* (Greely, CO: CreateSpace Independent Publishing).
Englade, Ken (1996) *Hot Blood: The Money the Brach Heiress, the Horse Murders* (New York, NY: St. Martins Press).
Englert, Rod and Kathy Passero (2010) *Blood Secrets: Chronicles of a Crime Scene Reconstructionist* (New York, NY: Thomas Dunne).
Epstein, Steven B. (2020) *Evil at Lake Seminole: The Shocking True Story Surrounding the Disappearance of Mike Williams* (Baker City, OR: Black Lyon Publishing).
Evans, C.D. and Lorene Shyba (eds) (2014) *Tough Crimes: True Cases by Top Canadian Criminal Lawyers* (Calgary, AB: Durvile Publications).
Ferry, Jon and Damien Inwood (1982) *The Olson Murders* (Chicago, IL: Cameo).
Fielder, Donna (2014) *The Vanished Wife: The Kathy Stobaugh Story* (New York, NY: Berkley).
Finkle, Derek (1998) *No Claim to Mercy: Elizabeth Bain and Robert Baltovich, A Suburban Mystery* (New York, NY: Viking).
Fleeman, Michael (2002) *"If I die…": A True Story of Obsessive Love, Uncontrollable Greed and Murder* (New York, NY: St. Martins).
Franke, David (1975) *The Torture Doctor: The Only True Account of the Greatest Criminal the Police Have Ever Handled* (New York, NY: Hawthorn).
Franscell, Ron (2019) *Alice and Gerald: A Homicidal Love Story* (Amherst, NY: Prometheus Books).
Freeman, E.H. (1871) *Edward H. Rulloff: The Veil of Secrecy Removed* (New York, NY: Lowood Press).
Gibson, A.M. (1965) *The Life and Death of Colonel Albert Jennings Fountain* (Norman, OK: University of Oklahoma Press).
Gilmore, John (1996) *Cold-Blooded: The Saga of Charles Schmid, the Notorious "Pied Piper of Tucson"* (Portland, OR: Feral House).
Gilmour, Walter and Leland E. Hale (2016) *Butcher, Baker: The True Account of an Alaska Serial Killer* (New York, NY: Open Road).
Glasgow, Michael and Phyllis Gobbell (2007) *An Unfinished Canvas: A True Story of Love, Family and Murder in Nashville* (New York, NY: Berkley).

Golab, Jan (1993) *The Dark Side of the Force: A True Story of Corruption and Murder in the LAPD* (New York, NY: The Atlantic Monthly Press).
Goldsmith, Jack (2019) *In Hoffa's Shadow: A Stepfather, a Disappearance in Detroit, and My Search for the Truth* (New York, NY: Farrar Straus & Giroux).
Graves, Jennifer and Emily Clawson (2013) *A Light in Dark Places* (Scotts Valley, CA: CreateSpace).
Hammer, Ron (1987) *The CBS Murders: A True Story of Greed and Violence in New York's Diamond District* (New York, NY: William Morrow).
Havill, Adrian (1999) *The Mother, the Son, and the Socialite: A True Story of a Mother-Son Crime Spree* (New York, NY: St. Martins).
Havill, Adrian (2001) *Born Evil: A True Story of Cannibalism and Serial Murder* (New York, NY: St. Martins).
Henderson, Tom (2006) *Darker than Night: The True Story of a Brutal Double Homicide - And an 18-Year-Long Quest for Justice* (New York, NY: St. Martins).
Herzog, Arthur (2012) *The Wood-Chipper Murder* (Wainscott, NY: Leslie Mandel).
Hoffa, James 1975) *Hoffa: The Real Story* (New York, NY: Stein and Day).
Holmes, William Leslie (2010) *Where Shadows Linger: The Untold Story of the RCMP's Olson Murder Investigation* (Victoria, BC: Heritage House).
Horner, Mark (2004) *September Sacrifice* (New York, NY: Kensington).
Horton, Sue (1989) *The Billionaire Boys Club: Rich Kids, Money and Murder* (New York, NY: St. Martins Press).
Humes, Edward (1991) *Buried Secrets: A True Story of Serial Murder* (New York, NY: Signet).
Hunter, J.T. (2015) *The Country Boy Killer: The True Story of Cody Legebokoff – Canada's Teenage Serial Killer* (Self-Published).
Jackson, Stanley (1953) *John George Haigh* (London: Oldhams Press).
Kackley, Rod (2020) *The Murder of Kelsey Berreth: A Shocking True Crime Story* (Grand Rapids, MI: Lyons Circle Publishing).
Karem, Brian J. (1999) *Above the Law: The Sensational Murder Case That Stunned the Nation* (New York, NY: Pinnacle-Kennsington).
Karpis, Alvin and Bill Trent (1971) *Public Enemy Number One: The Alvin Karpis Story* (Toronto: McClelland and Stewart).
Keppel, Robert and William Birnes (1995) *The Riverman: Ted Bundy and I Hunt for the Green River Killer* (New York, NY: Pocket Books).
King, Gary (2014) *Love, Lies and Murder* (New York, NY: Pinnacle Books).
King, Jeanne (2002) *Dead End: The Crime Story of the Decade – Murder, Incest and High-Tech Thievery* (New York, NY: M. Evans and Company).
King, Jeanne (2008) *Never Seen Again: A Ruthless Lawyer, His Beautiful Wife, and the Murder that Tore a Family Apart* (New York, NY: St. Martins).
Kolker, Robert (2020) *Lost Girls: An Unsolved American Mystery* (New York, NY: Harper Perennial).
Konigsberg, Eric (2009) *Blood Relation* (New York, NY: Harper Collins).
Larson, Erik (2004) *The Devil in the White City: Murder, Magic, and Madness at the Fair That Changed America* (New York, NY: Vintage).
Lavergne, Gary M. (1999) *Bad Boy From Rosebud: The Murderous Life of Kenneth Allen McDuff* (Denton, TX: University of North Texas Press).
Leake, John (2012) *Cold a Long Time: An Alpine Mystery* (Self-Published).
Lee, Henry K. (2010) *Presumed Dead: A True Life Murder Mystery* (New York, NY: Berkley Books).
Lefebure, Molly (1958) *Murder With a Difference: The Cases of Haigh and Christie* (London, UK: Heinemann).
Lillebuen, Steve (2012) *The Devil's Cinema: The Untold Story Behind Mark Twitchell's Kill Room* (Toronto, ON: McClelland and Stewart).
Ling, Justin (2020) *Missing From the Village: The Story of Serial Killer Bruce McArthur, the Search for Justice, and the System that Failed Toronto's Queer Community* (Toronto, ON: McClelland and Stewart).
Lookabill, Royce Glennwood (2016) *That's a Damn Good Dog: Commonwealth of Virginia vs. Stephen Metteson Epperly (1980) A Retrospective* (Ararat, VA: Laurel Hill Publishing).
Lowe, Gordon (2015) *The Acid Bath Murders: The Trials and Liquidations of John George Haigh* (Gloucestershire, UK: The History Press).
Maksymchuk, Andrew F. (2014) *Champions of the Dead: OPP Crime-Fighters Seeking Proof of the Truth* (Victoria, BC: Friesen).

Mayer, Robert (1991) *The Dreams of Ada* (New York, NY: Penguin).
McFarland, Gerald (1990) *The Counterfeit Man: The True Story of the Boor-Colvin Murder Case* (New York, NY: Pantheon Books).
McIntyre, Mike (2006) *To the Grave: Inside a Spectacular RCMP Sting* (Winnipeg, MB: Great Plains).
McNair, Cici (2010) *Never Flirt With a Femme Fatale: Lust, Money and Murder on the Island of Manhattan* (New York, NY: Fedora Press).
McQuillan, Alice (2000) *They Call Them Grifters: The True Story of Sante and Kenneth Kimes* (New York, NY: Onyx).
Mellor, Lee (2012) *Cold North Killers: Canadian Serial Murder* (Toronto, ON: Dundurn).
Moldea, Dan (1978) *The Hoffa Wars: Teamsters, Rebels, Politicians and the Mob* (New York, NY: Paddington Press).
Montgomery, John (2001) *Trials & Errors: The People vs. Brian Gordon Jack* (Winnipeg, MB: Watson and Dwyer).
Moore, Dot (2011) *No Remorse: The Rise and Fall of John Wallace* (Montgomery, AB: New South Books).
Moser, Don (1967) *The Pied Piper of Tucson* (New York, NY: Signet).
Mulgrew, Ian (1991) *Final Payoff: The True Price of Convicting Clifford Robert Olson* (New York, NY: Seal).
Mustain, Gene and Jerry Capeci (1993) *Murder Machine* (New York, NY: New American Library).
Nest, Michael, Deanna Reder and Eric Bell (2020) *Cold Case North: The Search for Jim Brady and Absolom Halkett* (Regina, SK: University of Regina Press).
Oates, Jonathan (2014) *John George Haigh the Acid-Bath Murderer: A Portrait of a Serial Killer and His Victims* (Barnsley, UK: Pen and Sword Books).
Olson, Gregg and Rebecca Morris (2014) *If I Can't Have You* (New York, NY: St. Martins).
Pearson, Edmond (1930) *Instigation of the Devil* (New York, NY: Charles Scribner).
Peterson, Rod (2018), *Under the Trestle: The 1980 Disappearance of Gina Renee Hall & Virginia's First "No-Body" Murder* (Bloomington, IN: IUniverse).
Phelps, M. William (2019) *Where Monsters Hide: Sex, Murder, and Madness in the Midwest* (New York, NY: Pinnacle Books).
Rasenberger, Jim (2020) *Revolver: Sam Colt and the Six-Shooter that Changed America* (New York: Scribner).
Recko, Corey (2008) *Murder on the White Sands: The disappearance of Albert and Henry Fountain* (Denton, TX: University of North Texas Press).
Reichart, David (2005) *Chasing the Devil: My Twenty-Year Quest to Capture the Green River Killer* (New York, NY: St. Martins).
Rother, Caitlin (2011) *Dead Reckoning* (New York, NY: Kensington).
Rule, Ann (1983) *Lust Killer* (New York, NY: Berkley).
Rule, Ann (2000) *And Never Let Her Go – Thomas Capano: The Deadly Seducer* (New York, NY: Simon and Schuster).
Rule, Ann (2001) *Empty Promises and Other True Cases* (New York, NY: Pocket Books).
Rule, Ann (2005) *Green River Running Red: The True Story of the Green River Killer* (New York, NY: Gallery Books).
Rule, Ann (2012) *Fatal Friends, Deadly Neighbors* (New York, NY: Gallery Books).
Rule, Leslie (2020) *A Tangled Web: A Cyberstalker, a Deadly Obsession, and the Twisting Path to Justice* (New York, NY: Citadel Press).
Russell, Haddeus (2001) *Out of the Jungle: Jimmy Hoffa and the Remaking of the American Working Class* (Philadelphia, PA: Temple University Press).
Scee, Trudy Irene (2009) *Tragedy in the North Woods: The Murders of James Hicks* (Charleston, SC: The History Press).
Schecter, Harold (1994) *Depraved: The Shocking True Story of America's First Serial Killer* (New York, NY: Pocket Books).
Schwartz-Nobel, Loretta (1987) *Engaged to Murder: The Inside Story of the Main Line Murders* (New York, NY: Viking).
Scott, Robert (2003) *Dangerous Attraction: A Walk on the Wild Side Would End in Rape and Murder for an All-American Girl* (New York, NY: Kensington).
Sharkey, Joe (1993) *Above Suspicion: An Undercover FBI Agent, an Illicit Affair, and a Murder of Passion* (New York, NY: Simon and Schuster).

Shenher, Lori (2015) *That Lonely Section of Hell: The Botched Investigation of a Serial Killer Who Almost Got Away* (Vancouver, BC: Greystone).

Sloan, Arthur A. (1991) *Hoffa* (Cambridge, MA: MIT Press).

Smith, Jay Charles (2008) *Joseph Wambaugh and the Jay Smith Case* (Philadelphia, PA: Xlibris).

Somerfield, Stafford (1950) *The Authentic and Revealing Story of John George Haigh* (Manchester, UK: Hood Pearson).

Sonnichsen, C.L. (1960) *Tolarosa: Last of the Frontier West* (Albuquerque, NM: University of New Mexico Press).

Springer, Patricia (2001) *Body Hunter* (New York, NY: Kensington).

Stewart, Bob (1996) *No Remorse: They Let Him Live; They Set Him Free to Kill and Kill Again* (New York, NY: Pinnacle).

Stobbe, Mark (2021) *The "Mr. Big" Sting: The Cases, the Killers, the Controversial Confessions* (Toronto, ON: ECW Press).

Strong, Marilee (2008) *Erased: Missing Women, Murdered Wives* (New York, NY: Wiley).

Sullivan, Randall (1996) *The Price of Experience: Money, Power, Image and Murder in Los Angeles* (New York, NY: Atlantic Monthly Press).

Turkus, Burton and Sid Feder (2012) *The Inside Story of the Syndicate Killing Machine Murder, Inc.* (New York, NY: Tenacity Media Books).

Turzillo, Jane Ann (2015) *Unsolved Murders and Disappearances in Northeast Ohio* (Charleston, SC: History Press Library).

Wagner, Diane (1986) *Corpus Delicti* (New York, NY: St. Martins Press).

Walker, Kent and Mark Schone (2001) *Song of a Grifter: The Twisted Tale of Sante and Kenny Kimes, the Most Notorious Con Artists in America* (New York, NY: William Morrow).

Walker, Robert (1984) *Silent Testimony: A True Story* (New York, NY: St. Martins).

Wambaugh, Joseph (1987) *Echoes in the Darkness* (New York, NY: Bantom).

Welch, Larry (2014) *Beyond Cold Blood: The KBI From Ma Barker to BTK* (Lawrence, KS: University of Kansas Press).

Worthington, Peter (2012) *Predator: The Life and Crimes of Serial Killer Clifford Olson* (Self-Published E-Book).

INDEX

For Product Safety Concerns and Information please contact our EU representative GPSR@taylorandfrancis.com Taylor & Francis Verlag GmbH, Kaufingerstraße 24, 80331 München, Germany